Detroit Perspectives

Glorious architecture of the 1920s: the Michigan Theater, now doing service as a parking structure. (Courtesy of Bob McKeown, 1986.)

Detroit Perspectives

Crossroads and Turning Points

Edited by Wilma Wood Henrickson

 Wayne State University Press   Detroit

03   02   01   6   5   4

Library of Congress Cataloging-in-Publication Data
Detroit perspectives : crossroads and turning points / edited by Wilma Wood
Henrickson.
      p.   cm. — (Great Lakes books)
      Includes bibliographical references and index.
      ISBN 0–8143–2013–9 (alk. paper). — ISBN 0–8143–2014–7 (pbk. :
alk. paper)
      1. Detroit (Mich.)—History—Sources.   2. Detroit (Mich.)—
History.   I. Henrickson, Wilma Wood, 1915–   .   II. Series.
F574.D457D5   1991
977.4'34—dc20   90–37064
                                                              CIP

GREAT LAKES BOOKS

Contents

Acknowledgments

The compiler of an anthology has many reasons to be grateful and many people to thank. One can only hope not to miss too many of those to whom gratitude is due.

Without good friends over many years, this work, of whatever worth it has, would not have been possible. First, to Philip Mason, head of the Walter Reuther Archives and Library of Urban Affairs, I owe a debt of untold measurement for his ready sympathy, warm encouragement, and demanding standards. I am also grateful to JoEllen Vinyard, of Eastern Michigan University, for being a strong supportive editor at *Detroit in Perspective: A Journal of Regional History.* I am thankful that for some years the Detroit Historical Society made *Detroit in Perspective* possible. Like most area history buffs, I shall continue to mourn its passing. Tom Jones, of the Historical Society of Michigan, has been helpful both currently and in the past.

Early encouragement was given by Jean Owen, former editor at the Wayne State University Press. Alice Nigoghosian, Anne Adamus, and editor Robin DuBlanc at Wayne State University Press have not only been unfailingly patient in the many stages of this work, but were able to secure rights to reprint several selections originally published by the press.

I thank the editors of the *New Republic* and Bill Newlin of New Republic Books for several acts of generosity. I feel an especially warm gratitude to old friend Bill Grant, not only for his brief history of a school crisis, "Integration's Last Hurrah," for the *New Republic*, but also for his encouragement in the early stages of this effort.

Among contributors there are many old friends. There is Jack Widick, who has written much great stuff, but is here represented by a single chapter of *Detroit: City of Race and Class Vio-*

lence, now reissued by Wayne State University Press, chosen because it describes the essence of Detroit's Camelot years under Mayor Jerome Cavanagh, years which have been so quickly forgotten by so many. I thank Kenneth Cockrel for his willing gift of material he had written for the Detroit Alliance for a Rational Economy (DARE), and mourn with many that his untimely death will make it impossible for him to add to service given his city.

There is Marie Oresti, of the Catholic Interracial Council. Our shared memories go back to wartime years with the Detroit Housing Commission, an experience also shared with Bette Jenkins (Downs). Both women shared a quiet fury at the obvious institutional racism of those years. Others, who are of course credited with their writings but whose personal help beyond that is gratefully acknowledged, include James Bell, Councilwoman Maryann Mahaffey, Harold Norris, the Reverend David Gracie, and Ernest Dillard.

Then there are Arthur Johnson, Victor Reuther, Jack Russell, Dan Luria, and Kathryn Kozora. Ron Williams also encouraged me through several appearances in that journalistic gadfly, *Metro Times*. Nor can one forget the gracious generosity of John Hersey in giving permission to use two telling chapters of *The Algiers Motel Incident*.

Special thanks go to David Lawrence along with Vivian Guilmette and Editor Neal Shine of the *Detroit Free Press* for patient and friendly help in arranging rights to reprint, and also for an introduction to Barbara Stanton, who made several helpful comments on the treatment of the 1967 riot.

At the *Detroit News*, Publisher Robert S. Giles willingly granted permission for the reprinting of several items, including the *News*-owned copyright of the *Detroit Times's* romantic story on the suicide of Janet MacDonald in 1939.

Thoughtful suggestions came from Steve Babson and Ron Alpern. Two other friends, Councilman Mel Ravitz and Carol Campbell, part-time poet and full-time assistant to Mayor Coleman Young, both graciously offered help and corrective advice during the course of this work.

Some who have taken on the painful task of reading some piles of manuscript include JoEllen Vinyard, Dale Vinyard, of Wayne State University, Philip Mason, and the Reverend Hugh White, urban affairs consultant to Bishop Coleman McGehee of the Episcopal Diocese of Michigan. Louis Goldstein, AIA, currently serving as Michigan coordinator of the AIA's Committee on Historic Resources, found time to read several sections pertaining to housing and planning. Stanley Solvick of Wayne State University read some material with a cautious, friendly eye, but not he nor any of these others should be blamed for surviving errors.

For access to good material in good libraries, I thank the entire staff at the Burton Library, most especially Alice Dalligan, retired director, Mary Karshner, Judy Barmatoski, and Deborah Evans, as well as Margaret Ward, now retired. Edward Weber, of the Labadie Collection at the University of Michigan, and Francis X. Blouin, director of the Bentley Library, have gone out of their respective ways to be helpful with troublesome requests. The Bentley Library provided reading access to the papers of an old friend, the late Josephine Gomon. None of this material is reproduced or quoted here, but it shed fresh perspectives on the trial of Dr. Ossian Sweet as well as Detroit life in the twenties. The very helpful staff at the Walter Reuther Archives and Library of Urban Affairs included Warner Pflug, Michael Smith, Kathleen Schmeling, and Tom Featherstone.

Access to materials not easily available has been made easier by Bill Lynch, bookseller and collector, who lent me several rare editions of books. I also wish to thank Anne Hinchman Berry for permission to include Theodore Hinchman's letter from the manuscript collections of the Burton Library.

Let us mention now those absent friends of long ago, believers in history, diggers of truth. In the thirties the history department at Detroit City College, which grew to become Wayne State University, was a more formal and completely masculine department. It was 1970 before I had the courage to call old friend William J. Bossenbrook "Bill." Among the faculty with whom I studied were historians Sidney Glazer, Raymond C. Miller, Alfred Kelly, Milo M. Quaife, and Winfred Harbison, as well as folklore specialist Thelma James and sociologist Donald C. Marsh.

Very especially I value the memory of Mary Ritter Beard, whom I first met through the help of Dr. Bossenbrook, who urged me to send her a copy of my thesis on Eleanor Roosevelt. Mary became my mentor, which lasted for some years—until I

15

foolishly decided that five children and the writing of history did not mix. Even then, she sustained and encouraged me, never failing to remind me that I would be a historian yet. To her and her work every American woman historian of a later vintage owes gratitude.

I am grateful to Bob McKeown, whose photographic insight into the city's dark corners is well known, and whose talent is to be credited for a number of the photographs in this book. One or two of these also appeared in *Metro Times*, whose editor and publisher, Ron Williams, should also be thanked. Some illustrations are credited to the Reuther or Burton collections. Credits are noted with each, though not the gracious searching help so freely given at each institution.

To Cameron Waterman I am indebted not only for his gift of a family photograph of the *Uarda*, but also for the sharing of his insights about one period in the life of old Detroit.

I thank Norman McRae, director of the social studies department of the Detroit Public Schools, not only for the material he has written but also for the informal information over the years and his perceptions of the black condition in Detroit.

My most continuing obligation is to my husband, Merle Henrickson, some of whose writings, spanning almost fifty years, appear here, and who, as a reader, can be counted on to be unfailingly critical. To our gently sharp-tongued daughter, Kirsten Brainard, I owe the comment that she had never realized while growing up in Detroit that she and her family occupied the center of the local universe. I can think of no more accurate, though embarrassing, perception of her mother's ego. It is clearly ego that has allowed me to make choices as to which events, decisions, and turning points in this city to include in the book. I am sure many of my readers will question my choices, and they have the clear right to do so.

My own hope is that this book will not only give some pleasure to those who care about history and cities and some insight to students, but also that it will open up areas that still need further questioning. Younger historians should find many dark corners worth exploring, and citizens some things worth fighting for.

Introduction

This is the story of 150 years of change in a city and its environs. Detroit was the capital of the huge area termed the Michigan Territory, the major trading center of the entire Northwest, and its oldest settlement. "A small city," Mr. and Mrs. William Woodbridge called it—with some contempt—in 1822, but in 1837, the year Michigan became a state, it was already more than 130 years old. Detroit's story is told here through a selection of readings focused on moments of change. Those cited in this work fall into several patterns, most of which have recurred several times in the years between 1837 and the present.

Perhaps the earliest, as well as one of the most persistent, of these turning points is the deterioration of the city's natural environment as Detroiters—sometimes mindlessly, more often under the direct pressure of making a living—marred the area's original beauty.

Other major changes in the life of the city came about through raw physical growth, growth that accelerated during an early land boom and three wars. At these times newcomers could hardly be absorbed, much less welcomed. They were times of unplanned urban sprawl, with further depletion of both physical and human resources.

Today there is a frightening shrinkage of the once-proud city, a shrinkage that is combined with a lopsided growth at the outer edges and in the half-dozen counties which make up the "Detroit Metropolitan Area," as the census-takers term it.

Some shifts in the direction of the city's life have been tied to the attractions of wealth. All too often the fat years have coincided with wars. Still, there has been money in Detroit. Dollars earned in Michigan created a local Gilded Age long before the automobile industry became the symbol of Detroit wealth.

Decisions that affect civil liberties or civil rights account for quite a few of the documents cited. Several relate to the care, or lack of it, given to children in the public schools, and others to those civic actions loosely termed "urban planning," which tend to lock us into living patterns we have not chosen.

Some accidental decisions have compelled the city to take new directions, closing off some options, opening others. Many major changes have been allowed to be made by simple drift. All too often a decision is arrived at by the few with no participation, perhaps even no awareness, by the many.

I assume, for instance, that in spite of the wide publicity given to the new City Charter Commission and its many study groups, during the 1970s, few realized fully what the new "strong mayor" government would mean in the political life of the city. In the years since the adoption of the charter, it has become the habit of both ordinary citizens and the daily press to deride the city council for its supposed personal weakness and lack of action. The coincidence of the election of a mayor, Coleman Young, whose own personal political style was that of the strong mayor, has helped to personalize the issue for the past fifteen years.

There have been trade-offs in the growth of the city, prices paid for decisions taken. Samuel Zug was a good businessman, given to religious and charitable works, an abolitionist, and a worker in the Underground Railroad. After the Civil War he bought a wooded island in the Detroit River. I suspect, but cannot prove, that its marshy inlets may have been useful earlier when he was helping in the escape of slaves to Canada. When the damp fogs of Zug Island made it seem an unpleasant place to retire, Zug sold the property to a group of developers. In later years Zug Island became synonymous with one of the ugliest features of industrial growth—the blight near the mouth of the Rouge River—where during times of full employment strange clouds arise to block the view of the riverfront from the decks of the Boblo boats cruising by. (This is not to mention what the same clouds of pollution do to the workers' families of southwest Detroit.) Pollution was long considered a necessary price to be paid for industrial growth, which of course meant jobs.

Trade-offs may involve changes other than physical: a number of those I have cited in documents are set primarily in human terms. The geometric expansion of Detroit's suburbs in the years following World War II did not just change maps dramatically or force the extension of utilities. There were many subtle human trade-offs made by the people moving outward. Most home buyers were tools of real estate developers and had little choice. With home financing sources and the Federal Housing Administration (FHA) working on the side of blandness, the new neighborhoods turned out to be as homogenized as to the age and income of their residents as they frequently were in design. It is also possible to pinpoint a turning point during the late 1940s and the 1950s when, by a fairly conscious decision, at least some Detroiters turned their backs on living among neighbors of other races. The process also destroyed many old ethnic neighborhoods, leaving children of the next generation dependent on the artificial support systems of "ethnic festivals" or the International Institute for a knowledge of other cultures. A series of local elections in the late forties, especially the 1949 choice of Mayor Albert Cobo, marked not only the acceptance of a segregated society, but also an outreach toward one.

Yet during those same years, there was at work a crosscurrent of change, triggered by the United Auto Workers (UAW). To labor's credit, the union was usually at odds with the trends developing toward a closed society. I have included some material on labor-sponsored housing and on a program for rescuing the schools from the dull straitjacket of "the System."

I am not trying to establish an anthology of the best-known writings on Detroit history, nor am I trying to ignore the classics in this field. A few selections from some of the early scholarship should encourage a further look into materials that are receding far enough into the past to become "endangered species" for most readers. There are selections from Silas Farmer, historian and son of the mapmaker John Farmer, and from Clarence M. Burton, who earned his living by authenticating abstracts and titles for real estate but whose massive personal historical collections became the basis of the department of the Detroit Public Library that bears his name. Along with historian-journalists Robert B. Ross and George Catlin, these are the early greats. I have omitted Francis Parkman's tale of the conspiracy of Pontiac to confine myself as much as possible to the years immediately before Michigan's statehood and the period of statehood itself—approximately the time from 1830 to the present.

Another sort of endangered species is the document written long ago in a style that now seems cumbersome and archaic. Few of today's readers would stand in line for a chance to read Lewis Cass's entire position paper on Indian removal—for such it was, a political document, probably aimed at getting the attention of the newly elected president, Andrew Jackson. Yet many of us have become sensitized to the experience of the Native American and are at least curious about the displacement of an entire people. Cass provides a statement of the rationalizations used by thoughtful white men to justify the actions of the times.

I have used both sources and secondary materials, whichever seemed to tell the story most effectively. There are included a number of newspaper articles and other fugitive materials. A good many of these are used simply because of the directness of the material, however incomplete, or tinged with its own bias, it may be. (Witness Mayor John Smith, basically a good man, challenging the Ku Klux Klan in 1925, yet somehow sure that the city's problems would go away if Negroes would just restrict themselves to neighborhoods where they were "welcome!")

I have also included as secondary accounts of events, some hard-won research by people who cared. It is a delight to bring to attention such superb research as that done by Alexandra Mc-Coy on the wealthy elite of the years before and after the Civil War and Jack Elenbaas's examination of the arrest of Alderman Tom Glinnan in 1912. Jorge Castellanos's article, "Black Slavery in Detroit," is one that deserves a more general public than it is likely to have. Few except scholars read scholarly journals, and one of the best of them in this area, *Detroit in Perspective*, is now dead. Castellanos's article appeared in the final issue of that periodical.

The Sojourner Truth housing riots of 1942 are cloudy in Detroit memories, dwarfed as they were by the troubles of 1943. I have included here a section of Bette Jenkins's courageous thesis on the role of her employer, the Detroit Housing Commission. Jenkins traces the thread of confusion running through the news reports of wartime violence by whites that many Detroiters ignored at the time.

Sometimes a style of writing is so evocative of the period that style alone does much to account for the document's inclusion, as with the obituary of Clara Ward. There is a sly, chuckling style behind the surface formality that John Lodge, a venerable Detroit politician, shared with his collaborator, Milo M. Quaife, which imparts a special flavor to Lodge's revelations of 1912 Detroit.

Walter Pitkin, onetime professor of journalism at Columbia University, was best known for his depression best seller, *Life Begins at Forty,* and is little remembered for his rambling, somewhat opinionated autobiography, *On My Own.* Long out of print, but with irreplaceable material on the Detroit of a century ago, this too is an endangered species among books.

One further criterion comes to mind: there still seems to be justification for making certain that materials by or about women or minorities are included. Over the years, such materials have not automatically gotten into print. Also, the writing of black local history by black scholars is a relatively recent, though growing, development. One of these scholars, Norman McRae, has worked in the field for a quarter of a century, and I am pleased to be able to include a selection from an unpublished manuscript by him.

This has not been an attempt to set forth a list of documents included, but rather to clarify the reasons for choice: interest to the reader, probability that it will not be easily found elsewhere, appropriateness to the themes involved, sometimes by a style or mood illuminating that theme, and, "other things being equal," the inclusion of women and minorities as both writers and actors. Preference has been given to direct source material, except when the historian's skill is needed to clarify the intentions of a somewhat murky original document. Given the frailties of historians, that does not happen often.

Part I

The River We Lost

The River We Lost

From the moment when the French first came to that nameless place on the narrows and called it "D'étroit," they were bewitched by the astonishing beauty of the river. The description given by the voyageurs is simply not believable in today's world. Was it ever really like that? Of course such paradise could not survive.

In exploring the Detroit River, we shall begin with the river of Cadillac's report, handed down to us through Silas Farmer, that tireless nineteenth-century historian. Then we shall move to the tale of the first major riverfront developer, the Cass Farm Company, organized by Detroit's leading citizens during the boom times of the 1830s. Its hopes and final failure are recorded by Clarence M. Burton, who remains the all-time expert on land titles and real estate transactions in early Detroit. This section will conclude with a modern evaluation of the old east side riverfront, prepared several years ago for the Detroit Recreation Department by historian Kathryn Kozora. The material used from her work covers the early and mid nineteenth century and shows the uses Detroiters made of their riverfront during the years of early commercial growth.

1. Cadillac's Account of Detroit

as reported by Silas Farmer

Since you [King Louis XIV of France] have directed me to render an account of it, I will do so, premising that Detroit is actually but a channel or river of medium breadth and twenty-five leagues in length, according to my estimate, . . . through which flows and escapes slowly and with sufficiently moderate current, the living and crystal waters of Lake Superior, Michigan, and Huron (which are so many seas of sweet water) into Lake Erie, Lake Ontario, or Frontenac, and which finally, together with the waters of the St. Lawrence, mingle with those of the ocean.

Its borders are so many vast prairies, and the freshness of the Beautiful waters keeps the banks always green. The prairies are

Silas Farmer, *History of Detroit and Wayne County and Early Michigan*, 3d ed. (Detroit: Farmer & Co., 1890; Detroit: Gale Research Company, 1969), 11.

bordered by long and broad rows of fruit trees which have never felt the careful hand of the vigilant gardener. Here, also, orchards, young and old, soften and bend their branches, under the weight and quantity of their fruit, towards the mother earth, which has produced them. It is in this land, so fertile, that the ambitious vine, which has never wept under the knife of the vine-dresser, builds a thick roof with its large leaves and heavy clusters, weighing down the top of the tree which receives it, and often stifling it with its embrace.

Under these broad walks one sees assembled by hundreds the timid deer and faun, also the squirrel bounding in his eagerness to collect the apples and plums with which the earth is covered. Here the cautious turkey calls and conducts her numerous brood to gather the grapes, and here also their mates come to fill their large and gluttonous crops. Golden pheasants, the quail, the partridge, woodcock, and numerous doves swarm in the woods and cover the country, which is dotted and broken with thickets and high forests of full-grown trees, forming a charming perspective, which sweetens the sad lonesomeness of the solitude. The hand of the pitiless reaper has never mown the luxurious grass upon which fatten woolly buffaloes, of magnificent size and proportion.

There are ten species of forest trees, among them are the walnut, white oak, red oak, the ash, the pine, white-wood and cotton-wood; straight as arrows, without knots, and almost without branches, except at the very top, and of prodigious size. Here the courageous eagle looks fiercely at the sun, with sufficient at his feet to satisfy his boldly armed claws. The fish are here nourished and bathed by living water of crystal clearness, and their great abundance renders them none the less delicious. Swans are so numerous that one would take for lilies the reeds in which they are crowded together. The gabbling goose, the duck, the widgeon, and the bustard are so abundant that to give an idea of their numbers I must use the expression of a savage whom I asked before arriving if there was much game. "So much," he said, "that they draw up in lines to let the boats pass through." . . . In a word, the climate is temperate, and the air purified through the day and night by a gentle breeze. The skies are always serene and spread sweet and fresh influences which makes one enjoy a tranquil sleep.

If the situation is agreeable, it is none the less important because it opens and closes the door of passage to the most distant nations which are situated upon the borders of the vast seas of sweet water. None but the enemies of truth could be enemies to this establishment so necessary to the increase of the glory of the king.

2.   The Cass Farm Company of 1835

Clarence M. Burton

One of the largest real estate enterprises that flourished at that period [1835–36] was what was known as the Cass Farm Company. This organization was similar to the corporations of our time, though in fact it was a copartnership. It was organized June 18, 1835. The organizers were the foremost business men of the city, ten in number: Edmund A. Brush, Charles C. Trowbridge, Eurotas P. Hastings, DeGarmo Jones, Shubael Conant, Elon Farnsworth, Oliver Newberry [and Henry Whiting, Augustus S. Porter, and Henry Cole].

. . . The company at first purchased all of the Cass farm south of Larned Street from Gov. Lewis Cass for $100,000 and they gave

Clarence M. Burton, "The Cass Farm Company of 1835," in *The City of Detroit, Michigan, 1701–1922*, ed. Clarence M. Burton, William Stocking, and Gordon K. Miller (Chicago: S. J. Clarke, 1922), 1: 341–43.

him a mortgage for the full amount. The additional security was the obligation of the purchasers and the moneys they expended in improving the property. Before we go further into the history of this company we will ascertain what the Cass farm was. It was a large farm of more than five hundred acres, reaching from Cass Avenue to Third Avenue of the present city and extending from the Detroit River three miles in depth to the railroads on the north. It had originally consisted of three farms and the origin of record title reaches back to the time when this country was under the French Dominion. . . . The property subsequently came to be owned by the estate of William Macomb and by the terms of his will passed on his three sons, David, William and John. Lewis Cass purchased the property from these heirs about the year 1816 for $12,000. It was practically unproductive, for aside from the small portion he wanted for the use of himself and family, it was leased for farm purposes at a small rental. But the times changed so completely between 1830 and 1835 that the front portion of the farm was now needed for business and dwelling purposes. The front, below Larned Street, was mostly covered with the waters of the Detroit River and this had to be all filled in to make it of any use. The work of filling in was begun in 1835. A contract was given to Abraham Smolk to do this work for the company. The entire tract was conveyed by the owners to Augustus S. Porter, August 17, 1835. Mr. Porter was to act as trustee for the company and make conveyances of the property as it was sold in parcels. Porter appointed Charles C. Trowbridge his successor to act in case of his death or disability. The formation of this company and the enterprise it demonstrated is thus referred to in the Free Press of March, 23, 1836:

City Improvements: We are highly gratified to learn from authentic sources that our enterprising fellow citizens Messrs. Newberry, Conant, Jones and others, proprietors for the Cass front, are making preparations for the erection of a splendid hotel on the site of Governor Cass' old residence. It is a subject of congratulation that our citizens are becoming alive to the importance of an addition to the comforts and convenience of travelers. It is true that we have two commodious and excellent hotels and a host of others good enough in their way but it is a subject of public notoriety that hundreds of passengers were compelled last season to remain over

night on board the steamboats, or leave the city, for want of lodg-
ings and even now at this inclement season when navigation is
closed, applicants are daily dismissed from public houses for want
of accommodations. . . .

We predict that the month of May will flood Detroit with persons seeking a temporary or permanent abode. The rapid growth
of this city, its situation on the great chain of lakes at the very center of Michigan and the important public improvements by railroads now being constructed, have attracted the attention of
foreign capitalists and thousands of men will seek an abiding place
among us. The construction of the Cass Hotel on the liberal scale
intended, will remedy many of those evils of which complaints
have justly been made, and its beautiful situation, commanding a
lofty view up and down the river, cannot fail to secure to it a large
share of public patronage. . . .

A year of work in filling in, building wharves and selling took
place before we find any report of their sales. The demand for
lots had been good and there were plenty of sales and many
buildings were erected. On October 20, 1836, the trustees reported that they had expended $53,388.27 in improvements and
had sold lots on contract and for cash to the amount of
$191,936.37. Of these sales $113,552.90 was considered good. Not
enough money had been received to warrant any payments either to Cass on his mortgage or to the members of the company.
Before this sale took place the following notice of it appeared in
the daily press:

GREAT SALE OF THE FRONT OF CASS FARM, DETROIT
The owners of this splendid property, comprising from 15 to 20
acres, having a front of wharfing on the ship channel of the Detroit
River of 1400 feet in length, well laid out in lots to suit the purpose
of warehousing and commerce, will be offered for sale at public
auction at the Michigan Exchange in the City of Detroit on Tuesday
the 20th day of September next. The improvements made by the
owners in wharfing this front and in reducing the high bank on
which the Mansion House of Governor Cass stood, to an easy and
convenient grade from Larned Street to the channel of the river, is
one of the most important and extensive that has been undertaken
by individuals in the west. . . . The proprietors have been engaged
in this work for about a year and are rapidly completing it, having
from 60 to 100 men constantly employed. . . .

The great financial depression that swept over the entire country in 1837 was not felt at once in Detroit and the sale of the Cass front went on at high speed. Messrs. Porter and Conant made an inventory of the property of the company on October 12, 1837, and found that they had in unsold lots $307,307.50 and in good contracts $113,552.90, making a total of $420,860.40. The times of depression had come, however, and it was not only impossible to sell more lots, but the contracts already made were being forfeited and the lands were falling back upon the company. The matter was a failure and it only remained now to make the best of it and get out with as little loss as possible. Nothing whatever on the principal had been paid to General Cass on his mortgage and the interest was paid only until January 1, 1837.

In 1839 Mr. Brush visited Cass in Paris, where he was living as the minister to France, and in the interest of the company made a proposition to him which was accepted. By this agreement the remaining lots were divided into ten portions and one portion allotted to each member of the company. The mortgage to Cass was discharged and in 1840 he took a new mortgage from each member for $10,000, covering the share of each. The ten members gave their unsecured bond for $17,500, the interest unpaid on the original mortgage. In November, 1840, Trowbridge gave up his interest to Henry R. Schoolcraft, John Hulbert and the Reverend William McMurray. These men had purchased interests under Mr. Trowbridge sometime before this, but now he stepped out of the company completely and turned over his shares to his successors completely without any further compensation. Affairs remained in this way for some years. The times were getting harder and harder and as no sales could be made the partners could not pay their mortgages. Their money was gone and to force payment for the mortgages would have compelled them to seek the court of bankruptcy. Farnsworth, Porter, the executors of the Cole estate, Whiting, Hastings, Brush and Conant all surrendered their interests to Cass in 1843. Oliver Newberry and Mrs. Catherine H. Jones [widow of DeGarmo] only retained their interests in the estate.

Thus ended in disaster one of the greatest real estate transactions that ever took place in Detroit. It started out on the wave of prosperity that swept over the country in 1835, and ended in the gulf of disaster and despair that followed in the wake of the financial crisis brought about by rotten wild cat banks and the depreciated currency of 1837.[1]

Editor's Note

1. As Mr. Burton indicates, the outcome of the Cass Farm deal was disaster for the partners. Historian Milo M. Quaife, in lectures given in 1936, said that while two or three partners escaped long term damage, August Porter handed over all his assets and died a poor man, and that only C. C. Trowbridge landed "butter side up." Trowbridge's escape involved the sale of his share to Henry Schoolcraft and two of Schoolcraft's associates at a time when land prices had begun to drop. Trowbridge also gave up to Cass a number of other land parcels in order to maintain his credit. Cass was a hard taskmaster. The partners, in varying degrees, had been close associates and friends of his before the venture. The Michigan legislature later outlawed the old practice of strict foreclosure that made it possible for mortgage holders to collect far more than the original investment.

     The lasting effects were not on some important Detroit pocketbooks but on the river's edge. This was the first clear loss of the shape of the shoreline and the extent of the river to industry and development. The Cass Company also seems to have made no effort to provide general public access to the water's edge. Access to the Detroit River is still something of a key bargaining point between public advocates and real estate developers.

     As for the land that Abraham Smolk once dredged and filled, it now lies firmly under a series of steel-fenced parking lots near the Joe Louis Arena.

3. Detroit's East Riverfront: People and Places of Yesterday

Kathryn Kozora

With the opening of the Erie Canal, the early 1800s brought steam navigation and the beginning of the settlement of the west. The Detroit River, now a water pathway connecting Detroit to the eastern seaboard and the Atlantic Ocean, put the city on the migratory route. The completion of a canal at Sault Ste. Marie connecting Lake Superior and Lake Huron joined Detroit to the Upper Peninsula of Michigan where accessibility to its lumber and mineral resources lured business and laborers to the north as well as industry to locations along the Detroit River. The changing land use patterns on the east riverfront reflected these new business interests as the heirs of the original French farm owners sold their land to those implementing the new economy.

Kathryn Kozora, *Detroit's East Riverfront: People and Places of Yesterday*. (Detroit: Detroit Recreation Department, 1982), 1–20.

In addition to the abundance of raw materials for industry—copper, iron ore, and coal—building materials were also plentiful. These included sand, plaster, and a large supply of brick clay and limestone. At this time, Michigan also produced more lumber than any other state. All these resources can be traced to activities on the east riverfront. The Hart Map of Detroit in 1853 shows a dozen saw mills with accompanying lumber yards, a shipyard and dry dock on the river between Riopelle and Dequindre, a large lime kiln located at the foot of DeQuindre and the city's Hydraulic works and reservoir at the foot of Orleans. . . .

From the early 1880s, various railroad companies had huge land holdings on both the east and west riverfront which provided lines for the movement of raw materials, finished products and people. The first of these companies on the east riverfront was the Pontiac and Detroit Railroad which occupied the land from Randolph to Beaubien and later to Riopelle. The Detroit and Milwaukee, the Great Western and the Detroit, Grand Haven and Milwaukee were some of the numerous companies that were associated with this section of the riverfront, often two or three companies at a time. A vast railroad complex was formed that became the center of much freight and passenger activity.

Shipbuilding became a successful early industry on the east riverfront which retained its importance until the early 1900s. At this time, new technology began to make wooden ships obsolete and the shortage of space on the riverfront property made it impossible to expand the facilities. In 1852, the first large vessel, a wooden propeller steamer designed to carry passengers and freight, was launched from what was to become the Detroit Dry Dock Company located at the foot of Orleans. As the center of wooden shipbuilding in Detroit, the Detroit Dry Dock Company supported numerous related industries. Among these were the Frontier Iron Works at 210 Chene which produced marine engines, the East End Boiler Works at 255 St. Aubin, the Taylor Water Tube Boiler Company at 1440 Franklin and the Murphy Iron Works at 3198 Guoin, manufacturers of marine and stationary engines. Under the leadership of Frank E. Kirby, one of the owners of the Detroit Dry Dock Company and a naval architect, many innovative vessels were developed including the "Lansdowne" a Detroit River railroad car ferry that was the largest ship on the lakes when launched in 1881. It is still in existence and there are plans to restore it as a floating restaurant. The Detroit Dry Dock Company was to become known for its major advances in wooden shipbuilding and enjoyed a nationwide reputation.

Other early industry on the east river front included the Schulte Brothers Soap Factory at Franklin and Rivard, one of the oldest establishments in Detroit. "German," "German Laundry" and "Indian Chief" were some of the soap varieties produced. The American Eagle Tobacco Company at 45–53 Woodbridge was started in 1848 and was one of a growing number of firms that created a viable industry around tobacco in Detroit. The Berry Brothers Varnish Manufactury opened in 1858 on the corner of Leib and Wight. Scattered around the area were a number of foundries and tanneries. These smaller industrial firms usually employed just one or two people and had apprentices training.

Next to Detroit Dry Dock Company was the reservoir of the City of Detroit. With increasing numbers of people in the city, supplying water became a problem. In the days of the French farms, planks had been extended into the river and water was drawn with buckets. Later, several wells were dug near the river and in 1824 a wharf was erected at the foot of Randolph Street where the Peter Berthelet family was in charge of the operation of the round house. . . . The plan for the hydraulic works was copied from the Old Manhattan works of New York City and had a 50-foot tower topped by a wooden tank that was 20 feet high. A narrow, winding stairway led to the top of the tower where "in olden times, a visit was one of the things to be enjoyed by all visitors." This system was in use until 1860 when another larger complex was built farther east on the river. . . .

Away from the main stream of commercial and financial activities which took place west of Woodward, the east riverfront took on an identity of its own. From a hodge-podge of mixed use starting with the mansions on Jefferson to the variety of industry found on the water's edge, neighborhoods emerged producing a kaleidoscope of activity. The resident population lived in small one and two story frame houses built along unpaved streets. Homes were clustered on Franklin, Woodbridge, Wight Streets or scattered throughout the area and interspersed with stores, shops and buildings of craft and industry. A myriad of small business and other services emerged—blacksmiths, barbers, bakers and butchers; shoemakers, saloon keepers, along with a seamstress or two. Grocery, drygoods, notion and drug stores provided for resident needs. Meat markets, machine shops and warehouses were side by side.

Boarding houses and a number of small hotels provided the housing for the transient population—sailors, travelers and the countless hangers-on of an immense new industry based on the world-wide movement of people and goods. . . .

There were fifty taverns and saloons listed in the 1855 Detroit Directory and a large number of them were located on the east riverfront, evenly divided between German and Irish ownership.

An editorial written in the 1885 Detroit Directory deplores the condition of the three mile Detroit riverfront. The writer observes that the various owners are protecting, improving or neglecting their property at will, "and in some instances have wholly barred the passage of the public from the water's edge." He states that the docks, with few exceptions, were in disrepair with "accidents and loss of life not uncommon." Also reported are a new line of docks being constructed from Orleans to the west side. Historically, there had been a continuous fill-in and expansion of the river's edge. As early as 1804, city officials approved the building of wooden cribs at the edge of the river that were to be filled with rubbish and other materials to create more land. In 1819, while giving permission for the building of a wharf at the foot of Randolph Street, it was noted that "as the city grew, an increasing amount of rubbish and refuse was deposited on the low grounds at the river's edge. This created an almost constant nuisance."

In 1826, permanent improvement of the riverfront was begun by depositing earth from the embankment of Ft. Shelby along the edge of the riverfront. This work continued until 1834. By 1889 an international agreement was made ending all further expansion of the river's edge.[1]

Editor's Note

1. This is one instance among many of Detroiters not taking seriously their agreements with Canada, whether about shorelines or air and water pollution. About five years after the 1889 agreement, Hazen

Pingree was urging a large extension of shoreline near the site of to-day's Cobo Hall.

The great expansions of the modern riverfront began in the late 1940s at the urging of the U.S. Army Engineers, with the cooperation of the Detroit City Plan Commission. Later river's-edge expansions made possible the building of Cobo Hall.

Part II

The Land

The Land

Land from the Indians: By Treaty and Expulsion

When the United States of America became a new nation, the Native Americans, whom other Americans universally spoke of as Indians, were in possession of the land and were not planning to go away. From the moment of the Europeans' arrival in North America, it was clear that the key to the newcomers' existence was land ownership. Clear, too, that the Indian's *use* of land, while it might include a private garden spot or a tribal claim to a hunting area, was not at all like the white man's concept of land *ownership*, with deeds, mortgages, and inheritance rights on paper. To the European, Indian land use was negligent, indolent, and inefficient. To the Indian, land and water were life-sustaining. It follows that the formalization of Indian treaties came about as an invention of the white man. Step by step, the land would pass from Indian hands to those of the white settler.

Early U.S. treaties were military in nature and had the purpose of establishing the sovereignty of the United States, making sure that the British could neither control the land nor the Indian tribes. As William Hull's negotiators put it to the "Chippewas, Ottawas, Pattawatamas [sic] and Wyandots" gathered at Detroit in 1807: "The said nations of Indians acknowledge themselves to be under the protection of the United States, and no other power, and will prove by their conduct that they are worthy of so great a blessing."

A considerable number of Michigan land gains were already made by the Americans under treaties drawn up before statehood. There were twenty-one treaties signed with the Chippewas alone, from 1785 to 1836, and many of these included Michigan lands.[1]

Some of the major land cessions made by treaty in the Northwest were:

1. *1785*, a treaty signed at Fort McIntosh. Much of the land deeded was in Ohio, but there were specific guarantees for Detroit, as well as Michilimackinac, from the "Wyandots, Delawares, Chippewas, and Ottawas." These were repeated in 1789, in a treaty made by General Arthur St. Clair.[2]

2. *1795*, Treaty of Greenville. Here General Anthony Wayne negotiated the cession of northern Ohio, northern Indiana, and "six miles square at the mouth of Chikago river, emptying into the southwest end of lake Michigan." This treaty repeats, with additions, the cessions of Michilimackinac and Detroit and the surrounding area, described as "The post of Detroit, and all the land to the north, the west and the south of it, of which the Indian title has been extinguished by gifts or grants to the French or English governments: and so much more land to be annexed to the district of Detroit, as shall be comprehended between the river Rosine [Raisin], on the south, lake St. Clair on the north, and a line, the general course whereof shall be six miles distant from the west end of lake Erie and Detroit river."

The treaty of Greenville was signed by representatives of the "Wyandots, Delawares, Shawnees, Ottawas, Chippewas, Pattawatimas, Miamis, Eel Rivers, Weas, Kickapoos, Piankeshaws, and Kaskaskias," in itself a good listing of Indian tribes who had at least some members in the old Northwest. With his accustomed and well-known pride, General Anthony Wayne declared, "Henceforth all hostilities shall cease; peace is hereby established and shall be perpetual."[3]

3. *1819*, Treaty of Saginaw. This treaty essentially covered the entire eastern half of the Lower Peninsula; it might better be described as involving the drainage areas of the Saginaw, the Rifle, the Au Sable, and Thunder Bay rivers in the eastern half of Michigan. The soft wetlands in the west central part of the state did not yet interest settlers. It was negotiated by Lewis Cass, governor of Michigan Territory and treaty-maker extraordinary. The

long-range result of this treaty was to open eastern Michigan for lumbering. This was a treaty marked by elaborate preparations and a hidden agenda for Indian removal that did not yet succeed.[4]

4. *1821, Treaty of Chicago.* Cass and Solomon Sibley obtained title to western Michigan south of the Grand River in a treaty negotiated with Potawatomis and Ottawas. Intended to make western Michigan—as well as the territories of Indiana and Illinois—more accessible to migrants, it was not popular with the Potawatomis when they had thought it over. It probably laid the groundwork for further hostilities in the West.

5. *1836, Treaty of Washington.* Change and distortion were the key factors in this treaty. In its final form, the treaty ceded to the United States all the remaining lands not included in tribal reservations in the Lower Peninsula and drastically cut those reserved lands. Extensive cessions were also made in the Upper Peninsula. Many individually owned areas that had belonged to Indian families of traders or Indian Agency employees were phased out. At this point, the government instituted a "buy-out" program on these, in the interest of what would today be termed cost efficiency. Among the signers for the government were a number of traders and officials who accepted cash payments "on behalf of their Indian families": John Holiday, John Drew, Rix Robinson, Leonard Slater, Louis Moran, Augustin Hamelin, and William Lasley.

The men and women who had owned these lands were often related to both the chiefs and the white negotiators across the table. Prominent Detroit families whose Indian children received early land grants included Rivard, Cicotte, Moran, Godfroy, and Beaubien, among others. Nor were there only French names. Sophia Biddle, given 640 acres near Mackinac, was an educated spinster and a welcome guest at the home of her relatives, the Biddles of Wyandotte. Her letters, in the Bentley library at the University of Michigan, show thoughtfulness and self-possession.

A major component in the 1836 treaty was the goal of Indian removal. Previously in the background, it was now accomplished by that harsh realist, Andrew Jackson. President Jackson's secretary of war and man in charge was Lewis Cass. They used as negotiator of the treaty Henry Schoolcraft, a scholar of Indian lore whose wife, Jane, was the daughter of the famed Ojibway chief Waub-Ojeeg. Schoolcraft was reportedly the official who was closer to understanding and caring about the Indians than any other prominent American of his time. Yet it fell to him to negotiate the treaty that set the wheels in motion for Indian removal. Both the removal of the Indians and the settlement of the Michigan-Ohio boundary were conditions that had to be met before Congress would grant statehood to the Michigan Territory.

The treaty was negotiated in Washington, subject to intense administration pressures. Even had he chosen to try, Schoolcraft could not have stopped the official urge to move the Indians westward and clear the land.[5] When the treaty was finally ratified by the U.S. Senate two months after it had been signed, it had been amended drastically. All the large tracts, for instance, in the areas of the Traverse and Père Marquette rivers that had been reserved for Indian use were now to belong to the Indians for a maximum of five years only. Worst of all, the Indians were no longer to have the option of relocating among the Chippewa of the Wisconsin and Minnesota regions. These changes and others made by amendment will be outlined in a section that will deal specifically with the Treaty of Washington.

To secure Native American agreement to the treaty, Ottawa and Ojibway treaty-signers remained in Washington at government expense for the two months it took Congress to ratify the treaty. Gifts were given. President Andrew Jackson took a personal interest; Jackson indeed had his own suit copied for one of the chiefs who admired it.

By May 27, when the revised treaty was ratified by Congress, the Ottawas and Ojibway had given up permanent title to almost all the reservation lands granted them in March. We cannot help but wonder how the phrase "Indian giver," used to describe a person who first gives and then takes away, crept into our language. Something is terribly wrong here.

Section readings begin with Lewis Cass's statement on Indian removal, written shortly before he became Andrew Jackson's secretary of war, responsible for carrying out that policy. Possibly meant as a "position paper" aimed at the president, it is a reasoned argument for Indian removal by the man who for years held power over Indian affairs in the Northwest. As such it represents the best rationalizations of the day.

I include sections of the Treaty of Washington, along with the significant distortions introduced by amendment. The section concludes with a speech given by a young Ojibway chief at Saginaw in 1819 and directed at Lewis Cass, who was negotiating the treaty with the Ojibway.

Editor's Notes

1. "Chippewas," in *Treaties between the United States of America, and the Several Indian Tribes from 1778 to 1837. . .* (Washington, D.C.: Commissioner of Indian Affairs, 1837; Millwood, N.Y.: Kraus Reprint Company, 1975), 650–58.
2. Some of the confusions and, perhaps, repetitions might have been wiped out if the advice of Henry Schoolcraft had been taken:

   A DEFECT IN MAKING INDIAN TREATIES
   "The cession of lands by Indians should invariably be made by a map drawn by them & appended to the original treaty. Countries are sometimes bartered by a wave of the hand. A bad or careless interpreter, who is explaining a written treaty, points his finger wrong in defining a boundary, leads a tribe to suppose they have not ceded, accessory to this wave of the hand. Millions of acres are thus, sometimes, put in dispute. Treaties are made to explain treaties, & purchases to cover purchases. All resulting from a bad interpreter, or the want of a line of a ms. or sketch map.

   The quotation appears in Schoolcraft's literary journal, the *Literary Voyager, or Muzzeniegun,* which he edited with his Ojibway wife. In his modern edition of Schoolcraft's Periodical (East Lansing: Michigan State University, 1962), Philip P. Mason described it as a "manuscript magazine produced by Schoolcraft during the winter of 1826–27." It is a tremendous source of material by and about Indians, including many Ojibway (Chippewa) folktales and beliefs.
3. *Treaties,* 54. An Indian view of General Wayne is reported in the *Literary Voyager* of December, 1826, under the heading "Conundrums" on p. 33: "When did a wagon crush the Western Indians? Ans. When Gen. Wayne drove over them at Maumee."
4. See the reminiscences of Ephraim S. Williams, "The Treaty of Saginaw in the Year 1819," *Michigan Pioneer and Historical Society* (hereafter referred to as *MPHS*) (1884): 262–70.
5. In a recent, rather unfriendly, biography, Richard C. Bremer states that by 1836 Schoolcraft had swung away from his earlier opposition

to Indian removal, probably under the influence of Cass, and was now dedicated to the effort to Christianize the Indians, with removal as a means of accomplishing this. See *Indian Agent and Wilderness Scholar; The Life of Henry Rowe Schoolcraft* (Mount Pleasant: Clarke Historical Library, Central Michigan University, 1987), 158–90.

1. Considerations on the Present State of the Indians and Their Removal to the West of the Mississippi

Lewis Cass[1]

The destiny of the Indians, who inhabit the cultivated portions of the territory of the United States, or who occupy positions immediately upon their borders, has long been a subject of deep solicitude to the American government and people. Time, while it adds to the embarrassment and distress of this part of our population, adds also to the interest which their condition excites, and to the difficulties attending a satisfactory solution of the question of their eventual disposal. . . . That the Indians have diminished, and are diminishing, is known to all who have directed their attention to the subject. . . .

The Indians have gradually decreased since they became first known to the Europeans. . . . There is no just reason to believe

Lewis Cass, *Considerations on the Present State of the Indians and Their Removal to the West of the Mississippi* (Boston: Gray and Bowen, 1928), 1–66.

that any of the tribes, within the whole extent of our boundary, has been increasing in numbers at any period since they have been known to us. This opinion is expressed by the Superinten- dents of Indian Affairs in the report submitted to Congress at its last session, by the war department; and from the favorable op- portunities possessed by those officers, of acquiring correct infor- mation upon this subject, their opinion must carry with it considerable authority. The whole amount of Indian population, within the United States, east of the Mississippi, is estimated in this report at 105,060. . . .

In the same report, the number of Indians west of the Missis- sippi is thus estimated . . . making a general aggregate of 313,130, within the United States. . . . And these are the remnants of the primitive people, who, only two centuries ago, possessed this vast country; who found in the sea, the lakes, the rivers, and forests, means of subsistence sufficient for their wants.

It would be miserable affectation to regret the progress of civ- ilization and improvement, the triumph of industry and art, by which these regions have been reclaimed, and over which free- dom, religion, and science are extending their sway. But we may indulge the wish, that these blessings had been attained at a smaller sacrifice; that the aboriginal population had accommo- dated themselves to the inevitable change of their condition, pro- duced by the access and progress of the new race of men, before whom the hunter and his game were destined to disappear. But such a wish is vain. A barbarous people, depending for subsis- tence upon the scanty and precarious supplies furnished by the chase, cannot live in contact with a civilized community. As the cultivated border approaches the haunts of the animals, which are valuable for food or furs, they recede and seek shelter in less accessible situations. The number of these animals may be dimin- ished, but cannot be increased, by the interference of men; and when the people, whom they supply with the means of subsis- tence, have become sufficiently numerous to consume the excess annually added to the stock, it is evident that the population must become stationary, or, resorting to the principal instead of the interest, must, like other prodigals, satisfy the wants of to- day at the expense of to-morrow.

. . . Whether the tribes upon this continent had attained the maximum of their population before the discovery, we have not now the means of ascertaining. It is certain, however, as well as from a consideration of their mode of life, as from a careful examination of the earlier narratives, that, greatly as they exceeded their present numbers, they were yet thinly scattered over the country. There is no reason to believe that vegetable productions were ever cultivated to any considerable extent by the Indians, or formed an important part of their food. Corn, and beans, and pumpkins were indigenous to the country, and were probably raised in small quantities around each Indian village. But they were left to the labor of the women, whose only instrument of agriculture was a clam-shell, or the shoulder-blade of a buffalo, tied to a stick. Their habits of life were then what they now are. They returned from their hunting grounds in the spring, and assembled in their villages. Here their few vegetables were planted. But although the seed-time came, no harvest followed; for before their corn was ripe, it was generally consumed, with that utter recklessness of the future, which forms so prominent and unaccountable a feature in their character. As the autumn approached, they separated and repaired to their *wintering* grounds, where, during eight months of the year, they were engaged alternately in the chase, and in those relaxations and amusements, peculiar to the condition of the hunter. This was the annual round of aboriginal life.

. . . Other circumstances cooperated in the work of [Indian] destruction. Fire-arms were introduced, and greatly facilitated the operations of the hunter. Articles of European merchandise were offered to the Indians, and they were taught the value of their furs, and encouraged to procure them. New wants arose among them. The rifle was found a more efficient instrument than the bow and arrow; blankets were more comfortable than buffalo robes; and cloth, than dressed skins. The exchange was altogether unfavorable to them. The goods they received were dear, and the peltry they furnished was cheap. A greater number of animals was necessary for the support of each family, and increased exertion was necessary to procure them. . . .

Herds of buffaloes were once found upon the shore of Lake Erie, and at the base of the Allegany mountains. They have now receded to the plains beyond the Mississippi, and are now migrating still further west. A few years since, they were unknown in the Rocky Mountains. They have now passed that barrier, and will ere long reach the Pacific. The beaver has nearly disappeared upon all our borders, and hunters and trappers have followed them to the waters of the Columbia. Even the common red deer, once so abundant, is rarely found east of the Allegany, and is becoming scarce in the western regions.

But a still more powerful cause has operated to produce this diminution in the number of the Indians. Ardent spirits have been the bane of their improvement; one of the principal agents in their declension and degradation. . . . [In areas close to white settlers it] has been found impracticable to prevent the sale of spirituous liquors. . . . The most judicious laws are eluded or openly violated. The love of spirits, and the love of gain, conspire to bring together the buyer and the seller. As the penalties become heavier, and the probability of detection and punishment stronger, the prohibited article becomes dearer, and the sacrifice to obtain it greater. We shall not attempt to investigate the cause of the inordinate attachment displayed by the Indians to ardent spirits. It is probably without a parallel in all the history of man. . . . This predisposition was the subject of observation and regret two centuries ago; and the earlier historians and travellers, while they furnish the record of its existence, furnish also the evidence of its overpowering influence and destructive consequences. . . . [2]

To the operation of the physical causes, which we have described, must be added the moral causes connected with their mode of life, and their peculiar opinions. Distress could not teach them providence, nor want industry. As animal food decreased, their vegetable productions were not increased. Their habits were stationary and unbending; never changing with the change of circumstances. How far the prospect around them, which appears to us so dreary, may have depressed and discouraged them, it is difficult to ascertain, as it is also to estimate the effect upon them of that superiority which we have assumed, and they have acknowledged. There is a principle . . . operating through all their institutions, which prevents them from appreciating or adopting any other modes of life, or any other habits of thought or action, but those which have descended to them from their ancestors. . . .

Many of [the Indians] were carefully taught at our seminaries of education, in the hope that principles of morality and habits of

Industry would be acquired, and that they might stimulate their countrymen by precept and example to a better course of life. Missionary stations were established among various tribes, where zealous and pious men devoted themselves with generous ardor to the task of instruction, as well in agriculture and the mechanic arts, as in the principles of morality and religion. The Roman Catholic Church preceded the Protestant in this labor of charity; and the *Lettres Edifiantes* are monuments of her zeal and liberality. Unfortunately, they are monuments also of unsuccessful and unproductive efforts. What tribe has been civilized by all this expenditure of treasure, and labor, and care? From the martyrdom of Le Père Brebeuf, in 1649, upon the shore of Lake Huron, to the death of the last missionary, who sacrificed himself in a cause as holy as it has proved hopeless, what permanent effect has been produced? Year after year sanguine anticipations have been formed, to be succeeded by disappointment and despondency. We are flattered with accounts of success, with explanations for the past and hopes for the future; and this, without the slightest intention to deceive. But the subject itself is calculated to excite these expectations. There are always individuals attending these establishments, who give fair promise of permanent improvement and usefulness. And as these prospects are blighted, others succeed to excite the same hopes, and to end in the same disappointment. . . .

The Wyandots, who occupied so much of the care of the Roman Catholic missionaries, have dwindled to about 700 individuals, who are seated upon a *reservation*, near the centre of the state of Ohio. Serious divisions of opinion exist among them, and a sedentary life begins to be irksome. Already their attention is directed to the trans-Mississippian regions. The Delawares, to whom the Moravians so long and faithfully devoted themselves, have already passed over the Mississippi, where they are resuming their pristine habits. A small society yet exists in Upper Canada; but they are diminishing, and certainly their appearance indicates neither prosperity nor improvement.[3] The Iroquois or Six Nations, the Shawnese, the Miamies, the Potawotamies, and the Ottawas, all of whom have engaged the care and attention of individuals and societies devoted to this object, furnish no evidence of any melioration in their condition, which has resulted from the prosecution of these efforts.

The cause of the total failure cannot be attributed to the nature of the experiment, nor to the character, qualifications, or conduct, of those who have directed it. The process and the persons have varied. . . . But there seems to be some insurmountable obstacle in the habits or temperaments of the Indians, which has heretofore prevented, and yet prevents, the success of these labors. . . .

Experience has shown, that the Indians are steadily and rapidly diminishing. And the causes of this diminution, which we have endeavored to investigate, are yet in constant and active operation. It has also been shown that our efforts to stand between the living and the dead, to stay this tide which is spreading around them and over them, have long been fruitless, and are now hopeless. And equally fruitless and hopeless are the attempts to impart to them, in their present situation, the blessings of religion, the benefits of science and the arts, and the advantages of an efficient and stable government. The time seems to have arrived, when a change in our principle and practice is necessary; when some new effort must be made to meliorate the condition of the Indians, if we would not be left with a living monument of their misfortunes. . . .

But after all, it cannot be denied, and ought not to be concealed, that in this transplantation from the soil of their ancestors to the plains of the Mississippi, some mental and corporeal sufferings await the emigrants. These are inseparable from the measure itself. But by an appropriation liberally made, and prudently applied, the journey may be rendered as easy for them, as for an equal number of our own people. By a continuation of the same liberality, arrangements may be made for their comfortable support, after their arrival in the land of refuge, and until they can accommodate themselves to the circumstances of their situation; until they can secure from the earth or the forests, that means of subsistence, as they may devote themselves to the pursuits of agriculture or of the chase.

The amount of the expenditure necessary for their migration and establishment is not a subject for serious consideration. All should be given, and no doubt will be given, that can be reasonably employed in their comfortable support. It is not a question of profit or loss, but a great question of national policy, involving the rights and feelings of those, from whom we have obtained much, and for whom we have done little.

Although the Indians are migratory in their habits, yet their local attachments are strong and enduring. *The sepulchers of their fathers* are as dear to them as they ever were to the nations of the East. . . . Now, when the time of severance has approached, we owe it to them, to ourselves, to the opinion of the world, that the process should be conducted with kindness, with liberality, and above all, with patience. The assurance of the Secretary of War[4] "that nothing of a compulsory nature to effect the removal of this unfortunate race of people has ever been thought of by the President, although it has been so asserted," is honorable to the government, and consolatory to those who are looking with most solicitude to the condition of the Indians. The intimation of the Secretary that the object of the President was "to explain fully to them and to the country, the actual ground on which it was believed they were rightly entitled to stand," is equally in accordance with justice, policy, and the public feeling.

Let the whole subject be fully explained to the Indians. Let them know that the establishment of an independent government is a hopeless project; which cannot be permitted, and which, if it could be permitted, would lead to their inevitable ruin. Let the offer of a new country be made to them, with ample means to reach it and to subsist in it, with ample security for its peaceful and perpetual possession, and with a pledge, in the words of the Secretary of War, "that the most enlarged and generous efforts, by the government, will be made to improve their minds, better their condition and aid them in their efforts of self-government." Let them distinctly understand, that those who are not disposed to remove, but wish to remain and submit to our laws, will, as the President has told the Creeks, "have land laid off for them and their families, in fee." When all this is done, no consequences can affect the character of the government, or occasion regret to the nation. The Indians would go, and go speedily and with satisfaction. A few perhaps might linger around the site of their council-fires; but . . . soon . . . they would dispose of their possessions and rejoin their countrymen. And even should these prefer ancient associations to future prospects, and finally melt away before our people and institutions, the result must be attributed to causes, which we can neither stay nor control.

53

Editor's Notes

1. The title page of the original document does not name Lewis Cass as author, yet the attribution to him is so accepted that all libraries fortunate enough to have a copy list him as such. Cass was in the habit of writing for literary journals using a pseudonym. The timing here suggests that the 1830 edition was indeed a "position paper" intended to catch the attention of the new president, Andrew Jackson. An Arno Press reprint (New York, 1975) is generally available in libraries.

2. Cass, who was personally a teetotaller, did not hesitate, when negotiating with the Ojibway at Saginaw in 1819, to have barrels of brandy available to speed the settlement, according to Ephraim Williams, trader in that area. Williams tells of the treaty in "The Treaty of Saginaw in the Year 1819," *MPHS* 7(1884): 262–70.

3. Cass himself had been a general during the War of 1812, which had led to the misfortunes of the Delawares in Upper Canada, and of the Moravian missionaries who lived among them. To his credit, he had at least arranged a pass for the refugees from a destroyed village to go to Ohio, where a number of them relocated in the area north of Columbus. For an extensive account of the little-known Moravians and the Delawares among whom they lived, see Elma Cray and Leslie Robb Cray, *Wilderness Christians* (Toronto: MacMillan, 1956).

4. Presumably Major John Eaton, Andrew Jackson's first appointee to this post, which Cass later inherited.

2. Change and Distortion: The Treaty of Washington, 1836

Commissioner of Indian Affairs

Reprinted here are major sections of the original treaty and the final revisions of those sections made by Congress before ratification. The amendments, which appeared at the end of the treaty in the original document, are rearranged here to follow directly the articles to which they apply, so that the reader may more easily follow the basic changes negotiated by the government after the Indians signed the original treaty.

I have kept the spelling and format of the original document intact.

OTTAWAS AND CHIPPEWAS
Concluded March 28, 1836—Ratified May 27, 1836.
Articles of a treaty made and concluded at the city of Washington, in the District of Columbia, between Henry R. Schoolcraft, commissioner on the part of the United States, and the Ottawa and Chippewa nation of Indians, by their chiefs and delegates.

[Article 2, omitted here, described the boundaries involved in northern Michigan and a part of Wisconsin and was not amended.]

ART. 2. From the cession aforesaid the tribes reserve for their own use, to be held in common, the following tracts, namely-:One tract of fifty thousand acres, to be located on Little Traverse

Commissioner of Indian Affairs, *Treaties between the United States of America and the Several Indian Tribes from 1778 to 1837* (Washington, D.C.: Commissioner of Indian Affairs, 1837; Millwood, N.Y.: Kraus, 1975), 650–58.

bay; one tract of twenty thousand acres, to be located on the north shore of Grand Traverse bay; one tract of seventy thousand acres, to be located on or north of the Pierre Marquetta river; one tract of one thousand acres to be located by Chingassanoo, or the Big Sail, on the Cheboigan; one tract of one thousand acres, to be located by Mujeekewis, on Thunder-bay river.

[AMENDMENT to] ART. 2. Line two, after the word "tracts," insert the following words, to wit: *"For the term of five years from the date of ratification of this treaty, and no longer;* unless the United States grant them permission to remain on said lands for a longer period" [Italics mine][1].

ART. 3. There shall also be reserved for the use of the Chippewas living north of the straits of Michilimackinac, the following tracts, that is to say: Two tracts of three miles square each, on the north shores of the said straits, between Point-au-Barbe and Mille Coquin river, including the fishing grounds in front of such reservations, to be located by a council of the chiefs; the Beaver islands of lake Michigan for the use of the Beaver island Indians, Round island, opposite Michilimackinac, as a place of encampment for the Indians, to be under the charge of the Indian department; the islands of the Chenos . . . Sugar island, with its islets in the river of St. Mary's; six hundred and forty acres at the mission of the Little rapids; a tract commencing at the mouth of the Pissisowining river, south of point Iroquois; thence, running up said streams to its forks; thence westward, in a direct line to the Red water lakes; thence, across the portage to the Tacqimenon river, and down the same to its mouth, including the small islands and fishing grounds in front of this reservation; six hundred and forty acres on Grand island, and two thousand acres on the main land south of it; two sections on the northern extremity of Green bay, to be located by a council of the chiefs. . . .

[AMENDMENT to] ART. 3. After the word "tracts," in the second line, insert the following words, to wit: "For the term of five years from the date of the ratification of this treaty, and no longer, unless the United States grant them permission to remain on said lands for a longer period." . . . It is understood that a place for fishing and encampment, made under the treaty of St. Mary's, of the 16th of June, 1820, remains unaffected by this treaty.[2]

ART. 4. In consideration of the foregoing cessions, the United States engage to pay to the Ottawa and Chippewa nations the following sums, namely: 1st. An annuity of thirty thousand dollars per annum, in specie, for twenty years; eighteen thousand dollars to be paid to the Indians between Grand river and the Cheboigan; three thousand six hundred dollars to the Indians on the Huron shore, between the Cheboigan and Thunder-bay river; and seven thousand four hundred dollars to the Chippewas north of the straits, as far as the cession extends; . . . Five thousand dollars per annum for the purposes of education, teachers, school-houses, and books in their own language, to be continued twenty years, and as long thereafter as Congress may appropriate for the object. . . . Three thousand dollars for missions. . . . Ten thousand dollars for agricultural implements, cattle, mechanics' tools, and such other objects as the President may deem proper. 5th. Three hundred dollars per annum for vaccine matter, medicines, and the services of physicians, to be continued while the Indians remain on their reservations . . . six thousand five hundred pounds of tobacco; one hundred barrels of salt; and five hundred fish barrels, annually, for twenty years. . . . One hundred and fifty thousand dollars, in goods and provisions, on the ratification of this treaty, to be delivered at Michilimackinac.

[AMENDMENT to] ART. 4. At the close thereof insert these words: "and also the sum of two hundred thousand dollars in consideration of changing the permanent reservations in articles two and three to reservations for five years only, to be paid whenever their reservations shall be surrendered, and until that time the interest on said two hundred thousand dollars shall be paid annually to the Indians. . . . "

[It is interesting to note how many of the obligations of the white man set out in Article 4 hinged on the continued Indian occupation of the reservation lands, a right that Article 4 in its final form denied.]

ART. 8. [italics mine]. *It is agreed that as soon as the said Indians desire it, a deputation shall be sent to the west of the Mississippi, and the country between lake Superior and the Mississippi, and a suitable location shall be provided for them, among the Chippewas, if they desire it and if it can be purchased upon reasonable terms, and, if not, then in some portion of the country west of the Mississippi, which is at the disposal of the United States. . . .* When the Indians wish it, the United States will remove them . . . provide them a year's subsistence in the country to which they wish to go. . . .

[AMENDMENT to] ART. 8. Strike out after the word "the," where it first occurs in line two, to the words "States," in the eighth line, and insert in lieu thereof these words: "Southwest of the Mississippi river, there to select a final place for the settlement of said Indians, which country, so selected, and of reasonable extent, the United States will forever guaranty and secure to said Indians. . . ."[3]

ART. 12. All expenses attending the journeys of the Indians from, and to their homes, and their visit at the seat of Government, together with the expenses of the treaty, including a proper quantity of clothing to be given them, will be paid by the United States.

ART. 13. The Indians stipulate for the right of hunting on the lands ceded . . . until the land is required for settlement.[4]

In testimony whereof, the said Henry R. Schoolcraft, commissioner, on the part of the United States, and the chiefs and delegates of the Ottawa and Chippewa nation of Indians, have hereunto set their hands, at Washington, the seat of Government, this twenty-eighth day of March, in the year one thousand, eight hundred and thirty-six.

Henry R. Schoolcraft
John Hulbert, *Secretary.*

Oroun Aishkum, of Maskigo,	his x mark
Wassangaze, of do [*sic*, ditto]	his x mark
Wabi Windego, of Grand river,	his x mark
Ainse, of Michilimackinac,	his x mark
Chabowaywa, of do	his x mark
Jawba Wadiek, of Sault Ste. Marie	his x mark
Waub Ogeeg, of do	his x mark
Apawkozigun, of L'Arbre Croche	his x mark
Keminitchagun, of do	his x mark
Mukuday Benais, of do	his x mark

Aishquagonabee, of Grand Traverse   his x mark
Akosa, of   do   his x mark

[Witnessed by·]

Lucius Lyon,   Leonard Slater
R. P. Parrott, Capt.U.S. Army   Louis Moran
W. P. Zantzinger, Purser, U.S. Navy   Augustin Hamelin, jr.,
                                      Henry A. Lenake . . .[5]

Editor's Notes

1. This effectively removed Indian claims to five reservation areas which amounted, in total, to 142,000 acres. The five-year limit, as opposed to perpetual ownership, would just represent time to pack up and move.
2. This not only has the same effect on many northern islands and spots in the Upper Peninsula, but would seem to account for some of the later legal confusions as to Indian fishing rights.
3. The key phrase seems to be "*Southwest* of the Mississippi." The original option of northwest lands would have allowed, though in a more restricted area, the continuation of traditional patterns of hunting and fishing. None of this would ever be possible, in the same way, "southwest of the Mississippi."
4. No changes are indicated here, but note that the final termination of the privilege is left completely in the hands of the U.S. government.
5. Signing for the government were John Holiday, John Drew, Rix Robinson, Leonard Slater, Louis Moran, Augustin Hamelin, and William Lasley, each of whom had agreed in the original treaty to cash settlements for land which had been owned by them on behalf of their Indian families, a trust relationship that was not always honored by the guardians.

3. You Do Not Know Our Wishes

Chief Oge-Maw-Keke-too

You do not know our wishes. Our people wonder what has brought you so far from your homes. Your young men have invited us to come and light the council fire. We are here to smoke the pipe of peace, but not to sell our lands. Our American father wants them. Our English father treats us better; he has never asked for them. Your people trespass upon our hunting grounds. You flock to our shores. Our waters grow warm; our land melts like a cake of ice; our possessions grow smaller and smaller; the warm wave of the white man rolls in upon us and melts us away. Our women reproach us. Our children want homes; shall we sell from under them the spot where they spread their blankets? We have not called you here. We smoke with you the pipe of peace.

Chief Oge-Maw-Keke-too, addressing Lewis Cass, as reported by Ephraim Williams, "The Treaty of Saginaw in the Year 1819," *MPHS* 7 (1884): 264.

The Land

Who Got the Land?

One of the political war cries in modern Michigan has been "Jobs, jobs, jobs!" We should translate this into "Land, land, land!" for understanding the past. No existence in Michigan Territory or in the new state of Michigan would have been possible without land as the basic commodity. Often the decision as to who got the land went to the one who had the swiftest horse to take him to the land office or the most force in facing down squatters and other claimants. Lumberman Dan Ward boasted in his autobiography of having beaten the *"landlookers"* of the St. Mary's Ship Canal Company to the land office to register the claim.

After the original people of the region—Chippewa or Ojibway, Potawatomis, Ottawas, and others—were forced out of their lands, the next project was the measurement and logical organization of land on which, of course, many settlers were already living.

Neat, square townships were formed, working out from a baseline road (called Eight Mile Road in the Detroit area). The charting of the new Territory of Michigan became a model for how such things ought to be done. Of course, occasional errors occurred on some of the maps, and some resurveying had to be done. Still, the work of John Mullett, William Burt, and Lucius Lyon, among others, was amazingly accurate given the hard conditions under which it had to be done. Descriptions of the planning process of those days and how it was accomplished are from a Detroit City Plan Commission document of 1954, *Trafficways for Three Million People.*

Order and straight-lined efficiency ended as one entered the city limits. Detroit, which once consisted only of military fort, parade ground, a few narrow farms on the river's edge, and common pasture, was becoming a town. Inevitably, the transition was accompanied by confusion and delay, argument and countercharges. There were lost records and auctions where it seemed almost everyone wanted their money back. The fire of 1805 that wiped out the town just as it was to make its first start at living under American rule did not help. Judge Augustus Woodward, friend of President Jefferson, provided elegant plans modeled on the work that famed engineer and city planner Pierre Charles L'Enfant and Benjamin Banneker, black mathematician, had done for Washington, D.C. Unfortunately, Woodward also came equipped with secretiveness and a disregard for anyone who asked for explanations. Practical home owners, according to Silas Farmer, looked at the Grand Circus that Woodward planned to be the hub of future parks and boulevards—and used it as a dumping ground for dead cats.

That land was of the greatest importance in the Michigan economy was shown in the boom years just before 1837 and in the tremendous crash in land values that followed. Both the madness of the boom and the later troubles are told of in the selection "U.S. Land Office" from Silas Farmer.

The biggest of all land acquisitions, scorned by many at the time, was the Upper Peninsula. Michigan got it by yielding seven miles across her southern border, including Toledo, to Ohio. A brief letter Senator Lucius Lyon wrote a Detroit friend does not detail either the transaction or the military skirmishes that surrounded it but does convey a sense of the machinations necessary for Michigan to achieve statehood.

This material on how the land was obtained and distributed just begins to cover the surface. There is the whole question of what became of the "school sections," those grants in each township for education, as mentioned in *Trafficways.* Some vanished in the early 1840s after bank failures, and especially that of the Michigan Bank, had wiped out both the state's credit and its cash. More public land went into grants to railroads—good lands, given as a reward to men who engaged in that most prosperous business. The grants seemed necessary at the time, but harder to understand later. Other entrepreneurs, such as canal builders, toll road builders, and lumbermen, found ways to get land for their efforts. Their rewards were based on the extent to which they provided access to the land. Land had to be easily available, and land too heavily wooded, swampy, or without roads would not attract the new immigrants who meant prosperity for all.

I will consider the matter of accessibility further in Part IV. For now I am more concerned with the distribution of the land itself. Still, it is clear that the rewards of providing access to land were frequently paid in the coin of land itself. The St. Mary's Ship Canal Company's membership of prominent Detroiters received hundreds of thousands of acres of good pine land for constructing the first of the locks at Sault Sainte Marie.

I recommend the exploration of land acquisition in Michigan for extensive further study for anyone interested in how grants were made, guidelines set, and rules broken, in Michigan lands.

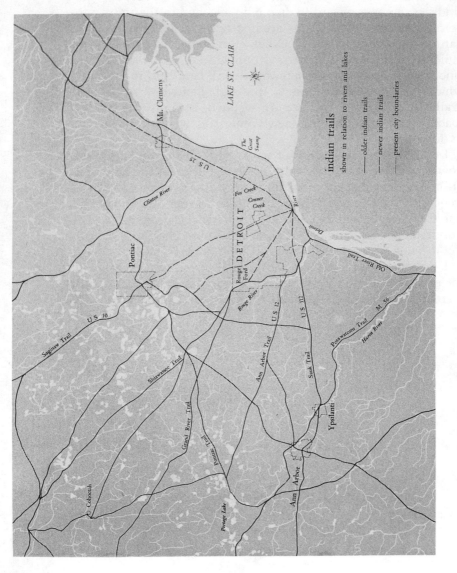

Indian trails created the routes of Michigan's later highways. (From *Trafficways for Three Million People*, Detroit City Plan Commission, 1949. Used with permission.)

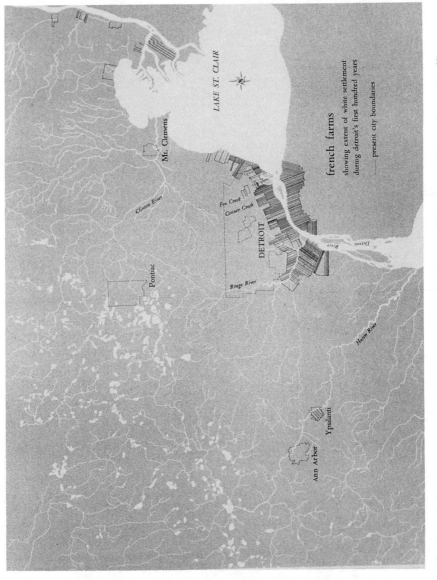

The French farms, in narrow strips, gave every man his own bit of waterfront. (From *Trafficways for Three Million People*, Detroit City Plan Commission, 1949. Used with permission.)

governor and judges' plan
—— portions of plan followed in
downtown detroit streets

Detroit River

The core of Judge Woodward's plan set the growth patterns for the
city. (From *Trafficways for Three Million People,* Detroit City Plan
Commission, 1949. Used with permission.)

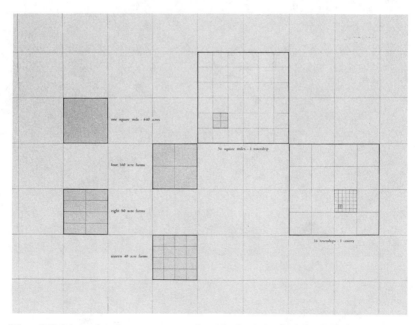

one square mile - 640 acres

four 160 acre farms

eight 80 acre farms

sixteen 40 acre farms

36 square miles - 1 township

16 townships - 1 county

How Michigan land was surveyed and platted after the Land
Ordinance of 1785. (From *Trafficways for Three Million People,*
Detroit City Plan Commission, 1949. Used with permission.)

1. Trafficways for Three Million People

Detroit City Plan Commission

French Farms

. . . The main French settlement was along the Detroit River where the French houses stood in a row all along the bank all the way from the mouth of the Rouge east to the great swamp just east of Belle Isle. As more French came they lined the shores of Lake St. Clair and the Detroit River to Lake Erie.

Settlements of the French moved up the Ecorse and Rouge Rivers at the time of the American Revolution from 1776 to 1783. Farms lined the Rouge River about eight miles to what is now the northern boundary of Dearborn. . . . In the years following the

Detroit City Plan Commission, *Trafficways for Three Million People*, text by Merle Henrickson, design and drawings by William Kessler, maps by Frederick Pryor (Detroit: Detroit City Plan Commission, 1949), 5–18.

American Revolution, French settlers began to fill in the banks along the Raisin and Clinton Rivers, and other smaller creeks. . . .

As the French settled along the rivers, each farm had a narrow frontage 400 to 900 feet wide on the river, and extended inland as much as three miles.

When more people came to Detroit to settle in later years, these old French farms were subdivided separately as each owner saw fit. Each subdivider laid out his farm according to his own notions of what would make good lots and good streets. Most of the owners laid out straight streets running back from the river for the length of their farms but very few of them bothered to provide continuous streets running parallel to the river. Jefferson Avenue already existed as an Indian trail. Harper Avenue runs along the northern boundary of the French farms. However, other east-west streets had offsets wherever some farmer disagreed with his neighbors about where the road should run.

Jefferson's Land Plan of 1785

When people from Michigan travel in Kentucky, Tennessee, Virginia, Missouri, or for that matter almost anywhere through eastern or southern states, they are often puzzled why the roads do not run straight north and south or east and west. Neither are there any square or rectangular farms.

Roads wind around following streams, and all the farms are irregularly shaped pieces of land with boundaries marked by big boulders, tall trees, or other landmarks.

When plans were being discussed for settling the Northwest Territory, including Michigan, Wisconsin, Illinois, Indiana, and Ohio, Jefferson suggested that there should be a more orderly way of measuring and dividing the land than had been followed before. His plan was to divide all the unsurveyed land into mile square pieces by running parallel roads one mile apart north and south, and east and west. Each mile square or section would contain 640 acres which could be divided again into four 160-acre farms, or eight 80-acre farms, or sixteen 40-acre farms.

By joining these square pieces of land together, Jefferson proposed to form the small divisions of government. Thirty-six one-mile squares, or a square six miles in each direction would be a township. Sixteen townships joined together, or a big square 24 miles in each direction would make a county.

The Land Ordinance of 1785 established this system as the basic pattern for surveying the land in the Northwest Territory which became the states of Ohio, Michigan, Indiana, Illinois, and Wisconsin. The same pattern was later followed in other states of the west.

Of course, many of the actual township and county boundaries were set up and changed several times by the territorial government as more people came to settle in this new territory. As a result the final boundaries adopted did not all match up as orderly squares. Oakland County, for example was five townships wide and five high, while Livingston County next to it was four wide and four high. Both follow the same basic square mile grid pattern, however.

The plan for dividing land also established a system of roads. The roads follow the survey lines which divided the land of the state into square miles. Eight Mile Road is called Base Line Road as it runs across the state because it is the east-west base line from which the rest of the state was measured. All across the state the roads follow these survey lines except where lakes, swamps, or high hills forced people to wind the roads around them.

Within Detroit we know the survey lines today as Livernois, Wyoming, Schaefer, Greenfield, Southfield, Fullerton, Fenkell, McNichols, Seven Mile and Eight Mile. These survey line roads form much of the network of main roads or thoroughfares for Detroit today.

Governor and Judges' Plan of 1807

Grand Circus Park, Washington and Madison Boulevards, Cadillac Square, and several small triangular parks in downtown Detroit make the city almost unique in American cities in having a street system in its central business area which departs from the rectangular pattern.

Viewed from an airplane, downtown streets converge on Grand Circus Park forming half of a six-sided block in the pattern of bathroom tile or a honeycomb.

The unusual plan of streets was drawn by Judge Augustus Brevoort Woodward after the town was destroyed by fire in 1805. Judge Woodward's plan was originally drawn to cover a much larger area than what exists today in downtown Detroit. Grand Circus Park is only half of the park originally drawn by Judge Woodward. Other boulevards were supposed to run northeast and northwest to other "circuses" and "campuses" about a half mile apart in all directions.

The owners whose buildings had been destroyed by the fire were given new lots in exchange for their old lots on narrow streets. Governor Hull and Judges Woodward and Bates would not permit people to rebuild their houses until the new plan had been drawn and approved.

The plan seemed so fanciful that Judge Woodward could not get people to follow it beyond the area affected by the fire. The Woodward plan extends to Cass Avenue on the west and Randolph on the east which were the boundaries of farms not yet subdivided when Woodward laid out the plan for the land between. On the north side the plan was stopped in the middle of what was to be a larger circular Grand Circus Park.[1]

Editor's Note

1. Several major expressways whose construction was begun in the fifties overlaid the remainder of the judge's handiwork.

2.   United States Land Office

Silas Farmer

From 1825 to 1837, the immigration from the Eastern States increased so rapidly that business flourished, and by the purchase and clearing of lands large sums of money were brought into and scattered about the Territory. As early as 1833 capitalists began to come from New York to invest in wild lands. In 1836 the number of immigrants amazed everyone; the steamers and sailing vessels were literally loaded down with people who came to settle in Michigan and the West. From five hundred to seven hundred frequently arrived on a single boat. During the month of May public lands were entered so rapidly that on Monday, May 9, the register [sic] had to close his door and receive applications through the window, and the receipts at the Land Office between the 1st and the 25th of the month were $278,000.

"United States Land Office," in Farmer, *History of Detroit*, 37–38.

The total amount received at the three Michigan land offices, namely Detroit, Kalamazoo, and Monroe, was over $1,000,000. During the year the total sales in Michigan amounted to the enormous sum of $7,000,000. Numerous associations were formed for the purchase of wild lands and embryo city sites, and at the mouth of every western river, and almost every township corner, towns were laid out. "On paper" creeks were magnified into streams, and comparatively insignificant streams were transformed into large rivers floating steamboats and other watercraft, while on the land the speculator's dreams took form in imaginary hotels, churches, schools, and railroads. Absolute forests were in imagination transformed into cities, and sold at ten thousand per cent advance. The laying out and making maps of these "paper cities" kept the few draughtsmen then in Detroit busy all day long and far into the night. Hundreds of dollars in the "wildcat" currency of the times, were frequently paid for a draughtsman's services for a single day. Leading men of both parties formed pools with fifty or a hundred thousand dollars, and committed the amounts to the discretion of agents who were to be compensated by a share of the profits in the lands purchased.

The details of some of these enterprises are so ludicrous as to be hardly credible. There remain to this day survivors of the crowds which, in the height of the season, occupied the entire width of Jefferson Avenue in front of the Land Office, each individual awaiting his turn to enter and secure his prize. Sometimes large sums were given to secure the services of the fortunate man at the head of the column by another who was far in the rear. Horses were mercilessly driven and killed in the race to reach the Land Office. In one instance, at midday, two men on horseback were seen turning the corner of Woodward and Jefferson Avenues, hastening at full speed to the Land Office. It turned out that they were victims of a cruel joker in Genesee County. Each of them had ridden all night, breaking down two horses apiece in the seventy-mile race, in order to be the first to enter a certain tract of land. The sequel showed that they wished to purchase entirely different parcels. . . .

It is utterly impossible to describe . . . the actual condition of the public mind at that period. This abnormal activity began to show itself in 1834, grew rapidly in 1835, and culminated in 1836; and when the panic came, the sites of many "paper cities" could be bought for less than the price of wild land, and to this day [1890] are owned and assessed as farm lands.

3.   The Biggest Land Deal of All

Lucius Lyon

In 1836 Lucius Lyon, a surveyor and friend of Cass and Schoolcraft, had already been named senator by the territorial legislature but could not take office until Michigan became a state. Ohio had the power in Congress to block statehood until it could have Toledo. Lyon waited in Washington and attended the boundary discussions. He claimed throughout that he was not part of any compromise or deal but insisted that if Ohio got its way, Michigan should make sure it benefited in the north. Michigan accepted a new southern boundary, seven miles north of the Ohio line, and received millions of acres in the Upper Peninsula. The arrangement was unpopular at home, and Lyon's enemies considered him what would today be called a "wimp." The fact that Lyon had been actively involved in setting up the 1836 treaty negotiations that wiped out most Indian claims in the Upper Peninsula meant little to Michiganders, who saw the whole thing as a defeat by Ohio. Lyon won statehood for Michigan but lost any chance of remaining a U.S. senator.

Excerpts from two of Lyon's letters revealing his anger and frustration are given here.

To Edward Mundy, Lieutenant Governor, Michigan, Feb. 26, 1836— I am awaiting with anxiety and impatience to see the report of the committee on the judiciary of the house of representatives on our boundary question and admission into the union. The report will be made in a day or two and on the boundary will be against us. All political parties here are courting the favor of Ohio, Indiana and Illinois and there no longer remains any doubt that the interests of Michigan are to be sacri-

"Letters of Lucius Lyon," *MPHS* 27 (1896): nos. 73, 52.

ficed. Our admission will be made to depend on the assent of the legislature to the boundary claimed by Ohio and Indiana. . . . Under this state of things there remains for Michigan no hope of redress. She will be compelled either to submit to the grossest wrong or make an attempt at revolution. . . .

To Col. D. Goodwin, Detroit, Feb. 4 [1836]— I thank you for the suggestions contained in yours of the 22d ult., relative to an addition to the state of Michigan on the west, provided Congress should break up our boundary on the south . . . which I yet hope will not be done. It if should be however, I for one, shall go in for all the country Congress will give us west of the lakes. It will only require the consent of the legislature to receive it, according to the doctrine which maintains that Congress can cut and carve the territory as they choose, and if that doctrine is to prevail, we will take advantage of it and let the "Devil take the hindmost" as gamesters say; for on this principle, all the legislation of Congress in relation to the boundaries of the states formed in the territory northwest of the river Ohio has been and is a mere bullying, and gambling operation where power and interest and artifice combine to insult and rob and cheat the weak and defenseless of their just rights.

Part III

The People of Early Michigan

The People of Early Michigan

It is most unfair to ignore those who were here long before statehood, but that is what we must do for the most part. Native Americans appear in the accounts of travelers and in the treaties they were compelled to sign. For the rest, we defer to the growing scholarship of Native Americans about their people in Michigan.[1]

Of the French there is also a good deal left unsaid. The earliest French were trappers and traders, less likely to have family with them than the British, and therefore most likely to find spouses among the Ojibway, Wyandot, and Ottawa women. These men who followed the fur trade into the northern woods were here before Cadillac, who was greeted by a Pelletier.

By the 1830s, the business emigrants from New York State and New England had closed their minds as to any French capacity in matters of importance. As they saw it, the French opposed sensible road expansions to help the city grow simply because the new roads divided their farms, sometimes even separated them from the river—which was the Frenchman's preferred method of transportation. To the Yankees, French families seemed always on the go, by boat or pony cart, to dances, weddings, and christening parties. Soon the French found themselves outvoted by the newcomers, but still Campaus and Beaubiens refused to sell their land, even when offered many times market value.

Slowly the French were backed into corners, and always accused of being thriftless. Yet there were still Morans in banking. A Marantette broker struggles with the current ills of the stock market and it was a Pelletier who helped found and direct one of Michigan's largest credit unions. One branch of a Ford family— banking more than automotive—is descended from the French wives of Elijah Brush and his father-in-law, John Askin. The genealogy of the French shows that a number of them, accused by the newcomers of too much love of parties, married into those respectable and sober families, and their descendants are now found on corporate boards of directors. As Alexandra McCoy suggests in her study of mid-nineteenth-century wealth excerpted in Part V, it is never wise to overlook the people who were here first.

The British came early to control Detroit after their victory in 1763. They left most reluctantly, having to be reminded several times that they had lost the war of 1812, even though they had forced Detroit's surrender in 1813. Among all British colonials of the old British Empire, one imperialist deserves to be remembered locally: John Askin, merchant and wheeler-dealer. When Askin finally prepared himself to leave for Canada, he insisted that a respectable government would honor his land claims. These claims numbered millions of acres, and included more than half of the lower peninsula of Michigan. Fortunately Askin was forced to leave the United States with his claims denied.[2]

Others who sometimes arrived with the earliest of settlers were black: slaves, usually, of the French or British, or captured by Americans or by Native American raiding parties. Because of their early arrival, even though in very small numbers, it seems appropriate to include blacks early in our discussion of the people of early Michigan during the years between statehood and the Civil War.

In a study of slavery in Detroit, Jorge Castellanos has set out three periods: the French, 1701–60; the British, 1760–96; and the American, 1796–1837. Here I quote from his introduction, then include one or two items from the French and British periods, following these with the section "Slavery in American Detroit."

Castellanos's work reflects a breadth of scholarship that is unusual in its use of both Canadian and United States sources. The interrelatedness of blacks in Canadian and American history of the early nineteenth century makes this a good area to explore.

Racism was in the Detroit area early, though it often appeared in that subtle, unaware form by which the master assumes the slave is happy, as Friend Palmer did when he wrote: "As a class the negroes were esteemed by our early time population . . . little cruelty was practiced by their owners . . . the negro was satisfied with his position . . . and was ever ready to help . . . against the treacherous Indians."[3]

Though it is possible to trust General Palmer much of the time, more credible accounts of blacks in Detroit's early days have been provided by Jorge Castellanos and Norman McRae. McRae contributes "The Thornton Blackburn Affair" from his Civil War Centennial study for the Michigan Historical Department. This was a case of escaped slaves that served to crystallize the fears of both races in Detroit during the 1830s.

On reading McCrae and Castellanos it becomes possible to believe, if not fully understand, that the promise of freedom wrapped into the Northwest Ordinance could be denied and postponed for almost a century. That is, of course, for blacks. Young Native American scholars insist that for their people, there was never even a meaningful promise in the ordinance.

By 1837, the balance of power had fallen into the hands of the New Yorkers and New Englanders because of the rapid increase in population that came after 1825, with the opening of the Erie Canal. These newcomers quickly formed the majority. They were mostly male, young, single, and geared to the expectation of early success. Lucius Lyon, born in Vermont, was just thirty-six when he took his seat as the first United States senator from Michigan and had already served two terms in Congress representing Michigan Territory. Michigan's most famous citizen, Lewis Cass, had served as federal marshal and state legislator in Ohio before coming to Michigan as territorial governor in 1813, at age twenty-nine.[4] Stevens Thomson Mason, the "boy governor" at barely twenty-one, was not too unusual against the backdrop of his times.

The places from which the young men came put their imprint on them and on their trades and politics. There were New York State men, canny and commercial; there were New Englanders who were no less interested in personal survival, but who were determined to import a measure of culture and morality as well.

New Englanders arrived first, bringing to Detroit the lyceum, the debating society, and the "reading circles" for leisure entertainment. Like the New York State people, they also brought account books and the Protestant church. They established Michigan's free public schools, surveyed lands, set up local governments. Unlike the soldiers and fur traders, they brought their women with them or sent home for them as soon as possible.

The feminine minority had its own problems on the frontier. New England men, with their cultural baggage of thrift, morality, and a tendency to elevate women, were apt to wound them in strange ways, never more so than when they were at their most well-meaning. When Mrs. William Woodbridge for a time received no invitations to the "Reading Circle" due to a supposed slight to Mrs. Cass, Woodbridge and Cass overreacted in many letters as they tried unsuccessfully to arbitrate a quarrel among ladies.

Then there was Zachariah Chandler, born in Vermont, up-and-coming young merchant in 1841—certainly one of Detroit's most eligible bachelors. A friend, attorney James F. Joy, introduced him into the home of one of the area's prominent families, the Stephen Trowbridges, who lived in rural Oakland County. Chandler was quickly attracted to twenty-two-year-old Elizabeth Trowbridge and began calling regularly. Her parents liked him and were not disturbed to learn that an understanding for their future had been reached between them.

One Saturday afternoon, Chandler arrived at the country home and the couple went horseback riding together. When they returned she was crying, and Chandler left immediately. In a tearful scene, she told her family that Mr. Chandler had broken off their engagement abruptly, saying only that he was not in love.

While the Trowbridge family was fuming with justified anger, Chandler worsened the situation by writing Charles C. Trowbridge, the girl's uncle, sending a check for three thousand dollars while trying to acknowledge that no "reparation" would make up for the destruction he had caused, or wipe out his sense of guilt for the broken promise. In 1841, a year of bank closings and failed land deals, three thousand dollars was no small sum.

Zachariah Chandler's idea was given a family veto through Charles Trowbridge and no money was allowed to change hands. Instead Miss Trowbridge survived grief and embarrassment to find her own solution. The following January she married a New Yorker and went to live, we hope happily ever after, in Brooklyn. Chandler became a United States senator and a millionaire but kept a certain aura of the outsider among the society of old Detroit.

As for the New York State men, a witty letter by Theodore Hinchman, written during the financial disasters of the 1840s and included here, shows that skillful interest in money which seems to have been in the baggage New Yorkers brought on the canal boats.

Among the next arrivals were the Irish, at least some of whom arrived well before the potato famine, which is usually thought of as the main cause for Irish migration. Their life in nineteenth century Detroit has been ably chronicled by JoEllen Vinyard in her extensive and sympathetic study, *The Irish on the Urban Frontier,* from which is reprinted a section on the working life of these newcomers.

The last of the major ethnic groups to arrive in sizable numbers before the Civil War were the Germans, who by the 1870s represented the very largest foreign-born population group in Detroit. Although not written until many years after the arrival of the early Germans, Walter Pitkin's study of the home and family of the prosperous miller Rickel during the 1880s is the best description I have found of the German culture in Detroit.

Another vital group in Detroit and southeastern Michigan comprised those German immigrants who were also Jews. Irving I. Katz points out that there were Jews among the early traders and trappers, and that one of them may well have furnished the inspiration for Stephen Vincent Benet's famous short story, "Jacob and the Indians." Their arrival in significant numbers, however, occurs at about 1850.

From *The Beth El Story,* I have selected a section that not only tells of some of the early arrivals but puts into sharp focus the state of Central Europe at that time, when Germans, Hungarians, and Austrians came to America to avoid the shadows of repression. The section will serve not only to sketch in the background particular to German Jews, but also to add to our understanding of other Germans, such as the socialist Dr. Herman Kiefer, who pioneered in public health, the farmers of Frankenmuth and Saline, and the storekeepers, craftsmen, and brewers (over fifty of them by 1860) of Detroit's East Side. From various sources we gain the impression that there were many cheerful social blendings among Jews and Gentiles in this early period. Anti-Semitism came later to the area, though it definitely came.

Editor's Notes

1. See for instance George Cornell, James M. McGlurken, and James A. Clifton, *People of the Three Fires: The Ottawa, Potawatomi and Ojibway of Michigan* (Grand Rapids, Mich.: Grand Rapids Inter-Tribal Council, 1986).
2. The late Milo M. Quaife, editor of Askin's voluminous papers in the Burton Historical Collection (BHC) at the Detroit Public Library, maintained in discussing the power of John Askin in dealing with both British and United States government officials that it was "a near thing" that Michigan was not lost to that fabulous entrepreneur.
3. General Friend Palmer, *Early Days in Detroit* (Detroit: Hunt & June, 1906), 104. A highly personalized and anecdotal collection of old memories, this is a good source for old locations and old families.
4. See Frank B. Woodford, *Lewis Cass: the Last Jeffersonian* (New Brunswick, N.J.: Rutgers University Press, 1950), 37.

1. Black Slavery in Detroit

Jorge Castellanos

Slavery in Detroit differed in many ways from the "peculiar institution" of the American South. It was introduced by the French and not by the British, and it developed initially under the influence of French law and custom as they were reinterpreted in colonial New France. Basically domestic in character, slavery never played a role in the economic life of the frontier town. It proved to be, however, extremely persistent and tenacious: it was retained by the British when they occupied Detroit in 1760; it survived when the city became part of Michigan Territory in 1796, in open violation of the anti-slavery provisions of the Northwest Ordinance of 1787; and it was not finally abolished until 1837 by the first constitution of the state of Michigan.

Jorge Castellanos, "Black Slavery in Detroit," *Detroit in Perspective: A Journal of Regional History* 7, no. 2, (Fall 1983): 42–57.

Slavery in French Detroit

. . . According to one source, there were 45 slaves in Detroit in 1706, when the total population of the city (excluding soldiers, but including the slaves themselves) had arrived at 563. Slaves represented then 7.99% of the total population. Most, if not all of them, were Indians or *Panis*, as they were called from the Indian tribe name Pawnee. The conversion of Indian slavery into Black slavery proceeded very slowly during the French period and was not completed until the British period, i.e., after 1760. At any rate, the population of Detroit and the number of slaves increased at a very slow pace under French rule. There were only 62 slaves in the city in November, 1760, when it was surrendered to a British force under the command of ranger Major Robert Rogers. There is no doubt that by then some of them were Black. . . .

Most of the first Black slaves in Detroit were obtained from the Indians who captured them in their raids against slave plantations in the South. Later some were brought to the city and its surrounding area by Southerners who moved in with their chattels. . . .

. . . Although relatively marginal in character, slavery was solidly entrenched in French Detroit society when the transfer of Detroit from France to Great Britain took place in 1763, after the Treaty of Paris officially ended the French and Indian War. . . .

Slavery in British Detroit

Paraphrasing a Gallic proverb it may be said that the more Detroit changed the more it remained the same. A new sovereignty meant a new power structure and new laws and regulations, particularly for control of the fur trade . . . but the post remained a small frontier town of fur traders and small farmers. . . .

Slowly, but continually, however, the city prospered under the new regime. Population increased. . . .

In March, 1779, by order of the commanding officer of Fort Ponchartrain, Captain R. B. Lernoult, a census of the settlement of Detroit was taken. . . . The census showed there were 294 households in Detroit in 1779. About 23% of them held slaves. [In 1782] the census showed there were 321 households in Detroit. Now 25.8% of them held slaves. . . . slaveowners represented about one-fourth of the number of households in Detroit, a respectable figure, indeed. And even more, the slaveowners tended to be the most influential members of the community. Slavery had become an important status symbol in the small frontier town. Although secondary in its economic influence, it was vital in many other respects. And that explained why it survived so long.

Black slavery increased in the British period, reinforcing itself numerically through several channels. After the occupation of the city, the economic system remained the same except that systematically British merchants took over the fur trade from the French until they controlled it absolutely by the 1780's. A number of Irish, Scotch and English traders, and also a few farmers, settled in the Detroit area. . . . A number of them were slaveowners and brought their chattels with them. A few residents also introduced slaves acquired in the American South.

. . . But [during the American Revolution] by far the most important sources of increase were the Detroit-based Indian raids against American settlements in the valley of the Ohio River and in Illinois. In those raids, the Indians often killed the whites whom they could not sell, but kept the Black slaves whom they could exchange for guns, ammunition and liquor. In 1780, a mixed force of whites and Indians, under the command of Henry Bird, attacked several forts in Kentucky. Some Black slaves were taken . . . some [were] sold in Detroit. For several years afterward, one of the owners of those slaves, Mrs. Agnes Le Force, tried in vain to repossess 13 of them who were in the hands of very prominent Detroiters. . . .

Generally speaking, the treatment given to the slaves did not differ substantially from that prevailing under French rule. Manumissions were not uncommon. . . . A few slaves received an elementary education and were placed in charge of activities requiring a certain level of culture. . . . Mullett, one of the ten Negroes owned by Joseph Campeau, acted as his master's clerk and earned the respect of the community for his integrity and shrewdness in business matters. Hector, who belonged to Gen. John R. Williams, was put in charge of the *Oakland Chronicle* plant. Crimes committed by white residents against slaves did not go unpunished. But sometimes the punishment dispensed to slaves for relatively minor felonies was disproportionately brutal, as in the case of Ann Wyley, who was condemned to death and executed for having stolen six guineas from the firm Abbott and Finchley. . . .

In 1793 the legislature of Upper Canada (to which Detroit was incorporated) passed a law providing for gradual abolition of slavery, thus setting a precedent within the British Empire. But that law freed not one slave this side of the Detroit River. When Great Britain evacuated the Detroit post on July 11, 1796, in conformity with the Jay Treaty, slavery in the city was at its historical peak numerically as well as institutionally.

Slavery in American Detroit

Under the new American regime, slavery abruptly declined. A large number of British residents moved to Upper Canada, settling about Windsor, Sandwich, Lake St. Clair, etc., and taking their slaves with them. So serious was this emigration flow that the population dwindled to about 500 in a few months. It was to take almost a decade for the Detroit population to reach the 2,000 plateau again. The abolitionist law in 1793 in Upper Canada was not really too radical. No slaves could be imported, and the children born to slave mothers after the act was passed would become free at age twenty-five, but those who were legally enslaved in 1793 would remain as such until death. Apart from patriotic feelings, the British slaveholders decided to leave because the antislavery provisions of the Canadian law seemed more promising to them than the abolitionist clause in the Northwest Ordinance of 1787, which they expected would become operative immediately after the occupation of the city by General Wayne's troops. Article VI of the Ordinance read:

> There shall be neither slavery nor involuntary servitude in the said (Northwest) Territory, otherwise than in the punishment of crimes whereof the party shall be duly convicted: provided always that any person escaping into the same, from whom labour or service is lawfully claimed in any one of the original states, such fugitive

may be lawfully reclaimed and conveyed to the person claiming his or her labour or service as aforesaid.

The Ordinance, however, did not put an end to slavery in Detroit. Slave owners petitioned Congress in 1802 to suspend it for ten years. Congress refused. But after a period of haggling with the slaveholders remaining in the city, Governor St. Clair interpreted Article VI as meaning that the extension of slavery was prohibited in the Territory (no slaves could be brought in), but those already in the Wayne County would remain indefinitely in their masters' possession. As so often happens in those cases, the struggle between freedom and property was decided in favor of the latter, that is, in favor of the privileged interests. The purgation of slavery from the lands becoming ready to enter the Union, which Thomas Jefferson considered essential for the future of the country, suffered a delay in Michigan Territory.

The slaves reacted to these disappointing events with massive desertions and with appeals to the courts for their freedom. A curious situation developed, due to the peculiar legal status of slavery in the adjacent territories of Michigan and Upper Canada. Since the introduction of new slaves was prohibited in both, any slave escaping from one side to the other was considered free. There were so many Canadian runaways in Detroit that soon after becoming the first Governor of Michigan Territory in 1805, William Hull gave them permission to organize themselves into a militia. However, Judge Woodward immediately brought charges of misgovernment against Hull, claiming that arming the Blacks was injurious to proprietors of slaves both in Detroit and in Canada. The Governor defended himself against the charges but the military club was disbanded.

A few slaves used the *habeas corpus* proceedings in attempts to obtain their freedom. In 1809 a Black woman called Hanna and "a mulatto boy" called Thomas were declared "free persons and not slaves." But most of the cases were decided in favor of the owners. The most famous of these decisions was *In the matter of Elizabeth Denison et al.*, issued in 1807 by Justice Woodward. It is so typical of the ambiguities of abolitionist legislation that it deserves detailed attention. In his conclusions, Judge Woodward begins by accepting without qualifications that "in this Territory slavery is absolutely and peremptorily forbidden." But immediately the question of property rights challenged the "absolute" principle of freedom. Woodward asked himself whether the provisions of the Ordinance were not nullified by that clause in the Jay Treaty of November 19, 1794, which established: "All settlers and traders shall continue to enjoy unmolested, all their property of every kind. It shall be free to them to sell their lands, houses or effects, or to retain the property thereof at their discretion."

The real issue, of course, was whether "property" included "slavery." Judge Woodward said yes. "Property" was used in the Treaty "with a latitude the most extensive of which it can possibly be made susceptible." Spain and Great Britain accepted the institution in their colonies, and even the United States of America, who claimed "the foremost rank of the world in protecting and maintaining the liberties of mankind," still recognized slavery. Since the Canadian slave law of 1793 confirmed the slave status for life for those who lived in the Detroit area at that time, all slaves in the possession of settlers on July 11, 1796 were the legitimate property of their holders. Therefore, Judge Woodward concluded, "I consider the return of the writ of *habeas corpus* sufficient, and I order Elizabeth Denison, James Denison, Scipio Denison and Peter Denison, Junior to be restored to the possession of Catherine Ineker Tucker." And so, the logic of class privilege defeated that of human justice, a treaty was made to prevail over an act of Congress, and the life of a moribund institution was legally prolonged for several years.

Meanwhile, the slaveholders—who were desperately in need of labor—tried to revitalize the declining system of indentured servitude. In 1803, John Reed, a runaway slave from Kentucky, appeared in Detroit during the summer. According to F. C. Bald: "Daniel Ransom provided bond for the Negro's release and had Solomon Sibley write to (Reed's owner) Colonel Grant, offering to buy the man. Sibley explained that he could not be held in Detroit as a slave, but that Ransom could probably persuade him to indent himself for a term of years." *Engagés* were employed side by side with slaves in Detroit at the turn of the century. John Askin had a gang of them working in a pinery close to the St. Clair River cutting timber. In 1799, Askin begged the McGills from Montreal to send him six or eight *engagés* in the spring. If more came than he could use it would be easy for him to sell their services at a very good price. The Detroit merchant wanted young men. He wrote: "Smart young boys does (sic) nearly as well as men and are much cheaper and easier managed."

The number of slaves continued to drop. The 1810 census enumerated 17 slaves in the city of Detroit, although the number at the time was probably higher; some slaveholders simply failed to report them. The 1820 census, for the first time, recorded none. But since slaves were made taxable property as late as 1818 it is doubtful that the 1820 figure was right. However, for all practical purposes, by 1830 slavery could be considered extinguished in Michigan. Simultaneously, the number of free Blacks increased from 67 in 1820, to 126 in 1830, and 138 in 1834. In 1837 there were 222 Blacks in Wayne County. The free Blacks were relatively few in numbers but extremely active in the defense of their rights and those of the fugitive slaves who happened to arrive in Detroit. In 1806, 1828 and 1833 angry demonstrations defeated the slave-hunters' intentions of using the fugitive slave law against runaways living in the city. The 1833 incident almost became a riot when the Blackburn family was freed from their captors and smuggled into Canada.

Slavery was legally abolished in Detroit by the provisions of the first Constitution of the state of Michigan. The Constitutional Convention met at the territorial capital of Detroit on May 11, 1835. On May 18, the leader of the Democrats, John Norvell, a delegate for Wayne County, proposed and the assembly unanimously accepted that a committee of seven be appointed to draft an article abolishing slavery in the future state. The committee reported two days later that it was in favor of the prohibition of the "peculiar institution" and proposed the adoption of the following article: "Neither slavery nor involuntary servitude shall ever be introduced into this state, except for the punishment of crimes, of which the party shall have been duly convicted." Norvell took the floor and said he was anxious that this article should be the first one adopted into the Constitution. By a vote of 81 to none, the assembly concurred.

The elimination of slavery, however, did not bring equality to the Black community. On May 22, the Convention committee on elective franchise proposed that the right to vote be restricted to "the white male inhabitants." Only the delegates, Joseph H. Patterson, Darius Comstock and Ross Wilkins, raised their voices against the discriminatory constriction. Wilkins was particularly vocal in his protest: "If . . . all men are free and equal, and we want to confine ourselves to the principles of the Declaration of Independence, where is the propriety of confining the right of voting exclusively to white male inhabitants?" He insisted that he was for allowing the "Negro to vote if he be intelligent and worthy of the privilege." His words were received with sneers by some and Wilkins insisted: "I see [some] gentlemen smile. . . . But I know many Negroes, or men of colour if the distinction be preferable, who are sober, industrious, intelligent, worthy members of society."

These good intentions were killed by John Norvell's intervention in the debate. The man who had urged the Convention to abolish slavery now demanded the limitation of the political and civil rights of the free Blacks. The right to vote, he argued, was not entirely a natural right, but a question of expediency. "Why, then," he asked, "should we invite within our limits; why hold out inducements to the migration hither, of a description of population confessedly injurious, confessedly a nuisance, to the community? It would not be denied that the Negro belonged to a degraded cast of mankind. We did not take them as equals to our homes, to our tables, to our bosoms. . . . Nature has marked the distinction. Society has, in all ages, recognized and sanctioned it." Norvell wanted to record his "solemn protest" against the "admission of the black to any association of equality, at the polls or elsewhere. . . . " In other words, slavery (which was dead anyhow), no; but segregation, which was very much alive, yes. The Convention once more agreed.

It was not the first time in Detroit's history that a piece of legislation purportedly designed to defend the Blacks was used against them. Only eight years before, in 1827, the infamous *Act to regulate Blacks and Mulattoes, and to Punish the Kidnapping of such Persons* was passed. Although pretending to protect the Black population, in practice it was an attempt to exclude them from the city and from the rest of Michigan Territory. Now the same Constitution that legalized their freedom, disfranchised them, deprived them of jury duty (a privilege only of electors) and closed the doors of the militia to them. Soon a statute was to prohibit inter-racial marriages in the state. It has taken more than a century of bitter struggles to correct some of those wrongs. Slavery was certainly scratched from the books in 1837, but racism proved to be much more stubborn than slavery had ever been.[1]

Editor's Note

1. Professor Castellanos's notes are extensive and include for the French period several references to *Liste du habitants du Détroit*, in the Burton Historical Collection, items in the John *Askin Papers*, vol. 1, edited by M. M. Quaife, also BHC. William R. Riddell is cited for "The Slave in Canada," *Journal of Negro History* 5 (1920): 267, and for his *Life of William Dummer Powell* (Lansing: Michigan Historical Commission, 1924).

   The source for several of the anecdotes of the British period is the anonymous but useful typescript, "Negroes in Detroit," BHC.

2.　The Thornton Blackburn Affair

Norman McRae

One of the ironies of Michigan history is that most of the American settlers in Michigan had come from the East and had brought along many of the New England values and ideas about education and human rights. Nevertheless, their relations with Negroes in Michigan were unduly influenced by the "black codes" of their sister states. "Black codes" were laws enacted by states to limit Negroes from participating in the full privileges and responsibilities of citizenship. These laws generally prohibited Negroes from voting, attending schools with whites, entering and using public facilities such as hotels, theatres, and restaurants, and in some cases, it forced them to post a bond

Norman McRae, *Negroes in Michigan during the Civil War,* ed. Sidney Glazer (Lansing: Michigan Civil War Centennial Observance Commission, 1966), 4–7.

with the local government to insure good behavior and to guard against indigency. . . .

On April 13, 1827, a law was passed which required all "black people to register at the county clerk's office after May 1, 1827." Those Negroes who did not have their "free papers" would not be permitted to reside in the territory. In addition, those Negroes who met all other requirements for residence had to post a five hundred dollar bond to insure their continuous "good behavior." All Negroes who could not meet the requirements were forced to leave the territory. Many merely crossed the river and entered Canada. Thus the Negro population of Detroit was reduced to sixty-six free Negroes.

This restrictive law of 1827 did not hinder Negroes from coming to Detroit on their way to Canada. Since the law of 1827 was never strictly enforced, many stayed here. Whenever their qualifications for residence were too closely checked, they merely crossed the river. One couple who stopped in Detroit rather than go into Canada was Mr. and Mrs. Thornton Blackburn. . . .

In 1831, Thornton Blackburn and his wife escaped from Louisville, Kentucky. They became members of the Negro community and were apparently well liked. In 1833, they were apprehended by their owner who invoked the Fugitive Slave Law of 1793, and had Sheriff Wilson place them in the city jail until they could leave on the steamer *Ohio* for Louisville. For this service the sheriff and his deputy received fifty dollars each. Meanwhile the Negro community was angered by the arrest which in their point of view was a miscarriage of justice.

The steamer *Ohio* was to leave on Monday. On Sunday, Mrs. Madison Lightfoot and Mrs. George French, two of Detroit's most prominent colored matrons were allowed to visit Mrs. Blackburn in the city jail. Mrs. Blackburn exchanged clothing with Mrs. French and in this disguise was quickly taken across the Detroit River to Amherstburg, Ontario. When Sheriff Wilson discovered the hoax, Mrs. French was threatened with the fate of permanently taking Mrs. Blackburn's place and this entailed being taken back to Kentucky where she would be sold into slavery to compensate the owner for the loss of one female slave. Later that day, however, Mrs. French was allowed to leave the jail.

The following day when Mr. Blackburn was to leave the jail to be returned to slavery a crowd of Negroes gathered outside the jail. They were angry, and the situation was rife with danger. As the sheriff, his deputy, the slave owner, and his slave approached the prison coach, the crowd drew closer. Blackburn asked the sheriff if he might speak to the crowd in order to allay their fears and to appease their anger. As the people crowded in to hear Blackburn, someone slipped him a pistol which he brandished and ran into the coach where he locked himself in, and promised to kill whoever attempted to recapture him. . . .

The group of white people who had been looking on immediately came to the rescue of Sheriff Wilson. In the melee that followed, Blackburn was slipped from the coach by Sleepy Polly, and Daddy Walker [a local black citizen] whisked him away to Canada. Sheriff Wilson was fatally wounded by an unknown assailant. The prison coach was disabled so that the pursuit of Blackburn was impossible. Daddy Walker threw any possible pursuers off the trail by going out Gratiot and then doubling back to River Rouge where he and Blackburn escaped by boat to Sandwich, Ontario. We have seen this particular scene played out in countless motion pictures. The only missing element is the man who said, "They went thata way."

Meanwhile back in Detroit a full scale race riot was in progress. In the subsequent examination, those persons involved were fined and sentenced to work on the street repair gang. Mr. Lightfoot was jailed for allegedly slipping the gun to Blackburn. Mr. and Mrs. French fled to Canada.

Many Negroes who had not been involved in the Blackburn affair planned a march in order to protest mob brutality and various injustices. Mayor Chapin issued a proclamation which silenced the planners of this demonstration. The proclamation stated that all Negroes who could not prove that they were free would be expelled from Michigan. And once more there was an exodus to Canada. Thus ended what the white citizenry of Detroit termed "The First Negro Insurrection."

3. A Young New Yorker in Detroit, 1841

Theodore Hinchman

During the winter of 1841, when Theodore Hinchman wrote the following letter to his brother in New York, Detroit was in the depth of the depression that followed the collapse of the land boom and the failures of local banks. Hinchman was working as a bookkeeper for John Owen, a businessman of varied interests: wholesale groceries, ship chandlery, and brewing. Still a bachelor who had not yet persuaded a certain teenaged Miss Chapin to come to Michigan, Hinchman was a careful observer of the local scene.

Dear Brother John

Having an opportunity to send you a line by Mr. Doremus who leaves here tomorrow for New York I will not let it pass.

Our state is in a great confusion and excitement in consequence of the failure of the Bank of Michigan to redeem its liability. The suspension law expired on the first. . . . [1] Since then the bank instead of giving six month Drafts, as it had previously, gives nothing. More than 80 suits have been commenced against it. Our circulation is composed almost entirely of its notes. Everybody became alarmed and lost confidence and endeavored to dispose of the bills they had on hand. The Detroit merchants,

Theodore Hinchman to John Hinchman, 19 February 1841, Hinchman Papers, BHC.

consequently, did a very good business. Instead of trying to sell goods as usual, it was our object to avoid it.

The legislature, which could have granted relief, refused to do anything, each party fearing to move in the matter.

The Merchants have held meetings, passed resolutions—and expended their breath & wisdom in discussing the matter, adopted resolutions & a memorial to the legislature praying them to loan the bank $750,000 state stocks. . . . The legislature have at least appointed a committee to examine the banks. They went into the bank, and wished to examine the items, which the bank refused to allow, so the investigation stands—

Some of the merchants, ourselves among the rest, have at last stopped taking the money in order to save from risk; and to bring the members of the legislature to terms, as all of the state funds are in the Bank of Michigan and the members will not get their pay at all if the money does not pass.

The Bank says they can pay give them time, and a loan, but if they do not get these, they will *wind up*. If so the money will fall 50 per cent immediately. We do a very small business in consequence. Mr. O. [Owen] has the *blues some*. I am on hand—as usual—will have more time to devote to reading & for Societies and Society—

The Young Men's Society have had excellent lectures by lernd [sic] and talented men this winter. A course of chemical lectures commenced the evenings. Our *Athenian Club* prospers. You ought to look in and see six egotistical *wise* young men, all ready to thrust their opinions on the club, all full of eloquence and self-esteem. Whether it be special talent, or only the character of a Wolverine, I leave you to judge.

Parties are all the rage, one almost every evening. The members of the legislature are almost always invited. They are beautiful monuments to politeness.

They afford some amusement to our city people. It is not uncommon for them to walk into the rooms, among the ladies, with their hats and cloaks on. Wisdom—unpolished! Unpresuming! 300 & 400 invitations are often sent out. Instead of dancing, we find only a crowd of people. I have been invited to three or four large ones lately. I don't enjoy myself very much, however, as I never flourish very extensively in a large crowd. . . .

Yr Brother Theodore

Editor's Note

1. Refers to the Currency Act passed by the Michigan Legislature a year earlier. This had given the bank power to issue drafts by which the state could pay the cost of internal improvements such as railways or canals. When the legislature did not renew the law, much of the program collapsed.

4. The Irish on the Urban Frontier

JoEllen Vinyard

By midcentury Detroit housed Irish who had left their native land with education and resources, Irish who had left with nothing but managed to parlay work and chance into wealth and position, and Irish whose disadvantages of a lifetime continued to weight them down. There was work to be done in the city on top, in the middle, and at the bottom. The range of opportunities accommodated the spectrum of Irish abilities, if not always in precise proportion to the newcomers themselves. Like the children's nursery rhyme, the Detroit Irish community in 1850 had its "rich man, poor man, beggar man, thief."

At midcentury, while the Irish were the largest immigrant group, they had not arrived in numbers so overwhelming as to

JoEllen Vinyard, *The Irish on the Urban Frontier: Nineteenth Century Detroit, 1850–1880* (New York: Arno Press, 1976), 48–79.

disorganize the existing economy or undermine their own position. In Detroit, with opportunity considerable and religious prejudice negligible, assets or liabilities of background most often determined the work that Irish immigrants could get.

Early in the nineteenth century, years when the prosperous eastern counties were contributing the most steady flow of emigrants, Detroit fell heir to several of that small number of Irishmen with resources of wealth and talents. Those who arrived in America with a profession or a skill had high aspirations; sharpened perceptions made them more critical of inadequacies in the seaboard cities where they landed. . . . Some made several shifts in the course of their continuing search and many such immigrants leapfrogging westward, began to arrive in Detroit by the late 1820's. . . . According to some reports the westward bound Irish usually had resources of at least $100 a family and some had as much as $5,000.[1]

Indeed, the act of getting to Detroit took some money. Coming from New York City before midcentury the traveler had to pay twenty-five to fifty cents for the Hudson River trip to Albany, then $5 for the railroad fare to Buffalo unless he endured the cheaper but longer canal trip. Finally $1.50 to $5 for a steamboat ticket from Buffalo to Detroit. . . .[2]

The Irish who had collected in Detroit by 1840 were prospering. That year the parish roster for the Irish Catholic church, Most Holy Trinity, bore witness. Of the 189 male pew holders, 59 were businessmen, 52 were in skilled occupations such as carpentry and masonry, 44 were laborers, and 16 were tailors or shoemakers. Four men were clerks, one was a collector for the United States customs, four were farmers. The Irish church had three judges, two medical doctors, two teachers and an architect.[3]

A number of these early arrivals stayed on in the city. In 1850 at least 267 of the 647 families headed by Irish men had been in the country for five years or more, many of them in Detroit for some time. There was, by then, a sizeable contingent among the Irish that had accumulated a stability of residence that stretched back 10 to 25 years.

Within the decade of the 1840's, however, the Detroit Irish community had expanded to include increasing numbers of poor and uneducated, the men and women who were more represen-

101

tative of the overwhelming peasant masses in Ireland. Like his wealthier countrymen, the Irish farmer-turned-American laborer often arrived in Detroit after a series of moves; moves made gradual by straitened means and stops marked always by a sameness of low-paying, unskilled work. Occasional immigrants arrived without luggage. Finding themselves unable to afford the whole passage to Detroit, they had to promise it as security along the way. . . .

In 1846 Detroit began to accumulate still another group of Irish immigrants: the fugitives from the failure of the potato crops. At midcentury at least 52 Irish families in the city had crossed the ocean within the preceding four years along with the famine migration. These were the years when peasants from the poorest areas from the South and West were cleared from the land with little or no reimbursement; when droves of subsistence cotters finally resigned themselves to emigration; when jobless townsmen from the cabin districts crowded into the steerage sections of departing ships.

The most destitute of the desperate famine refugees were not likely to make their way at once to Detroit unless they had contacts in the city who offered encouragement, aid, and comfort. Over four-fifths of the Irish family heads who came to Detroit between 1845 and 1850 were credited with the ability to read and write, a rate almost the same as that of the earlier arrivals. This suggests that Detroit did not gather in many from the lowest levels of Irish society even during the famine years. . . .

Longer residents jibed that on a Saturday night one could spot an Irishman just off the boat by his beaver hat, "high water" trousers, and short clay pipe. The reality of the maladjustment bit deeper. While the number of newly arrived Irish who fell upon charity was not staggering, the number who managed quickly to get good jobs was not impressive. At midcentury the Irish who had arrived in the United States after 1846 differed significantly in occupation from those who had come earlier. Among the pre-famine immigrants, 40% worked as laborers, whereas 79% of those who had come after 1846 were in that category.

Irishmen compelled to make their way as common laborers often preferred the jobs considered in Ireland to be more manly. Occupations that called for physical strength and prowess were greatly admired. In the 1850's, over 400 men were regularly employed by the 43 sawmills along the Detroit river front and many Irish were among the number. Others found work in the iron furnaces and related industries. By 1858 there were five iron furnaces in the county. Production had increased tenfold since 1840 and jobs had grown apace. Allied to the smelting works had come factories that manufactured cars, wheels, axles, locomotives, boilers, steam engines and stoves. In 1854 Captain Eber Brock Ward built the Eureka Iron and Steel works. Soon after the Wyandotte Rolling Mills located nearby. [Both plants, according to Vinyard, had deliberately located in Ecorse township on the edge of one of Michigan's finest remaining forest tracts, where charcoal supplies were still available.[4]] The two factories were the largest industrial employers in Wayne County in the 1850's. Jobs were available there for the unskilled, for those willing to do the hauling and heaving. Scores of Irishmen hired on. There were scores of unskilled jobs to be had on the roads being built on all sides of Detroit. . . .

In keeping with the entrepreneurial organization of the city, dozens of Irish laborers were self-employed. Over fifty of the more than 300 Irish laborers were draymen. Several owned their team and wagon and many worked along with their sons or brothers. The fleet of draymen hauled wood, coal and freight to and from the docks and railroad yards.

The pushcart or backpack with assorted household wares provided another means of self-employment. Here was a chance to work when, where and if one chose. In Ireland, however, hawkers were regarded contemptuously as the lowest outcasts of society, along with the tinkers, wanderers and itinerant beggars. Because of the old stigma, the poor profits to be accrued, or both, a scant five Irish family men and five single men fell back on this way of making a living. . . .

Chronic unemployment among the Detroit Irish population was confined to only a few, according to census reports. In 1850 eight Irish family men and 15 single men had been without work for at least six months. An additional 5% of the male family heads did not list any occupation; this too was a small number even if most were potentially employable but out of work. The low rate of unemployment attested to the job possibilities of the city, and perhaps to the assets and efforts of the Irish who selected Detroit as a home. . . .

Countless men worked only sporadically, separated from the chronically unemployed neither by state of mind nor state of being. For most families the way of life provided by a breadwinner who was a casual day laborer was one of privation and economic insecurity. . . .

The average daily earnings of a common laborer in Michigan in 1850 amounted to $.88. . . . Over the decade of the 1850's, along with a general trend, workers in Michigan increased their daily earnings to a level of $1.04. By 1860 draymen in Michigan averaged about $1.34 a day.[5]

Whatever day work a man did, money came uncertainly and often seasonally. The amount was small recompense for work that, however manly, was predictably hard and frequently dangerous. The laborer's continued strength and good health meant everything to his family, but the odds were not favorable. With less chance to accumulate savings, family crises, whether continuing or sudden, fell especially hard upon the laborer and his family. To a considerable extent the frontier economy and the culture of Detroit, much like the agricultural society from which the Irish came, viewed the family as a work unit. It was a matter of course and of honor that the family members were mutually self-sustaining.

Notes

1. Robert Ernst, *Immigrant Life in New York City* (New York: King's Crown Press, 1949), 62, quoting *The Irish-American* (26 August 1849).
2. Edward H. Thomson, *Emigrant's Guide to the State of Michigan* (New York: State of Michigan Emigration Department), 45.
3. Richard R. Elliott, "First Irish Catholic Parochial Organization Established in the Western States, Trinity Church, Detroit, 1835," *American Catholic Historical Researches*, no. 12 (January-October 1895): 134–37.
4. Vinyard, *Irish on the Urban Frontier*, 96.
5. Stanley Lebergott, *Manpower in Economic Growth* (New York: McGraw Hill, 1964), 541, 219.

5.　Germans

Walter Pitkin

One day Harry Rickel asked me to come over to his house. I went. And that simple act was one of the three or four main turning points of my life. It brought me into a new culture which was complete and exciting. It was the first one I had entered, next to the one I grew up in. . . .

It was our second high school year when I met Harry. He was different. He had a certain serious interest in things that few other students showed. At the same time he was hail-fellow-well-met. He was utterly unlike the Germans around us in Fourteenth Street. I soon learned how and why.

The Rickels lived in a big brick house on the north side of Adelaide Street. To us of Fourteenth Street it was a king's palace. Yet it was only a comfortable dwelling with high ceilings and many rooms, all furnished well but plainly.

One by one, the family appeared. First the mother, a sweet, simple woman who reminded me in some ways of my own mother. Then the two oldest brothers, both so much older than I that to them I was just a kid. They heeded me little. Then Martha and Armin, the two youngest. Martha was a darling of eight or nine years; I quite fell in love with her. Armin was a clever boy with a bright smile. He won me, too, on the spot. All was well. Yes, but what was that noise outside?

A harsh noise. A loud noise. A noise from a human throat. A noise indicating anger. And so in came Mr. Rickel, lord of the manor. A small, slightly bent man, with thin, tight lips, he was trying to shake off a bad temper. Somebody who had come up the walk with him had enraged him, and he did not try to suppress his fury.

The family hushed. Mr. Rickel rumbled and bumbled around, uttering something in German. Then Mama Rickel said something to him in German. Then the older sons. I fell out of the parade.

When we sat down for supper, the old man had subsided. Then he said to me, in excellent, crisp English: "If you want to be around here much, you must learn German."

Thenceforth he was sprightly, told stories, poked fun at the boys and girls, was altogether charming.

"You study Greek, under Sherrard?" he lifted his brows. "Now, see here, you fool!—" this to Harry. "You should learn Greek. But you are too lazy." And then into a rasping diatribe against the unambitious Rickel children.

The victims sat mute throughout it. That was the custom. How different from us Yankees! We'd have talked back. And not too sweetly, under criticism.

What was this? A tall, slender bottle of Rhine wine being poured into glasses around the table. Wine! None of that wicked stuff in our Prohibitionist home. When Uncle Walter craved wine, he sneaked off with me to Put-In-Bay. Here the family drank it unashamed. Yes, this was a new culture indeed.

Such wine! Put-In-Bay never grew its equal. Old man Rickel grinned, and poured me another glass, and then another. Oh, yum! Incidentally I ate like two pigs too. And such food! A potato salad the like of which had never hypnotized my tongue. Cold cuts of every sort, all the finest. Black rye bread. Heaps of strong cheese. . . . But enough! I must get back to trivial matters.

Did Harry and I sit on the porch? Did we lie on the lawn? Did we go upstairs? Did we fall asleep at the table? Who knows? Not I. All I recall is my wandering home late that night, vowing that German pumpernickel was the best pumpernickel to be had for a nickel, and that some day I must go to Germany where that wine came from. Hooray!

I took to dropping in once a week, then twice.

"You must take German lessons from Hermann," Mr. Rickel insisted. "It is a shame you do not understand us half the time. Yes, you go see Hermann, tomorrow."

So to Hermann I went. The teacher dwelt along the railroad tracks on the east side. He was a hulk of beery fat through which two merry little eyes peered, for all the world like a little pig looking under a fence . . . or something.

"We begin now," he said and set a stein of beer in front of me. He uttered sundry short sentences having to do with beer and drinking in company. He began with *"Prosit"* and worked up. After an hour of this, he brought in a china coffee pot which we drained while I babbled at my best.

My best was bad. Sherrard was getting my best. I didn't have genius enough for two bests. So I gave Hermann my second best and made a fair start. And before winter set in, I had caught my stride. Hermann was pleased. But old man Rickel was delighted, although he was stingy with compliments.

Harry began taking me around to the *Harmonie Verein,* the best German club within many hundred miles. There I met the grand old Germans, the Marxhausens, the Carstens, the Muellers, the Breitmeyers and a score more. There too I began to discover that my German was a wretched blend of the real stuff and second-generation American German. The latter was what I heard and used with boys and girls of my own age. It enraged old man Rickel. He used to berate Harry by the hour for getting words out of order or using the wrong gender. But little did that help anybody. The second generation was growing up American. The larger background of culture that made German what it was no longer existed in Detroit. But the German elders didn't understand that one must have the total situation in order to develop habits suited to it.

As this was the first alien culture into which I moved, I observed it closely and came to many conclusions about it. Some of these came much later, of course; but they may be stated here, without ruining my story. I liked enormously the willingness to work hard, the eagerness to learn everything about a subject, the almost brutal frankness, the neatness and the marvelous plain food. I could not understand the mania for singing and for games. And I powerfully disliked the power of the elders over the young. This marked the widest breach between our old Yankee world and the German.

The older men puzzled me for a long time. They worshipped Abe Lincoln. Old man Rickel would speak of Abe as if Abe were God. I never could do that, though I too admired Abe in my own way. Other men of the passing generation then would praise America and our democracy more fervently in private talks than any Fourth-of-July orator could. At length this grew clear.

Old man Rickel was a little boy back in Germany when in 1848 Carl Schurz and his band joined the revolution, to overthrow the old regime. Failing, Schurz and the others fled to America, where they were received with hurrahs by our own patriots. Many of them grew rich, famous and powerful here. Our people took them in warmly. These revolutionists later joined the Union Army and fought to preserve the Union. Abe was their Commander-in-Chief.

Alert, ambitious German boys followed the blazed trail. Between 1850 and 1880 thousands of the keenest, most democratic among the youth of the Fatherland came over here. And out of their number grew up the German community centering around the *Harmonie Verein*. . . .

Merchants, manufacturers, chemists, engineers, physicians, professors,—of such was the group made up. No wonder that I came to dislike the French and Irish and Poles and other groups out our way! I did not understand at the time that I was making an unfair comparison. I was setting over against the cultured, prosperous upper class Germans our own rabble of poor, struggling toilers, not one of whom had ever enjoyed what we today call a high school education.

Thus are our prejudices formed.

Old man Rickel shaped my life as much as anybody else. He never knew it. I wish I might have told him before he died. He would have been pleased.

He had a fanatical love of German learning. Germans knew best, Germans studied hardest. Germans made the greatest discoveries. The only thing wrong with Germans in the old country was that they were political morons. They allowed the Hohenzollerns to kick them around.

"Philosophy and psychology?" said he many a time. "If you ever wish to amount to anything in those fields, you must study at Berlin."

"Arabic?" said he again. "If you don't go to an Arab country to learn it, you must go to Berlin."

In this he was supported by his son-in-law, Dr. Osius, a keen physician lately arrived from Germany. Osius was German of the Germans. In time I found out how and why. He laughed softly when anyone mentioned Johns Hopkins Medical or Harvard Medical.

"In time, I am sure," he would say, "these will become great institutions. But as yet—" And then a polite and devastating shrug . . .

6. German-Jewish Immigrants

Irving I. Katz

There were Jewish fur traders and trappers in Michigan from shortly after the arrival of Cadillac. However, this selection is about those late-comers from Germany who came to the area in the years after 1837.

Mid-century brought a new influx of Jews to American shores immediately before and after the abortive European revolutions of 1848. The revolutionary fire which swept across Europe in the 40's fed on many fuels—nationalism, socialism and liberalism. Within the multi-national Austrian Empire especially, political, social and economic dissent raged high. The Austrian Empire was a hodgepodge of national and ethnic groups—Germans, Slavs, Magyars and Italians. It extended into Bohemia, Hungary, Italy and the Germanies, all spliced together by the Hapsburg monarchs into a motley and loose-jointed empire.

The rising currents of liberal and nationalist sentiment in Europe in the 30's and 40's lifted these people to rebellion against

Irving I. Katz, *The Beth El Story; with a History of the Jews in Michigan before 1850* (Detroit: Wayne University Press, 1955), 50–58.

the aristocratic government of Prince Metternich and the monarchy. Throughout most of the Germanies, led by independent Prussia, there was a clamor for liberal reform and the formation of a German federation which would exclude Austria. In Germany, it was largely a middle class movement which drew its recruits from the ranks of university professors, students and literati as well as from merchants and some workers. In 1848 revolutions erupted throughout the Austrian Empire and in almost every continental country but Russia. Liberals and nationalists, often allied, fought for the independence of subject nationalities and for governmental reforms. Socialists also joined in the general revolt.

Within a year, however, those new revolutionary governments which had been formed either failed or were snuffed out by the Hapsburgs as quickly as they were established. The elements of idealism and optimism of the pre-1848 years gave way to those of reaction and bitterness. Nationalism became a militant and aggressive religion. The age of "Blood and Iron" was being ushered in.

During these years, there began the early exodus of many central and southern Europeans to the United States. Among them were Jews from Germany and Hungary, where nationalist and racist feelings were on the rise. A number of these Jews, particularly from Bohemia, Silesia, Bavaria and Hungary finally settled in Michigan.

Michigan was now attached to the East by a transportation network of water and rail lines. The Michigan Central Railway provided a number of commercial opportunities to merchants and peddlers. Many Jews continued west from the Atlantic seaboard to Buffalo, then on to Michigan, settling in Detroit and those cities linked to Detroit by rail. Many German Jews settled in Ann Arbor, where there was already a large German-speaking population.

Ann Arbor and Ypsilanti were among the first communities where Jews settled in the 1840's. In 1850, the entire population of Washtenaw County totaled 28,567. Ann Arbor counted something less than 5,000 citizens; Ypsilanti only about 3,000. In the decade from 1840 to 1850 Detroit had increased its population from 9,102 to 21,019. Michigan itself had grown from about 212,000 to almost 400,000 by 1850. Saginaw was a mere village with about 900 citizens. . . . Grand Rapids and Kalamazoo both ran about 2,500. . . .

Ann Arbor and Ypsilanti were chosen by the new Jewish immigrants for two principal reasons: first, because in the 1840's Washtenaw County was the best county for farm stock, wool and hides; second, because many of the farmers in this county were recent German immigrants themselves and the Jewish arrivals found here the language of their native land and a place where they could earn a living, mostly as peddlers, until they could establish themselves as merchants, manufacturers or craftsmen.

Among the first to come to Ann Arbor from Bohemia were the five Weil brothers, who arrived as follows: Solomon in 1843, Moses and his wife in 1844, Leopold in 1845, Marcus in 1846 and Jacob in 1848. The Weil brothers formed a nucleus of a colony of Jews and their home became the headquarters of all German-Jewish arrivals. Here the humblest peddler always found a hospitable welcome. The brothers were orthodox in their religious observances, maintained a kosher household, and conducted the first *Minyanim* (services) held in Michigan. The first Sabbath and festival services were held, in 1845, in a house in the lower town of Ann Arbor which was jointly occupied by Leopold Weil and his brother-in-law, Judah Sittig, who came to Ann Arbor about 1845. Later they gathered at the home of Leopold and Moses on Washington Street, or at that of Solomon and Marcus on Huron Street. After their parents arrived in 1850, services were held uniformly at the parents' home, a brick house on Washington Street, near their tannery.

For the rites which followed the birth of Solomon Weil's eldest son, in 1848, a *mohel* (circumcizer) was brought all the way from Cleveland, Ohio, and it is said that when, in 1850, the parents of these brothers were sent for, the father, at their request, purchased a *Sefer Torah* in Prague and piously bore the Scroll of the Law in his arms all the way to Ann Arbor.

. . . Leopold Weil and Judah Sittig attempted farming in Lima Township, as did Moses Weil, together with one Weidel, a Bohemian Jew, in South Lyon Township, but all gave it up after a year or so because of the wildness of the locality and the rampage of the savage beasts of the forest.

Other German-Jewish immigrants who came to Ann Arbor and Ypsilanti before 1850 were: Charles, Adolph, and Louis

Bresler with their father, Leo Bresler; Charles, Henry, and Emanuel Lederer; Moses Rindskoff, Charles Fantle, Solomon Bendit, David Weidenfeld and brother, Adam Hersch, Isaac Altman, Simon Sloman, the Fantes brothers, one Hayman, one Feder, and possibly Alex and Martin Guiterman, Solomon Sondheim and Benjamin Goodkind. Many of these later moved to Detroit, when the city began its commercial rise.

Lewis F. Leopold, whose name was Freudenthaler in his native Baden, Germany, his wife Babette, who was a member of the Oesterreicher (Austrian) family, their infant son, Lewis' sister, Hannah, and Lewis' brother, Samuel, were located on the island of Mackinac in 1845. The brothers became the first pioneers in this locality in the fishery business and were soon shipping a thousand barrels of salted fish to Cleveland each season. This business, together with the sale of supplies to fishermen, Indian trading, and the purchase of furs, laid the foundation for an extensive business and they became prominent as owners of Lake Michigan vessels and merchants in the ports of the Great Lakes. . . .

Within a few years after 1850, the Leopolds and Austrians established leading stores in Michigan, at Eagle River, Eagle Harbor, the Cliff Mine, Calumet, and at Hancock, Joseph Austrian having selected the latter place as the site for his first store and warehouse.

Edward Kanter, a native of Breslau, Germany, who came to Detroit in 1844, was a resident of Mackinac in 1845, where he was employed by the American Fur Company. In 1846, he worked for the Leopolds and Austrians mentioned above. He remained in Mackinac until 1852 when he moved to Detroit. Kanter became the first Jewish banker in the city by founding the German-American Bank. He was a very colorful personality and the first Detroit Jew to be active in politics, having been elected among other offices a member of the state legislature in 1857. He was also a great friend of the Indians and because of his bustling activity was named by them "Bosh-Bish'gay-bish-gon-sen," meaning "Fire Cracker." The Indians always had a great liking for Kanter; they never missed an opportunity to call on him in Detroit or to send greetings to him. The merchants of Detroit in the early 1860's were at a loss one day to account for a circle of Indians gravely squatted in front of Kanter's store on the main business street, Kanter making one of the circle, the whole company smoking and maintaining a strong silence until they (the merchants) were informed that the Indians were a delegation of chiefs on their way to see the Great White Father at Washington, who would not pass through Detroit without smoking a pipe of peace with "Firecracker". . . .

A study of the city directories of Detroit published before 1850 disclosed the following:

The 1837 *Directory*, the first to be published, contains 1,330 names, but not one that can be safely claimed as Jewish.

In the second *Directory*, issued in 1845 and containing 2,800 names, we find Solomon Bendit and Company, dry goods; Goodkind and Freedman, fancy and dry goods; and Moses Rendskopf (later Rindskof).

In the third City *Directory*, published in 1846 and containing 3,238 names, the following known Jews are listed: S. Bendit and Company, dry goods; Frederick Cohen, portrait painter; Solomon Freedman, fancy and staple dry goods; Adam Hersch, cigar maker; Moses Rendskopf; Jacob Silberman. The *Directory* also contains an advertisement by Frederick E. Cohen. . . .

In the 1850 *Directory*, the fourth, in spite of the large increase in the population, which then numbered 20,019, only the following Jewish firms and individuals are listed: A. Amberg and Company, merchant tailors; S. & H. Bendit and Company, dry goods; F. E. Cohen, portrait painter; Solomon Cohen, peddler; S. Freedman and Brothers, dry goods dealers; Alexander Grunwald, clothing store; Adam Hersch, firm of Silberman and Hersch; Leopold Pappenkeimer (later Pappenheimer), fancy store; Silberman and Hersch, cigar manufacturers; Jacob Silberman, firm of Silberman and Hersch. . . .

The list of Jews in the 1850 *Directory* is not complete, however, for we know that several other Jews resided in the city. By the fall of 1850, there were in Detroit more than the traditionally required *minyan* (ten males over the age of thirteen), to start a congregation, and on September 22, 1850, the little band of Jews in Detroit organized the Bet El Society (now Temple Beth El), Michigan's first Jewish congregation, thus founding the first Jewish community in the state of Michigan.

Part IV

Getting Around in Michigan: Problems of Internal Improvements

Getting Around in Michigan: Problems of Internal Improvements

In the beginning Michigan traveled by foot or canoe, later on horseback. Those with means might secure an Indian guide. Soon the growing daily business of Michigan made these devices impractical. The Erie Canal, opening in 1825, brought newcomers by the thousands, but it did not solve the problem of how they would move about in Michigan. Swamps and rumors of swamps kept many settlers out of the interior.

Silas Farmer remarks that in the boom days of 1834 there was great excitement because of a new stagecoach line. "The entire distance from Detroit to Chicago," exulted a newspaper editor, "may be performed in less than five days."

"A Fortnight in the Wilderness" is a report by Alexis de Tocqueville of a trip from Detroit to Saginaw in 1831. That most urbane of foreign travelers conveys a sense of beauty and loneliness in a strange land.

Neither land nor water assured safety for the traveler. Getting from place to place soon became not only an inconvenience but a major political issue for the area. The internal improvements program has often been labeled a political pork barrel, a view still standard in many textbooks of American history. The alternatives are rarely considered: mud above wagon wheels, ships lost in lake storms, without lighthouses, the isolation of families in the wilderness.

Senator Zachariah Chandler begged Congress for roads, lighthouses, channel dredging, and railroads from the time of his first election to Congress in 1856. The internal improvements issue was to him a case of North versus South from his first day in Congress. Later known for his strong antislavery views and his sponsorship of the Reconstruction Amendments, he should also be remembered for his fight to unlock the Northwest.

1.   A Fortnight in the Wilderness

Alexis de Tocqueville

We reached Detroit at three o'clock. It is a little town of between 2,000 and 3,000 inhabitants. . . . We had crossed the State of New York, and steamed 400 miles on Lake Erie; we now were on the frontier of civilization. Still we did not know what course to take. To cross almost impenetrable forests; to swim deep rivers; to encounter pestilential marshes; to sleep exposed to the damp air of the woods;—these are efforts which an American easily conceives, if a dollar is to be gained by them—that is the point. But that a man should take such journeys from curiosity he cannot understand. Besides, dwelling in a wilderness, he prizes only man's work. He sends you to visit a road, a bridge, a pretty village; but that you should admire large trees, or wild

Alexis de Tocqueville, "A Fortnight in the Wilderness," in *Memoir, Letters, and Remains of Alexis de Tocqueville* (Cambridge and London: MacMillan, 1861), 140–207.

scenery, is to him incomprehensible. We could make no one understand us. . . .

We soon saw that it would be impossible to obtain the truth from them in a straightforward manner, and that we must manoeuvre.

We therefore went to the United States' Agent for the sale of wild land, of which there is much in the district of Michigan. We presented ourselves to him as persons who, without having quite made up our minds to establish ourselves in the country, were interested to know the price and situation of the Government lands.

Major Biddle, the officer, now understood perfectly what we wanted, and entered into a number of details to which we eagerly listened. "This part," he said, (showing us on the map the river of St. Joseph, which, after many windings, discharges itself into Lake Michigan), "seems to me to be the best suited to your purpose. The land is good, and large villages are already founded there; the road is so well kept up that public conveyances run every day." Well, we said to ourselves, now we know where not to go, unless we intend to travel post over the wilderness.

We thanked Major Biddle for his advice, and asked him, with an air of indifference bordering on contempt, towards which side of the district the current of emigration had, up to the present time, least tended. "This way, . . . towards the northwest. About Pontiac and its neighborhood some pretty fair establishments have lately been commenced. But you must not think of fixing yourselves farther off; the country is covered by an almost impenetrable forest . . . towards the northwest, full of nothing but wild beasts and Indians. The United States propose to open a way through it immediately; but the road is only just begun, and stops at Pontiac. I repeat, that there is nothing to be thought of in that quarter."

We again thanked Major Biddle for his good advice, and determined to take it in a contrary sense. We were beside ourselves with joy at the prospect of at length finding a place which the torrent of European civilization had not yet invaded.

On the next day (the 23rd of July) we hired two horses. . . . Having bought a compass, and some provisions, we set off with our guns over our shoulders, and our hearts as light as if we had been two school-boys going home for the holidays.

Our hosts at Detroit were right in telling us that we need not go far to see woods, for a mile from the town the road enters the forest, and never leaves it. The ground is perfectly flat, and often marshy. Now and then we met with newly-cleared lands. As these settlements are all exactly alike, whether they be on the outskirts of Michigan or of New York, I shall try to describe them once for all.

The little bell which the pioneer takes care to hang around the necks of his cattle, that he may find them in the dense forest, announces from a great distance the approach to the clearing. Soon you hear the stroke of the axe; as you proceed traces of destruction prove the presence of man. Lopped branches cover the road; trunks half calcined by fire, or maimed by steel, are still standing in the path. You go on, and reach a wood, which seems to have been maimed by sudden death. Even in the middle of summer the withered branches look wintry. On nearer examination a deep gash is discovered around the bark of each tree, which, preventing the circulation of sap, quickly kills it. This is generally the planter's first measure. As he cannot in the first year cut down all the trees on his new property, he kills them to prevent their leaves overshadowing the Indian corn which he has sowed under their branches.

Next to this incomplete attempt at a field, the first step of civilization in the wilderness, you come suddenly upon the owner's dwelling. . . . Here the trees have been cut down, but not uprooted, and they still encumber with their stumps the ground that they formerly shaded; round these withered remnants, corn, oak saplings, plants, and weeds of every kind spring pell-mell, and grow side by side in the stubborn and half-wild soil. Like the field around it, this rustic dwelling is evidently a new and hasty work. . . .

We did not reach Pontiac till after sunset. Twenty very neat and pretty houses, forming so many well-provided shops, a transparent brook, a clearing of about a square half-mile surrounded by the boundless forest: this is an exact picture of Pontiac, which in twenty years may be a city. . . .

We were taken to the best inn in Pontiac (for there are two), and as usual we were introduced into the barroom; here all, from the most opulent to the humblest shop-keeper, assemble to smoke, think, and talk politics on the footing of the most perfect equality. The owner of the house, or rather the landlord, was, I must not say a burly peasant, for there are no peasants in America, but at any rate a very stout gentleman, whose face had about as much frankness and simplicity as that of a Norman horse-dealer. . . . [He] never looked you in the face when he spoke, but waited till you were engaged in talking with someone else to consider you at his leisure. . . . .

We said to him, "Before fixing in your country, my dear land-lord, we intend to visit Saginaw, and we wish to consult you on this point." At the name of Saginaw, a remarkable change came over his features. It seemed as if he had been suddenly snatched from real life and transported to a land of wonders. His eyes dilated, his mouth fell open, and the most complete astonishment pervaded his countenance.

"You want to go to Saginaw!" exclaimed he; "to Saginaw Bay! Two foreign gentlemen, two rational gentlemen, want to go to Saginaw Bay! It is scarcely credible." "And why not?" we replied. "But are you well aware," continued our host, "what you undertake? Do you know that Saginaw is the last inhabited spot towards the Pacific; that between this place and Saginaw lies an uncleared wilderness? Do you know that the forest is full of Indians and musquitoes; that you must sleep, at least for one night, under the damp trees? Have you thought about the fever? Will you be able to get on in the wilderness, and to find your way in the labyrinth of our forests?"

After this tirade, he paused, in order to judge of the effect which he had produced. We replied, "All that may be true, but we start tomorrow for Saginaw Bay. . . . "

He asked us: "Perhaps you are sent by the Canadian fur company to establish relations with the Indian tribes on the frontier?"

We maintain our silence.

Our host said no more; but he continued to muse on the strangeness of our scheme.

"Have you never been to Saginaw?" we resumed. "I," he answered, "I have been so unlucky as to go there five or six times, but I had a motive for doing it, and you do not appear to have any." "But you forget, my worthy host, that we do not ask you if we had better go to Saginaw, but only how we can get there most easily."

Brought back thus to the matter in hand, our American recovered his presence of mind and the precision of his ideas. He explained to us in a few words and with excellent practical good sense how we should set about our journey through the wilderness. . . . He took the candle, showed us a bedroom, and after giving us a truly democratic shake of the hand, went to finish his evening in the common room.

On the next day we rose with the dawn, and prepared to start. . . .

We had been advised to apply to a Mr. Williams, who, as he had long dealt with the Chippeway Indians, and had a son established at Saginaw, might give us useful information. After riding some miles in the forest, . . . we saw an old man working in a little garden. We spoke to him, and found out that he was Mr. Williams.

He received us with much kindness and gave us a letter to his son. We asked him if we had anything to fear from the Indian tribes through whose territories we were about to pass. Mr. Williams rejected this idea with a sort of indignation. "No, no," he said, "you may proceed without fear. For my part, I sleep more fearlessly among Indians than among white people."

I note this, as the first favorable impression given to me of the Indians since my arrival in America. In the thickly-peopled districts, they are always spoken of with a mixture of fear and contempt; and I think that in those places they deserve both. . . . If the reader, however, will go on with this journal, and follow me among the European settlers on the frontier, as well as among the Indian tribes, he will form a higher, and at the same time a juster idea of the aborigines of America.

After we left Mr. Williams, we pursued our road through the woods. From time to time a little lake (this district is full of them) shines like a white tablecloth under the green branches. . . .

Still travelling on, we reached a country of a different aspect. The ground was no longer flat, but thrown into hills and valleys. Nothing can be wilder than the appearance of some of these hills.

In one of these picturesque passes, we turned suddenly to contemplate the magnificent scene which we were leaving behind, and, to our great surprise, we saw close to us, and apparently following us step by step, a red Indian. He was a man of about thirty, tall, and admirably proportioned. His black and shining hair fell down upon his shoulders, with the exception of two tresses, which were fastened on the top of his head. His face was smeared with black and red paint. He wore a sort of very short blue blouse. His legs were covered with red *mittas*, a sort of pantaloon which reaches only to the top of the thigh, and his feet were defended by mocassins. At his side hung a knife. In his right hand he held a long rifle, and in his left two birds that he had just killed.

The first sight of this Indian made on us a far from agreeable impression. The spot was ill-suited for resisting an attack. On our right a forest of lofty pines; on our left a deep ravine, at the bottom of which a stream brawled along the rocks, hidden by the thick foliage, so that we approached it, as it were, blindfold! To seize our guns, turn round and face the Indian in the midst of the path was the affair of an instant. . . . He halted in the same manner, and for half a minute we were all silent. . . .

I said, that when we turned round, arms in hand, the Indian stopped short. He stood our rapid scrutiny with perfect calmness, and with steady and unflinching eye. When he saw that we had no hostile intentions, he smiled: probably he perceived that we had been alarmed. I never before had remarked how completely a mirthful expression changes the savage physiognomy. . . . An Indian grave and an Indian smiling are different men. . . .

Making signs, we asked him for the birds which he carried; he gave them to us for a little piece of money. Having made acquaintance, we bid him adieu, and trotted off.

At the end of half an hour of rapid riding, on turning round, once more I was astonished by seeing the Indian still at my horse's heels. He ran with the agility of a wild animal, without speaking a single word or seeming to hurry himself. We stopped; he stopped; we went on; he went on. We darted on at full speed; our horses, natives of the wilderness, leapt easily every obstacle: the Indian doubled his pace: I saw him, sometimes on the right, sometimes on the left of my horse, jumping over the brushwood and alighting on the ground without the slightest noise. He was like one of the wolves of the North, which are said to follow horsemen in hope of their falling and thus becoming a more easy prey.

The sight of this strange figure, now lost in the darkness of the by our side, became at last an annoyance. . . . It occurred to us that he was leading us into an ambush.

We were full of these thoughts, when we discovered, right in front of us in the wood, the end of another rifle; we soon came alongside of the bearer. We took him at first for an Indian. He wore a kind of short frock-coat, tight at the waist, showing an upright and well-made figure. His neck was bare, and his feet covered by mocassins. When we were close to him, he raised his head; we saw at once he was an European, and we stopped short. He came to us, shook us cordially by the hand, and we entered into conversation.

"Do you live in the desert [forest]?" "Yes; here is my house." And he showed us among the trees, a hut even more miserable than the ordinary log-house. "Alone?" "Alone." "And what do you do with yourself here?" "I roam about the woods, and I kill right and left the game which comes in my way, but the shooting is not good here now." "And do you like this sort of life?" "Better than any other." "But are you not afraid of the Indians?" "Afraid of the Indians! I had rather live among them than in the society of white men. No, no; I am not afraid of the Indians; they are better people than we are, unless we have brutalized them with strong liquors, poor creatures!"

We then showed to our new acquaintance the man who followed us so obstinately, and who at that moment was standing stock still, a few paces off. "He is a Chippeway," said our friend, "or, as the French would call him, a *sauteur*. I would lay a wager that he is returning from Canada, where he has received the annual presents from the English. His family cannot be far off."

So speaking, the American signed to the Indian to approach, and began to talk to him in his language with great fluency. The pleasure that these two men, so different in race and in habits, took in exchanging their ideas, was a striking sight. . . . After examining carefully the rifle of the savage, the white man said to us,—"This is an excellent musket; the English no doubt gave it to him, that he might use it against us, and he will certainly do so, in the first war. This is how the Indians call down upon their heads their own misfortunes,—but they know no better, poor things!" "Are the Indians skilful in the use of these long heavy guns?" "There are no shots like the Indians," replied our new friend, in tone of the greatest admiration. "Look at the little birds which he sold you, sir; there is but one shot in each, and I am sure that he fired at them only twice. There is no man so happy as an Indian in the districts whence we have not yet frightened away the game; but the larger sorts scent our approach at a distance of more than 300 miles; and, as they retire, they leave the country before us a waste, incapable of supporting any longer the poor Indians, unless they cultivate the ground.". . .

We proceeded on our way. We maintained the same rapid pace, and in half-an-hour reached the house of a pioneer. Before the door of the hut an Indian family had encamped. An old woman, two young girls, and several children, were crouching round a fire to the heat of which were exposed the still palpitating limbs of a whole kid. A few steps off an Indian was lying quite naked on the grass, basking in the sun, whilst a little child was rolling about in the dust by his side. Here our silent companion stopped: he left us without bidding us adieu, and sat down gravely among his countrymen.

What could have induced this man to follow our horses for five miles? We never could guess.

After breakfasting in this spot, we remounted, and pursued our journey through a wood of thinly scattered lofty trees. The underwood had been burnt away. . . . The ground was covered with fern, extending under the trees as far as the eye could reach.

Some miles further on, my horse lost a shoe. . . . Not far off, happily, we met a planter, who succeeded in putting it on again. [He] advised us to make haste, as the daylight was beginning to fail, and we were at least five miles from Flint River, where we intended to sleep.

Soon, indeed, we were enveloped in perfect darkness. We were forced to push on. The night was fine, but intensely cold. The silence of the forest was so deep, the calm so complete, that the forces of nature seemed paralysed. No sound was heard but the annoying hum of the musquitoes, and the stamp of our horses' feet. Now and then we saw the distant gleam of a fire, against which we could trace, through the smoke, the stern and motionless profile of an Indian.

At the end of an hour we reached a spot where the roads separated; two paths opened out in different directions—which should we take?. . . . One led to a stream we did not know how deep; the other to a clearing. The moon just rising showed us a valley full of fallen trees: further on, we descried two houses. . . .

We determined to take advice before proceeding My companion remained to take of the horses, whilst I, with my gun over my shoulder, descended into the valley.

Soon I perceived that I was entering a new settlement. Immense trunks of trees, their branches as yet unlopped, covered the ground. By jumping from one to another, I soon was near the houses. But the stream separated me from them. Happily, its course was impeded in this place by some huge oaks that the pioneer's axe had no doubt thrown down. I succeeded in crawling along these trees, and at last reached the opposite side.

I warily approached the two houses which I could see but indistinctly. I feared they might prove Indian wigwams. They were unfinished. The doors were open, and no voice answered mine. I returned to the edge of the stream whence I could not help admiring for a few minutes the awful grandeur of the scene. . . . The moonlight played upon the shattered remnants of the forest, creating a thousand fantastic shapes. No sound of any kind, no murmur of life was audible.

At last I remembered my companion, and called loudly to tell him . . . to cross the rivulet and join me. The echo repeated my voice over and over again in the solitary woods, but I got no answer. I shouted again, and listened again. The same death-like silence reigned.

I became uneasy, and I ran by the side of the stream till I reached the place lower down where it was fordable.

When I got there, I heard in the distance the sound of horses' feet, and soon after Beaumont himself appeared. Surprised by my long absence, he had proceeded towards the rivulet. He was already in the shallow when I called him. The sound of my voice, therefore, had not reached him. He told me that he, too, had tried by every means to make himself heard, and, as well as I, had been alarmed at obtaining no answer. If it had not been for this ford which served as a meeting place, we should perhaps have been looking for each other half the night.

We resumed our journey with the full resolution of not again separating, and in three quarters of an hour we at last came upon a settlement, consisting of two or three huts and, what was still more satisfactory, a light. A violet-coloured line of water in the hollow of the valley proved that we had arrived at Flint River. Soon,indeed, a loud barking echoed in the woods, and we found ourselves close to a log-house, separated from us only by a fence. As we were preparing to climb over it, we saw in the moonlight a great black bear, that standing on his hind-legs, and at the very extremity of his chain, showed as clearly as he could his intention to give us a fraternal embrace.

"What an infernal country is this," said I, "where they keep bears for watchdogs.". . .

We halloed at the top of our voices and with such success that at last a man appeared at the window. After examining us by the light of the moon: "Enter, gentlemen," he said, "Trink, go to bed! To the kennel, I say, they are not robbers."

The bear waddled off, and we got in. We were half dead with fatigue. We asked our host, if we could have oats for our horses. "Certainly," he replied, and began to mow the nearest field with American *sangfroid*, and as if it were noon-day. Meanwhile we unsaddled our horses. . . .

. . . There was but one bed in the house; it was allotted to Beaumont. I wrapped myself in my cloak, and lying down on the floor, slept as soundly as a man does who has ridden forty miles.

On the next day (July 25th) our first care was to inquire for a guide.

A wilderness of forty miles separates Flint River from Saginaw, and the road is a narrow pathway. . . . Our host approved of our plan, and shortly brought us two Indians whom he assured us we could perfectly trust. One was a boy of twelve or fourteen; the other was a young man of eighteen . . . [who had] taken care to paint his face with black and red in symmetrical lines; a ring was passed through his nose, and a necklace and earrings completed his attire. His weapons were no less remarkable. At one side hung the celebrated tomahawk; on the other, a long sharp knife, with which the savages scalp their victims. Round his neck hung a cow-horn containing his powder; and in his right hand he held a rifle. . . . his eye was wild, and his smile benevolent. . . .

. . . We asked him his price for the service he was about to render to us. The Indian replied in a few words of his native

128

tongue; and the American immediately informed us that what he asked was about equivalent to two dollars.

"As these poor Indians," charitably added our host, "do not understand the value of money, you will give the dollars to me, and I will willingly give him what they represent."

I was curious to see what this worthy man considered to be equal to two dollars, and I followed him quietly to the place where the bargain was struck. I saw him give to our guide a pair of mocassins and a pocket-handerkerchief, that certainly together did not amount to half the sum. . . .

However, the Indians are not the only dupes of the American pioneers. Every day we were ourselves victims to their extreme cupidity. It is true that they do not steal. They are too intelligent to commit any dangerous breach of the law; but I never saw an innkeeper in a large town overcharge so impudently as these tenants of the wilderness, among whom I fancied I should find primitive honesty and patriarchal simplicity.

All was ready: we mounted our horses, and wading across the rivulet (Flint River) which forms the boundary of civilization, we entered the real desert. Our two guides ran, or rather leapt like wild cats across the impediments of the road. When we came to a fallen tree, a stream, or a bog, they pointed to the right path, but did not even turn to see us get out of the difficulty. Accustomed to trust only to himself, the Indian can scarcely understand that others need help. . . .

From time to time our Indians halted. They placed their fingers on their lips in token of silence, and signed us to dismount. Guided by them, we reached the spot whence we could see the bird for which we were searching. It was amusing to observe the contemptuous smile with which they led us by the hand like children. . . . .

As we proceeded, we gradually lost sight of the traces of man. . . . Before us was the scene that we had been so long seeking—a virgin forest.

Growing in the middle of the thin brushwood . . . was a single clump of full-grown trees, almost all pines or oaks. Confined to so narrow a space, and deprived of sunshine, each of these trees had run up rapidly, in search of air and light. As straight as the mast of a ship, the most rapid grower had overtopped every surrounding object. . . .

But it is time to return to our journey to Saginaw. We had been riding for five hours in complete ignorance of our whereabouts, when our Indians stopped short, and the elder, whose name was Sagan-Cuisco, traced a line in the sand. He showed us one end, exclaiming, *Michi, Conte-ouinque* (the Indian name for Flint River), and pointing to the other, pronounced the name of *Saginaw*. Then, marking a point in the middle, he signed to us that we had achieved half the distance, and that we must rest a little.

The sun was already high, and we should gladly have accepted his invitation, if we could have seen water within reach; . . . we motioned to the Indian that we wished to halt where we could eat and drink. He understood us directly, and set off with the same rapidity as before. An hour later he stopped again, and showed us a spot where we might find water about thirty paces off in the forest.

Without waiting for us to answer, or helping us to unsaddle our horses, he went to it himself; we followed as fast as we could. A little while before the wind had thrown down a large tree in this place; in the hollow that had been filled by the root was a little reservoir of rain water. This was the fountain to which our guide conducted us, without . . . [it] having occurred to him that we should hesitate to partake of such a draught. We opened our bag. Another misfortune! The heat had entirely spoilt our provisions, and we found our dinner reduced to the small piece of bread, which was all we had been able to procure at Flint River.

Add to this a cloud of musquitoes, attracted by the vicinity of water, which we were forced to fight with one hand while we carried our bread to our mouths with the other, and an idea may be formed of a rustic dinner in a virgin forest. . . .

We soon began to think of starting, but we were dismayed to find that our horses had disappeared. Goaded, no doubt, by hunger, they had strayed from the road in which we had left them, and it was not without trouble that we succeeded in tracing them; we blessed the musquitoes that had forced us to continue our journey.

The path soon became more and more difficult to follow. Every moment our horses had to force their way through thick brushwood, or to leap over the large fallen trees that barred our progress.

At the end of two hours of an extremely toilsome ride we at length reached a stream. . . . We waded across it, and from the opposite side we saw a field of maize and two huts that looked like log-houses. As we approached, we found that we were in a little Indian settlement, and that the log-houses were wigwams. The solitude was no less perfect than in the surrounding forest.

When we reached the first of these abandoned dwellings, Sagan-Cuisco stopped. . . . He again traced a line in the sand and showed us by the same method as before that we had accomplished only two-thirds of the road; then he rose and pointing to the sun, signed that it was quickly sinking into the west, next he looked at the wigwam and shut his eyes. . . . He wished us to sleep in this place. I own that the proposal astonished us as much as it annoyed us. It was long since we had eaten, and we were but moderately inclined to sleep without supper. The sombre savage grandeur of scene that we had been contemplating ever since the morning, our utter loneliness, the wild faces of our guides, and the difficulty of communicating with them, all conspired to take away our confidence.

There was a strangeness too in the conduct of the Indians. Our road for the last two hours had been even more untrodden than at the beginning. No one had told us that we should pass through an Indian village, and everyone had assured us that we could go in one day from Flint River to Saginaw. We could not therefore imagine why our guides wanted to keep us all night in the desert.

We insisted upon going on. . . . Sagan-Cuisco had paid particular attention to a little wicker bottle that hung by my side. A bottle that could not be broken. . . . I signed to him that I would give him the bottle if he would take us immediately to Saginaw. He then seemed to undergo a violent struggle. He looked again at the sun, then on the ground. At last he came to a decision, seized his rifle, exclaimed twice, with his hand on his mouth, *Ouh! Ouh!* and rushed off before us through the bushes.

We followed him at a quick pace, and we soon lost sight of the Indian settlement. Our guides continued to run for two hours, faster than before.

Still, night was coming on, and the last rays of the sun had disappeared behind the trees, when Sagan-Cuisco was stopped by a violent bleeding at the nose. . . . It was evident that fatigue and want of food had exhausted their strength. We began to fear lest our guides should renounce the undertaking, and insist on sleeping under a tree. We therefore proposed to mount them in turns on our horses.

They accepted our offer without surprise or shame. It was curious to see these half-naked men gravely seated on English saddles, carrying our game-bags and guns slung over their shoulders, while we were toiling on before them.

At last night came. The air under the trees became damp, and icy cold. In the dark the forest assumed a new and terrible aspect. Our eyes could distinguish nothing but confused masses without shape or order; strange and disproportioned forms; the sort of fantastic images which haunt the imagination in fever. The echo of our steps had never seemed so loud, nor the silence of the forest so awful. The only sign of life in this sleeping world was the humming of the musquito.

As we advanced the gloom became still deeper. Now and then a fire-fly traced a luminous line upon the darkness. Too late we acknowledged the wisdom of the Indian's advice; but it was no longer possible to recede.

We therefore pushed on as rapidly as our strength and the night permitted. At the end of an hour, we left the woods, and entered a vast prairie. Our guides uttered three times a savage cry, that vibrated like the discordant notes of the *tam-tam*. It was answered in the distance. Five minutes afterward we reached a stream; but it was too dark to see the opposite bank.

The Indians halted here. They wrapped their blankets round them, to escape the stings of the musquitoes; and hiding in the long grass, looked like balls of wool, that one might pass by without remarking, and could not possibly suppose to be men. . . .

In a few minutes we heard a faint noise, and something approached the bank. It was an Indian canoe, about ten feet long, formed out of a single tree. The man who was curled up in this frail bark wore the dress and had the appearance of an Indian. He spoke to our guides, who, by his direction, took the saddles from our horses, and placed them in the canoe.

As I was preparing to get into it, the supposed Indian touched me on the shoulder, and said, with a Norman accent which made me start,

"Ah, you come from old France! . . . stop—don't be in a hurry—people sometimes get drowned here."

If my horse had addressed me, I should not, I think, have been more astonished.

I looked at the speaker, whose face shone in the moonlight like a copper ball. "Who are you, then?" I said. "You speak French, but you look like an Indian." He replied that he was a "Bois-brulé," which means the son of a Canadian and an Indian woman. . . .

Following the advice of my countryman, the savage, I seated myself in the bottom of the canoe, and kept as steady as possible; my horse, whose bridle I held, plunged into the water, and swam by my side, meanwhile the Canadian sculled the bark, singing in an undertone to an old French tune some verses, of which I caught only the first couplet,—"Between Paris & St. Denis, there lived a maid,"&c.

We reached the opposite bank without accident; the canoe immediately returned to bring over my companion. All my life I shall remember the second time that it neared the shore. The moon, which was full, was just then rising over the prairie behind us, half the disk only appeared above the horizon. . . . Its rays were reflected in the stream, and touched the place where I stood. Along the line of their pale, tremulous light, the Indian canoe was advancing. We could not see any sculls, or hear the sound of rullocks [rowlocks]. The bark glided rapidly and smoothly—long, narrow, and black, resembling an alligator in pursuit of his prey. Crouching at the prow, Sagan-Cuisco, with his head between his knees, showed only his shiny tresses. Further back, the Canadian was silently sculling, while behind followed Beaumont's horse, with his powerful chest throwing up the waters of the Saginaw in glittering streams. . . .

[We proceeded to a house] about a hundred yards from the river. . . . we should probably have repaired our strength by a sound sleep if we could have gotten rid of the myriads of musquitoes that filled the house; but this was impossible. . . .

These insects are the curse of the American wilderness. They render a long stay unendurable. I never felt torments such as those which I suffered from during the whole of this expedition, and especially at Saginaw.

We went out very early, and the first objects that struck us were our Indians, rolled up in their blankets near the door, and sleeping by the side of their dogs.

This was our first daylight view of the village of Saginaw, which we had come so far to see. A small, cultivated plain, bounded on the south by a beautiful and gently flowing river; on the east, west, and north by the forest; constitutes at present the territory of the embryo city. . . .

The village of Saginaw is the furthest point inhabited by Europeans to the north-west of the vast peninsula of Michigan. It may be considered as an advanced post; a sort of watch-tower, placed by the whites in the midst of the Indian nations. . . .

After breakfast we went to see the richest landowner in the village, Mr. Williams. We found him in his shop engaged in selling to the Indians a number of little articles of small value, such as knives, glass necklaces, earrings &c. It was sad to see how these poor creatures were treated by their civilized brother from Europe.

All however, whom we saw there were ready to do justice to the savages. They were kind, inoffensive; a thousand times less given to stealing than the whites. It was only a pity that they were beginning to understand the value of things. But why a pity? "Because trade with them became every day less profitable." Is not the superiority of civilized man apparent in this remark? The Indian in his ignorant simplicity would have said that he found it every day more difficult to cheat his neighbour; but the white man finds in the refinement of language, a shade which expresses the fact, and yet saves his conscience.

On our return from Mr. Williams' we went a short way up the Saginaw to shoot wild ducks. . . . The report of a gun in the woods roused us from our dream. At first it sounded like an explosion on both sides of the river; the roar then grew fainter, till it was lost in the depth of the surrounding forest. It sounded like the prolonged and fearful war-cry of advancing civilization. . . .

The facts are as certain as if they had already taken place. In a few years these impenetrable forests will have fallen; the sons of civilization and industry will break the silence of the Saginaw; its echoes will cease; the banks will be imprisoned by quays; its current, which flows on unnoticed and tranquil through a nameless waste, will be stemmed by the prows of vessels. More than 100 miles sever this solitude from the great European settlements; and we were, perhaps, the last travellers allowed to see its primitive grandeur. . . .

It is this idea of destruction, with the accompanying thought of near and inevitable change, that gives to the solitudes of America their peculiar character, and their touching loveliness. You look at them with a mournful pleasure. You feel that you must not delay admiring them. The impression of wild and natural greatness so soon to expire, mingles with the lofty thoughts to which the progress of civilization gives rise—you are proud of being a man; and yet you reflect almost with remorse, on the dominion which Providence allots to you over nature. . . .

We wished to quit Saginaw on the next day, the 27th July, but one of our horses was galled by the saddle, and we resolved to remain a day longer. . . . At five A.M. we resolved to start [the return journey to Detroit]. . . . In three hours we reached a deserted wigwam on the lonely banks of the river Cass. . . .

On leaving the wigwam we found several paths. . . . After due examination and discussion, we could think of nothing better to do than to throw the bridle on our horses' necks to leave them to solve the difficulty. In this way we forded the river as well as we could, and were carried in rapidly in a southwesterly direction. More than once the roads became nearly invisible in the brushwood. . . we were not completely reassured till we reached the spot where we had dined three days before.

We knew it again by a giant pine, whose trunk, shattered by the wind, we had before admired. Still we rode on with undiminished speed, for the sun was getting low. . . . As night was coming on, we came in sight of the river Flint; half-an-hour later we were at the door of our house. This time the bear received us as old friends, and rose upon his hind legs to greet our happy return.

During the whole day we had not met a single human face; the animals, too, had disappeared. No doubt they had retired from the heat. All that we saw, and that at rare intervals, was now and then, on the bare top of a withered tree, a solitary hawk standing motionless on one leg, and sleeping quietly in the sun, as if cut out of the wood on which he was resting.

THE CHEAP, PLEASANT& EXPEDITIOUS ROUTE.

BETWEEN THE

EAST AND WEST

IS NOW BY THE

Detroit & Milwaukee R. R.

Fare $3.00 less than by any other Route.

1871.   *1872.*

Two Express Trains Leave Detroit Daily with Passengers for

PONTIAC, HOLLY, FENTONVILLE, FLINT, SAGINAW, OWOSSO, ST. JOHNS,

Lansing, Grand Rapids, Grand Haven,

MUSKEGON, MILWAUKEE, CHICAGO, ST. PAUL, ST. ANTHONY,

AND ALL POINTS ON THE MISSISSIPPI RIVER.

First Class Staunch Steamships

Built expressly for this Line, ply on the Lakes to and from each Train.

CLOSE CONNECTION MADE AT DETROIT WITH THE

GREAT WESTERN RAILWAY

OF CANADA,

For Buffalo, Rochester, Boston, New York, Philadelphia, Toronto, and with Grand Trunk Railway f
Montreal, Quebec, and with Cleveland and Lake Superior Line of Steamers.

For Emigrants this Line offers Cheap and Comfortable Transit.

For particulars see Company's Time Table to be had at any of the Stations on application.

THOS. BELL, Gen'l Supt.

D. M. R. R. Office, Detroit, 1871.

"Getting around" in Michigan gradually became easier. Clark's *Detroit City Directory* of 1871 advertised the combination of lake and rail travel that came to serve the public. (Courtesy of Bill Lynch.)

2.   Zachariah Chandler's Fight for Internal Improvements

Detroit Post and Tribune

Upon the day following that on which Mr. Chandler first took his seat in the Senate Judah P. Benjamin of Louisiana[1] offered a resolution providing that thereafter the standing committee of that body should be appointed at the commencement of each session of Congress. The Committee on Commerce then consisted of seven members . . . composed of Messrs. Clay of Alabama, chairman, Benjamin of Louisiana, Bigler of Pennsylvania, Toombs of Georgia, Reid of North Carolina, Bright of Indiana, and Hamlin of Maine. Mr. Chandler was assigned to the committee on the District of Columbia. . . . Mr. Hamlin was also appointed to this inferior committee, giving it two Republican members, where the Committee on Commerce had but one. The

"Zachariah Chandler: An Outline Sketch of His Life and Public Services," *Detroit Post and Tribune* (1880): 164–181.

general assignments of places to the minority was so inadequate and unfair that a Republican caucus (the first Mr. Chandler had attended) had been called to consider the matter. Mr. Chandler, although a new member, was one of its speakers and gave strong expression to his sense of the injustice with which both his party and the Northwest had been treated. It was decided to make a formal protest. There was but one [Republican] member to represent the country of the Great Lakes and the whole of New England and New York. . . . But the Republican protest, well-grounded as it was, proved then unavailing.

In his first speech before the entire Senate, Chandler commented:

> I rise, sir, to protest against this list of committees as presented here. Never before, in the whole course of my observation, have I seen a large minority virtually ignored in a legislative body upon important committees. This is the first time that I have ever witnessed such a total, or almost total, ignoring of a large and influential minority. But, sir, whom and what does this minority represent? It represents—I believe I am correct in saying—more than half—certainly nearly one-half—of all of the free white inhabitants of these United States; and yet this minority, representing the commerce and revenues of the nation, is expected to be satisfied with one place on the tail end of a committee on Commerce. I may almost say that that committee is of more importance to the Northwest than all the other committees of this body; but the great Northwest is totally ignored upon a committee in which it takes so deep an interest. Not a solitary member of this body from that portion of the country is honored with a position on that committee, and yet you have been told of the hundreds of millions of dollars' worth of commerce which is there looking to protection from this body. . . .

Before Mr. Chandler entered the Senate there had been some work done by the United States upon the most serious natural obstacle to the navigation of the Great Lakes, the tortuous channels and extensive shoals at the mouth of the St. Clair river, known as the "St. Clair Flats." Largely through Senator Cass's efforts an appropriation of $45,000 had been made in the Thirty-Fourth Congress (it was passed over Franklin Pierce's veto) for this work, and this sum had been expended under the supervision of Major Whipple in the clearing out of a channel through the shoals of about 6,000 feet in length, 150 feet in width, and nine feet in depth at low water. This improvement, valuable as it was, did not prove at all adequate, and was made much less useful in the few following years by a lessening in the depth of the waters of Lake St. Clair. The rapidly growing commerce of the lakes manifestly demanded the early construction and permanent maintenance through these shoals of a first-class ship canal, which could be safely used in all conditions of water and weather by vessels of the largest class. Mr. Chandler. . . commenced at once his attack on the great obstacles in its way—namely the disposition of the older States to undervalue the commercial importance of the Northwest, and the traditional hostility of the Democracy [sic] to all internal improvements. The first measure . . . was a bill "making an additional appropriation for deepening the channel of the St. Clair Flats;" when it was introduced it was referred to the Committee on Commerce. There an effort was made to strangle it by persistent inaction. Accordingly, on April 24, Mr. Chandler introduced in the Senate a resolution instructing the Committee on Commerce to report back this bill, for action in the Senate. This resolution not receiving immediate consideration, on May 3 he called it up and demanded a vote. Mr. Clay, the chairman of the committee, opposed it with much temper, and moved to lay it on the table, but this motion was lost by one vote. Mr. Clay then attacked Mr. Chandler's resolution as insulting to the Committee on Commerce. . . . Mr. Hamlin, the sole Republican member [on the Committee] expressed his gratification at the fact that the Senator from Michigan (Mr. Chandler) had offered this resolution; he thought that it was appropriate and that the action of the committee called for such instructions. . . . Mr. Benjamin . . . moved as a substitute for the pending resolution, a general order to the committee to report on all public works on which there had been any expenditure, and this motion prevailed. Mr. Chandler, who was after a specific point and not a mere generality, accepted this as a defeat, and began anew by giving notice on the spot that he should ask leave at a subsequent day to introduce a bill for the improvement of the St. Clair River Flats, making an appropriation of $55,000, this being the amount estimated by the United States Engineers as being necessary at that time. On May 10 he presented this bill, but the

Senate refused to refer, and adopted a motion to lay it upon the table. Mr. Chandler met this second defeat without discouragement, and later in the session did succeed after two efforts in procuring the addition of this item of $55,000 to the civil appropriation bill. But the threat of an executive veto of the whole measure, if this appropriation was not omitted, proved potent with the Senate, and it was ultimately stricken out. Mr. Chandler closed his last speech on this measure at that session, with a demand for a vote by yeas and nays, and these words: "I want to see who is friendly to the great Northwest and who is not—for we are about making our last prayer here. The time is not far distant when, instead of coming here and begging for our rights, we shall extend our hands and *take* the blessing. After 1860 we shall not be here as beggars."

Mr. Chandler said in an address at St. Johns, in Michigan, October 17, 1858:

> When I took my seat in the Senate I supposed every section of the country would be fairly heard in the details of business. There were twenty Republican Senators representing two-thirds the revenue, business, and wealth of the country. How were they placed on committees? Out of seven on the Committee on Commerce they had one. I call attention to this fact. It bears the mark of design. How does this work? . . . I introduced at an early date a bill appropriating money for the St. Clair Flats, and it went to this Southern Committee on Commerce. I procured all the necessary plans and maps and estimates and gave them into their charge. One hundred days rolled away and they had not deigned to examine them. I then introduced a resolution, instructing them to report. Subsequently I introduced a bill myself which was laid on the table. By the most untiring efforts I succeeded in getting the desired appropriation tacked upon a appropriation bill and passed. But the President's friends threatened a veto of the whole bill unless this was stricken out—and that was done. Thus committees were packed against us and we were thwarted at every turn. Thousands of dollars can be obtained for almost any creek in the South, while the inland seas of the North are denied a dollar, and we are left to take care of ourselves the best we can.

The second session of the Thirty-Fifth Congress began in December, 1858. . . . Mr. Chandler moved to take his St. Clair Flats bill from the table. This time it was passed by a vote of 29 to 22,

and sent to the House, . . . [where it] was finally passed, its in-
troducer working for it with the utmost energy in the committee-
rooms, on the floor, and by private solicitation. It reached Mr.
Buchanan in the last days of that Congress, and he killed it by
withholding his signature but without a formal veto. The Thirty-
Sixth Congress met in December, 1859, and on the 4th of January
Mr. Chandler's bill to deepen the St. Clair Flats Channel made its
appearance. On February 2 Mr. Buchanan informed Congress, in
a special message, of his reasons for "pocketing" the measure at
the last session. This veto took the position that the improvement
of harbors and the deepening of rivers should be done by
the. . . . States, and Michigan . . . with Upper Canada should
provide the necessary means. . . . Mr. Chandler reviewed this
message at length. . . . Jefferson Davis at once came to the defense of the veto on constitutional grounds and a running debate
followed, on the subject, between Messrs. Chandler and Bing-
ham of Michigan, Hamlin, Crittenden, Davis, Toombs, Wigfall
and others. Mr. Crittenden condemned the veto, while Toombs
and Wigfall joined Davis in its defense. Thus the plotters of rebellion assumed a hypocritical attitude as defenders of the constitution. . . as they assumed a virtue that they never had, that of
being patriots with a deep regard for the the fundamental law of
the land. No action followed this debate, but on February 20 Mr.
Chandler moved that his bill be made the special order for the
23d. . . . when that day arrived the Senate refused to proceed . . . no action was taken before adjournment. The second
session of this Congress commenced in December, 1861, with
civil war imminent and no chance for the consideration of any
project for internal improvement. At the meeting of the next
Congress the Democracy found itself in a petty minority, and remained powerless at Washington for many years. As soon as it
became plain that rebellion could not destroy the life of the nation, Mr. Chandler brought forward again his bill for the improvement of the channels at the head of Lake St. Clair, and with
the powerful support of his colleagues and the commercial interests of the Northwest obtained without difficulty from Republican Congresses such appropriations as were required for the
construction of a great ship-canal. . . . [2]

Mr. Chandler was the firm friend of an intelligently-planned
and general system of internal improvements. His labors, and

those of men like him, have borne fruit in manifold aids to commerce scattered over river, lake and ocean—light-houses, breakwater, harbors of refuge, straightened and deepened channels and improved natural highways. He was prompt to recognize the claims of all sections, but was especially vigilant in regard to the necessities of the Northwest, and his memory will long be cherished throughout the region of the Great Lakes as that of the most ardent and efficient champion of its commercial development.

Editor's Notes

1. Judah Benjamin is better known for his role as treasurer of the Confederacy than as senator from Louisiana.
2. The "great ship-canal" was, of course, the St. Marys River at Sault Sainte Marie.

Part V

Detroit and the Civil War: Glory and Ambivalence

Detroit and the Civil War: Glory and Ambivalence

At first the men of Michigan went off bravely and hopefully to the Civil War. The spirit of those early days is well captured by Frank B. Woodford's essay, "Thank God for Michigan!" But the war years were tangled, unhappy ones for many Detroiters; many men from Detroit did not return from Spottsylvania, from Wilderness, from Andersonville. Some Michigan men were ordered by General George Custer to accompany him to the West at the war's end when they thought the war was over and they would be coming home.

Not everyone of importance favored the war. Some saw it only as disunity. The handsome, socialite Episcopal Bishop McCoskry could not bring himself to encourage his own chaplains in the field. Late in 1860, Democrat Lewis Cass resigned his cabinet post as secretary of the interior in disgust when he saw he was powerless to stop the drift of United States armaments to Southern forts. President Buchanan, a Southerner, was clearly less than interested in the problem of the rapid depletion of Northern arsenals. Yet Cass remained, for all that, a Democrat. Never a copperhead, Cass was simply one who believed in the Union, thought of abolitionists as single-issue men who spoiled good politics, and felt his life work was draining away. The elderly widower sat out the war years at the home of his daughter, Mrs.

Canfield, widowed by the Mexican War, while Detroit changed around him.

Perhaps the most significant change was one of attitude. As the war progressed, the joy that had attended the first departing militia was gone, replaced by a new ambivalence. In this city—where once black and white abolitionists had contrived escape to Canada for hundreds of slaves, where once Sojourner Truth and Frederick Douglass had spoken—the average citizen had somehow changed sides.

Abolitionism was no longer embraced. The *Detroit Free Press*, never in favor of a war it thought unnecessary, allowed its most sensation-seeking reporter to write an incendiary account of the trial of "the Negro Faulkner." Faulkner, a black man of conservative, non-integrationist views, was falsely accused of sexual improprieties involving two young girls. A would-be lynch mob formed at the jail following his trial, and the militia was called out. One of the white rioters was shot by a soldier, and in the rioting that followed over two hundred black family homes were destroyed by fire. Most of the homes were on the near east side, in the Brush-Beaubien area now known as Greektown. Some reports of the riot from the *Detroit Advertiser and Tribune*—the *Free Press*'s ideological rival—are included in this section. One probable factor in the white working-class anger was that this was during the time of the draft quotas. In 1863, the war appeared to be going badly for the North, and men were advertising for substitutes to serve in their stead, offering steadily growing bounties.

Detroit stubbornly retained "Colored School #1," "Colored School #2," and "Colored School #3." These nameless schools were officially held by the board of education to be equal to other schools; the board claimed that a majority of white parents and children were so prejudiced that it dare not permit black and white children to attend school together. Yet, to many parents of the time, and to black teachers such as Fannie Richards and Delia Pelham, the segregated solution was no longer acceptable.

Five years after the Faulkner riot, Detroiters had a clear chance to choose direction. A proposed new state constitution included a provision for black male suffrage. Every ward of the city voted it down, with working-class precincts defeating it by the widest margins.

The Thirteenth, Fourteenth, and Fifteenth Amendments on which Senator Chandler had labored were needed nowhere more than in his home state of Michigan. Because of them, the state could no longer deny the vote to any of its male citizens, and Justice Cooley of the Michigan Supreme Court ruled in an opinion reprinted here that Detroit's "colored schools" were unacceptable as well. Justice Cooley had a certain advantage over Thurgood Marshall a century later. In chiding Detroit for racism that might damage children, Cooley was writing the majority, not the minority, opinion of his court.

Last in the Civil War documents is Alexandra McCoy's account of the changes in wealth that occurred between the 1840s and the end of the Civil War. Though many of Michigan's prewar leaders, or their families, were still among the wealthy, there were newcomers, and new industries as well. The stage was clearly set for the Gilded Age that was to follow.[1]

Editor's Note

1. Friend Palmer states that when Peter Henkel heard Chandler remark that the war would be a long one, he promptly bought up pork and storage space. John Bagley stored pipe tobacco and other men stocked up on "high wines" (i.e., port and sherry) before new special revenue taxes pushed up the prices. Palmer observed that he heard and saw it all, but had no money to invest. Palmer, Scrapbook no. 28, BHC.

1. "Thank God for Michigan!"

Frank B. Woodford

William H. Withington went to war, but on the way he stopped long enough to buy a corset for his wife at Mrs. McAdam's shop in Jackson, Michigan. To remind himself of what he had to purchase—a "No. 28, fasten in front with strap, $2"—he jotted down the essential information and specifications in his little pocket notebook. On the opposite page, he registered the number of his service revolver. It was 1107. Withington was a careful man; a written record was much more reliable than a frail memory.

Having done his errand at Mrs. McAdam's, Withington boarded the Detroit train. The date was April 16, 1861. He made

Frank B. Woodford, *Father Abraham's Children* (Detroit: Wayne State University Press, 1963), 25–35.

the journey, in all probability, with his fellow townsman, Governor Austin Blair, whose business in Detroit was urgent.

Besides being an up-and-coming businessman, of whom everyone in Jackson expected great things, the twenty-six-year-old Withington was captain of the local militia company, the Jackson Greys. It was in his capacity as a military man that the governor might have wished his company. Governor Blair was embarking on a fateful journey. He was on his way to meet his advisors and see what could be done about raising an infantry regiment to fill Michigan's quota under President Lincoln's call for 75,000 volunteers for three months service.

The call to arms came as no great surprise to Captain Withington. He had been expecting it, and, with the thoroughness which was typical of everything he did, he started early to get ready for war. A native of Dorchester, Massachusetts, there was enough Yankee in him to make him methodical and precise. The entries in his notebook reveal a good deal about him. A careful man with a dollar, as every young man on his way up should be, he noted every penny he spent.

The following week Withington paid his dues to the Jackson Greys—another twenty-five cents. It was a sound investment, because on February 15 he was elected captain of the company.

What Withington had been anticipating happened April 15. When the news of Fort Sumter's surrender was announced, the Jackson Greys assembled immediately in their armory and voted to offer their services, which, their captain proudly recorded, "were tendered by me to the Gov. this day." It was with satisfaction that he pointed out that in the aye-and-nay voting on the question all thirty-one votes were ayes. . . .

When it came to raising a company of volunteers or buying a corset, Withington gave the matter at hand his close personal attention.

The enthusiasm with which the Jackson Greys embraced the goddess of war was duplicated all over Michigan in every town which had a militia company. Each unit was as eager as Withington's to offer its services. Each began to fill up its ranks to the authorized strength of seventy-eight men with a spirit which was as competitive as it was patriotic. Orders were that the first ten companies ready would be accepted; the laggards would have to wait until they were needed.

First of all, though, there were certain necessary preliminary steps which had to be taken before a regiment could be put in the field. There had to be a staff. Governor Blair took care of that by appointing one while he was in Detroit on April 16. Alpheus S. Williams, or "Pap" Williams, as his men called him, a fatherly veteran of the Mexican War, was made brigadier general. . . .

Captain Whittlesey, his pockets stuffed with the money that Treasurer John Owen had been able to borrow or beg, set off to New York to purchase cloth for uniforms.

The week following Governor Blair's call for troops was one of feverish activity and excitement. In the preparations to go to war, the experiences of the Detroit Light Guard were typical of what all the militia companies went through.

The Light Guard was a venerable military association which traced its origins back to the Black Hawk War when it was organized as the Brady Guard. Prior to the outbreak of the Civil War it was primarily a social organization which attracted gentlemen of standing in the community as members. Military training consisted of occasional drills and parades, but much more frequently there were dances and banquets. Now and then, the Light Guard journeyed to another city to fraternize with some other militia company, playing host in turn, and trying to outshine the other in a display of hospitality. Several militia companies occasionally joined in a summer encampment for three or four days, and vied for prizes in drill competition.

An encampment was held for three days in Jackson in August, 1860, and the Light Guard attracted "much attention by their uniform step and easy line." . . . Each man received a bouquet from the belles of Jackson, a token which fired the Detroiters up to such a pitch that they handily won the competitive drill prize— thirty-five dollars. Most of the money, unfortunately, had to be paid to farmers to reimburse them for fences torn down to supply firewood. . . .

Being a member of the peacetime militia was something like belonging to a uniformed lodge or fraternity.

Then came April, 1861, and everything changed!

The Light Guard met in its armory on Woodbridge Street the evening of April 17 and, as Withington's Jackson Greys had done two days earlier, voted to "tender our services as a company to the commander-in-chief of the Michigan Militia, and ask to be enrolled in the regiment called for in his proclamation of the 17th inst."

Several of the members, substantial business and family men, some well on towards middle age, had to resign because of their personal circumstances. . . .

The rolls were filled by April 19 with seventy-five of the most promising applicants from the throng which clamored to join.

"Recruits came in by the hundreds, and many were so anxious to enlist with the famed Light Guard that money was liberally offered for the honor and privilege." So said Frederick Isham, a Detroit newspaperman who later went to the front as a war correspondent.

Of those accepted, almost all were Detroit residents. The average age of the company was twenty-three. Columbus Starkweather, Otis Cook, and Irving Garrison, at eighteen, were the "babies" of the company. Eventually, twelve men were dropped, but for every vacancy thus created there was a score of eager applicants.

Training began immediately, and on April 20 rookies with two left feet were learning the rudiments of squad drill in the open spaces of Campus Martius, the plaza adjoining City Hall. . . . Recruits who considered themselves as seasoned veterans after two or three days in the awkward squad became impatient. They had expected to be off for the front within a few hours after enlisting. . . .

Old campaigners, watching the preparations and recalling their experiences in former wars, were free with suggestions to the recruits about how to survive the rigors of the field. . . . The Free Press (April 25, 1861) printed the following sound advice from an "Old Soldier."

1. Remember that in a campaign more men die from sickness than by the bullet.

2. Line your blanket with one thickness of brown drilling. This adds by four ounces in weight and doubles the warmth.

3. Buy a small India rubber blanket (only $1.50) to lay on the ground or to throw over your shoulders when on guard duty during a rainstorm.

4. The best military hat in use is the light colored soft felt; the crown being sufficiently high for air to stir over the brain.

5. Let your beard grow, so as to protect the throat and lungs.

6. Keep your entire person clean; this prevents fevers and bowel complaints in warm climates. Wash your body each day if possible. Avoid strong coffee and oily meat.

7. A sudden check of perspiration by chilly or night air often causes fever and death. When thus exposed do not forget your blankets.

April 24 brought the awaited general order forming the regiment—the 1st Michigan Infantry—and listing the companies which had been selected, giving them their designations. . . .

"The makeup of the companies," said the state adjutant-general, "was composed of young men from all the professions and trades, and really embraced a class of the most respectable of the community." He might have added that for most part the members of the 1st were from the first families, and socially elect, of their various towns.

From April 18 to 24, all drilling was in company armories, but after the formation of the regiment, a shift was made from the companies' home bases to Fort Wayne, the army base on the Detroit River near the western limits of the town. . . . [By Monday, April 29] all companies had reported in and Colonel Willcox [Orlando B. Willcox of Detroit] took command of the regiment. Later the same day a detail of regular troops which had been stationed at Mackinac joined the 1st Michigan at Fort Wayne. Their arrival was delayed by their transport running aground on Belle Isle. Several hours were required to free the vessel.

Willcox and his officers had a problem of discipline on their hands from the outset. The light-hearted rankers, fresh from their roles as store clerks, bookkeepers, students, and young gentlemen about town, weren't accustomed to the restrictions of military life. They regarded their induction as the beginning of a glorious, carefree outing which would reach an exciting climax some afternoon when they would smash the rebellion with one blow.

Companies A and F discovered they didn't have much to do at the Fort before the rest of the regiment arrived. Playing cards and reading soon palled, and the men saw no reason for not returning to town for an evening of pleasure. Strict orders had been given that no one was to leave the Fort without a written pass. That posed no problem. The men simply wrote out their own. A stop was put to that after twenty men had passed the guard, but others discovered a convenient exit through an unwatched sally port. Most of them spent the night in Detroit, but all of them were on hand in the morning for reveille.

The first few days were devoted to giving the recruits the outward appearance of soldiers. On May 1, the first consignment of rifles arrived and was distributed. The arms which the men had brought with them were turned over to the home guards. The new weapons, described only as "minie guns", were probably Springfield 1855 muzzle-loading rifles of .58 caliber. This assumption is based on the statement that the regiment was equipped with the most up-to-date weapons. The records fail to show where they came from . . . the rifles of the 1st Michigan may have been Federal issue, sent down from the United States Arsenal at Dearborn.

It was time to put away the fancy uniforms of the independent companies which the men had been wearing since they moved into the Fort. The colorful trappings of hussars, dragoons, and zouaves, were shipped home and the new uniforms were donned.

Captain Whittlesey had returned to Detroit with $20,000 worth of cloth which he had purchased from the A. T. Stewart Department Store in New York. Detroit tailors, working on contract, made up to each man's individual measure the uniforms, which were described as "gray petershams for overcoats, navy blue for coats, and navy flannel for pants." The headgear was the familiar kepi, or forage cap, and the ladies of Detroit held sewing bees at which they made havelocks [attached head and neck scarfs] for the men. These, it was said, would be most useful as protection against sunstroke when the regiment marched victoriously through the hot, sunny South. . . .

About a thousand troops were crowded into space [at Fort Wayne] which lacked facilities for that many. To relieve the overcrowding, the passenger steamer *Mississippi* was borrowed from the Michigan Central Railroad and moored alongside the Fort. It was used to quarter four companies, and provided a mess hall for the entire regiment.

At first the mess was catered by a hotel man, Hiram R. Johnson. It came as something of a shock to the young gentlemen to discover that they were expected to eat at bare pine tables "with tin cups and plates, with iron spoons and cutlery." The menu was described as similar to that served in the average dollar-a-day hotel. Apparently it did not compare favorably with mother's cooking. The soldier's indignation exploded into a small riot one day when their dessert consisted of rice pudding instead of pie!

Gradually, however, the regiment began to shake down. Squad drill gave way to company and battalion exercises, and the 1st Michigan began to feel very soldierly. The Fort was visited daily by hordes of admiring civilians—friends, relatives, and plain sightseers who were impressed by the progress the troops were making. The easiest access to the Fort from the city was by boat, and the Windsor ferry line scheduled regular trips, with hourly sailings on Sunday. One day alone it was estimated that ten thousand people visited the Fort. . . .

The daily routine was strenuous. Reveille sounded at sunrise; sick call was at 6:30, and breakfast at 7. The guard was mounted at 8; dinner call came at 1 p.m., and the evening parade was held one hour before sunset. Tattoo was blown at 9, and all hands were expected to be in their straw-stuffed pallets half an hour later.

On May 1, the regiment was mustered into Federal service. That required new physical examinations, and there was a weeding out of the unfit and the under-aged—some of the recruits having lied about how old they were. There were also opportunities, before induction, for second thoughts, and those who wished to do so were permitted to resign. Few availed themselves of that privilege. . . .

After three weeks of preparation, the 1st Michigan was deemed ready. Orders were issued to start for Washington on May 13, and go by way of Cleveland, Harrisburg and Baltimore. . . . Friends and relatives came in droves for final goodbyes, and on the night of departure, it was said, the "pillows of their sisters and sweethearts were wet with tears."

Departure time was late afternoon. At 5 p.m. two Michigan Central steamships, the *Illinois* and the *May Queen*, drew alongside the Fort, and the 1st Michigan, 798 strong, went aboard. Slowly the two vessels moved up-river to Woodward Avenue, where a brilliant fireworks display was touched off as a civic farewell. Then . . . with the regimental band stationed in the bow of one of the ships, playing "The Girl I Left Behind Me," the two vessels turned their prows downstream.

The 1st Michigan was off to war!

The self-esteem which the regiment carried with it was not lessened during its trip East. . . . People lined the railroad tracks through Ohio and Pennsylvania to see them pass. At every stop delegations brought food to the men; young ladies presented locks of their hair and occasional kisses to the gallant-looking fellows from the Wolverine state, who, in turn, were feeling more heroic by the minute.

At Harrisburg the regiment was issued rations and for the first time was told to do its own cooking. This was a new and baffling experience, and the results were something less than a gourmet's delight. Despite orders not to leave camp, many of the men chucked underdone beef and scorched coffee into the bushes and lit out for the restaurants in town.

Colonel Willcox and staff were being entertained by Governor Curtin of Pennsylvania at a late dinner in a fashionable Harrisburg hotel. During the course of the festivities Willcox did a little boasting about the firm discipline with which he controlled his men. As proof he declared that the regiment was caged up in camp, strictly observing his orders to remain there. The colonel was in the midst of this self congratulatory dissertation when its effect was completely spoiled. For at that moment about twenty privates of the 1st Michigan filed into the dining room and sat down. The Colonel's face "when his eye fell on us—was a sight for the gods!", one of the men recalled later. . . .

It was 10 o'clock the night of May 16 when the Michigan regiment arrived in Washington, but even at that late hour it was warmly welcomed. In those uncertain days Washington was in a state of perpetual jitters. Rebel flags could be observed from time to time on Arlington Heights across the Potomac. Many Washingtonians sympathized openly with the South. There was no assurance that enough loyal Union troops could be assembled to hold the city against a Confederate coup or attack.

Then, out of the night, came those fine, soldierly-looking men from Michigan, the first Western regiment to reach Washington. Loyal citizens breathed easier.

155

"The Michigan Rifle Regt. came into town last night about 10 o'clock, marching from the depot up the Avenue to Eleventh Street," the Washington correspondent of the *New York Evening Post* informed his newspaper. "They were preceded by a splendid band of music which soon aroused our citizens, and long before they had reached the quarters assigned to them, hundreds of people were out to give them welcome. The enthusiasm of the crowd was irrepressible, for this was the first Western regiment which had arrived at the capital."

To a lonely, burdened man in the White House, the band's blare and the tramp of feet brought the answer to a question which had bothered him: Would the Western states remain loyal to the Union and support it with men and resources?

Now he knew.

"Thank God," said Abraham Lincoln, "for Michigan!"

2.   The Faulkner Riot

Detroit Advertiser and Tribune

The headlines below graced the front page of the Detroit Advertiser
and Tribune *on Saturday, March 7, 1863. In themselves they formed a synopsis
of the horror story that followed. William Faulkner, a downtown saloon-keeper,
who happened to be black, had been accused of sexual assault by two nine-year-
old girls, Ellen Hoover, black, and Mary Brown, white. He was bound over for
trial and was then found guilty by a jury on March 6.*

*The wave of violence that swept over the city is chronicled here. After seven
years in Jackson prison, Faulkner was proven to have never committed a crime.
Mary Brown confessed that the girls had made up the tale to avoid being punished for coming home late.*

CASE OF THE NEGRO FAULKNER
He is Convicted and Sent to the State Prison for Life
Attempt to Lynch Him on his Way to Jail
He is Protected by the Military
The Soldiers Assailed by the Mob Fire Upon it and Kill One Man
General Assault Upon the Negroes Throughout the City
Several Negroes Believed to be Murdered
A Large Number Horribly Beaten
Great Destruction of Property by Arson
Several Fires Under Way at the Same Time
Military Called on from Ypsilanti and Fort Wayne

"Case of the Negro Faulkner," *Detroit Advertiser and Tribune* (7 March 1863): 1–2.

Scenes, Incidents, &c.
Full Particulars Up to Two O'Clock this Morning

What Transpired in the Court Room

This (Friday) afternoon the Court assembled, and the jury were promptly in their seats, the Courtroom being densely crowded. Judge Witherell charged the jury in the only manner which the law seemed to justify. The jury retired, and after an absence of about ten minutes, brought in a verdict of guilty. His Honor then told the prisoner to stand up, and asked him if there was any reason why the sentence of the law should not be pronounced in his case, to which the prisoner replied that there was. He was then told to come forward and give his reasons, which he did. He said that the saloon which he keeps is a place of public resort; that the girls Mary Brown and Ellen Hoover, for reasons which he could not at the time comprehend, were—and had been for several days—in the habit of calling into the saloon; that he remonstrated against it and on several occasions, in the presence of one or two of his customers, he told them to leave. He was satisfied, since this crime had been laid against him, that they were accessories to a plot to get him removed from the building he occupies. He said that he had no time to get testimony, his principal witness being a tall young man who boards somewhere near the Michigan Central Depot, and he believed he was a map peddler, who came frequently to the saloon to get a lunch or dinner. He again expressed his belief that this was a plot got up by his enemies to injure his character and drive him from his place.[1]

His Honor, the judge, replied that if his statements were true, or had been established in evidence during the trial, this would have mitigated his case to some extent; but as there was no evidence to that effect, and as the jury after a careful hearing of the testimony, and a full knowledge of the law, had pronounced him guilty of one of the highest crimes known on the statute book, it only remained for him to pronounce the sentence. "You are therefore," said the Judge, "sentenced to the State Prison at Jackson, there to be confined during your natural life." The sentence was highly applauded by the crowd present. . . .

The Scene in Front of the City Hall and Vicinity

An order was then issued that the Courtroom be immediately cleared. A large concourse had already assembled in front of the City Hall and was constantly increasing, and violent threats were made to take the life of the prisoner. The officers were firm and resolute in their determination to convey him safely to the jail and, as a precaution, a detachment of the Provost Guard from the Barracks, under the Lieutenant Van Stam, was called to aid. When the troops arrived at the Campus Martius, they were hooted at and assailed with a variety of offensive weapons, but they behaved coolly and prudently. The prisoner was brought down from the Courtroom, and proceeded, escorted by several of the police and the soldiers up Monroe avenue and Randolph street to Gratiot street, followed by several thousand people, many of them bent upon seizing the prisoner. . . . Stones, brick-bats, mud and sticks were hurled against the soldiers, in a perfect shower. . . .

Upon reaching Gratiot street, the crowd had largely increased, and became more violent, until the officers reached the intersection of Gratiot and Clinton, when several of the soldiers were seriously injured by bricks and stones . . . an order was given to fire. The first volley was probably composed of blank cartridges. . . .

In Front of the Jail—A Man Killed

When the crowd had reached the front of the jail on Beaubien street, brickbats, stones, mud, and every available missile was thrown at the soldiers. . . . The soldiers were again ordered to fire a second volley, which they did, with fatal effect. One man, Charles Langer, daguerrotype artist, . . . was shot dead, the ball striking in the pit of his stomach. . . .

The authorities succeeded in securing the prisoner in jail, and the soldiers passed on to the Barracks. . . . The mob then seemed determined to wreak their vengeance upon Negroes that could be found in the street. A portion of the crowd then passed down Beaubien street, and assailed several Negro houses on the way. Some of them took a turn up East Lafayette, and stoned every house known to be occupied by negroes, and broke in windows, tore down fences, and committed many other outrages. . . .

Morris Horan, blacksmith, who keeps shop on the corner of Larned and Wayne, was shot from the inside of a house occupied by negroes, next to the cooper shop on Beaubien street, near East Fort.

Soon after this the cooper shop was fired by the mob, which together with the dwelling house adjoining it, and a barn nearby, were completely destroyed.[2]

A dwelling house belonging to colored people, on the corner of Beaubien and Lafayette streets, was completely riddled. Almost the entire floor of the house was torn out, and the furniture piled up in the street in front and burned. . . .

The mob was composed, to a large extent, of young fellows brought up in the "street school"—rowdies and vagabonds, ignorant, unreasoning, and crazy with whisky and prejudice. Their spirit and their shouts were full of bitter and violent hatred for the negro. "Kill the nigger!" "D——n the nigger!" "Butcher all niggers!" "Stone that nigger house!" "Tear down that nigger dive!" "Every d——n nigger ought to be hung!" We will do the mob the justice to suppose that but few of them could read, and that they despised, above all things, the free school and the church. They are exactly the fittest material for political demagogues to work with. . . .

Nearly every respectable person in the crowd, and there were many present, from that pardonable motive, curiosity— condemned the rioters and endeavored to quiet them.[3] But arguing with the rioters was useless. . . . The mob had caught the political slang, and fiercely demanded the lynching of some "d——d Abolitionists," seeing the negroes had mostly hidden themselves. We saw fellows plunge across the muddy streets and dash along the sidewalks—in their insane fury to "kill a nigger,"—at a rate of speed that a loafer of their style was never known to practice except when running from an officer.

Occurrences in the Evening

A number of small wooden buildings on Lafayette street between Beaubien and St. Antoine were fired, and six of them with their furniture, were entirely destroyed. In one of the tenements, the inmates were locked in, and were threatened with death if they attempted to escape. But even the mob spirit relented when the wretches begged for mercy and burst the doors open to escape from being burned to death.

Robert Bennett, a molatoo [sic], was badly cut and rushed to the Biddle House. . . . Dr. Steward, a respectable colored Physician, residing on Clinton street, opposite the jail, an old grey headed negro, was fearfully beaten. . . .

While the main body of rioters were engaged in the destruction of the houses on Lafayette street, a large crowd of boys and men, probably forty in number, discovered an inoffensive colored man in an alley in the rear, and immediately assailed him with bricks, stones, and clubs, knocking him down in the ditch. Boys from eight to ten years of age seized bricks and stones and with the most fearful imprecations, such as "Pray, you d——n nigger, we will kill you!" rushed upon him. The negro was beaten very badly and has probably since died. We have not learned his name.[4]

Editor's Notes

1. It would be satisfying to have more information as to whether there was some basis in fact for Faulkner's fears. However, William Faulkner's name and address are not listed in any city directions, even in the later years when he had a market stall provided for him by an embarrassed citizenry.

2. The cooper was Whitney Reynolds. He lost seven hundred dollars and his tools.

3. Among the "respectable persons" involved was John J. Bagley, later governor of Michigan, and a worker for school equality and Catholic Bishop Lefèbvre. Most praise went to a courageous Irish police officer, Daniel Sullivan.

   Not so good as people went was the fire marshal, W. M. Champ, who admitted he had not allowed the fire hoses to be turned on the black homes while they were in flames because the mob had threatened to cut them if he did so. He saw his duty as protecting city property. He ordered adjacent white homes to be hosed down, however, "for the greatest good of the greatest number."

4. The victim, Joshua Boyd, was featured in later news accounts. Boyd was an escaped slave who had come north to "freedom" a few years earlier.

Other riot incidents were reported in the *Advertiser* during the following days, several due to research by the Reverend S. S. Hunting, Unitarian minister. Families with small children were forced to spend the rainy weekend in the woods east of town. Many went to Canada, as people had following the Blackburn incident a generation earlier.

3. A Northern Victory Does Not Create Equality

Detroit Advertiser and Gazette

The Detroit Advertiser and Gazette *worked persistently but without success for the passage of a new Michigan constitution that would give the vote to black males. I quote from two editorials, one published immediately before and the other immediately after the special election.*

Our readers will bear in mind that but a few days remain before they will be called upon to vote upon the new Constitution. We have very thoroughly discussed the provisions of this instrument, and if we have at all succeeded in our purpose, we have shown that it is superior to the present organic law. That it has no defects we have not pretended. . . . There is no such thing as unanimity to be attained in the support of the Constitution of a State. If on the whole, a Constitution is a good one, and we shall have future opportunity of remedying by amendment the more salient objections, it ought to secure the support of all good citizens. . . . The proposition for revision originally came from the Democratic press, the *Free Press* of this city, leading off

"Close Up the Column," *Detroit Advertiser and Gazette* (3 April 1868): 2.
"Election Results," *Detroit Advertiser and Gazette* (7 April 1863): 2.

163

in the discussion. Democrats, in common with Republicans, felt that we had outgrown our organic law, and were it not that the new Constitution secures Equal Suffrage, a large number of Democrats would vote for it. Leading Democrats in the State helped make it, and voted in detail for all of its principal provisions. It is opposed by the Democratic party now, not because they wish to defeat the Constitution as a whole but because they wish to defeat negro suffrage in it. . . .

We earnestly appeal to Republicans who for any cause, are meditating a vote against the Constitution, to temperately weigh the considerations we present. To defeat Equal Suffrage after liberating a race and pledging ourselves to their protection, is to prove recreant to our principles and to deny our record. To defeat Equal suffrage in Michigan, where there are about a thousand colored voters, and to establish it in South Carolina where the newly enfranchised colored citizens actually constitute a majority of the people—to enforce possible negro government in another state, while we will not permit one colored man when offset by one hundred white men, to vote in our own State, is disgraceful inconsistency and hypocrisy. . . .

[In commenting on the election results, the editors make their disappointment clear.]

The new Constitution is badly defeated. It was opposed by all the enemies of Impartial Suffrage in this region, and in many sections of the interior by the Prohibitionists, who feared the success of the revised instrument without the Prohibitory clause. It also encountered every adverse vote in the Republican party on the ground of its increased salaries, its exemption clauses, the railroad question, the agricultural college location, and other points involved in the various sections. These questions invited the scattering fire of thousands in the aggregate, all over the State. . . . We labored to the best of our ability to secure its adoption, we deeply regret its defeat, and in giving our last kick as its advocate we console ourselves with the reflection that we died game.[1]

Editor's Note

1. The constitution lost in every one of Detroit's ten wards, and most heavily in the working-class neighborhoods, where blacks may have been seen as potential job competitors.

   At the Fourth Ward voting place, August Thiele's grocery store at Hastings and Croghan (now Monroe), the vote was 93 for and 584 against the constitution. This was the neighborhood most affected by the brutal house burnings during the Faulkner riot five years earlier. In no other ward did voting rights do quite so badly, though in the Michigan Avenue home of John Kiely, "cigar maker," the measure was defeated by 729 to 133, and in William Wunsch's home-and-saloon polling place on Clinton Street, there were 149 votes for to 527 against.

   Among the business and professional voters, things were somewhat better, though there were no victories for black suffrage there, either. Voters from the great houses downtown voted at City Hall, and 144 of them favored the constitution, with 171 against. The votes from the elegant homes along Cass, Woodward, and Second north of Grand Circus Park were tallied at Steam Engine House No. 3 on Clifford Street. There were 508 for, with only 613 against.

   These statistics appeared in the late edition of the *Advertiser* of April 7.

4. School Desegregation and the Workman Case

Supreme Court of Michigan

Joseph Workman was listed in the city directory as "porter (col'd) [colored]." He was also the father of a ten-year-old son on whose behalf he brought suit to force the admission of his son to the school nearest his home, the Duffield, rather than the nearest "colored school." The Detroit Board of Education fought the case all the way to the Michigan Supreme Court—and lost.

Reprinted here is an abridged version of The People ex. rel. Joseph Workman v. The Board of Education of Detroit, *including the arguments before the Michigan Supreme Court and the majority opinion in favor of Workman, delivered May 12, 1869, by Chief Justice Cooley.*

H. M. & W. E. Cheever, for relator [argument for Workman]:

The board of education of the city are a body corporate, . . . to them is committed the direction and regulation of the free schools of the city. . . . Section one of the act of 1842 provided that "the city of Detroit shall be considered as one school district, and hereafter all schools organized therein, . . . shall . . . be public and free to all children residing within the limits thereof, between the age of five and seventeen years, inclusive." . . .

[The legislature's] intention clearly was to commit the care and custody of the free schools of the city of Detroit to the respondents . . . to be by them carried on as nearly as possible in accor-

Supreme Court of Michigan, Workman v. Board of Education, *Michigan Reports* (April Term 1869): 399–499.

dance with the general state law, not to be "regulated" in such a way as to be virtually closed against one class of citizens, while open to others.

. . . By the law of the state, children must attend in the district where they reside . . . .

A "regulation" requiring children to go from the tenth ward to the ninth, a distance of over two miles, and pass other schools on their way, becomes virtually a prohibition of the benefits of the school system.

Again, the Duffield has its grades; the colored school is a primary school only; and the exclusion of the colored child from the union school is an absolute prohibition of an enjoyment of the higher grades of the free schools.

The power to regulate is not the power to prohibit. . . . The primary intention of the act is to give free schools to all children in the city. . . .

D. B. and H. M. Duffield, for respondents[1] [summing up for the board]:

Respondents insist that the [Workman child] is not entitled to the *mandamus* [the right to attend Duffield School], prayed for the following reasons:

1. Because it is at this time impossible for the respondents to comply with it on account of the lack of room in the schools. . . .

2. Because the relator has no such interest in the matter as entitles him to ask for a *mandamus*.

The petition should be made by the child excluded, by its next friend: . . .

3. Because the resolution of respondents requiring colored children to attend separate schools, established and maintained exclusively for them, is:

First. Authorized by statute.

Second. An exercise of their discretion, with which this court will not interfere; and,

Third. A reasonable regulation "for the good government and prosperity of the free schools of said city." . . .

There has been no exclusion of relator's child from the public schools of said city. The return expressly avers that the relator's child can, at any time, upon proper application, be admitted to the colored schools. . . .

167

This power to regulate the classification and distribution of the school children must be placed somewhere outside the scholars. . . .

Can it be said to be unreasonable for respondents to separate colored from white children in the public schools as long as stated? Comp. L. [Compiled Laws of Michigan] p. 950 . . . forbids intermarriage between them. . . .

. . . The fact is averred and admitted that there exists among a large majority of the white population of Detroit a strong prejudice or animosity against colored people, which is largely transmitted to the children in the schools, and that this feeling would engender quarrels and contention if colored children were admitted to the white schools.

Whether the association together of black and white children in the same schools would not equally foster and engender this prejudice may well be doubted. . . .

We submit that both upon principle and authority the *mandamus* should be denied.

COOLEY CH. J. [Chief Justice]:
. . . The legislature of 1867 passed an act amendatory of the primary school law, one section of which is as follows: "All residents of any district shall have an equal right to attend any school therein. Provided that this shall not prevent the grading of schools according to the intellectual progress of the pupils, to be taught in separate places when deemed expedient." . . .

It cannot be seriously urged that with this provision in force, the school board of any district which is subject to it may make regulations which would exclude any resident of the district from any of its schools, because of race or color, or religious belief, or personal peculiarities. It is too plain for argument that an equal right to all the schools, irrespective of all such distinctions, was meant to be established.

Does this provision apply to the city of Detroit? That city, as we have seen, is expressly declared to be "one school district", and is, therefore, within the words of the act of 1867. That the legislature seriously intended their declaration of equal rights in the schools to be partial in its operation, is hardly probable. . . .

The declaration is incorporated in the general primary school law. I am not aware that there is any organized portion of the state that does not come under some of the provisions of that law. The specially created union school districts [the larger towns and cities] are subject to it, except so far as the special legislation creating or governing them is inconsistent. The declaration in the Detroit free school act that the city shall constitute one school district, is idle for any other purpose than to connect the city with the primary school system which the general law establishes. . . . It is not true, therefore, that the primary school law has no application in the city of Detroit, or that we may say of any of its provisions respecting districts that Detroit is exempt from them. . . .

. . . And as all other portions of that law not inconsistent with the free school act apply to the city of Detroit, so must the section establishing equality of right in the schools apply also, unless it can be shown to be inconsistent. No inconsistency was pointed out on the argument, nor was any reason suggested as likely to have influenced the legislature to make that city an exception. . . .

. . . Yet, if we were to look outside the act of 1867 for the occasion of its passage, we should probably find that occasion to exist only in the city of Detroit, and in some two or three of the union or graded districts where distinctions based on color were kept up, which were unknown in other portions of the state. . . .

. . . We do not discover that there is anything in any of those statutes—and we include particularly in this statement the Detroit free school act—that overrules or modifies the requirement of the general law, that the right to attend the schools shall be possessed equally and impartially by all classes of residents.

The conclusion is inevitable that the legislature designed the impartial rule they established to be of universal application.

It remains to be seen whether there are any formal objections to the writ prayed for. It was suggested by the respondents that the father, as such, could not apply for a *mandamus* on behalf of his infant child, but that the child should apply by guardian. . . . The father is the natural guardian of the child. . . . Although the proceeding is for the benefit of the child, the duty of placing him in school is the parent's, and the father is entitled . . . to appeal to the courts for the removal of any unlawful impediments. It was also urged that the application for the writ did not show affirmatively that the child possessed the necessary qualifications for admission to the school. It shows, however, that the father applied for his admission, and offered to submit him to all the rules, examinations and regulations of the board with regard thereto, and was refused because of the child's color. . . .

As the statute of 1867 is found to be applicable to the case, it does not become important to consider what would otherwise have been the law [italics mine].[2]

Editor's Notes

1. For the Workman case the board of education hired the attorneys Henry and Divie Bethune Duffield, sons of the prominent minister for whom the school was named.

   Among their many arguments the Duffield brothers claimed "that there is a strong prejudice against the colored people among the majority of the population of the said city, and among many of the children in said schools, . . . and that the abolition of said colored schools, and the indiscriminate union and mingling of colored with white children in all the public schools, would be greatly prejudicial to the best interests of said public schools, and would engender strife and discord among the scholars thereof."

2. Ruling in favor of Joseph Workman, the court, speaking through Justice Cooley, held that the Detroit Board of Education was required to give equal access to education to Workman's son. Although Justice Cooley's other decisions have been widely studied in law schools for a century, this one apparently never reached the state's colleges of education. Though the labor-backed reform coalition of 1955–70 went far in removing the evils of discrimination, it was from a belief that "quality integrated education," the phrase of the late UAW attorney and board member Abe Zwerdling, was a good in itself. The statute of 1867 on which Cooley based his opinion was clearly essential if Michigan was to conform to the provisions of the new Fourteenth Amendment, which forbade the states to legislate inequality. It is still amazing that the Detroit Board and its lawyers tried so stubbornly to ignore its validity.

   Historians concerned with the history of Michigan blacks are well aware that racial integration has been late in coming to the schools—if indeed one believes that it has! However, few Michigan scholars or educational administrators have been aware how completely Cooley's decision on behalf of Joseph Workman and his son made innumerable, persistent actions of discrimination by the Detroit Board of Education over many years (and no doubt actions by some other Michigan boards of education) simply outside the law.

5. A New Power Structure: Wealth before and after the Civil War

Alexandra Ueland McCoy

To Alexandra McCoy we owe a specific knowledge of who were the wealthy of Detroit and Wayne County before and after the Civil War, as well as significant factors that may have helped determine their good fortune. For this story of wealth and power, I have chosen excerpts from McCoy's work describing the economic elite of 1844 and that of 1860 through 1866.

The research methods used for tracing the wealthy are thorough and innovative. For the 1860s group there were the extra resources of the federal census and the records of a special federal income tax levied during the Civil War. Information from the latter is referred to under the title "tax rolls" in Table 2.

The Economic Elite of 1844

Ninety-seven individuals made up the economic elite of Wayne County, Michigan, in 1844. These men were selected primarily on the basis of their known wealth with important economic roles as a secondary consideration. Tax assessment rolls for real and personal property for the city of Detroit and Wayne County provided the comprehensive measurement by which the men were ranked.[1] Wealth figures were based on the assessment formula then in operation, which was to rate property at 30% of actual cash value.[2] Therefore, Lewis Cass, whose real and per-

Alexandra Ueland McCoy, "Political Affiliations of American Economic Elites: Wayne County, Michigan, 1844, 1860, as a Test Case" (Ph.D. diss., Wayne State University, 1965), 55–92.

sonal property was assessed at $73,383, appears on Table 1, as being worth $244,365. . . .

Property in Wayne County was, of course, not as precise a measurement of wealth as an income tax would have been. It left out extensive ventures into land in other Michigan counties and in other states.[3] Personal wealth did not reveal itself entirely on the tax rolls where personal property was usually itemized as horses, carriages and furniture. Farmers and Mechanics Bank was assessed for $20,000 worth of stock, but nowhere does individual ownership of bank stock show up.

Nor is there any evidence of the investments of twenty-three men known to be involved in burgeoning copper companies.[4] Robert Stuart, a former American Fur Company official, who negotiated a treaty of sale of copper lands with the Indians, owned 125 shares "given gratis". Charles Moran, a leading landowner, held fifty shares in the Eagle Harbor Mining Company, along with Charles Howard, John Hurlburt, Shadrach Gillett and Fred Wetmore.

The predominance of realty in the tax rolls, while undoubtedly reflecting the major source of wealth, obscures the relative liquidity of individuals. Elon Farnsworth's plea for ten dollars from Solomon Sibley (valued at $19,330 and $33,093, respectively) suggests an occasional dire lack of cash as late as five years after the crash of 1837: "I am obliged to raise some money today and take the liberty to ask you for the ten dollars for which I gave you a receipt and was credited to your account in the Henry estate. I would not trouble you, but I suppose this fund is lying in the bank and I find it impossible to collect any old debts".

Indebtedness undoubtedly plagued many of these men. . . . The affairs of C. C. Trowbridge reveal the long struggles of a debtor struggling to pay off the obligations incurred when the banks went under after 1837. Trowbridge complained: . . . "the failure of the bank brought down upon my head the consequences of acts with which I had no more connection than the Grand Turk himself. I lost by this and another bank $25,000 which added to my other losses left me almost hopelessly in debt".

Trowbridge was probably sounding poor to Olcutt, his creditor, because in 1845 he was buying property worth over $1,000 in Allegan County, and in 1846 his friend Robert Stuart congratulated him on his expanding opportunities: "I am truly gratified at the good state of your affairs. Will you make anything out of the railroad? . . . "

Other evidence of economic standing to complement known wealth was sought for two reasons: first, to sustain the selection of men at the lower ranks, worth less than $15,000, and second, to include people in key positions who simply did not turn up on the tax rolls. Thus, nine individuals worth between $10,000 and $15,000 holding key positions were added to these seventy-two over $15,000 who were clearly of the top elite on the basis of wealth alone. The positions were members of the Board of Trade, officers in banks or corporations or manufacturers of concerns employing more than twenty hands. Sixteen who did not appear on the tax rolls were selected if they were officers or manufacturers of large concerns. . . . George Russel, for example, owned ferry boats and an iron foundry and engaged in land speculation but did not appear on the tax rolls.

Key positions were shown to be reliable indicators when careers were followed beyond 1844. Many of the men at the lower ranks had the enterprising qualities which would make them men of great wealth in 1860. Though not rich in 1844, H. P. Baldwin, Christian H. and Frederick Buhl, and James F. Joy showed their abilities by buying up the stock of the Michigan State Bank for 15% of face value before it re-opened in 1845.[5] It was the enterprise of these men which gave them a foothold, because during the early forties most of the capital for railroads and banks came from eastern sources. James F. Joy's promotion of the sale of the Michigan Central brought him out of the limited scope of debt-collecting for banks into the large sphere where he was to make his fortune.

Manufacturers were identified from a study of Detroit industry made in 1848. This list [from the *Detroit Daily Advertiser* June 16 and August 22, 1848] was of inestimable value because it described the 139 establishments then operating either as to number of employees, annual value of product, or in the case of lumber, total [board] produced.[6]

Once selected, the elite was divided as to economic role, degree of wealth and time of arrival in Wayne County. . . .

The attempt was to assign roles according to probable major source of income. All men chosen from the tax rolls were land-

Industry in old Detroit. *Detroit City Directory* of 1859. (Courtesy of Bill Lynch.)

owners, for example, but only men who had no other apparent major source of income were identified as landowners. To recognize its importance to a frontier economy, fur was listed where it represented rise to wealth, even though the actual trade had passed its peak. . . Classified as non-specialized entrepreneurs were men who had interests diversified beyond one business and a directorship. Josiah L. Dorr, for example, was a merchant, part owner of the Detroit Iron Company, and a director both in a copper company and a bank. Bankers were often lawyers; they are classified solely on their active officership in 1844. Thus, Elon Farnsworth, a lawyer in 1844, became a banker in 1860.

The wide divergence in wealth suggested an investigation of the relationship of economic roles to wealth. Landowners and fur fortunes were almost exclusively concentrated among the top (above $50,000) and medium ($25,000 to $50,000) brackets. . . .

All other roles were concentrated in the low bracket, with lawyers, bankers and manufacturers conspicuously lacking among the highest incomes. This division, favoring roles natural to a frontier economy, suggests that early arrival was also a key factor. It is therefore not surprising to note that 72% of the men at the top of the wealth scale were in Wayne County before 1820, in contrast to the majority of the lower ranks who came after 1830.

The value of arriving early might seem to suggest that the top members of the elite were self-made men. Quite the contrary was true. Out of a total of thirty-two well-to-do fathers known for the entire ninety-seven [members of the elite], twelve of these belonged to the eighteen men worth more than $50,000.

The likelihood is that a much larger number of these men enjoyed an advantaged early environment to enable them to start a business in the West, where $5,000 or $6,000 was required to purchase a good stock.

. . . There was an easy manner, a democratic stance among the economic elite in the early days. Jacob Farrand recalled: "The people here in the earlier days of Detroit went along just about as they were; men of business lived along in a conservative sort of way, one year and another, devoid of any aristocracy. All the old inhabitants were people of a social nature inviting to each others houses and lived along in an enjoyable way".[7]

[Some merchants who retired] . . . became capitalists or bankers. These were the men who saw the new avenues for making great fortunes. They became the leaders of the group designated as the economic elite of 1860.

Table 1
The Economic Elite of 1844—Bases for Selection and Economic Role

Listed According to Wealth		To Detroit	Economic Role
Lewis Cass	$244,365	1813	Landowner
Oliver Newberry	$179,553	1820	Shipping
DeGarmo Jones	$116,150	1818	Non-Specialized
Shubael Conant	$110,882	Born	Merchant
John R. Williams	$117,459	Born	Landowner
James Abbott	$116,523	Born	Fur, copper
John Biddle	$116,207	1820's	Fur
Joseph Campau	$111,791	Born	Fur
Barnabas Campau	$103,672	Born	Fur
Peter Desnoyers	$ 92,241	Before 1820	Merchant
Josiah R. Dorr	$ 79,144	1825	Non-Specialized
Edmund A. Brush	$ 77,704	1802	Landowner
Antoine Beaubien	$ 75,124	Born	Landowner
William Brewster	$ 71,878	1815	Fur
Franklin Moore	$ 58,308	1833	Merchant
Zachariah Chandler	$ 58,275	1833	Merchant
Charles Moran	$ 56,809	Born	Landowner
John Drew	$ 51,521		Merchant
Jonathan Kearsley	$ 48,151	1819	Landowner
John Hurlburt	$ 47,892		Fur
Robert Stuart	$ 46,959	Before 1820	Fur
Thomas C. Sheldon	$ 46,786	1817	Landowner
Jonathon L. King	$ 43,872	1829	Merchant, Mfr.
Francis Eldred	$ 39,294	1816	Merchant, Mfr.
Dominique Riopelle	$ 39,160	Born	Landowner
John McDonnell	$ 37,395	1812	Landowner
David Cooper	$ 35,407	1799	Merchant
Darius Lamson	$ 34,132	1830's	Merchant
John Owen	$ 34,054		Merchant
John Palmer	$ 33,699	1818	Merchant

Table 1 (cont.)

Listed According to Wealth		To Detroit	Economic Role
Solomon Sibley	$ 33,093	Before 1810	Mfr., Quarry
Thomas Rowland	$ 32,733	1812	Landowner
Pierre Teller	$ 29,304	Before 1830	Merchant
Chas. C. Trowbridge	$ 27,579	1819	Banker
Alex C. McGraw	$ 26,640	1809	Merchant, Mfr.
Theodore Romeyn	$ 25,363	1835	Lawyer
Levi Cook	$ 25,557	1815	Merchant
Louis Davenport	$ 25,041	1830's	Shipping
William Woodbridge	$ 24,718	1812	Lawyer
Douglass Houghton	$ 24,598	1830	Banker
David Thompson	$ 23,829		Landowner
Shadrach Gillet	$ 23,676	1815	Non-Specialized
John Watson	$ 23,476		Merchant
Moses L. Dickinson	$ 23,176	1831	Merchant, Mfr.
Eustache Chapoton	$ 23,026	Born	Builder
Charles Desnoyers	$ 22,693	Born	Merchant
Henry N. Walker	$ 22,680	1834	Banker, Lawyer
Eurotas P. Hastings	$ 21,934	1825	Merchant
Frederick Wetmore	$ 21,811	1841	Merchant
Richard H. Hall	$ 21,645	1836	Merchant
Alanson Sheley	$ 21,534	1831	Builder
W. N. Carpenter	$ 21,328	1826	Merchant
Charles Brush	$ 21,078	Born	Landowner
Harmon DeGraff	$ 20,313	1837	Merchant, Mfr.
Buckminster Wight	$ 20,273	1832	Sawmill
George F. Porter	$ 20,855	1829	Banker, Lawyer
Thomas Coquillard	$ 19,906	Born	Mason
Elon Farnsworth	$ 19,330	1822	Lawyer
Alexander Newbould	$ 19,064		Merchant
Lewis Goddard	$ 18,697		Banker
James F. Joy	$ 18,564	1836	Mich. State Bank, Lawyer
James A. Van Dyke	$ 18,691	1834	Copper, Lawyer
John Scott	$ 17,649	1829	Builder
Peter DesNoyers	$ 17,629	Born	Merchant
William Chittenden	$ 17,149	1835	Central R.R.
J. Nicolson Elbert	$ 16,899	1840	Non-Specialized
John Roberts	$ 16,816	1820	Merchant, Mfr.

Table 1 (cont.)

Listed According to Wealth		To Detroit	Economic Role
Alpheus S. Williams	$ 16,533	1836	Non-Specialized
Francis Cicotte	$ 16,317	Born	Landowner
Alexander D. Fraser	$ 16,137	1823	Lawyer
John G. Atterbury	$ 15,984	1830's	Lawyer
Alvah Ewers	$ 14,418	1829	Merchant
Samuel Pitts	$ 14,069	1831	Mfr., Lumber
Theodore Williams	$ 13,852	Born	Merchant
Henry P. Baldwin	$ 12,820	1838	Manufacturer
Chauncey Hurlbut	$ 12,654	1825	Merchant
Benjamin Kercheval	$ 12,097	1821	Merchant
Orville Dibble	$ 11,655	1830's	Hotel Prop.
Alfred Dwight	$ 11,655	1833	Non-Specialized
George Bates	$ 10,000	1834	Copper, Lawyer, Banker

[Most of the following names on the list have only sources of wealth indicated, sometimes judged by number of employees. There are also more gaps in the information available about this group. "Non-specialized" includes such mixtures as ferry boats and foundries, or newspapers and copper. Robert Banks used his "25 hands" in the manufacture of clothing and is the only black who was wealthy enough to make the list.]

Table 1 (cont.)

Listed According to Wealth		To Detroit	Economic Role
Robert Banks	25 hands		Merchant, Mfr.
William Barclay	45 hands		Mfr., Iron
Christian Buhl	25 hands	1833	Mfr., Merchant, Banker
Frederick Buhl	25 hands	1833	Mfr., Merchant, Banker
Charles Howard	Banker	1840	Non-Specialized, Copper
Oliver Hyde	56 hands	1832	Mfr., Foundry

Table 1 (cont.)

Listed According to Wealth		To Detroit	Economic Role
Silas Kendrick	64 hands	1837	Mfr., Foundry
George B. Russel	Ferry	1836	Non-Specialized, Iron, Builder
William F. Smith	Sawmill	1841	Manufacturer
George B. Throop	Bank Pres.	1832	Banker, Lawyer
Wesley Truesdail	Non-Spec.	1836	Banker, Copper Sawmill
John Welles	Bank Cashier		Banker
Gurdon Williams	Railroad		R. R. Pres.
Charles Jackson	$15,700	1816	Builder
Horace Hallock	60 hands	1831	Merchant, Mfr.
Francis Raymond	60 hands	1832	Mfr. (with Hallock)
William Gooding	120 hands		Mfr., Steamboats

Notes: [The first] eighteen men having property over $50,000 are classified as "High".

[The next] twenty men, representing approximate wealth of between $25,000 and $50,000, are classified as "Medium".

The next [group of men] with wealth over $25,000 are classified as "Low".

[Throughout the table, gaps occur when the information was not available. Some interesting "economic indicators" have been deleted, such as membership in the Board of Trade, or additional directorships held, but all information given for the basic categories has been included.]

The Economic Elite Of 1860

. . . One hundred and thirty-five men worth more than $50,000 made up the economic elite. In 1844 there were only eighteen individuals who surpassed this qualifying lower limit and more than half of the elite were worth less than $25,000. Wealth therefore was a sufficient basis for selection without regard to economic role. Selection was buttressed by the existence of two sources listing property, the Detroit tax rolls and the census of 1860.[8] Income was also used as an indicator of wealth. Thanks to the Civil War income tax and the custom of printing lists of taxpayers in the local papers, the top Detroit incomes for 1864 could be identified.

The formula worked out for combining income and property as criteria was as follows: Only the thirty-four incomes over

$10,000 were used as a basis for selection because the figures were for 1864 rather than 1860. Since anyone in 1860 with an income between $5,000 and $10,000 was accounted among the "rich", those over $10,000 would seem to be economic leaders, even interpolating back to 1860. Furthermore, these high incomes undoubtedly concealed greater wealth. The tax of 1864 excluded [such] income as dividends or interest received from banks, trust companies, railroads, canals or turnpike companies, or gains from the sale of real estate held more than one year. Thus the $91,037 received by millionaire E. B. Ward did not reflect his extensive property in steamboats, railroads, plank roads and banks.

With property evaluations ranging from $50,000 to $1,000,000, only those worth over $200,000 were ranked "High", bracketed with men having incomes over $10,000. . . . The existence of two sources for 1860 on real and personal property provided an excellent check on the identity of the elite. Although the Census evaluation and local property value did not always coincide, the existence of two records showed unmistakably who the rich men were. The great majority show up as men of considerable property on both lists. Those who appeared on one list with property between $100,000 and $200,000 were ranked "Medium" and those between $50,000 and $100,000, "Low. . . . "

The rise in the value of rich men's holdings since 1844 appears more striking when one considers that 1860 was not a boom period—prices had remained depressed since the crisis of 1857 with only a slight improvement in the middle of 1860. . . . Although Detroit was far from matching New York City's seventy-nine men who reported incomes of $100,000 or more in 1864, 315 incomes over $2,000 was not a bad showing next to New York's 10,900 in 1863. Compared against the incomes of the general population of New York, the wealth of Detroit's elite stands out sharply: in the 1860's only about 1% of the population of New York received incomes of $842 or more. When it is also remembered that burgeoning dividends were omitted from income calculations, the wealth of the Wayne County elite supports Rufus Tucker's conclusion that during the Civil War period "the wealthy were wealthier in relation to the mass than now, although there were fewer of them".

A breakdown of the composition of the 1860 elite according to economic roles shows significant changes in the economy. The non-specialized entrepreneur gives way to the capitalist. Instead of engaging in banking, selling, and small manufacturing, the successful merchant now invests the proceeds of his successful business in other firms and becomes the director of several. The Buhl brothers are good examples of the merchant turned capitalist, although Frederick Buhl modestly referred to himself in the 1860 Census as "hatter". Their early venture as fur merchants and hat manufacturers came to a profitable close in 1853. C. H. Buhl bought out a hardware firm, invested extensively in railroads and by 1863 had enough to put one million dollars into iron manufacturing in Pennsylvania.

Despite industrial growth, landowners were the leading group, representing 26% of the 1860 elite. Their predominance reflects the vital role land values played in the growth of American fortunes. . . . Eight were heirs of large landowners and six were retired merchants. Others were actually modern real estate operators. Partners William B. Wesson and Albert Crane dominated the field and made fortunes as pioneers in land-dividing. They were the first to sell lots on time with only a small down payment. That these men did differentiate their roles is seen by their designations in the 1860 Census. While Crane and J. W. Johnston referred to themselves as "real estate dealers", David Thompson and Alexander Newbould were "speculators", Wesson called himself a "landowner", and seven put themselves as "gentlemen". John C. Williams was a "farmer". George Duffield was actually a leading Presbyterian clergyman, but since this role would hardly have been the direct route to a fortune worth $50,000, he has been called a landowner. Like other landowners, he was alert to the possibility of making money elsewhere. . . .

Quite predictably, manufacturers also outnumber the merchants among the elite. . . . Eleven of these "industrialists" were in lumber manufacturing, typically combined with large operations in lumber lands. Samuel Pitts and Buckminster Wight continued from profitable beginnings in the forties, surpassed, however, by New England lumbermen, F. Adams, N. W. Brooks, Charles Merrill and Henry Benson, who came to Detroit in the fifties. New men and earlier starters shared other fields. E. B. Ward, who made a fortune in the forties as a vessel owner, began his enormously successful career as iron manufacturer when he established the Wyandotte Rolling Mill in 1853. D. M. Richardson built the first match factory in 1856 and two others got rich with tobacco; K. C. Barker and Company was built in 1848, John J. Bagley's firm in 1853. Alexander McGraw and Henry P. Baldwin had expanded their shoe manufacturing and merchanting operations—Baldwin's income was next to Ward's in 1864 at $33,647. Other basic products which supported the elite were beer (William C. Duncan and Richard Hawley), meat (John Hull), and leather (George Curtis and George Kirby).

An interesting type was the doctor turned capitalist. Doctors, who required only the most rudimentary training to practice, were attracted to growing towns where the opportunities in non-medical pursuits engaged them to such an extent that it was "often difficult to differentiate between their merchandising activities and professional practice". Dr. George Russel abandoned his practice as early as 1837 to begin his career as a manufacturer in the construction of ferry boats. Dr. Eliphalet M. Clark's medical practice was so subservient to his industrial pursuits that even a medical source considered only his "first grain elevator at the foot of Fort Street and his enterprise to manufacture locomotives in 1855". There is no available evidence of Dr. Samuel Truedell's activities as a businessman, but it is doubtful that he could have accumulated his estate on the basis of medical practice alone. With professional man William Woodbridge, whose skyrocketing wealth had placed him fourth among the elite, Truedell has been called a landowner.

A man's economic activity did not seem to have as great a bearing on his relative wealth as it did in 1844 when landowners and fur fortunes monopolized the higher ranks. . . . Capitalists and manufacturers had the greatest likelihood of attaining the high and medium brackets of the wealthy. Bankers and lawyers were, predictably, still in the low brackets.

Mobility, seen as the achievement of wealth by men of lower class origins, was difficult to determine. Evidence was too scanty to determine with any certainty to what extent the elite of 1860 were self-made men. The forty-one men known to have well-to-do fathers divided among the various ranks as follows: High 18; Medium 12; Low 11.

There was, however, a marked persistence in holding on to wealth once gained. The carry-over from the elite of 1844 was pronounced. Taking into consideration those known to have died or moved away, only one-fifth of the 1844 elite failed to qualify in 1860. The old elite divided themselves in the different ranks as follows: High 27%; Medium 27%; Low 46%. Those who were at the top in 1844 tended to stay there. Only one took a fall. John Drew, who had been worth more than $50,000 in 1844 as a merchant, had become a retired "gentleman" with a modest estate of $22,000.

As a postscript to the discovery that wealth tended to multiply and perpetuate itself, seventeen of the men of 1860 or their inheriting descendants were listed among Detroit's forty-two millionaires in 1892.[9] [Those names included on the earlier list are indicated by asterisks.]

Table 2
The Economic Elite of 1860—Bases for Selection and Economic Role

High: Property worth over $200,000 and / or income over $10,000

	Property (Census)	Property (Tax Roll)	Income (1864)	Economic Role
Joseph Campau*	$3,400,000	$ 380,653		Landowner
Lewis Cass*		$1,189,725	$22,700	Landowner
E. B. Ward	$1,007,000	$ 89,743	$91,037	Capitalist
Wm. Woodbridge*	$ 330,000	$ 599,916		Landowner
Albert Crane	$ 210,000	$ 474,704		Landowner
Charles Merrill	$ 210,000	$ 409,923	$11,026	Lumber
Z. Chandler*	$ 300,000	$ 433,288	$56,236	Merchant
E. A. Brush*		$ 392,646		Landowner
James F. Joy*		$ 365,584	$19,918	Capitalist
William Hale		$ 354,228		Landowner
George B. Russel*		$ 333,166		Capitalist
Wm. B. Wesson	$ 105,000	$ 313,592		Landowner
C. H. Buhl*	$ 250,000	$ 217,682	$33,400	Capitalist
J. C. D. Williams	$ 125,000	$ 249,750		Landowner
John Owen*	$ 180,000	$ 245,254	$19,522	Capitalist
Alex M. Campau		$ 232,184		Landowner
Luther Beecher		$ 221,944		Merchant
David Cooper*	$ 93,000	$ 208,500		Landowner
H. P. Baldwin	$ 115,000	$ 208,291	$33,647	Capitalist
Henry E. Benson		$ 141,774	$30,480	Lumber
David Whitney			$30,000	Lumber

Table 2 (cont.)

High: Property worth over $200,000 and / or income over $10,000

	Property (Census)	Property (Tax Roll)	Income (1864)	Economic Role
K. C. Barker		$ 48,285	$29,611	Manufacturer
Chas. DuCharme	$ 55,000	$ 50,449	$29,400	Merchant
Allen Shelden		$ 40,950	$27,500	Merchant
Reuben Town		$ 49,950	$27,500	Merchant
Edward Orr			$27,498	Merchant
N. W. Brooks		$ 38,000	$24,100	Lumber
E. Ward	$ 18,000	$ 52,558	$24,508	Shipping
J. J. Bagley			$23,180	Manufacturer
Richard Hawley		$167,998	$22,205	Manufacturer
Francis Adams		$ 38,661	$18,803	Lumber
Franklin Moore*	$ 41,000	$ 74,259	$19,181	Merchant
F. Buhl*	$ 83,000	$ 82,750	$16,280	Capitalist
S. Pitts*		$140,526	$19,829	Lumber
John Stephens	$140,000	$143,134	$18,730	Merchant
Ira Davis	$ 65,000	$ 27,072	$14,777	Shipping
D. M. Richardson			$14,650	Manufacturer
George Curtis			$14,500	Manufacturer
C. W. Jackson	$ 32,300	$ 77,439	$14,226	Manufacturer
J. Wiley		$ 66,200	$14,179	Manufacturer
George Kirby	$ 45,000	$ 66,933	$12,708	Manufacturer
G. F. Bagley			$11,326	Merchant
George Peck			$10,913	Capitalist
S. Mandelbaum		$ 50,782	$10,000	Capitalist
Francis Palms*		$ 25,641		Landowner [lumber]

Medium: Property worth between $100,000 and $200,000

	Property (Census)	Property (Tax Roll)	Economic Role
Charles Moran*	$101,000	$198,468	Landowner
Alexander McGraw	$135,000	$192,773	Merchant, Mfr.
Wm. S. Biddle	$120,000	$191,308	Landowner
J. Mott Williams	$ 52,000	$163,236	Landowner
John P. Clark	$162,600	$ 62,637	Shipping
Jacob Beeson	$160,000	$ 29,304	Banker

185

Table 2 (cont.)

Medium: Property worth between $100,000 and $200,000

	Property (Census)	Property (Tax Roll)	Economic Role
John Hull	$156,000	$129,397	Merchant
Jacob S. Farrand	$145,000	$ 59,440	Banker
Henry Haigh	$154,000	$ 17,482	Merchant
Richard H. Hall*		$155,993	Merchant
Samuel Lewis	$ 77,500	$144,062	Capitalist
N. P. Stewart	$ 60,000	$142,357	Banker
Theodore Eaton	$ 95,000	$141,247	Capitalist
J. W. Johnston	$110,000	$140,397	Landowner
H. H. Emmons	$140,000	$102,064	Landowner
William A. Butler	$ 42,000	$139,860	Banker
Shubael Conant*	$121,500	$134,348	Capitalist
Moses Dickinson*	$ 35,000	$130,039	Landowner
Alanson Sheley*		$124,125	Capitalist
W. C. Duncan	$ 55,000	$121,794	Manufacturer
David Thompson*	$120,000	$100,982	Landowner
O. M. Hyde*	$120,000	$ 62,271	Capitalist
Eustache Chapoton*	$ 24,000	$112,809	Builder
Ebenezer Penniman	$112,500		Merchant
E. M. Clark	$ 76,000	$111,205	Capitalist
Jonathon L. King		$110,556	Merchant, Mfr.
Peter Desnoyers*	$ 36,000	$107,026	Landowner
W. N. Carpenter*	$105,000	$ 61,605	Landowner
Albert Ives	$100,000	$104,678	Banker
Francis Eldred*	$ 50,000	$102,897	Merchant, Mfr.
Samuel P. Brady		$101,614	Merchant
John C. Williams	$101,000	$ 94,155	Landowner
Gabriel Chene	$ 53,000	$101,731	Landowner
C. C. Trowbridge*	$100,000	$ 62,853	Banker
H. N. Strong	$146,000	$101,481	Shipping

Low: Property worth between $50,000 and $100,000

	Property (Census)	Property (Tax Roll)	Economic Role
A. D. Fraser*		$99,067	Lawyer
Buckminster Wight*	$33,000	$99,594	Lumber

Table 2 (cont.)

Low: Property worth between $50,000 and $100,000

	Property (Census)	Property (Tax Roll)	Economic Role
Ashael S. Bagg	$80,000	$99,733	Hotel Prop.
Henry T. Backus	$80,000	$18,731	Lawyer
Alex. H. Newbould*	$66,000	$94,738	Landowner
Dominique Riopelle, Jr.		$94,821	Landowner
Hugh Moffat	$50,000	$92,407	Lumber
William Barclay*	$66,800	$91,575	Manufacturer
George F. Porter*		$91,297	Banker
Gurdon Williams	$90,000	$43,883	Capitalist
George Foote	$87,000	$53,280	Merchant
Chauncey Hurlbut*		$86,945	Merchant
James Burns		$86,746	Merchant
Theodore Williams*		$84,781	Landowner
Oliver Bourke	$85,000	$21,395	Merchant
Caleb Ives		$85,364	Banker
Ransom Gardner	$75,000	$83,333	Merchant
C. A. Trowbridge	$75,000	$79,920	Manufacturer
Henry A. Wight	$35,000	$79,254	Lumber
Stanley G. Wight	$33,000	$79,254	Lumber
Francis Raymond*	$20,000	$76,590	Merchant
F. B. Sibley	$60,000	$75,880	Manufacturer
S. B. Scott	$75,000		Merchant
Caleb Van Husan	$70,000	$73,593	Capitalist
George Duffield	$50,000	$70,096	Landowner
Alexander Stowell	$70,000	$11,655	Landowner
Henry N. Walker*	$70,000		Banker
John Palmer*	$12,000	$67,832	Landowner
Alexander Chapoton	$40,000	$67,732	Builder
Jared C. Warner	$66,000		Landowner
George B. Truax	$60,000	$65,054	Lumber
Eugene St. Amour	$65,000	$94,821	Builder
William Ten Eyck	$64,130	$61,921	Landowner
Charles Jackson*	$64,000	$50,749	Builder
Colin Campbell	$23,000	$63,603	Merchant
William Kieft Coyl	$60,000	$62,637	Landowner
Giles B. Slocum		$61,921	Merchant
Frederick Wetmore*		$61,671	Merchant
Levi Cook*	$60,000	$60,772	Banker

Table 2 (cont.)

Low: Property worth between $50,000 and $100,000

	Property (Census)	Property (Tax Roll)	Economic Role
Samuel Truedell	$60,200	$60,106	Landowner
Darius Lamson*		$60,106	Landowner
Thomas Lockwood	$60,000	$26,007	Lawyer
Elon Farnsworth*	$50,000	$58,774	Banker
Thomas F. Abbott	$55,000		Merchant
Geroge W. Bissell	$50,000	$48,701	Merchant
F. J. B. Crane	$50,000	$49,726	Landowner

Other members of previous elite [1844]

	Property (Census)	Property (Tax Roll)	Economic Role
Horace Hallock	$30,000	$44,788	Merchant, Mfr.
A. S. Williams	$39,000		Gentleman
Thomas Coquillard	$13,520	$33,300	Builder
George C. Bates		$22,105	Lawyer
John A. Welles	$25,000		Lawyer
John Drew	$22,000		Capitalist
John Roberts	$14,000	$15,251	Retired
Theodore Romeyn	$15,000		Lawyer
J. N. Elbert	$16,500		Postoffice Clk.

Notes

1. "Detroit Real and Personal Property Tax Assessment Roll, 1844," Burton Historical Collection, (hereinafter referred to as BHC); "Wayne County and Personal Property Tax Assessment Roll, 1844", BHC. "Springwells Real and Personal Tax, Assessment Roll, 1845", in William Woodbridge Papers, BHC. The existence of more than one record provided a good check. The Detroit records were more complete and therefore the main source. A few individuals qualified on the basis of land owned in the townships outside the city.
2. Michigan Historical Records Survey Project, Division of Professional and Service Projects, Works Progress Administration, *Inventory of the*

Municipal Archives of Michigan, City of Detroit, No. 10, City Treasurer (Detroit: The Survey, 1940), 18.

3. Abbott Papers, BHC; E. P. Hastings Papers, BHC; C. C. Trowbridge Papers, BHC; "Land Book of Alfred Dwight", A. A. Dwight Papers, BHC; Robert Stuart Papers, BHC.

4. Jacob Houghton, Jr. and T. W. Bristol, *Reports of Wm. A. Burt and Bela Hubbard, Esqs. on the Geography, Topography, and Geology of the U.S. Survey of the Mineral Region of the South Shore of Lake Superior for 1845* (Detroit: C. Wilcox, 1846, 92–102). Officers of working companies: Degarmo Jones, Gurdon Williams, Charles Howard, John Owen, George E. Bates, Wesley Truesdail, A. H. Newbould, Pierre Teller, James A. Van Dyke. Officers of organized companies: C. M. Hyde, A. S. Williams, James Abbott, James Van Dyke, Peter Desnoyers, F. Cicotte, John Drew, Theodore Williams, George C. Bates.

5. Also George F. Porter, Z. Chandler, C. C. Trowbridge, President, Alex H. Adams, Cashier, Burton, *Wayne [County]*, II, 1224.

6. *Detroit Daily Advertiser*, June 16, 1848, August 22, 1848. . . . The twenty-two largest firms—employing more than 25 hands, doing annual business worth $50,000 or more or producing more than 2,000,000 [board feet] of lumber were: S. N. Kendrick, Machine Shop, 64 hands, $70,000 per annum; H. (Wm.) Barclay, Michigan Foundry, 45 hands, $70,000 per annum; William Gooding, Ship and Steamboat Building, 120 hands; William Smith, Eagle Steam Saw Mill, 36 hands (partner Alfred Dwight); Robert Banks, Clothing Manufacturer, 25 hands; Hallock and Raymond (Horace Hallock and Francis Raymond Clothing), 60 hands, $50,000 per annum; O. M. Hyde, Hydraulic Foundry and Machine Shop, 56 hands; F. and C. H. Buhl, Hat Manufacturers, 25 hands, $30,000 per annum; Wight's Steam Saw Mill, 2,000,000 feet (Buckminster Wight); Moore's Lumber Yard, 2,600,000 feet (Franklin Moore); Black River Lumber Yard, 2,500,000 feet (Alanson Sheley, manager). . . .

7. "Detroit in History", Palmer Scrapbooks, IV, BHC, 210.

8. "Finance City Treasurer Tax Roll Real and Personal Property, 1860", BHC; Eighth Census of the United States, 1860. Michigan. Microfilm Copy, BHC.

9. E. Alfred Brush and Lillie Thompson (son and granddaughter of E. A. Brush), Christian H. Buhl, Mrs. Dr. Book and Francis Palms (daughter and son of Francis Palms), Estate of John J. Bagley, Theodore H. Eaton, Estate of Jacob S. Farrand, James F. Joy, William B. Moran (real estate inherited in part from Charles Moran), Mrs. T. W. Palmer (daughter of Charles Merrill, inherited), Allan Shelden, Alanson Sheley, Estate of William B. Wesson, David Whitney, Jr., Luther Beecher, William Butler.

Editor's Note

Government record sources listed under notes 1, 2, and 5 should be of considerable value to other scholars, especially the inventory of municipal archives conducted by the Works Progress Administration, listed in note 2. I have deleted a number of McCoy's notes for reasons of length. I have also renumbered the second data table (Table 5 in original work) for clarity.

Part VI

The Gilded Age Comes to Detroit

The Gilded Age Comes to Detroit

The period we know as the Gilded Age appears abruptly after the Civil War, and somehow it is surprising to find it occurring in Detroit. We are used to tales of the great fortunes of New York and Philadelphia, or of the California railroad barons. In Detroit, however, that midwestern port city, a supply center for the backcountry, the changes were profound. Industrialization seemed to be almost concurrent with the war. Of course, this was a Northern city and, more than that, a city in the state that claimed the Republican party as its own—winning people on a winning side. The war economy and party loyalty helped to create new wealth.

We have noted from Alexandra McCoy's list of the wealthy of 1866 a number who had been wealthy in 1844. Some of those names will continue to occur in any discussion of Detroit's elite through the next years: Buhl, Joy, and Ward, among others. But the base for wealth had already begun to shift from land ownership or "merchant" to other means of getting or keeping wealth. There were newcomers. 1866 is a bit too early for either Strohs or Fords. Yet a Henkel daughter married a Stroh, even if neither family was a part of the Gilded Age. Industrial growth would add new names and new industries for those who became, or remained, wealthy. The McMillans produced railroad cars but had been lumbermen. Lumber and railroading were strongly linked together from 1865 on. Senator McMillan was said to have the largest yacht on the Great Lakes and one of the more opulent mansions in Washington.

Even more lavish was the home of Congressman Hale of Maine. Hale was described as a "bon vivant" who had his money by way of his wife, the only child of Senator Zachariah Chandler. Eber Ward, as Vinyard informed us, moved from shipping to heavy industry. Industries expanded to include others, usually related, and the banks and insurance structures that strengthened them. The interlocking directorships of these firms were held by the new wealthy and, always, some of the old. The scope of Detroit's wealth and its far-flung ambitions is illustrated by the fact that before and after the Spanish-American War several prominent Detroiters had land investments in Cuba. Homer Warren, Detroit's preeminent realtor, even opened an office in Havana for a time.

In general, land ownership remained important but became an auxiliary, rather than a main source, to major wealth until the real estate expansion of the 1920s. Some land within the city of Detroit, however, was useful as homesites. On East Jefferson, beginning to crowd out the old French homes, and on downtown Lafayette, Fort, and Washington streets (later Washington Boulevard), rose the new mansions of the wealthy, complete with carriage houses. In a few years they would extend northward out Woodward Avenue, to be followed by luxurious apartments. By the turn of the century a rental in the Palms on East Jefferson or the Addison on Woodward (now a check-cashing center for the poor) was enough to guarantee a young couple a place in the social register.

In the homes, managed by women, even more than in the clubs dominated by men, we catch the flavor of Detroit's Gilded Age. Downtown, on West Lafayette Street, the ladies were "at home" on Tuesdays, with flowers and music in the drawing rooms. Other streets chose other afternoons when the lady of the house waited at home for callers. The evenings saw still more music, as well as cards, dinners, or supper parties after the guests returned from a play at one of several downtown theaters.

Included in this section is an account of summers on a small (compared to Senator McMillan's) ninety-five-foot yacht. It was possible, however, to operate even a yacht with informal intimacy. That was the case with the steam-and-sail *Uarda*. Steam-and-sail yachts were of relatively short duration on the Great Lakes, but to Cameron D. Waterman, the *Uarda*'s owner, steam seemed the only rational way to get to the north shore of Lake Superior or Georgian Bay. Sailing, along with fishing of course, was the most fun when you got there.

With any size of boat, it was possible to run up to the "Old Club" at Harsen's Island, where a large informal dining room welcomed members. At other times many of the same crowd might be found enjoying simple foods and good fun at Harbor Springs, several hundred miles northwest on the eastern shore of Lake Michigan. A still smaller section of this elite might be found a long way from home at the Huron Mountain Club, which was—and remains—a remote wilderness area in the Upper Peninsula.

The Gilded Age was the age of the gentleman's club. Clubs served as an escape from the niceties of home. There were dozens of clubs, lodges, and "secret societies" listed in the city directories. There was something for everyone. There was the "Order of Chosen Friends," the "United Ancient Order of Druids," the "Centennial Boating and Athletic Association," which shared a dock at the foot of MacDougal Street with the Detroit Yacht Club. The Detroit Boat Club took the foot of Joseph Campau for its boat house and demonstrated its considerable status by holding its winter meetings in the Russell House, at Woodward and Campus Martius. There were three curling clubs for Scotsmen. The German community had a choice of Turnverein for gymnasts and the Harmonie for singers and musicians. Hunting and fishing clubs included the Lake Ste. Claire Fishing and Shooting, already called the Old Club and already elite. There were the Detroit Club and the Yondotega, the Prismatic and the Witenagemote. In the latter two, members took turns presenting a learned topic for discussion. There is a legend of a Witenagemote member who, unable to afford a horse and carriage, walked seven miles to meetings because "the talk was good."

A final indicator of Detroit's Gilded Age was the ability of its wealthy daughters to marry titled Europeans. This midwestern city had its full share of countesses, baronesses, and princesses. They came from such Detroit families as Cass, Lothrop, Palms, Walker, McMillan; daughters and granddaughters of politicians, distillers, lumbermen, landowners, and Indian traders.

First was Isabelle Cass, who became the Baroness von Limbourg in 1858. Most famous was her niece, Maude Ledyard, the granddaughter of Lewis Cass who became Baroness von Ketteler. The baron, who was Germany's ambassador to China, managed with foolhardy bravery to get himself shot down early in the Boxer Rebellion. His young, widowed bride spent the next year or two sewing rare old silks into sandbags for defense from Chinese gunfire.

It was left, however, to the daughter of one of Michigan's wealthiest and most tough-minded capitalists to exploit to the fullest the possibilities of foreign marriage and a life that included any number of mistakes. Clara Ward, daughter of Captain Eber Brock Ward, became in 1890 the Princess Chimay. Her obituary is included here.

From this we move to an account by Walter Pitkin on how the "rest of us" lived during the Gilded Age. In "Castle Garden Days," Pitkin describes several widely differing Detroit neighborhoods of the 1890s, but he is mainly oriented to the near West Side, the Grand River-Trumbull area, not too far from the ballpark.

1. Summer Escapes: Life on the Steam Yacht *Uarda*

Wilma Wood Henrickson

From 1891 through 1893, the crew of the easy-going steam yacht *Uarda*, skippered by its owner, Cameron Davenport Waterman, included as cabin-boy and all purpose deckhand, Will Wood, the editor's father. Will was 16 when he came to Grosse Ile to work on the *Uarda*, but he had already formed the habit of keeping a diary.

Saturday, June 17 [1891]. . . . Between 12 & 1 we started on her [*Uarda*] for Detroit, landed at M.C.R.R. [Michigan Central Railroad] dock and took on a party of about 20 men. . . . Started down the American channel and crossed Lake Erie to Kingsville.

Wilma Wood Henrickson, "Summer Escapes: Life on the Steam Yacht *Uarda*," *Chronicle of Michigan History* (Fall 1984): 6–9.

By now Will had learned that Mr. Waterman expected to pay for all food his crew consumed on shore. There would be no skipping dinner or economizing for the sixteen year old boy: " . . . had roast beef, sliced potatoes, spring lamb, mint sauce, string beans, peach pie, and tutti-fruitti ice cream."

> Sun. 19. Done all the work and went to breakfast. Had mutton-chops, baked potatoes, omelet, French rolls, and chocolate. Started away at 11. Landed the party in Detroit. Before this one of the men went around and then handed me a handful of change, amounting to $1.80.
>
> Mon. 20. . . . Went out at 2:30. Took on a party of 31 at Detroit, mostly ladies. The waiter was on board and we served French pineapple ice-cream (in small bricks), raspberries, and cake. Came down the main channel a little below the stock farm and up the Canadian. . . .

On August 2, the *Uarda* began her first northern cruise of the year with an overnight stay at the Old Club, at the "Flats," the delta of Lake St. Clair on the American side.

> I have hardly anything to do after morning work is done. We have two regular meals a day: breakfast between 7 & 8 and dinner between 6 & 10 p.m. Can help ourselves to lunch at any time. Landed Campbell at Somerville [near Marysville, south of Port Huron] and Douglas and Russel at Port Huron. Reached Lake Huron at noon. Squall came up during the afternoon. The wind blew and the water looked black, but here was very little rain. Had the foresail up. Are lying at a long pier a mile long, forming a harbor of refuge [Sand Beach Harbor, now known as Harbor Beach]. Run 100 mi.

The next day's sailing followed a favorite pattern of Captain Waterman's: they left at 4:20 in the morning and sailed until 6:30 in the evening, to reach Detour at the edge of the Upper Peninsula.

> Crossed Saginaw Bay—75 mis. by noon. Out of sight of land for three hours. Detour is a mile above Point Detour, the entrance to St. Mary's River. A straggling village of one street, one store, and two hotels. People fish in summer and lumber during winter. Run 161 miles.

During the next few days, Will saw "the hole for the new lock," the sunken S. S. Pontiac, and "the finest scenery yet. Rock covered with trees," in the North Passage. Then "Let Douglas off at Point Detour. He gave me 50 cents."

From Algomah Mills, Ontario, on the North Channel's north side, they were headed for home. At Goderich, the diary records:

> Left Kilarney 4:30 a.m. Arrived 8 p.m. Crossed the mouth of Georgian Bay. Out of sight of land. Steered while they were at dinner. Run 168 miles. This beats the record. Went uptown. 161 steps up the hill. The business part of the town is around the courthouse in a 16 sided polygon. Geo. and I went around it and had started on the second trip before finding it out.

George White, cook on the *Uarda*, was the first black Will Wood came to know. He was to appear frequently in the diary over the next three summers. An entertaining raconteur, at home in the ship's galley, he was also able to build a fire on land in the rain to grill Lake Superior whitefish for a party depressed by a damaged boat. He bargained with Indians for berries and maple syrup that went with the blueberry flapjacks and fried perch. He had a talent for making friends quickly in faraway ports, which eased the loneliness of the uncertain adolescent who served as cabin boy.

The *Uarda* reached home on August 31, and fall chores began on both yacht and farm. The yacht remained in use all fall. On October 7, the Watermans watched the race between the yachts *City of the Straits* and the *Papoose*, from their boat deck in Lake St. Clair.

On December 13, Will was paid off for the season. His check that day for $84.75 covered the past four months at $20 wages per month and $4.75 for out-of-pocket expenses. He had received $20 earlier. With the help of Mr. Pitman, owner of a coal company and drydock, and a frequent passenger on the *Uarda*, he opened an account at the Mechanic's Bank, and then enrolled at the Detroit College of Commerce, paying $22.50 for three month's tuition, $6.15 for books. "They socket [sic] to one for everything." On Sundays that winter he wore his "new red tie and derby" to St. Thomas Episcopal Church in Trenton. The Watermans, following their custom, sailed on a passenger liner for Europe, where Mrs. Waterman and the children would spend most of the winter in France while Mr. Waterman returned for a businessman's winter in Detroit.

An anxious spring without work after finishing business college ended when Will was rehired to help get the *Uarda* ready for summer. On July 27th: "Went to Detroit with the yacht. Got a new carpet for the cabin and had the compasses adjusted." On August 1 the *Uarda* docked at Pitman's for taking on supplies and the next evening the Watermans again started their August cruise with a night at the Old Club on Harsen's Island. "We have eleven on board and the same cook as last year."

The *Uarda* resting on a beach near Tobermory, Ontario, c. 1895. (Courtesy of Cameron Waterman, grandson of the steam yacht's owner, Cameron Davenport Waterman.)

This year they went west from Mackinac to Charlevoix and Northport on Lake Michigan, then to North Manitou Island where Will lost a quarter to the lake, but "talked with several nice young Chicago Minnehahas summering here."

There followed several stops along the south shore of Georgian Bay and the shores of the Bruce Peninsula, then called the Saugeen.

200

Sun. 28, Meaford, Ont. Stood watch at breakfast time about an hour. Arrived here 7 p.m. Ran nearly the entire length of Georgian Bay—110 miles. Had trouble keeping kids off [at the dock]. . . .

Tues. 30, Owen Sound. . . . Went up-town after dinner. Met a young fellow outside the Methodist church and went to Epworth League with him and afterwards around town. Went abroad the *Pacific, Baltic, Marine Hearse, City of Midland* and *Athabasca*. The last has twice as much brass on her engine as we have on the whole yacht. Saw two steam shovels unloading her cargo of wheat. . . .

A storm in Georgian Bay forced them off their route, and made the trip home difficult:

With every pitch the water would spout up the hawse-pipes and the propeller wheel would come half out of the water. In turning around we gave such a roll that half the dishes were smashed. . . . Was so rough that we could have no tables set for breakfast, but we are bound to reach Detroit by Sunday. . . . The *Western Reserve* broke in two, ten miles off Whitefish Point in last Thursday's gale, and all but a wheelman were drowned. . . .

Will worked that winter at the Detroit Club, but the following June he was once again on Grosse Ile, doing farm chores while waiting for the *Uarda* to get under way. There was hay to be loaded, currants and cherries picked, and then on June 30, the *Uarda* went to Detroit "to see the Spanish caravels going to Chicago." This was one of the early excitements leading up to the Columbian Exposition that fall. The *Uarda* "had small flags up. Great tooting of steam vessels in the river. The new fire tug *Detroiter* was out showing off."

Will was more sophisticated now. The "trip to 'Mettawas' " is noted mainly for a $2 tip from Mr. Waterman's guests. He tries to be casual about his day off on the Fourth of July:

Spent the "Glorious" at Grosse Ile until 10 a.m. Then to Slocum's Island [later known as Elizabeth Park]. . . . Over sixty gallons of ice-cream sold. $155 made by the K.L.M. [Knights of Labor Marching Band]. Dancing, racing, boat racing, girling as usual. . . . Was introduced to Miss Pearl—of whom I have heard ever since coming to Grosse Ile. Her reputation as a flirt is unequalled. . . . I was in her company for three hours. Went for a row uptown and back. She wished me to come down next Sunday afternoon.

On July 10, a minor disaster struck. "*Uarda* refused inspection on account of boilers." The "new Almy tubular" purchased the previous year had never lived up to expectations.

> Thurs. 13. Started about 8:30 with a special permit to go to the dry-dock. Mr. Waterman had appealed to Supervising Inspector Westcott and he inspected and passed the boat today. Went in dry-dock p.m. Got part of bottom scrubbed. . . .
>
> Friday, August 4, Thessalon, Ont. North shore of the Northern Passage of Georgian Bay. . . . Run through the beautiful North Passage & the Devil's Gap to this small town. A great ice jam in April carried away part of the dock and sank a tug. Temperance camp meeting in progress.

There followed several days of crisscrossing paths in an effort to locate supplies which had been due to arrive on the *S.S. Telegram*. Trips to Kilarney, "Dog River," and Pilot Harbor proved useless but not uneventful. On Monday they saw the boiler of the *City of Montreal*, "lost eight years ago. Just raised from Bonner's Bay. . . . Scaled a bluff for huckleberries . . . 150 feet."

On a Tuesday which ended at Otter Cove, there were more adventures.

> Ran twenty miles to Gravel River. Too windy to anchor. Back 15 miles to cove. Anchored. George and I went to the falls on the side of the bluff. I never saw anything like it before. A shallow fall of water—150 ft. zig-zagging down. In ascending we crossed six times. Ira [Waterman child] fell in.

The party now planned to relax and enjoy fishing in Lake Superior, but the diary entry of Saturday, August 19, is headed ominously: "Sunk at Bachawamung."

The *Uarda* lived again, after expensive and ingenious repairs. With a style appropriate to Detroit in those times—perhaps the best of the Gilded Age, the Watermans continued to enjoy cards and charades on the boat, good fishing and the company of friends. Let Newport and Manhattan have their monstrous occasions. Let Senators Zach Chandler or James McMillan imitate the eastern style. Some Detroiters could—and did—live well.

2.   The Age of the Gentleman's Club

Detroit Free Press

Recognizing the importance of clubs on Detroit's social scene, the Free Press undertook a survey of a wide range of them in 1893. They found the Detroit Club to be an all-around leader. Though its membership frequently overlapped with the "thinking men's" or the "sporting men's" clubs, it combined substantial prestige with a willingness to have business deals made over its linen tablecloths.

This is a series of excerpts from their survey.

DETROIT AS A CLUB CITY
Some of the Places Where Men Do Congregate
And Where They Follow the Bent of Their Inclination

Of the social clubs the Detroit Club, with a beautiful modern home at the corner of Cass and Fort streets, is the richest and most influential. It is just 11 years old, and has erected a home at a cost of something like $120,000. Clergymen, lawyers, army and navy officers, professors, doctors, merchants, hotel proprietors, editors, manufacturers, bank presidents, railroad presidents, architects, contractors, real estate dealers, and men of leisure are the component parts of the contented family that calls this club its intermediate home. The dullest understanding can comprehend the advantages resultant to the welfare of the city from the interchange of ideas between these men of affairs.

"Detroit as a Club City," *Detroit Free Press* (2 July 1893): 25.

Money has not been spared to make of this club a resort to fill the most exacting with a sense of satisfaction. There is a reception room unsurpassed in the west, a library of valuable books and a wealth of interesting current literature; a large fully-equipped dining-room, several smaller dining-rooms for private use, a cafe, a billiard and pool room, bowling alley, card rooms, barber shop, complete toilet facilities in every part of the building. Members may escort their wives, daughters and sweethearts to the club with the knowledge that what they see there will be only of the purest and best. The reception room set aside for the use of the gentler sex is a bower of beauty, and by a large and constant attendance they show their appreciation of what has been done for them. The dinners and suppers held within its walls are marvels of completeness and elegance.

Celebrities who favor Detroit with their presence are invariably, when not too difficult of access, escorted to this social circle, which shines all the brighter for the introduction of a new gem. Upon its registers may be seen the names of men whose achievements ring out from across the ocean. Others there are, now dead, remembered and revered because of their deeds.

The man of business has found the club an invaluable convenience in one respect. He is frequently visited by patrons who have come to negotiate a sale or a purchase of goods, or a piece of land or an interest in somebody's business. It is desirable that he treat these visitors as guests, and show them courtesies not demanded in the routine of life. What is more inviting than a visit to the club, where a luncheon is partaken and an hour is spent in the company of our foremost men of affairs?

The Harmonie Society

This club is a forty-niner. Detroit was a muddy little village in those days, but it had within its borders a gathering of honest, fun-loving Germans who thought to strengthen their friendships in social organization. Then was born the Harmonie Society. . . . It has seen Detroit grow from a swamp-fringed village to a prosperous metropolis, and it has taken pride in that growth because its own members have individually assisted in it.

It has been progressive, too, has grown with the city, kept pace with advanced ideas and shown its liberalism in every action. . . . The club has primarily a large hall, with stage and roomy gallery, and, secondarily, a basement containing a bar, billiard and pool tables, and a long, roomy dining-room with kitchen. With very simple accessories the mind and the stomach are amply provided for.

Though the society is famous for its musical strength as evidenced in its concerts, the principal feature is its yearly masquerade, which is given in February. . . . Appropriate costumes of the richest material are secured, and the young men and women excite their minds with pleasurable anticipation. A series of tableaux, well staged and costumed with historical accuracy are prepared, and orchestras are provided. When the night of pleasure arrives, the singers contribute of their talent to these harmonies, and it is talent that even a New York audience could with pleasure listen to. . . .

The Germans are by nature an amusement-seeking, sociable race. They enter into their sports with a heartiness and a zest that add cent per cent to their effectiveness. Drop into the building any evening in the winter season and you will see knots of men gathered here and there, usually around a table, discussing news and current topics and playing dominos, whist, skat and kindred games or telling yarns and singing fatherland songs. They have their beer, too; one must admit there would be something lacking without it. . . .

The Phoenix Club

This club is well along in its teens. It has a series of large well-furnished rooms above the drug store at the corner of Woodward avenue and Duffield street. It was organized by Hebrews, and is composed mainly of members of this race, though a few of the most prominent Gentiles also take an interest in its doings. No class in Detroit more heartily enjoy themselves than do these same Phoenixers when gathered at their club. They are fond of cards and light wines, dances and private theatricals. When you see these rooms ablaze with lights and a crowd of well-dressed people leaving carriages to pass through a canvas hallway stretched across the walk and leading up to the entrance, you may infer that a young Jewish man and woman have been married but an hour before and that a reception at the Phoenix Club is to follow.

The Prismatic Club

But little is known of the Prismatic Club. Its members abhor publicity and talk about their club affairs but little.

The members are all men of responsibility and culture, discuss the latest religious controversy, the new navy, the financial situation, the world's fair and kindred topics, and, as they are all readers and students as well, an evening in their society is equal to a month of close perusal of the magazines and newspapers.

There are no young men in this society, or, more properly speaking, fraternity, and the attractions necessary to hold them are missing. A few rooms, tables, chairs, and standard books answer all demands. The cigars and other good things may be brought, if necessary, to meeting. Sometimes the members are disposed to poke fun at each other, after the manner of Philadelphia's famous Clover Club, and it is surprising how much wit, humor, and sarcasm can be showered forth upon the unfortunate who happens, for the moment, to be the butt. They are genial, congenial, spirits, these, and they can select the best things intellectual with a discriminating judgment that nets a high standard of excellence. Though it has been said they discuss questions of vital interest, yet they have about them an originality that permits of license of a different character. There is not, perhaps, one man among them who has not seen life in its sterner aspects, whether in early privation or in war, who has not traveled somewhere in America or Europe or Asia or South America, and absorbed material for future use. There is not, moreover, a dull man in the Prismatic Club. An author, a historian, a journalist, might sit out two or three sessions of the club and every magazine or newspaper in the land would eagerly publish to the world those tales of adventure and observation as retold by himself. That's the Prismatic Club. . . .

The Witenagemotes

They are a choice lot of spirits—young and middle-aged men, every one of whom is well-known in Detroit. But their movements at Witenagemote are deep, dark, mysterious as the grave. Somebody asks why, but nobody has found out enough about them to answer. They have a banquet at the Russell House once a year, at which time they get back in the ordinary, in full evening dress, with a clown's high pointed white hat in addition, lock the doors and sing, drink champagne, make addresses, drink champagne, tell stories, and drink champagne. Of course, they are not adverse to good imported cigars. It is said the wit and humor that emanates from this banquet is plentiful enough to be cut into slabs and finish the Woodward avenue paving. . . . [1]

Editor's Note

1. The Detroit Club maintained its magnificence, like other clubs of its time, because there was a working class willing to serve its needs, even if this meant long hours and split shifts. One of these workers was the same Will Wood who had worked on the yacht *Uarda*. Through Charles Rathbone, a property manager who had been a frequent guest of the Watermans on the *Uarda*, Will was able to secure a job at the Detroit Club. Will started work in December of 1892, just as its "new building" was opened. The same building at the corner of Cass and Fort streets still serves as the home of the Detroit Club, almost a century later. Extracts from Will's diary follow.

> December, 1892 Tues. 13. Went up to Detroit and saw Charles Rathbone. He told me to meet him at the Det. Club house at 12:30. I went there and he got me a job as "door-boy" at $15 a month and board but not lodging. Am to commence Friday. . . .
> Friday 16. Came up on 9:35 train [from Trenton] to Detroit and went to the club-house. Went to Hudson's and was measured for a uniform. Worked until 6 carrying from the old to the new house corner of Fort and Cass sts. Hard work climbing upstairs. Hired a room at 156 3rd st. at $1 per week.
> Sat. 17. Moving all day. Had supper to-night in new house. They had an informal opening to members to-night. We live very plain here. Just meat, potatoes and bread. 18 yrs. old today.
> Sun. 18. Went to work in my new uniform as door-boy. Worked until six. My hours will be from seven to six every-days and from twelve to six Sundays. . . .

Mon. 19. From 12:30 to 2:30 there was such a rush (about 80) that I thought I could never stand it.

Thur. 22. Cold. Had a grand reception this evening. Had a fine orchestra. We used the bowling-alley for a coat-room, and it looked like a railroad collision and an earthquake. The things were checked without order and we had to look all over for any certain number, unless the owner remembered where it was put. Came away at 12:10. Seventeen hours on duty! . . .

Sun. 25 Snow nearly all day. The most lonesome Christmas I ever spent. Went to work at 12:15. . . .

3. Clara Ward, Detroit's Prodigal Princess of Chimay

Detroit News

Clara Ward, daughter of Captain Eber Brock Ward, the Great Lakes shipper, lumberman, and industrialist, became the Princess Chimay in 1890. Self-proclaimed mistress of King Leopold of Belgium, she is best defined by her flowery, romantic obituary in the Detroit News *of December 19, 1916. It summarizes for us one aspect of the Gilded Age.*

A score of years ago, Clara Ward was the idol of Detroit young womanhood. Wealthy and beautiful, she left her native Detroit to marry the Prince de Chimay and Caraman, a Belgian nobleman closely allied to the royal family. Her light burned brightly in the capitals of Europe. She was favored of kings, the leading figure in many startling escapades, the toast of Paris. She was a princess, an American princess, who had captured the old world by her wit and her daring as much as by her lovely face.

Today she lies dead in her home in Padua, Italy—a prodigal daughter spurned by her mother, shunned by her former companions, her life ended, if not in poverty, as least in unlovely cir-

"Clara Ward, Detroit's Prodigal Princess of Chimay," *Detroit News* (19 December 1916): 1–2.

cumstances. She died a woman without illusions. She had gone the pace. She had lived intensely, a slave of her desires; she died an outcast, an old woman of 43 years, just when she should have been in her prime. . . .

The story of Clara Ward reads like a romance of the Duchess. At the age of 17, in 1890, when the country was stormed by impecunious noblemen of Europe, seeking gold for their damaged titles and equally damaged selves, Miss Ward, daughter of a multi-millionaire lumberman, was married in Paris to the prince. . . . A papal nuncio officiated, and the witnesses were the British and American ambassadors. . . . She had a yearly income of $50,000 from the estate of her father, and besides the fortunes of her mother and uncle were hers to draw on. . . .

For several years the prince and his American wife lived contentedly in Belgium. Two children were born to them. . . . But beneath the surface the fires that were later to consume her were burning fiercely. At last they burst out and the princess began to go on trips to Paris incognito. Once there, making the rounds of the gayest cafes and music halls, she squandered money riotously, everywhere dazzling with her beauty and startling with her prodigality. On one of these unbridled tours of the French capital, she met in a restaurant a Gipsy fiddler. He was—and is— a man of unprepossessing appearance physically. He is short and slender, his shoulders stooped. He wears a black moustache, and his black hair sweeps romantically back from his forehead. And in his eyes burn searing lights. These eyes kindled anew the tempestuous fires within the girl. These eyes won the princess from her husband and made her for years the slave of the Gipsy, [Jancsy] Rigo. . . .

Just as she had climbed up from a Detroit schoolgirl to a princess, so now she put aside her coronet and made the descent. And a turbulent time it was! In 1901, her uncle, Thomas R. Lyons, who was appointed conservator of her estate, showed that in seven years his niece had spent nearly a million dollars, $750,000, and most of it frittered away in company with the sparkling-eyed Rigo. Two years in Egypt cost $150,000; six weeks in Paris $32,000. She paid $35,000 for a pair of diamond earrings and then, tiring of them, pawned them for $4,000. . . . Shortly after her marriage to Rigo she gave a frank interview:

A final flare-up of Gilded Age elegance: J. L. Hudson display window, November, 1916. (From J. L. Hudson File, BHC. Used with permission.)

The true cause of my elopement with Rigo lies at the king's door [Leopold of Belgium]. I did not leave home from caprice, but because I had lost my position and was too proud to remain anywhere under sufferance. From the very first moment that I arrived in Brussels King Leopold showered me with attentions. At last came the celebrated garden party at the palace at Laeken.

The king neglected his guests for me. By his favoritism, the jealousy and hatred of the entire court was aroused against me. I defied them, as I have all my life defied everyone. The attentions of the king were pleasing to me, and I encouraged them. . . .

At last, at a certain fete, during a moment which will live in my memory till I die, I stood alone on one of the steps of the great staircase leading to the palace conservatories.

As I entered the great hall every woman there turned her back on me, or gazed at me contemptuously.

211

What I suffered in that moment of insulted pride, no one will ever know. Then it was that I broke the strictest law of court etiquette, which demands that no one shall retire from the assembly until the queen has left.

An officer stood near me. I turned and asked him to give me his arm out of the palace. He refused. I left alone, banishing myself from the court forever.

I am done with it all. I wanted to be free. I am at least out of the rotten atmosphere in which modern society lives. It does not want me, and I do not want it—so we are quits.

The last chapter in her life, as far as Detroit is concerned was written two years ago, when Rigo, her gipsy lover, was engaged by a local cafe to feature its cabaret. Relatives of Clara Ward— there are many of them living in the city and vicinity—could have seen her fiddler husband jauntily stepping about the smoke-filled cafe, ogling the women and playing his sensuous Hungarian airs on his eloquent violin.

Here is a man who cut a wide swath through Europe with one of the world's most beautiful women as his companion. . . .

While he was here he recalled what she had said to him about her home. "Once we thought we would go back to her native city together," he described the incident, "and she said, 'Ah, Jancsy, la belle Paris is not more beautiful than Detroit when the lights are shining on the river.' "[1]

Editor's Note

1. Clara Ward married four times; the obituary writer seems particularly shocked that one husband was an Italian railroad porter. Rigo divorced Clara, as had the Prince of Caraman and Chimay earlier. The prince was a cousin of King Leopold of Belgium, and there are some implications that he might have divorced Clara earlier, except for the social impossibility of naming his kinsman the king as corespondent.

   Clara was not allowed to see her children after the divorce, and her mother, although she herself had been a target of gossip when she had displaced the first Mrs. Eber Ward some years earlier, turned off all attempts Clara made at reconciliation.

4. Castle Garden Days

Walter Pitkin

Not everyone lived in luxury during the Gilded Age. Then, as now, ordinary folks outnumbered the elite. Walter Pitkin, who was born in 1878, describes the working-class neighborhood of his childhood. Ethnic and racial groups were less defined by neighborhood than they would be in another decade or two. Pitkin also contrasts his own neighborhood with some others in late-nineteenth-century Detroit.

For years I carelessly assumed that I grew up in old Detroit. But I didn't. I lived west of Trumbull Avenue and south of Grand River Avenue. What's more to the point, I was one of the first inhabitants of this area. But old Detroit lay east of Trumbull Avenue and north of Grand River Avenue. It differed from my Detroit as greatly as Park Avenue differs from First Avenue, in New York City. Look first at my Detroit—and laugh, if you want to.

We Connecticut Yankees were first to arrive in what later became our neighborhood. And we were one of the first families to settle the great triangle enclosed by Grand River Avenue, Poplar

Walter Pitkin, excerpted from "Castle Garden Days" in *On My Own.* Copyright 1944 Walter Pitkin. Reprinted with the permission of Charles Scribner's Sons, an imprint of Macmillan Publishing Company.

Street and the Belt Line Railway. Who followed us? Everybody except Yankees. Those were Castle Garden Days. Our Detroit became an annex and an outlet for Castle Garden.

You don't know what that means. Why should you? There was no Ellis Island until I was thirteen years old. That mighty immigration station did not open up for business until New Year's Day of 1891. Before then aliens came in through Castle Garden, at the foot of Manhattan Island, now called the Battery.

During the decade before Ellis Island the stream of newcomers became a torrent. . . . A heavy leakage from that stream reached us. It came all of a sudden, shortly after 1886.

First came the Bergers, from Holland. Then the Stanleys, originally out of England. Then the mighty swarm of Scots—the Murrays and McKees and Maddoxes and Kerrs, mostly from Edinburgh. Then the mightier swarm of Considines and Magees and Shaughnessys and Donohues and Coxes and Hughes out of Ireland. Then the tidal waves of Poles, who moved in half a mile west of us and became a little Poland once and for all time. Then a thin scattering of Germans, Danes, Norwegians and Belgians: the Zimmermans, the Sorensons, and others.

Along with these folks from Castle Garden came two lesser streams out of Canada. One was old French Canadian, the other was freshly out of France but by way of Montreal and Quebec; the Fontaines, Labadies, and a few others. Finally came a mere spatter of English and old-stock Americans from many sources; the Grinnells, the Hudsons, the Edgecombes and others.

By 1890 almost every lot had a house on it. Everybody worked hard, stuck to his own job, held fast to his own culture, and left everybody else free to do the same. We had no paupers, no rich; no loafers except Charley, the tramp; and no society folks.

At the time I failed completely to understand my environment. I missed the significance of my easy contacts with people of many races, religions, nationalities, and crafts. No boy in a New York slum could have enjoyed the wide variety of acquaintances I did. The later immigrant groups kept to themselves, created colonies, clung to their languages and cultures, and sought no outside connections. Not until the children of these immigrants grew up did the old colonies break down a little. But in my Detroit, every family had broken away from its sources. We had no Scotch quarter, no Irish quarter, no German quarter, no

French quarter. There was a Polish quarter, but it lay far outside of our neighborhood.

Nor was there any one business, trade, or craft that overshadowed the others. Starting at Grand River and working down one side of Fourteenth Street and then back up on the other side, I recall a druggist, a carpenter, a fisherman, a civil engineer, a ship carpenter, a school teacher, a printer, a livery stable man, a tug boat captain, a mason, a cattleman, a newspaper editor, a candy maker, a customs officer . . . as far up and down the street as memory's mare pulls me through the dust. Then up a side street, Joe Labadie, the writer of dime novels, a saloonkeeper, a carpenter. . . .

Some were Catholics, most were Protestants, but several were Free Thinkers and atheists. Some were drunkards, while others were rabid Prohibitionists. Some were thugs and thieves, but most were honest and hard working. Neither Republicans nor Democrats claimed many, for these newcomers had as yet formed no strong political convictions. They had to work too hard. For politics they had little time.

As yet there was no true community. The group was purely arithmetical, a mere sum of its parts, and all the parts stood out alone, free, unfused. The place was likewise crude. Through most of our early years there the road was dirt, the ditches just deep holes, the sidewalks made of rough pine boards nailed to two frame timbers. . . . Many of us kept a few chickens and let them forage for themselves half of the year.

. . . About five hundred feet west of Trumbull Avenue, as you go down Grand River Avenue, you smell something not too good. You see a huge red building on an alley. You walk around to the rear and look in. Two huge men are slaughtering steers hung from high tackles. The floor runs deep in warm blood. The men are blood from head to foot. The warm carcasses hang on hooks, covered with a million flies. A few small boys loiter around to get certain cuts for their home kitchens. The Magees sold these cheaply on the spot.

This, the Magee slaughterhouse was—as I say—a scant five hundred feet from one of the most charming mansions and gardens of old Detroit, the home of James E. Scripps, the great newspaper publisher. And this propinquity, in a far from poetic fashion, symbolizes the two Detroits, the world of difference between two cultures. Our Detroit came right up to the steps of the Scripps fence. The stenches from the slaughter house breezed in upon the Scripps family when the wind took a certain turn.

Scripps had transplanted a fairy fragment of old Surrey to the back door of Donnybrook Fair. He had copied a fine old English manor house and set it about with a delightful garden. He had cut off the world with a fancy fence which cost more than any house in our block. He kept a gardener. He installed an art gallery. . . .

This frontier of frills and fashion, the east side of Trumbull Avenue north of Grand River Avenue, lay far beyond the mass of Quality Folks. There were blocks and blocks of plain folks between Scripps and Woodward Avenue; but these plain folks were not like those of Fourteenth Street. They were Yankees out of Massachusetts, Yankees out of the Western Reserve, alias Ohio; a medley of middle-class lawyers, doctors, dentists, engineers. . . . Finally you reach Quality Street, which some would have said was Cass Avenue and others Second. There began one of the two areas that made up the heart and soul of old Detroit. It spread out irregularly on both sides of Grand Circus Park about to Willis Avenue, then faded out into green fields and dirt roads.

The other area was Jefferson Avenue, roughly from Chene Street out to Belle Isle Bridge, the end of the old Boulevard. Here dwelt many of the old French families, some in shabby genteel fashion, but most of them in a quiet, unstudied magnificence hard to equal anywhere else on earth, then or now. Row upon row of elms, maples, and oaks. Immense, dreamy lawns, stretching from the front gates clear down to the river; little boat houses on the shore, sheltering canoes and launches and sail boats and a few launches; mansions of brick, rather plain on the outside, but luxurious inside. . . .

[Old Detroit] was the most leisurely of American cities. Off the beaten tracks of westbound pioneers, it was not backwash, for it had more old wealth and old culture by far than did any of the cities in the great line of march between the Atlantic and the Pacific. Beside it, Buffalo was a mere outhouse. . . . Beside it, Chicago was a dung heap. Bostonians declared it was more like Boston than any other place. Yet it was no more Boston than I am Lillian Russell. It was, in truth, Detroit and nothing else.

In the Eighties I saw it as wide, cool streets, as brick houses set far back in soft lawns; as a riverside refreshed with breezes out of every quarter and down from every cloud; as a place where prominent citizens chatted by the hour with one another on park seats and at street corners; as a place where nobody hurried except to fires; as a place where people read important books and discussed them endlessly; as a place where a well read man was more welcome to dinner than a rude lumber baron who had just made another million by cheating homesteaders up back of Alpena.

All this I saw even when young. But never was I a part of it. Nor did I even taste it until after 1892. So you see it is only by a legal fiction that I call myself a citizen of old Detroit. True, our neighborhood had been recently taken into the city. We were, officially speaking, in the Tenth Ward. But we might as well have been called the Violent Ward, so far as old Detroit was concerned. Judged by Detroit's standard, we were violent. In 1885 we were living in 1865. We were the laggards in the cultural lag.[1]

Editor's Note

1. Though ethnic and racial groups have changed more than once since Pitkin's time, this near West Side area still retains its reputation for diversity and takes pride in violence. The mansion of James Scripps was razed some years ago, but part of his garden is occupied by the Frederick Douglass Library. Across Grand River Avenue the square tower of Trinity Episcopal, the very British church Scripps built, dominates the skyline, dwarfing even the golden arches of a nearby MacDonald's.

Part VII

The Progressives and Other Reformers

The Progressives and Other Reformers

Detroit venerates strong mayors. In the line that stretches from Solomon Sibley to Coleman Young, there have not been many. Among the dozens of mayors, Zina Pitcher, Hazen Pingree, James Couzens, Jerome Cavanagh, and Frank Murphy come to mind, with, of course, the current incumbent, Mayor Coleman Young. Of them all, Pingree stands the tests of history as well as any.[1] In Detroit he also served as an advance guard for the Progressive movement that sprang up in other cities.

Though Pingree dominates Detroit's Progressive period, he could not have succeeded had the climate of the times not shifted to reform. Some of the shift is to be found in the columns of the *Detroit Evening News* under the editorship of James Scripps, who was dedicated to producing a newspaper for the working class. His stance is reflected in the very first document of this section: two editorials from his paper on Belle Isle, which he termed the "People's Park." Militant support was given to the purchase of Belle Isle by ordinary people. Clearly the time was ripe for reformers, Mayor Pingree among them.

Best known for his "potato patches"—land made available to the unemployed for growing food—Pingree showed that he was a reformer in many other, more significant, ways. Like Franklin Delano Roosevelt later, he came from a secure financial position to befriend workers and was therefore considered "a traitor to his class." His ultrarespectable church refused to renew the family's reserved pew after Pingree's first term in office.

The mayor sided with strikers when their picket lines were attacked by the police. He fought diligently, though with only minimal success, against the combine controlled by the McMillans and Hendries that owned the franchise of the Detroit City Railway. He fought for the establishment of the Public Lighting Commission and urged public ownership of all utilities.[2] He demanded an end to the toll road contracts, which he believed were a device to rob Detroiters whenever they left the city limits. He cut government costs, installed tax reforms, opened the assessment process, and encouraged citizen appeals.

Pingree is also notable for his championing of both riverfront development and park improvements, arguing that a good way for the city to make money was by preserving and developing its aesthetic advantages. His idea of extending outward the river shoreline downtown in order to build a large assembly hall and convention center has, of course, been a feature of Mayor Coleman Young's administration, almost a century later.

Believing that state government stymied his reform efforts in Detroit, Pingree ran for governor to correct the ills of his beloved city. He was elected governor while continuing to serve as mayor of Detroit, apparently believing that he could hold both offices at the same time. The Michigan Supreme Court thought otherwise. Pingree's abrupt resignation as mayor, early in 1897, was forced by that body.

There were weak spots in Pingree's reform efforts. They grew directly out of his anxiety to provide good, cheap government for the workingman, but sometimes the odds were just too great. His long battle with the transport monopoly headed by the McMillans was not finally settled until a quarter of a century after his term of office.

In dealing with public education, his concern with what he believed to be workers' interests led him astray. Pingree was certain that in the Detroit Board of Education he had found the center of corruption. He was not content with sending angry veto messages, several relating to the new high school building, whose location and cost he heartily distrusted. Later it would become "Old Main" to generations of Wayne State University students.[3] One summer evening in 1894, Pingree arrived at a board of education meeting with several policemen and had four board members arrested on the spot for receiving bribes from a furniture company. The mayor failed to win his court case, partly because the furniture salesman needed as a witness had opportunely left town, but also because his sweeping attack was too general. It incurred, for instance, a libel suit brought by one innocent board member who was not arrested but who resented the mayor's inclusive tirade.[4]

I have included two of the mayor's typical veto messages, both addressed to the board of education.

Pingree's cause was less just when he tangled with the growing forces of progressive education represented among the board's employees. In what now seems a total misunderstanding of the facts, Pingree believed that the liberal educators, and particularly their spokesperson, Assistant Superintendent Mathilde Coffin, were proposing an elitist curriculum that sidestepped the needs of the children of the working poor. Coffin was a formidable reformer in her own right, and the broad curriculum she proposed was in a number of ways more clearly related to young people and jobs in Detroit than Pingree ever realized. However, Coffin never had the mayor's support, and on one occasion he vetoed the budget line item that represented her salary.

I have included my own article on Coffin from the late journal *Detroit in Perspective.*

There were several other reformers who showed a casual disregard for standard opinion in their pursuit of ideas. Sketches appear here of Jo Labadie and Eliza Burt Gamble. There could have been others, such as D. Farrand Henry, scientist; Carrie Van Oostdyke, suffragist; Judson Grennell, single-tax economist; the lawyer and journalist Mary Stuart Coffin (no relation to Mathilde); the Pelham brothers, who were publishers of a black newspaper before they were government servants; and any number of others. All of them carried on a variety of crusades in casual disregard of standard opinion. All of them, in a less kind age, would be termed eccentrics.

Blacks were largely left out of the Progressive period. For them, the achievements of Reconstruction had not come easily, and the triumphs did not last long. Mayor Pingree failed to help. We think it was only a sad coincidence, rather than any purposeful effort. When his own commitment to eliminating patronage got in the way of blacks who had achieved through machine politics the offices for which many were thoroughly qualified, but could never have hoped to win by election, this does not seem to have been a fact that he noticed. His first concern was the effort to avoid deal-making and special favors. Forrester Washington calls the period one of "recrudescence" for blacks and in a telling historical essay tells us why.

Editor's Notes

1. Though Melvin G. Holli's *Reform in Detroit: Hazen S. Pingree and Urban Politics* (New York: Oxford University Press, 1969) is the outstanding biography of Pingree, much personal information about the Pingree family and their life-style is to be found in the unpublished typescript "Pingree," by Cyril Arthur Player, BHC.
2. Detroiters lost interest in public ownership after the Progressive period. When, in the 1970s, someone suggested selling the Public Lighting Commission Pingree had established to Detroit Edison, the rationale for public ownership seemed to be understood by only one or two city officials. Fortunately, Councilman Kenneth Cockrel was able to carry the day for maintaining the yardstick function of PLC.
3. Although Pingree himself lived at Woodward and Farnsworth, sharing what is now the site of the Detroit Institute of Arts with D. M. Ferry, he felt that the neighborhood was too elite to be welcoming to high school students. The site chosen at Cass and Warren was a part of the Cass estate and was being marketed under the name of the Cass Farm Company.
4. Emma Fox Papers, BHC. Fox, a clubwoman and parliamentarian, served a single term on the Detroit Board of Education as one of two women members during a period when the Michigan Legislature permitted women to run for that office as well as to vote in local school elections. (Eliza Gamble was particularly scornful of this small sop to motherhood.)

1.   Belle Isle: The People's Park

Detroit Evening News

When the city, after much debate, purchased Belle Isle in 1879, there remained stormy political discussion about its maintenance costs. Ten years later the arguments reached a climax as a bond proposal for the park conflicted with rival efforts to secure bonding for Grand Boulevard, which was to circle the city three miles from downtown. The Evening News *took up the fight for Belle Isle, calling it the "People's Park." Two of its many editorials on the park are reprinted here.*

Boodlers Hate the Park

"We love him for the enemies he has made", said Gen. Bragg at the democratic convention of 1884 when eulogizing Governor Cleveland. Belle Isle Park does not need such a commendation as that, for the people love it for its own sake, and for its own beauties; but the same words might be used of it, whenever its interests come up in the common council. It is an enterprise solely for the people's benefit; it has catered to no private interests. . . .

"Boodlers Hate the Park," *Detroit Evening News* (16 February 1889): 2.
"Shallow Politics," *Detroit Evening News* (18 February 1889): 2.
Both are also in Randall Scrapbook, no. 23: 22, 29, BHC.

At one time, not long ago, a well-organized conspiracy was hatched in the council, led by a leading boulevard alderman,[1] to get rid of it altogether by selling it, and this was only defeated by an angry manifestation of popular feeling, which subsequently swept the proposer out of office. The report of the committee on parks last night, favoring the recommendation of the mayor for park improvement bonds, was the signal for another uprising of the enemies of the park. Every man of them is tarred with the same stick. For years past, they have been the constant source of scandals in the city government, and some of them have escaped indictment and prison only on legal technicalities. Every man of this sort opposes bonding the city for the improvement of the People's Park,[2] but warmly endorses the scheme for handing the resources of the city over to the Speculator's Boulevard.

Shallow Politics

If the story be true that the Republican aldermen propose, as a measure of party politics, to resist the bonding of the city for the improvement of the island park, they will commit a very foolish political blunder. It is said that taking advantage of the mayor's recommendation of bonds for the park and for sewers, some political Smart Alecks among them imagine they see an opportunity to place their party in the attitude of the champion of municipal economy by resisting all bonds for whatsoever purpose and put the local democracy in a hole at the same time, as the champion of extravagance, and that they have suddenly seized upon this program for use in the next municipal election. . . .

The same [as of sewers] may be said of the island park. The rich do not need it. Their own dooryards are in many cases beautiful parks. In summer they go to the seaside, and if they wish an airing without going away, their fine horses and carriages can whirl them off to their villas at Grosse Pointe. They will probably take little comfort in the island park even when it is completed, for the poor will be there in their homely garments, and with their homely ways, to offend the eyes and ears of my lord and my lady. But the council will make a mistake to accept this indifference of the rich towards the park as an index of popular opinion. The masses of the people want it. It is seaside, villa, air,

Young women sketching on Belle Isle, 1905. (From BHC. Used with permission.)

water—everything in the way of rest and comfort—to which they can escape from the squalid and often unwholesome surroundings of their homes. They are frightfully in earnest about it. They have watched its progress and marked its enemies, and they will mark for destruction any political party which will place itself in the way of its speedy completion.

It cannot be completed by the niggardly annual appropriations which the council doles out to it. They are eaten up by the cost of maintenance; nothing is left for the work of improvement. . . .

Editor's Notes

1. This reference is very likely to James Randall, politician and developer, who was nicknamed "Boulevard Randall." He also kept the scrapbook that provides the sources noted here.

2. The role of Belle Isle as a "people's park" began early. Thorough histories of Belle Isle, formerly Isle au Cochons, or Hog Island, appear in Farmer, *History of Detroit*, 75–79 and Burton, *City of Detroit*, vol. 1, 438–62. The island was originally bought from the Ottawa and Chippewa Indians by a British lieutenant, George MacDougall, in 1768 for "5 barrels of rum, 3 rolls of tobacco, 3 lbs. of vermilion, a belt of wampum and 3 lbs. of paint." Extra rum and paint were given on possession.

   According to an unidentified news clipping in a Burton scrapbook, sometime in 1912 two enterprising members of the Chippewa group, Rising Sun and Oscar Beaver, tried to have the property returned to their nation, stating that the original bargain was obviously unfair. See Burton Scrapbook, no. 72:195, BHC.

2.   Excerpts from the Mayor's Annual Messages, 1891 and 1896

Hazen Pingree

As early as January, 1891, in his second annual message to the Detroit Common Council, the mayor was casting wistful eyes at New York's Central Park and urging Detroit to take it as an example. By the time of his seventh and final annual message, in 1896, Pingree was able to focus his plans on the riverfront. Both messages are lengthy and are excerpted here.

A Central Park

Those who have kept track of the growth of Detroit in the past 25 years, have noticed that the city has scattered like a large village, spread out over much more territory than has been necessary for its real size, as indicated by its population. The result has been that there is property within a block or two of the City hall, which is as valuable as much that is two or three miles away. This central property has not been desired for residence purposes, it is too high in price for factories, and it is being gradually abandoned by wholesale houses. No state is better located

Hazen Pingree, Annual Message of the Mayor, *Journal of the Common Council*, City of Detroit (13 January 1891): 2–9.
Hazen Pingree, Annual Message of the Mayor, *Journal of the Common Council*, City of Detroit (20 January 1896): 2–14.

than Michigan, and no city than Detroit for building up and conducting large manufacturing interests. Neither is there any city in the country that could be made to draw so many outsiders within its limits, by its beauties, as Detroit. In other words, it can be made a great manufacturing city, and a great place of resort for strangers, both winter and summer. By taking advantage of its location, its climate, and its natural beauties, it could be made a veritable Paris of America. And this means a good deal, when it is considered that fully one-half the population of Paris, is supported by strangers attracted to that city by the reputation of its parks and boulevards.

A large park, in the center of the city, would boom Detroit more than the establishment of half a dozen Union Depots or of 18 or 20 factories. The Grand Circus Park was wisely designed by the governor and judges who replatted Detroit after the fire as the hub of a park system, consisting of broad avenues radiating from it as a common center.

The only mistake which they made was in not making this Central Park large enough for the subsequent growth of the city. They undoubtedly had the same thing in mind as those who laid out Boston, who reserved for the perpetual common use, that magnificent Central Park now known the world over as "Boston Commons". Bostonians regard it as of such great advantage to them that no sum of money would induce them to part with it; and they have of late years added to it, by purchase, another Central Park of nearly equal size, known as the "Public Gardens". It is a well-known fact that after the purchase and improvement of Central Park in New York City, the rapid rise in the taxable value of the land near it more than met the interest on its cost.

A glance at the map of the city will show that the spaces, southeasterly and southwesterly from the Grand Circus are so cut up into small parks, avenues and alleys, that private property is less than one-half of the whole. And that property, from its irregularity, and for reasons before mentioned is held at comparatively low figures. It could be obtained by the city either by purchase or condemnation, for a reasonable amount. The space south of Elizabeth east to Brush or Beaubien streets; south to Gratiot avenue; up Miami [later Broadway] avenue, crossing Woodward avenue at Park street, down Washington to Grand River, and up to its intersection with Elizabeth street, if made into a common or central park would be of untold advantage to every other part of the city, and to the country in general. Such a magnificent space of 82 acres, of which only 43 acres would have to be purchased, would be a lasting monument to the wisdom of the city fathers who procured it, and would justly entitle all who aided in the cause to the gratitude, not only of this generation, but of generations yet unborn.

Waterfront Improvement

Among our public spirited citizens there have been discussions from time to time during the past year looking to the formulation of some plan whereby Detroit can extend its reputation as one of the most beautiful cities of the United States and add to the volume of the steadily increasing stream of visitors.

Already Detroit has become a favorite resort for visitors from the Southern States during the summer months, and an attractive city for the conventions of the various State and inter-State organizations for the promotion of private enterprises.

But although the city has attained to the dignity of the first class in point of population, and of public improvement in nearly all lines, there is a lack of facilities for the accommodation of conventions of the first class, such, for example, as the national conventions of the political parties.

During the discussions alluded to, attention has been chiefly directed to the waterfront of the city along a river unsurpassed for volume and excellence of water in the world. It is a magnificent stream, worthy of any expense of ornamentation and of works of utility, yet the entire sweep of the river front is without that character of improvement in docks, buildings and breathing places for citizens in any way worthy of the great river, or of the business presenting itself.

While it cannot be expected that Detroit, like New York, can adopt the policy of acquiring the entire water front, as New York City did in 1871, and enter into the construction of piers, roadways and parked spaces, and meeting the expenses of construction and the employment of an army of men by the rental of piers and the receptacles for freight, it is not impossible that Detroit can afford to . . . select some section of the water front for improvement.

My attention has been directed to the acquiring by the city through condemnation proceedings, or ordinary purchase of the property along this front bounded by the river, Woodbridge street and Third street, upon which I find the total assessed valuation to be $1,496,030, and I present this matter to your honorable body for your consideration, and also for the consideration of the general public, and this special section of the water front is put forward as much for its general suggestiveness as for making it a possible objective point with which to start the project of water front improvement.

I would recommend that your honorable body refer this important subject to some committee that can afford the time for the consideration of it, and that such committee invite the cooperation of the Manufacturer's club.[1]

Editor's Note

1. We note that Pingree's plans for the riverfront included an extension into the river to provide a great assembly hall for national political conventions. There is a surprising similarity to the dreams of Mayor Coleman Young a century later. Both men saw the river as a political and economic asset to the city, and, as with his championship of a greatly expanded Grand Circus Park, Pingree shared the later mayor's dream of Detroit as a traveler's paradise.

3.   Board of Education Vetoes, 1893–94

Hazen Pingree

Mayor Hazen Pingree could be quick to anger, and often used his veto power. There was a particularly harsh quality in his relations with the board of education, which he identified with corruption. After all, it was their meeting he once invaded with policemen and arrest warrants for four members.

The following two letters from Pingree to the board are less sensational than that action, but give the flavor of his annoyance and are typical of his routine expressions of displeasure.

January 26, 1893

To the Board of Education:

GENTLEMEN:—I am informed that it has been the custom of your Committee on Real Estate and School Buildings to open bids for construction of school buildings, heating, ventilation, etc., in the Secretary's office, behind closed doors, to which the representatives of the various newspapers and the bidders themselves are denied admission. This plan may be pursued from the purest of motives and the opening conducted with the most absolute impartiality and fairdealing. But the fact that this important work is done in secret, when it should be open to public

Hazen Pingree to the Detroit Board of Education, 26 January 1893 and 8 October 1894, *Proceedings of the Detroit Board of Education, 1893–1894* (Detroit: James H. Stone & Co.).

scrutiny as the sunlight of Heaven, engenders suspicion of wrong-doing, where perhaps none actually exists. Your board is handling the public money, and a large amount of it; and not only your actions, but also those of all your committees, should at all times be open to public inspection. As Mayor of the city, and as an ex officio member of your board, I would respectfully advise the adoption of a resolution directing that hereafter the opening of bids for any kind of public work in charge of the Board of Education be open and public, instead of private and secret, as at present.

Very respectfully,
H. S. PINGREE,
Mayor

Detroit, October 8, 1894.

To the Board of Education:

I herewith return to you without my approval so much of the proceedings of your honorable body by which you have selected as a High School site the block bounded by Warren, Hancock, Cass and Second Avenues.

My reasons for this action are as follows: The building of a High School is a matter in which almost every citizen of Detroit is deeply interested. I have endeavored to get an expression of opinion upon the question of this location and find that while there is a great diversity of sentiment, the majority of the citizens who take an interest in the matter are opposed to a location so far north. The selection of a site within the mile circle would be more satisfactory. . . .

Very respectfully,
H. S. PINGREE,
Mayor

4. "Too Bright for the Schools?" —Assistant Superintendent Mathilde Coffin

Wilma Wood Henrickson

> The schools have been going to the dogs . . . for nearly a generation. . . . Rooms are crowded with children who should have been educated in the essentials in a few short years and permitted to go out in the world and assist their parents to earn bread. . . .
>
> People who can afford it and have a grain of sense no longer send their children to the public schools, which are becoming more incompetent every day—and more costly to the taxpayer.
>
> —*Detroit Evening News*[1]

So what else is new? The year was 1896, and the angry quotations are from the *Detroit Evening News*, forerunner of to-day's *Detroit News*. . . . Detroit was entering a third year of major depression. This would not be the first, nor the last time that hard-up Detroiters would ask to have Detroit's children educated cheaply, for entry-level, even dead-end jobs.[2] Yet most were proud of their schools. Throughout the nineties Detroit's public

Wilma Wood Henrickson, " 'Too Bright for the Schools?'—Assistant Superintendent Mathilde Coffin," *Detroit in Perspective: A Journal of Regional History* 7, no. 2 (Fall 1983): 26–39.

schools had been making exciting gains. Natural science, physical education, a school for the deaf had all been added, kindergarten re-introduced, music and art strengthened. New schools had been built: the elite and controversial new high school out in the country at Cass and Warren, plus the Poe, the Harris, the Campbell, the Columbian. Even her enemies agreed that many, perhaps most, of the educational changes within the new buildings were due to the resourcefulness of one woman—Assistant Superintendent Mathilde Coffin.

Under the friendly, hands-off leadership of Superintendent William Robinson, Coffin had reduced class size which in some cases had reached as many as 75 students, and revised the entire elementary school curriculum. . . .

Coffin was determined to break with rote learning and drill. "Too much of just such work in the past is what has helped produce so many stupid people," she wrote tartly. To avoid teachers being "enslaved by a single textbook," she brought a range of texts and newspapers into the classroom. Children were to be urged to check varied references and prove the truth of their statements. Teachers were urged to get rid of the printed "Plan Books" which contained canned lessons and bulletin board ideas for the year ahead. Fresh work, related to today's world, would be the thing.

Times were hard in the spring of 1896, but Coffin was at the height of her powers. She had been effectively serving as Assistant Superintendent of Schools for five years, though not always with that title. Her $250 a month salary made her one of the more highly paid women executives in the country. It meant that she could live at a good address, . . . on Woodward Avenue, between Charlotte, and Peterboro, it meant that she could be one of the few Detroiters to have a telephone. . . .

Less than a year after Coffin was at her peak of influence, however, she would be jobless, "released from her duties for the good of the schools," struck off the payroll, and forced to go to court for her salary.

On Saturday evening, March 14, 1896, Miss Coffin returned from a Teachers' Institute in Monroe County. She told her audience there of her latest experiment—the introduction of the newspaper in the form of a sample abridged edition of the *Evening News* into the classrooms of Detroit. Coffin opened her own copy of the *Evening News* to find her ideas the subject of sharp attack under the headline: "EDUCATION FADS RUN MAD":

> God help the poor children. . . . This new fad is not proposed for the purpose of making them better readers, but solely to stuff their poor brains with the press of rubbish that is called the news of the day. . . . Wise fathers and mothers, while their children are still at school, try to keep the newspapers out of their hands. . . .
>
> It is astonishing that anyone in authority in the schools would have the impertinent audacity to propose forcing into the child's hands reading matter which his father or his mother would shrink from giving him access to at home.

Coffin immediately, and recklessly, took up the challenge. In one of many letters to the editors of the *Evening News* she undertook a serious defense of the courses her critics had labelled "fads":

> Your free use of the word "fad" prompts me to ask what you mean by it. . . . Are drawing, physical culture, and nature study fads? . . . You plead for the three R's. Nature study furnishes something to read and write about. We do not find that the presence of something to say "dissipates the minds of the children" in writing. If our children are allowed to continue this study of nature and history, they are in danger of forming the habit of saying something when they write.[3]

The *Evening News* did not back away, but continued to argue for traditional methods, such as arithmetic drill, rather than the individual problems Coffin urged. One editor openly stated that employers would prefer not to hire young bookkeepers whose training in mathematics might cause them to raise awkward questions.

Coffin retorted, "A boy is more than an adding machine." In a direct challenge to the editor of the *Evening News* [James Scripps], she stated:

> A man's prejudice against the public schools may be so strong as to paralyze his thought power in that direction and render him incapable of making judgments based upon facts. Your loose writ-

ing about educational matters shows a lack of acquaintance with the schools and the work which is doing in them at the present time. One purpose of education is to develop responsibility to truth; this, I take it, is even more important than the three R's.

The behind-the-scenes uproar was sufficient to cause Coffin to offer her resignation. The Board refused to accept it, but the genie was out of the bottle now. . . .

Coffin had strong defenders, among them Mrs. Carrie Oostdyke, president of the Independent Voters' Association and Attorney D. Augustus Straker, a leader in Detroit's black community.

School Inspector Marr, who would later fall by the wayside, went so far as to say: "Miss Coffin stands for the main question, whether we are to go ahead or to turn back. . . . There are two classes among the teachers, those who are in favor of Miss Coffin and those who are opposed and they can be divided by the measure of their skill and enthusiasm in their work. The better teachers are unanimously for Miss Coffin. . . . "

However, stories on Coffin's progressivism would soon be obscured in all the papers by the Board's actions in the growing fiscal crisis.

. . . During this period, control was vested in sixteen Board members termed "School Inspectors," one elected from each of the city's sixteen wards, with eight to be chosen in each biennial election. The Board of Estimates, in part appointed by the mayor, had substantial power over the budget, though, within the framework outlined, the Board of Education could maneuver to rearrange expenditures within categories. The mayor himself had veto power, and Mayor Pingree often used it. He clearly felt his vetoes were necessary to curb extravagance which could hurt working taxpayers. . . . He fought the plans for the new high school, for instance, every inch of the way. . . .

In March the *Evening News* carried a small item congratulating Inspector Hall [a west side dentist], for his shrewdness in making friends with the Board of Estimates in his efforts to get the "fads" out of the school budget. Inspector Hall seems to have felt he had a mandate to return the curriculum to the three R's. He was probably an enemy of Coffin's even before she made a stinging remark that children would continue to sing whether or no Inspector Hall succeeded in eliminating music in the schools. Until now most of the Board had been united in its warm support of Robinson and Coffin. Always members stood together against the Board of Estimates, their natural enemy at budget time.

In April, the Board of Estimates, certainly with the approval of Mayor Pingree, slashed the education budget mercilessly. Building funds, cut severely in previous years, were now all but gone. No matter that many of Detroit's school children could not have a full day of school because there was no place to put them, or that . . . the average child stayed in school only five years, [or that] . . . Detroit's school age population during the nineties was one of the fastest growing in the country.

The Board of Estimates not only slashed the salary category, but made it clear that they expected some of the savings to come through the elimination of the "special teachers"; this meant Coffin and the supervisors of the various departments who were working under her.

. . . The Board of Education determined to make a number of budget decisions on its own. . . . Two weeks were abruptly slashed from the remainder of the school year; there was discussion of an even shorter year for 1896–97, and general salary cuts were put into immediate effect. Coffin's pay would now be reduced to $235 a month. The pensions of retired teachers . . . would be cut $5 a month, leaving them with $30. . . . Teachers of many years seniority, including well-known kindergarten specialist Fannie Richards [the first black woman hired by the Detroit Public Schools], were cut from $72.50 to $70 a month.

When the schools reopened in the fall, everything that could go wrong for Coffin did. . . . Someone with an eye for small economies suggested that teachers pay a dollar fee to cover the costs of . . . the monthly teachers' meetings arranged by Coffin; letters of protest appeared in the papers. The writers pointed out that a dollar was a lot of money when you had taken a pay cut above the lost time in June. . . . One writer noted also that the speakers Miss Coffin chose always seemed to want teachers to read more and to work much more, with the idea of constantly changing the lesson plans to fit the children. Teachers had little enough free time as it was. . . .

Coffin invited even more public notice by her active part in a women's group that championed educational reform. . . . Coffin seems to have enjoyed the full confidence of Robinson, and the warm support of most of the Board. The Women's Educational Union would change all that.

The first mention of this group occurs in the fall of 1896. Feminist, radical, and mushrooming in growth, in sixty days it had gained the support and membership of the top staff of the public schools. Coffin was elected vice-president, and the Superintendent's wife served as treasurer. George Brown, labor editor of the *Evening News*, writing in its Sunday edition, the *News-Tribune*, predicted that membership might easily go to 10,000 and that the political strength of Detroit women, who were allowed by Michigan law to vote in local school board elections, could lead to sweeping changes in the schools.[4]

The Union was the brain-child of feminist author Mrs. Eliza Burt Gamble, described by one school inspector as a "man-hater . . . on a rampage." For over two months, the Union, meeting constantly in the schools after hours, seemed on the edge of power. Coffin . . . addressed over four thousand mothers at its various meetings during the fall. What happened between October, when school officials, including Board President Caleb Pitkin [father of Walter Pitkin], had warmly endorsed the Women's Union, and December when it was a major factor in Coffin's firing?

From the outset, meetings were held at a feverish pace, at first in Mrs. Gamble's home, then, after the Board with some hesitation approved, in the schools after classes. Soon major meetings of the organization were scheduled in the Board of Education building on Miami Avenue—later Broadway. . . . Conflict surfaced with the prospectus of the main message the Union would deliver to mothers. . . . Harriet Scott, principal of the Normal School, understood that she had been chosen to write it. Gamble, a published writer, without prior consultation, used her own skills to prepare a separate document directed at the mothers of Detroit's school children. This was a surprise to everyone, but most of all to Mrs. Scott, and that particular meeting was a disaster. . . .

The Superintendent's wife . . . believed there were secret meetings to which she was not invited. . . . [Mrs. Robinson] quickly came to believe that the whole group represented a plot against her husband's best interests. She decided that Coffin herself really wanted to be Superintendent of Schools. With appar-

240

ent naivete, she blurted out at a committee meeting of the Union that her husband had told her he didn't enjoy working with women's groups, and planned to have as little as possible to do with the Women's Educational Union. . . .

Coffin then tried to discuss the role of the Union directly with Robinson. On Saturday morning, October 24, meeting with him in his office, she asked him to assure the principals that the group had his firm support. She stated that he then became "very angry," "paced the floor," and finally said, "There's too much of this female business. I'm tired of it." Coffin reports, "I rolled up my coat collar and left the office. Afterwards, . . . he explained to a friend of mine that he made no reference to myself, which, however, did not lessen the indignity."

During November, Gamble had a open, angry break with Robinson and called a press conference in which she accused him of "throwing cold water" on the Women's Union. Unfortunately, Coffin was again present, and Robinson later suggested to her that she was over-tired because of the long hours she had put in doing organizing work with the group, and that it was time to get back to her regular duties. Coffin was angry enough at this that she went over Robinson's head to Inspector Marr, as chairman of the board's Committee on Schools and Teachers, and asked him to seek a definition of her responsibilities as Assistant Superintendent. The reply came from Robinson early in December in a written memo. The memo listed routine jobs and managed to seem both derogatory and hostile.

Coffin was to report each Friday exactly what she had done during the week, to provide efficiency ratings on teachers in any buildings she visited, and to be available in her office every afternoon between four and five, Monday through Friday. The sting was in the last requirement. This was precisely the time that the Women's Educational Union was conducting its meetings. . . .

Coffin only had to live by the new rules a short time before the game was over. "IT'S OUT! *That Dark Secret the Board of Education Would Keep: The Women Can't Be Muzzled, And Here It All Is; Breach Between Superintendent Robinson and Miss Coffin*" were the headlines the *Detroit Free Press* used on its page one story on December 18, covering the rift between Coffin and Robinson.

On December 17, apparently obsessed with the public's right to know, Coffin released to all Detroit papers the story of her troubles on the job over the past two months. Just a day later she also announced her candidacy for the position of Superintendent of Schools. Jokingly, she told reporters that she had been "nominated" by Mrs. Robinson. Before the Superintendent's wife spread those rumors, it had not occurred to her to try to displace him. However—when the issue had been raised, it had suddenly occurred to her that she had been doing the major share of Robinson's work for several years now; his contract would expire in July—and why not?[5]

It was on December 17, too, that Gamble proposed the dissolution of the Women's Union, at an angry meeting at which she was booed by a faction of women principals. . . .

That same evening the Committee on Schools and Teachers of the Detroit Board of Education recommended that the full Board "relieve Miss Coffin of her duties." The Board made it official at its next meeting on Tuesday, December 22. "DECAPITATED" said the *Evening News*.

When the vote was taken [to fire Coffin] only long-time Board member Dr. Lucien Ellis dissented. . . . He explained to reporters that no one could give a reason for the board action. He seems quite correct. The official board minutes remain abrupt and sketchy, referring only to "the good of the schools."

If the Board was not saying much officially, much was being said by the press. . . . the *Journal* sadly urged her to resign. In both the *Evening News* and the *Free Press*, Coffin almost knocked the Cuban revolution out of the headlines. Coffin was accused of claiming to have written most of Robinson's reports and speeches, a point which may have been true. . . . She was accused of having schemed to get Robinson's job for herself. (Her version of her decision to seek the appointment, inept as it sounds, is probably the true one.) She was accused of being influenced, even "spoiled" by a mysterious male friend. She was accused of bewitching Robinson. Always she was accused of making too much money.

William Voigt, Jr., a brewer and former Board member, was candid above all others: "She is a very bright woman. In fact, she is too bright for the good of the Detroit schools. In her ambition and exploiting of scientific education, she has overshot her mark."

On Christmas Eve the *Evening News* carried its second mention by name of Franklin Ford, the mystery man accused by some

242

of giving her ideas and urging her on to covet the Superintendency. . . . In the words of the men interviewed: "He has some great ideas, but they are too deep for me" . . . "A dreamer. He wants to correlate everything" . . . "I do not understand just what his interest is in our schools" . . . "I believe he has been an itinerant newspaperman. I understand that at one time he was connected with Bradstreet's " . . . "In fact, he is a sort of conundrum to me, as he is to everyone else."

Ford had, in fact, been an editor with Bradstreet's, predecessor to Dun and Bradstreet's, for the ten years prior to 1887. He was an investigative journalist with a special interest in banking and credit; he tried to persuade the University of Michigan to establish a school of journalism. . . . "Conundrum of the day," the *Evening News* summarized Ford, and seemed to forget him.[6]

In its angry meeting of December 22, Board Attorney William Baubie had offered his legal opinion on breach of contract to a Board which refused to listen. Baubie angrily, and as it turned out accurately, predicted, "You'll ask me for an opinion when she takes you to court!"

On January 28, 1897, the Board, in a notably chiseling effort to save money, voted not to pay Coffin her January salary, with Lucien Ellis and a few others dissenting. Miss Coffin sued. She asked for the balance due on her contract and $5,000 damages. She was represented by . . . former judge John J. Speed, Master in Chancery, one-time Corporation Counsel, codifier of the City Charter. The Board remained stubborn in its refusal to pay and was summoned to Circuit Court in April.

From the start, Coffin dominated the trial and charmed the jury. . . . Board members who appeared as witnesses against her . . . were unable to substantiate their allegations. They could prove she was in the Van Dyke School one afternoon instead of in her office, but they were forced to admit she was there on official business. They could prove she was active in the Women's Educational Union, but no one could remember ever ordering her not to be. Circuit Court ruled in her favor, and the Board promptly voted to appeal to the Michigan Supreme court, which refused the appeal, seeing no evidence that Coffin had either violated directions or refused to perform her duties.

Judge Carpenter, of Circuit Court, handed down his decision favoring Coffin on Friday, April 30. Three days later, on Monday,

May 3, 1897, Mathilde Coffin and her "excellent friend," Franklin Ford, were married at the Church of the Transfiguration on Park Avenue in New York. William Livingstone's friendly *Detroit Journal* headlined the event "NEEDS NO SCHOOL!" and announced that the Fords would live in New York.

What happened after in the schools? Most of the new work remained in place. True, Miss McGrath was now able to sell the Board her arithmetic drill book, which epitomized the methods to which Coffin had objected. The political and economic geography researched and promoted by Coffin, with its emphasis on Great Lakes shipping and Detroit resources and industry, slowly sank without a trace. But when the principals petitioned that natural science be kept in the elementary schools, it was. Kindergarten, after a brief cut-back, appeared again. Physical education, art, music, shop, homemaking, and a special school for the deaf were here to stay. After a one year lapse, new schools would be built again. Coffin and Robinson had set in place the notion that the public schools must make room for a full day's schooling for every child. Never again would Detroit teachers be proud to say out loud that they were still using their unchanged lesson plan book left over from college days. Certainly never again would a Detroit newspaper claim that its own pages were too immoral for classroom use.

As the *Free Press* had correctly predicted in December, the Women's Educational Union would show no political clout whatever in the spring elections. Or ever.

Superintendent Robinson, a victim of the controversy, would fail to keep his contract after the Board's annual meeting in July, and retire to sell insurance. Popular and politic young-man-in-a-hurry Wales Martindale would succeed him.[7] Among the new schools built by Martindale, one of the very first would be appropriately named the James Scripps, for the publisher of the *Detroit Evening News*.

Hazen Pingree, who had believed that the new methods were not in the interest of the worker's children, became Governor of Michigan in January, 1897. A school would be named for Pingree in 1902, as there would be, in time, for many of Coffin's one-time women subordinates: the Myra Jones, the Isabel Thirkell, the Ella Fitzgerald, the Fannie Wingert, the Jennie Fleming. No statues with pigeon droppings are dedicated to Mathilde Coffin in any park, nor would any school be named for her—nor, for that matter, for black educator Fannie Richards, who was another genuine pioneer of the era.

In December, 1897, attorney Speed was able to force out of the Board a belated paycheck for Coffin's services from her December release to the date of her wedding—$993.62, plus $21 costs, for a total of $1014.62. [The Board first went to the Michigan Supreme Court, which refused to overturn the Circuit Court's decision in favor of Coffin.]

The woman who wouldn't appear in Detroit's history books left the schools with a progressive statement of how—and why—history should be taught:

> You [the editor of the *Evening News*] believe history should be taught in the schools, but you would have the past taught as something separated from the present. Is it thus separated in fact, or would you simply teach it so? . . . Is it your idea that the best preparation a child can have for living in this world is to know nothing about it? . . . Is the living, growing, moving, wonderful world about us to be excluded from the schools? . . . Are we to have only the past—a dead past torn from the present? Some day, regardless of obstacles, the school will connect with life. . . . [8]

Notes

[For the convenience of the reader, no attempt has been made to reproduce here the full notes that accompanied the original article in *Detroit in Perspective*.]

1. *Detroit Evening News* (14 March 1896): 3.
2. The earliest was the Lancastrian experiment 1818–1824, a system whose aim was to teach up to 1,000 students, with one teacher. Sister Mary Rosalita, educational historian, called it "a system under which education was superficial, and discipline a negative quality. . . . it could not long be upheld simply because it was cheap . . . a scheme in which the memorizing and reciting of lessons glibly was the be-all and end-all, . . . a makeshift for genuine education." *Education in Detroit Prior to 1850* (Michigan Historical Commission, 1928), pp. 187–204. See also Moehlman, *History of the Detroit Public Schools*, (Bloomington, Ill., Public Schools Publishing, 1925), pp. 45–57.

3. Coffin, Mathilde, "The School and the Newspaper, Letter of Mathilde Coffin to the Detroit Evening News, Replying to the Editorial of March 14," March 17, 1896. Excerpts and Miscellania File, BHC.
4. *Sunday News-Tribune*, Nov. 22, 1896.
5. *Detroit Free Press*, Dec. 17, 1896. All local papers carried some of this material, or made reference to it over the next few days.
6. *Detroit Evening News*, Dec. 24, 1896. Ford's own statement of his goals for himself and U. of M. are outlined in *Draft of Action*, Ann Arbor, 1892, (E & M Files, BHC.)
7. In December 23, 1896, the *News* had termed Martindale a "pushing man" who had been criticized for "having a political turn." Times had changed by July!
8. Coffin, Mathilde, Reading Room File, BHC.

5.   The General Strike

Jo Labadie

The capitalists don't like the general strike. Do you know why? Because it is the most effective weapon the workers have thought of. Capitalists don't want to do the hard work themselves, and what are they to do with their capital if their slaves refuse to use it? If it isn't used, there is no profit for the idler. There is no income for the mere owner. Capital deteriorates from want of use. The life of capitalism depends upon the use of capital for usury's sake. Usury is the heart of capitalism, and when this stops the thing is a dead one.

The general strike is not an invasion of anyone's rights or freedom. If you refuse to work for any reason whatever, how is this an invasion of anyone's rights? . . . If one has not the right and freedom to quit work when he wants to then is he slave indeed.

Jo Labadie, "The General Strike," in *Essays by Jo Labadie*, The Labadie Shop, 1911, 38–43, BHC.

The traitorous workers who act as shooters and beaters of strikers and [as] strikebreakers are impotent against a general strike that embraces even a quarter or a third of the workers in fundamental industries. The general strike is direct. You don't need to depend on someone else to do your striking for you. It is an old saying that if you want a thing done, do it yourself. This is a thing you must do for yourself if it is to be done. No politician or agent or middleman comes between you and what you want done. The politician is eliminated from the problem. That is why the politicians, good, bad, and indifferent, are against it.

The ballot isn't a comparison [sic] the general strike in effectiveness. For nearly a century and a half the working men of this country have voted. What have they accomplished by it? During all this time the grafter, the skin brigand, the industrial, commercial, and political pirates have absorbed the land, the machinery, the money and everything else necessary for the production and distribution of the material comforts of life.

And how about the bullet? Why hasn't the killing of man by man during the hundreds and thousands and possibly millions of years settled these questions of men's relations to the rest of their kind if war and violence can do it? Is it time the old ways are discarded and new and less destructive, less violent and invasive ones be tried? . . . There is only one thing that can defeat the general strike. Hunger is a powerful taskmaster. It will drive men back to industrial slavery if their loved ones come within reach of its lash. But the general strike need not last long. It ought to be so general and complete as to stop the wheels of commerce and industry in the wink of an eye. It should be so universal as to paralyze the arm raised against it. It can do it. It will prevent violence if it be widespread enough. It is more effective than guns. It is less noisy and dangerous than powder and dynamite. It is the ultimate manifestation of the worker's self-ownership. . . . [1]

Editor's Note

1. An excellent brief account of Labadie's pampleteering and labor activities, written by his granddaughter, Carlotta Anderson, is to be found in "Jo Labadie, Detroit's Gentle Anarchist," *Michigan History* (June–July 1986): 32–39.

6.   The Sexes in Science and History

Eliza Burt Gamble

> With the progress of civilization and since women as sexual and economic slaves have become dependent upon men for their support, no male biped has been too stupid, too ugly, or too vicious to take to himself a mate and perpetuate his imperfections.
>
> —*Eliza Burt Gamble*

I had reached the conclusion, as early as the year 1882, that the female organism is in no wise inferior to that of the male. For some time, however, I was unable to find any detailed proof that could consistently be employed to substantiate the correctness of this hypothesis.

In the year 1885, with no special object in view other than a desire for information, I began a systematized investigation of the facts which at that time had been established by naturalists relative to the development of mankind from lower orders of life. It was not, however, until the year 1886, after a careful reading of *The Descent of Man*, by Mr. Darwin, that I first became impressed with the belief that the theory of evolution, as enunciated by sci-

Reprinted by permission of the Putnam Publishing Group from *The Sexes in Science and History* by Eliza Burt Gamble. Copyright © 1916 by G. P. Putnam's Sons.

entists, furnishes much evidence going to show that the female among all the orders of life, man included, represents a higher stage of development than the male.

Notwithstanding the superior degree of development, which according to the facts elaborated by scientists, must belong to the female in all the orders of life below mankind, Mr. Darwin would have us believe that so soon as the human species appeared on the earth, the processes which for untold ages had been in operation were reversed, and that through courage and perseverance, or patience, qualities which were the result of extreme selfishness, or which were acquired while in pursuit of animal gratification, man finally became superior to woman. . . .

. . . Although women are still in possession of their natural inheritance, a finer and more complex organism comparatively free from imperfections, and although, as a result of this inheritance, their intuitions are still quicker, their perceptions keener, and their endurance greater, the drain on their physical energies, caused by the abnormal development of the reproductive energies in the opposite sex, has, during the ages of man's dominion over her, been sufficient to preclude the idea of success in competing with men for the prizes of life. Although an era of progress has begun, ages will no doubt be required to eradicate abuses which are the result of constitutional defects, and especially so as the prejudices and feelings of mankind are for the most part in harmony with such abuses. . . .

If we examine the subject of female apparel, at the present time, we shall observe how difficult it is to uproot long-established prejudices which are deeply rooted in sensuality and superstition; and this is true notwithstanding the fact that such prejudices may involve the comfort and even the health of half the people, and seriously affect the welfare of unborn generations. . . .

Although the female of the human species, like the female among the lower orders of life, is capable of appreciating fine colouring, and to a considerable extent, the beautiful in form, the style of dress adopted by women is not an expression of their natural ideas of taste and harmony. On the contrary, it is to Sexual Selection that we must look for an explanation of the incongruities and absurdities presented by the so-called female fashions of the past and present. The processes of Sexual Selection, which, so long as the female was the controlling agency in courtship, worked on the male, have in these later ages been reversed.

For the reason that the female of the human species has so long been under subjection to the male, the styles of dress and adornment which have been adopted, and which are still in vogue, are largely the result of masculine taste. Woman's business in life has been to marry, or at least it has been necessary for her, in order to gain her support, to win the favour of the opposite sex. She must, therefore, by her charms, captivate the male.

. . . It is not singular that in the struggle for life to which they [women] have been subjected they should have adopted the styles of dress which would be likely to secure to them the greatest degree of success. When we remember that the present ideas of becomingness or propriety in woman's apparel are the result of ages of sensuality or servitude, it is not remarkable that they are difficult to uproot, and especially so as many of the most pernicious and health-destroying styles involve questions of female decorum as understood by a sensualized age. . . .

Ever since the dominion of man over woman began, a strict censorship over her dress has been maintained. Although in very recent times women are beginning to exercise a slight degree of independence in the matter of clothes, still, because of existing prejudices and customs they have not yet been able to adopt a style of dress which admits of the free and unrestricted use of the body and limbs. It is believed that woman, the natural tempter of man, if left to her own sinful devices, would again as of old attempt to destroy that inherent purity of heart and cleanliness of life which characterizes the male constitution. Woman's ankles and throat seem to be the most formidable foes against which innocent man has to contend, so the concealment of these offending members is deemed absolutely necessary for his protection and safety. . . .

When we consider that apparel is but one, and a minor one, of the strictures under which women have laboured during the latter era of human existence and when we consider all the ignoble and degrading uses to which womanhood has been subjected, the wonder is not that women have failed in the past to distinguish themselves in the various fields of intellectual labour in

251

which men have achieved a limited degree of success, but that they have had sufficient energy and courage left to enable them even to attempt anything so far outside the boundary of their prescribed "sphere." . . . [1]

Editor's Note

1. Very little is known about the personal life of Gamble. In spite of the bitterness attributed to her by the press, there are no recorded objections from Mr. Gamble to his wife's outspoken feminism. John Gamble was a real estate developer with considerable property at Orchard Lake. The couple had two children. In a 1912 letter to Jo Labadie, in which she states that she has "always thought of herself as a socialist," she complains of the colds and bronchial trouble she suffered at Orchard Lake, where Mr. Gamble's work took them in the summers. It all sounds amazingly docile for a woman whose historical scholarship has set the tone for much later research. Mary Ritter Beard, in 1945, praised her work in early history. Beard also hunted in vain for Detroit traces of Gamble's work for the Women's Archives on which she was working.

7.　Progressivism Skips Detroit Blacks

Forrester Washington

While the Progressive reformers came more and more to identify good government with the curtailment of ethnic variation, one group, as usual, suffered more than others. Looking back on this period in 1920, sociologist Forrester Washington called it a time of "recrudescence" and loss of power. He was describing the same period that a later historian, Rayford Logan, would term nationally the "nadir" of hopes raised during the Reconstruction period.

Period of Political, Social, and Economic Recrudescence—1895 to 1915

A. Loss of Occupational Status

Beginning with 1895, Negroes gradually lost their hold on the good paying positions in the hotels. Some hotels, even some of the larger establishments, have retained Negro waiters down until today. But the majority of the larger ones, as well as many of the smaller ones, supplanted their Negro employees with white foreigners, chiefly Greeks, in the late 90's.

Forrester Washington, "History," in *The Negro in Detroit: A Survey of the Conditions of a Negro Group in a Northern Industrial Center during the War Prosperity Period* (Detroit: Associated Charities, 1920).

About the same time, there began a gradual replacing of Negro barbers with white barbers in the better shops.

In other occupations, also, Negroes began to lose the monopoly of employment which they had possessed for years. There was a notable decrease in the number of Negro coachmen, butlers, gardeners, etc.

The chief reason given for these changes was the craze at that time on the part of the fashionable classes to copy the styles of Europe. Hence, the supplanting of Negro coachman with English coachman; Negro hotel cooks with French cooks, etc. It is also said that the change in the class of personal service workers was due to the large immigration from Europe at that time which enabled employers to obtain highly trained servants at a lower wage than they had been paying Negroes.

One result of this loss of status in the personal services field was the attempt of Negroes to get a footing in the manufacturing and mechanical field. In 1897, a committee of Negroes, among whom were Albert Johnson, William Ernst, and Robert Williams, was formed for the express purpose of obtaining jobs in industry for Negroes who were losing out in hotels and domestic service.

This committee took as its premise the fact that the Negro constituted one-fifteenth of the population, and that, therefore, one-fifteenth of the employees in any establishment having at least fifteen workers, should be Negroes. The committee was not successful in creating a large number of openings for the Negro but it was responsible for the introduction of Negro conductors and motormen on the street railways[1] and for the introduction of a few Negro laborers into one of the stove companies.

The occupational status of the Negro continued to retrogress down to the year 1915.

B. Loss of Political Power

The change from the convention system of nominating candidates to the primary system of nominating candidates which occurred about 1895, acted as a blight on the Negro politically. Up until that year, Negroes had held many important municipal, county and state appointive and elective position. One Negro had been elected to the City Council.[2] Four Negroes had been elected to the State Legislature. One Negro had been elected Circuit Court Commissioner. But since the year 1894, when William Ferguson was re-elected Estimator of the City of Detroit, no Negro had been elected to public office.

C. Loss of Social Privilege

Beginning with 1890, there developed an increasing rift in the cordial relations which had existed in the white and colored races in Detroit. Evidence of this was the "Ferguson suit against Geiss" [sic; Geis] a prominent restaurateur, for discrimination in a public restaurant. Ferguson's suit against Geiss was only the beginning of similar acts of discrimination in theatres and restaurants. Few of the suits after the Ferguson-Geiss case ended as satisfactorily as did that case for the colored people. In many cases judgment was awarded to the Negro when he had been refused admission or set aside in public places but the judgment was usually from one to six cents, so that the offending parties were encouraged to repeat their acts of separation.

Among the reasons given for this development of racial antipathy was the increasing number of Negroes in the state and, secondly, an undesirable migration of race-track followers that began before 1890.

This undesirable migration began shortly after 1885, when race-tracks were established at the 8-mi. Road and Grosse Point. Most of the track followers were undesirable elements of both races from the South. Both of these elements went into the quiet restaurants and amusement places of Detroit and conducted themselves in such a boisterous manner that their patronage became very undesirable. However, the colored "sports" were the chiefest sufferers, as they were the only ones discriminated against.

In 1895, the betting feature of horse-racing was eliminated all over the United States. Consequently, the race-tracks were abolished in Detroit but almost simultaneously other tracks were established at Windsor, Ontario, on Canadian soil, just across the river from Detroit. The proximity of Windsor attracted the touts, gamblers, book-makers and the undesirable followers of the race-track from all over the country, so that down until the present day Detroit has had to suffer from the behavior of this race-horse class.

Soon after the abolition of race-track betting the famous "Reform Wave" struck Chicago and eliminated at least a large part of the colored "red light" district. A great many proprietors of disorderly resorts in that city and their hangers-on, came to Detroit because it had the reputation of being a "wide open town".

Whatever the reasons for the declining of the old friendly relationship between the white and colored people of Detroit, the fact remains that policies of separation have grown gradually more common since 1895.[3]

Editor's Notes

1. This was a battle that had to be fought all over again by the NAACP and others when it was discovered in 1940–41 that blacks were systematically being screened from employment as conductors, motormen, or bus drivers for the Detroit Streets and Railways Commission (DSR). The usual device was an apparent failure of preliminary health examinations; it was widely reported that at least one doctor would insist that any black applicant coming before him had failed the Wasserman test.

2. The position was actually one with the Board of Estimates, comparable in power but not the same as that of alderman. William Patrick was the first black elected to the Detroit Common Council.

3. It is likely that some of Washington's information came to him from older Detroiters during the years of 1917–18, when he served as executive secretary of the fledgling Detroit Urban League. It is probable that families such as the Coles, the Lamberts, the Johnsons, the Swans, and the Pelhams instructed the newcomer in area history. However, Washington brought to the local history of his people a young man's anger.

Part VIII

July, 1912: Business
Dominates Reform

July, 1912: Business Dominates Reform

After the exit of Pingree from local and state politics, it was downhill all the way for Detroit as far as the Progressives went. Some of the uglier aspects of petty election fraud reasserted themselves but, more importantly, the aims of the reform movement underwent a distortion.

As the automobile became an industrial force to be reckoned with, so did the former makers of wagon wheels, or marine engines, or bicycles, who were now making cars. Their drive toward Americanism came at the very moment when whole new groups of foreigners were arriving, mostly from southeastern Europe. Long-defined political neighborhoods and enclaves of the foreign-born received diminished respect, as people were encouraged to identify them with corruption, saloons, vote-buying, and mysterious radicalism.

The city hoped for responsible and efficient government, the kind that Mayor Pingree had tried for and almost achieved. It was willing to pay by devaluing its ethnicity.

There were relatively few blacks in Detroit until the very end of this period; they were not a particular target of the reformers of 1912. However, their rapid increase during the labor shortages of World War I made the group more visible by 1918, when the new city charter was adopted. By then it was clear that the reformers looked forward to a millennium of good government, preferably controlled by white Anglo-Saxons. All in all, to gain a superficially clean city government, the first steps were taken in an effort to homogenize the people.

All Detroit was stunned by the newspaper headlines of July 26 and 27, 1912. Not since Mayor Hazen Pingree's school board arrests almost twenty years earlier had there been such a demonstration that politics was, indeed, a dirty business. In all, twenty-six of the city's thirty-six aldermen were arrested for allegedly taking bribes. Many would, in fact, shortly be released, and the prosecution's case would finally revolve around Tom Glinnan, an alderman—comparable to a member of today's city council— from the city's newest ward, the eighteenth, in southwest Detroit. That Glinnan would eventually escape all charges would be regarded as either a triumph of civil liberties or proof that a new system of urban government was needed, depending on point of view.

The new system did indeed come to pass with the charter of 1918, which replaced the board of aldermen, elected by wards, with a nine-member council elected at large, a system that survives today.

I have chosen two interesting, differing accounts of the incident. One version comes from the memoirs of elder statesman John C. Lodge, who served many years as alderman, councilman, and mayor. Lodge's memoirs, *I Remember Detroit*, were dictated by him in 1948 and published by Wayne University Press the following year. The other account is by Jack Elenbaas, urban and political historian of the Progressive period. His analysis in *Michigan History* (Winter, 1970) shows an awareness of the civil liberties issue that is generally lacking from the contemporary accounts.

1. I Enter Politics

John C. Lodge, with Milo M. Quaife

Henry M. Leland was an able engineer who at the beginning of the century designed the Cadillac automobile. He rose to prominence as President of the Company and in later years created the Lincoln automobile. For practically a third of a century he was one of Detroit's foremost industrial and civic leaders. He was an earnest advocate of good government, who believed the city was "going to the demnition bowwows."

Pliny W. Marsh was a young lawyer who had served as attorney for the Prohibition party of Michigan . . . in 1909 Mr. Leland brought him to Detroit and with the cooperation of Divie B. Duffield and a few others they created a little organization with a name which nearly killed it—the Detroit Civic Uplift League.

John C. Lodge, with Milo M. Quaife, "I Enter Politics," in *I Remember Detroit* (Detroit: Wayne University Press, 1949), 84–88.

Imagine, if you can, trying to accomplish anything in politics with a name like that. By the man in the street it was dubbed the "Goo-goo League." When Mr. Leland came to seem me about the organization I told him that the first thing they should do was change its name. "It is rather difficult to uplift people," I said. "Just call it the Detroit Citizen's League." This change was made, and the name, Detroit Citizen's League, was adopted. . . . a couple of years passed before it was able to exert any material influence upon the city government, which continued to be dominated by the Wets.

Then came the blowout of 1912. Early in the spring a resolution was introduced to the Board of Aldermen requesting the President of the Board to appoint a committee to go to Pittsburgh and interview the officials of the Pennsylvania Railroad on the possibility of extending its services to Detroit. [Lodge, Mayor Thompson, and a number of others went to Pittsburgh without effect.] . . .

It was just at the beginning of the era automobile men like to refer to as "the game", and our output of automobiles was rapidly becoming tremendous. We who were on the ground knew what was happening to our city, but the officials of the Pennsylvania Railroad at Pittsburgh could not see it. . . .

Although I was a member of the Board of Aldermen, I had no knowledge of the wholesale bribery that was going on until I read the exposure of it printed in the late afternoon edition of the *News* on July 26, 1912. That was a tremendous newspaper scoop. About two weeks prior to this, Homer Warren [Detroit postmaster, who was also serving as president of the board of commerce] telephoned me one morning to ask if I could come to his office, as he wanted me to meet a couple of gentlemen who were coming in at eleven o'clock.

So I went over to the post office, where Mr. Warren introduced me to Walter Brennan, a real estate man from the Wabash Railroad. With him was Rufus Lathrop, who was the local attorney for the Wabash. They proceeded to say that they wished to have Seventh Street closed from Fort to West Jefferson (then called River Road), and Mr. Warren asked me what I thought of the project.

I replied that I had gone to Pittsburgh two or three weeks before that to offer every possible aid to the Pennsylvania Road if it would come into Detroit, and that I did not see how I could consistently oppose the Wabash proposition, a road that was already here. I then said to Mr. Brennan that I hoped nothing would happen between then and the time the Aldermen acted to make me change my mind; any boodling on this, and I would be off the reservation.

I said this because I had some suspicion concerning the action of certain Aldermen in the past. But the proposal seemed to be entirely proper, and it received the vote of the entire Board with the exception of one Alderman from the ward which contained the local opposition to the measure. It subsequently appeared that Andrew H. Green, Manager of the Solvay Company, and a group of associates had raised the sum of $10,000 with which to employ the Burns Detective Agency of New York in an attempt to smoke out the whole bunch of saloon grafters, and that Brennan, who was in fact Walter Burns [of the Burns Detective Agency, an early security company], had been sent to Detroit to trap them.

This brings me to the point of narrating the handiwork of Edward R. Schreiter. At that time an Alderman could draft an ordinance for submission to the Board. Now this has to be done by the Corporation Counsel, or at least must be approved by him. Schreiter, who was a clever fixer, had promoted an ordinance creating the office of Secretary of the Board of Aldermen, to be filled, of course, by himself. Thereafter he had about half of the Aldermen eating out of his hand. He provided them with free theater tickets, tickets to the race track over in Windsor, and I don't know what else, until the matter of the Seventh Street closing came up.

Although I knew nothing of the bribery in this connection, the existence of a smelly situation generally was publicly suspected, and in fact all through the arraignment and trial that followed, the *Journal* kept saying: "You haven't attacked the wart on the face of city politics—Ed Schreiter." So I concluded it was time to get rid of him, and although Bert Allen, another Alderman whose name wasn't in the list of bribe-takers, objected that I was prejudging the case, we had more than a quorum, and my ordinance to abolish the office of Secretary to the Board was passed by unanimous vote, which disposed of Mr. Schreiter.

Seeing that he was through, I supposed he figured that he had better play the rat, and he went to Brennan with a printed list of the Board of Aldermen which I still have, on which he had inserted the sums—ranging from $1,000 downward—which each of the bribe takers would accept, and one by one they trooped into Brennan's office in the Ford Building, where they were paid the sums Schreiter had indicated. Highest on the list was Thomas E. Glinnan, bellwether of the flock, who received $1,000. Most of the others were given sums ranging from $100 to $300. Brennan had installed a dictaphone in his office to record the transactions and when the men came out policemen waiting in the corridor arrested them and took them over to headquarters.

This was the story the *News* published that afternoon of July 26. The scandal was a stench in the nostrils of the whole city, but it had the incidental benefit of ridding us of Schreiter, who had provided the brains for the dishonest Aldermen who stupidly followed his leadership. Bad as their conduct was, however, there was some extenuation for it. The enactment of the ordinance for the closing of the street-end was wholly proper. Their fault lay in the acceptance of pay as a reward for their votes. Yet, although I have never indulged in it, the acceptance of theater passes and other favors by public officials is commonplace. Of course, the only motive for such gifts is the desire to influence the action of the recipients.

Thomas E. Glinnan, who was an Alderman from the Eighteenth Ward, in which Green's business was located, was the only one of the bribe-takers who was ever brought to trial, and he was acquitted. Although he admitted that he had received the money, his attorney, James MacNamara, argued successfully that it had been forced upon him by Brennan without his consent. He was the big boss, and following his acquittal there seemed to be no point in prosecuting the other Aldermen. The Eighteenth Ward extended westward from about Military Avenue to the City Limits. It was an industrial section inhabited largely by railroad and working men.

Glinnan had been elected Alderman of the Eighteenth Ward twice. Subsequently the city created three new wards—increasing the number from eighteen to twenty-one—by making the Nineteenth and Twenty-first wards out of the Seventeenth, and taking the southwesterly part of the Eighteenth Ward to make the Twentieth. After the debacle of 1912, Glinnan was re-elected to the Board of Aldermen three times, once from the Eighteenth and twice from the Twentieth Ward. He was a strong-minded man, and though he had but little or no formal education, he had a great deal of native force and ability. Evidently he was the kind of representative the people down there wanted. In 1918 he filed his petition for the new City Council, but in the election he ran number 18, the lowest in the list of nominees.

2. The Excesses of Reform: The Day the Detroit Mayor Arrested the City Council

Jack D. Elenbaas

As I have suggested in the introduction to this section, Elenbaas sees different villains in his look at urban politics.

The 1912 Detroit city council scandal and trial of Alderman Tom Glinnan revealed the dark side of that zealous reformer who worked out his strategy during the Progressive Era. Ambitious politicians on the outside looking in, brutally competitive newspapers fighting for survival, plus influential businessmen with a desire for more political influence over city hall, all came together in that summer in 1912 to create one of the most sensational scandals in the history of American municipal government, and all of it was done in the name of reform. . . .

[Long before the trial] . . . all of the Detroit papers agreed that the case against Tom Glinnan was especially airtight. The prosecutor's office had the marked money, it had witnesses, it had a

Jack D. Elenbaas, "The Excesses of Reform: The Day the Detroit Mayor Arrested the City Council," *Michigan History* 54, no. 1 (Winter 1970): 1–18.

confession, and it had recordings of the conversation that had taken place between Glinnan and Detective Brennan at the time the bribe was made. The Burns Agency prided itself on being scientific, which included the latest in wire tapping devices. Detective Brennan declared: "Mayor Thompson, I want to congratulate you. It is refreshing to come to a city like Detroit and find a man big enough and willing to go out and clean up grafters not for the sake of putting them in prison but for the good of the municipality. . . . "

The plight of the arrested aldermen, however, continued to remain uncertain long after the 1912 mayoral election was over. It was not until the spring of 1915, over two and a half years later, that their fate was finally decided.

After two months of examination, during which time seven of the seventeen aldermen arrested August 9 were released, the court bound over for trial the remaining ten. The Prosecuting Attorney, Hugh Shepherd, then announced that he would try the case of Thomas Glinnan first. He believed that the case against the alderman was a strong one and that the prosecution could with certainty count on a conviction.

Glinnan's defense council was headed by James A. MacNamara, a successful Detroit attorney. . . . For the next nineteen months Shepherd and MacNamara engaged in a series of legal maneuvers that included two requests for changes of venue and the challenging of hundreds of prospective jurors. . . .

The selection of a jury proved to be a never-ending task, as the defense successfully challenged whole lists of names of prospective jurors. In his challenges MacNamara charged that the jury commissioners, whose job it was to submit the list of names for jury duty, had been quite selective in carrying out their task; so selective, in fact, argued the defense, as to insure the conviction of Tom Glinnan. On the stand Pontius Wood, one of the jury commissioners, admitted that no names were selected from the defendant's ward. He also testified that the commissioners had agreed to exclude from the list politicians, saloonkeepers, and Negroes. Judge Phelan asked: "Do you mean that you would not put the name of a good law-abiding citizen upon the jury list because his color happened to be different from yours? Why if we allowed that it would be easy to take the next step and bar citizens on account of their nationality or religion."

"Well, we barred saloonkeepers," replied Wood.

It was also revealed by the defense in the examination of the jury commissioners that the prestigious Detroit Board of Commerce had secretly submitted to the commissioners a list of names of men that it would like to see serve on the Glinnan jury. With this kind of evidence and this kind of aggressive defense, Tom Glinnan's attorneys were able to challenge 750 names and to delay the start of the trial nineteen months.

Finally on July 6, 1914, the last juror was seated, and Alderman Glinnan was brought to trial. The prosecution's case rested on its witnesses which included Detectives Brennan and Burns, Andrew H. Green, Jr., and the two arresting officers. The prosecution also claimed that it had the roll of marked bills taken from Glinnan at the time of the arrest and the recordings of the conversation that took place between Glinnan and Brennan at the time the bribe was received. The final piece of evidence that filled out the prosecution's case was the alleged statement made by Glinnan after his arrest.

The defense, seemingly faced with an impossible task, attempted to develop three lines of argument in the hope of freeing the alderman. The first approach of the defense was to destroy the credibility of the prosecution's witnesses. A second approach was to establish reasons why some men wanted Glinnan out of the way. And finally, a third line of argument used was to disprove the charge that a conspiracy had ever existed between the alderman and the detective who posed as a Wabash Railroad official. If it could be proved that at no time before the vote on the petition did Glinnan agree to accept money from Brennan, then of course, the prosecution did not have a case.

Two of the prosecution's major witnesses, Detectives Burns and Brennan, received very rough handling by Defense Attorney MacNamara. In the cross-examinations the defense established the fact that the detectives had been invited by Mayor Thompson and had been financed by Andrew H. Green to "test the integrity" of certain aldermen believed to be corruptible. The defense charged that in effect the Burns Agency came to Detroit to encourage aldermen to commit a crime which, MacNamara argued, was a crime in itself.

The past record of the Burns Agency was gone over thoroughly by the defense, and the two detectives were forced to admit that their organization had gotten into trouble in various cities such as Omaha, Atlanta, and New York. Some of the detectives employed by Burns Agency, it was revealed, were still under indictment for perjury in some of the cities mentioned. The record also showed that William J. Burns, the head of the agency, had been removed as an officer of the Association of Police Chiefs for "unprofessional conduct." MacNamara described Burns as an "assassin of character deadlier than a cobra" who engaged in reckless and lawless methods. On a number of occasions the defense managed to get the two detectives to contradict one another. . . . The defense charged that these men were simply hired witnesses brought to Detroit to do a job using any means necessary and that they had used illegal means in the past and were using them again. In their treatment of the defendant, argued the defense, they had used the whole gambit including bribery, perjury, and the third degree.

Another star witness of the prosecution was Andrew Green. He also received a severe grilling at the hands of the defense. Mr. Green was a prominent Detroit businessman with a record of civic involvement. He had provided the money to finance the investigation as well as the bribes, and he had been present in the room where Glinnan was alleged to have made the confession. During the cross-examination Green estimated that the whole affair had cost him around ten thousand dollars, more or less. . . . Green did admit that he had promised Glinnan a job in his company, the Solvay Process Company, if the alderman would confess. . . .

Other witnesses for the prosecution included the county detectives, the stenographer, and the dictograph operators. All claimed to have been in the room where Glinnan had produced the money and had made the alleged confession. In the cross-examination the defense established that Detective Burns had shouted at Glinnan and had threatened him. They also testified that Burns had ordered Glinnan to remove the money from his left-hand coat pocket immediately after his arrest. The question then posed by the defense was, how did Mr. Burns know which pocket the money was in, unless he had schemed with his cohort Brennan to have it planted there?

As for the recordings of the conversation between Glinnan and the bribe-offering Detective Brennan, the defense brought in as expert Fred Ireland, the chief stenographer for the United States Congress, who testified that the dictograph machine could not have operated effectively under the conditions present in that office at the time of the arrest. The witnesses also disagreed as to whether or not Glinnan had confessed, and as a result the court refused to allow any statement made by Glinnan at the time of the arrest to be used as evidence, because it obviously had been obtained by threats and because its contents could not be substantiated. When Glinnan's defense counsel had finished with the prosecutor's witnesses, not one left the stand with his credibility intact.

A second line of argument developed with great care by the defense counsel was the establishment of motives for the arrest of Alderman Glinnan. In the testimony of the two detectives, Burns and Brennan, it was revealed that they had received large sums of money from both Green and from the county treasurer. The defense concluded that the detectives had been hired to "get Glinnan" and that the amount of money they received depended on how successful they were.

As far as the motives of Andrew Green were concerned the defense promised that: "We shall show you . . . it was a scheme to assassinate the character of a fellow citizen by hired crooks masquerading as private detectives . . . to make a political holiday for Andrew Green and to make a pay-day for the Burns Detective Agency."

Green's role in this whole affair was shrouded in mystery. He had a reputation for contributing money to various causes, and on one occasion he had posted bail for two labor organizers who had been arrested in connection with an alleged dynamiting conspiracy. More recently he had contributed money and effort in the fight to get the Thompson-Hally [street railway] ordinance passed. After its defeat, there was talk about Green becoming the Democratic candidate for mayor in the upcoming local election. Glinnan and Green had recently locked horns over the Thompson-Hally proposal, and it was quite evident that a certain amount of antagonism and political rivalry had built up between the two men.

On the stand Green testified that after the defeat of the Thompson proposal, he had met with the mayor to discuss why it was so difficult to get necessary reforms passed. The mayor explained, said Green, that too many aldermen in the city council had to be paid before anything was done. Green then suggested to the mayor that they devise a plan that would expose the bribe-takers. In a letter to Thompson dated February 14, 1912, Green wrote: "I wish to say that I will undertake whatever you wish me to do in regard to this matter." By that time Thompson had already conferred with Burns, the price had been set, and now Green had agreed to foot the bill.

Green admitted that he had decided to run for mayor but then withdrew his name on July 24, 1912, which was just two days before the first arrests were made. He explained that his decision to withdraw was caused by his employer's refusal to continue his salary during his term as mayor. The defense offered another explanation, claiming that Green, who at first thought that his financial backing of the investigation of the aldermen would help him to win votes, suddenly realized that the detectives had no evidence against the aldermen, but were going to frame them. Green then . . . decided to drop out of the mayor's race before the whole thing blew up in his face.

The motives of Mayor Thompson in this case were also explored by the defense although the ex-mayor never took the stand. . . . Brennan testified that Thompson had indicated to him that, "if you reach Glinnan you reach them all." The conclusion drawn by the defense was that Thompson had hoped to salvage his sagging political career by posing as a "graft-hunting" mayor and that he had called in private detectives to trap in any way they could his opponents in the city council, especially the "Boss of the Common Council" Tom Glinnan.

All of the prosecution's witnesses had reason to want Alderman Glinnan out of the way, reasoned the defense. For the Burns Agency it was simply money as it had been at other places across the country where they had operated. For Andrew Green it was a combination of a desire for reform, plus public recognition and possible political opportunity. And for Mayor Thompson it was a chance to escape political defeat and at the same time bring down upon his political tormentor, Tom Glinnan, the righteous wrath of vengeance in the disguise of reform.

After having raised serious doubts concerning the credibility of the prosecution's witnesses and after having established certain underlying causes for Glinnan's arrest, the defense now moved to discredit the charge that a conspiracy had existed between Detective Brennan and the defendant before the final vote on the Wabash petition had been taken. The key to the prosecution's and the defense's case on this point was the testimony of Detective Brennan. . . .

Brennan arrived in Detroit February 23, 1912, and a few days later he met with Van Dyke and Thompson in Van Dyke's office. At this meeting Brennan received instructions to "test the integrity" of certain aldermen mentioned by Van Dyke and by the mayor. Among those mentioned was Tom Glinnan. . . .

Brennan's testimony further showed that for the next two months he had nosed about the saloons and hotels that were located around city hall, hoping to uncover information about the illegal activities of those aldermen mentioned by Mayor Thompson. . . . Finally they [Brennan, Burns, Thompson, Green, and Van Dyke] hit upon the idea of submitting a bogus petition to the city council and then seeing which aldermen would sell their votes. The Wabash Railroad Company was contacted and it consented to allow the name of the company to be used on the petition, and on May 7, Glinnan as a member of the Street Opening Committee introduced it to the council. The first vote on the petition came July 9, and all the councilmen except one voted in favor of it. . . . On July 11, two days after Glinnan had recorded a vote in favor of the petition, the defense pointed out, Brennan stated that he met with Glinnan at the phony Wabash office and offered him $750 for his vote. Glinnan testified at this point that Brennan did not offer him any money but had invited him to the Wabash office to discuss a possible position on the railroad. Here the case rested on the word of Brennan or Glinnan, and the jury had to decide which to believe.

A few days after the July 11 meeting between Glinnan and Brennan, a final vote on the Wabash petition was taken and it passed. On July 24 Brennan met Alderman Glinnan on the street and invited him to drop by his office on the 26th and pick up his money. Glinnan testified on the stand that Brennan had said nothing about money but instead had suggested that he come to his office on the 26th with letters of recommendation for the job they had discussed earlier. . . . Glinnan's story was that . . . he had turned over the letters of recommendation to Brennan, and then he was ushered out the door into the hands of the waiting detectives who immediately placed him under arrest. Following his arrest he was hurried into an adjoining office where Detective Burns demanded that the harried alderman turn over the roll of money he had in his coat pocket. Then Glinnan was subjected to a three hour ordeal in which Burns threatened, Green pleaded, and the assistant prosecutor waited for a confession which Glinnan insisted he never made.

The defense concluded its case by maintaining that the whole incident was a frame-up to get Glinnan. Glinnan had never at any time, argued the defense, agreed to accept money nor in fact did he take any money. Instead Burns and Brennan, after having failed to come up with any proof of wrongdoing on the part of the alderman, had gone to Thompson and Green and had concocted this desperate scheme as a last resort. Glinnan, stated the defense, had favored the railroad's petition before his discussion with Brennan on July 11 when the detective alleged he had offered Glinnan the money. As a matter of record, Glinnan had supported the petition on the first vote taken on July 9. The defense also maintained that on the day of the arrest, the alderman was lured to the Wabash office with the promise of a job and then had marked money planted in his outside coat pocket. After the plant was made, . . . the hapless Glinnan was then subjected to the third degree for three hours in a futile attempt to get a confession out of him. It all boiled down to one fact, declared the defense, and that is do you take the word of Brennan, a "hired witness," or the word of Tom Glinnan, a "dedicated public servant?"

The jury deliberated forty-five minutes and returned a verdict of not guilty. The courtroom went wild. The following spring the Wayne County prosecutor's office asked that charges be dropped on the remaining nine aldermen still waiting to be tried. . . . The court agreed and the cases of the other nine aldermen were dropped.

It has been stated that the arrest of the ten aldermen and the trial of Thomas Glinnan helped move Detroit closer to the new charter she finally received in 1918. The new city charter abolished the board of aldermen and the partisan system of ward representation and in its place established a nonpartisan, highly centralized system of local government designed to be more efficient and less corrupt. Although no convictions had been obtained, the board of aldermen had been disgraced, and now reform organizations such as the Detroit Citizen's League and the Board of Commerce used this scandal to good advantage in bringing about the changes in Detroit's government that would give these groups more control than they had had under the old ward system. This was all done, of course in the name of reform. The partisan ward system of government which had based its strength on an intricate relationship between aldermen, ward bosses, and organized blocs of voters was done away with in the new 1918 charter. In its place a more centralized nine-man council elected at large was established which would be out of the hands of the ward bosses and in many cases out of touch with the needs of the wards. City council elections would now be susceptible to well-financed campaigns in which the newspapers and organized civic groups would have a much greater degree of influence.[1]

Editor's Note

1. In the preparation of this article, Elenbaas made extensive use of Wayne County Court records and the Scallen Papers, BHC, as well as the newspapers of the time. Other scholars working within this period during the last few years have made use of the insights shown here.

Part IX

Agents of Change: The Automobile and World War I

Agents of Change: The Automobile and World War I

Detroit's trademark, the automobile, arrived well before 1900. Manufacturers of products that characterized Detroit industry during the second half of the nineteenth century—marine motors and steam engines, bicycles, carriages, wagons, and farm implements—were led naturally to attempts at production of the automobile, the newest excitement spreading through the business world.

Throughout the early 1900s, several imaginative automotive inventors were eliminated by the competition. Automotive history is a whole separate field for the historian. I will only comment that the scope of those early deletions, long before the "Big Three," can be seen in the panorama of unfamiliar car names. Just a few of those that no longer exist are: the Maxwell, the Detroit Electric, the Dort, the King, the Huber, the Herreshoff, the Sommer, the Aerocar, the Welch, the Peerless, the Leland, Reo, and Durant. Other names, such as Packard and Olds, were absorbed into new management and financing structures, and there is, of course, an Oldsmobile today. Just one early inventor, the first Henry Ford, would head the greatest individually owned auto plant of them all.

The world war brought no cessation in automobile manufacturing; in addition there were government contracts for armaments and for a time even airplanes.

As industry grew, so did the responsibilities its leaders took on. There came to be a unity of stance. When the President of the "Good Citizens League," a Negro organization, wrote angrily to the chamber of commerce, "when it comes to the Negro you have just one opinion"; he was speaking only a part of the truth. More and more industrialists shared one opinion about not only the Negro, but a great many matters—the Industrial Workers of the World (IWW), the open shop, "Americanism" programs for factories and schools . . .

While World War I speeded up industrial development and helped to channel its direction into automotive and auto-related areas, it did not fundamentally change the direction toward Americanism in which the city's leadership had been moving since 1912.

The businessmen reformers of 1912 brought into the war years their notion of the ideal worker for the new factories. If he (and it was usually "he") were not born an American he would be taught to become a good imitation of one. Thrift and temperance were important, too. Liquor went with political corruption, even rebellious anarchism. (After the Russian Revolution in October, 1917, "Bolshevism" came to be the new term used to disparage those "outside agitators" who carried on the struggles of labor.)

Employers pointed out, with reason, that intemperance, which they often associated with foreigners, could lead to factory accidents. Yet a careful reading of state labor inspectors' reports, with their urgings to cover a wheel, repair electrical equipment, or install guards on punch presses, does make one wonder what priority was really given to accident prevention.

A fear of being thought German or pro-German pervaded the ordinary people of the city. Carl Schmidt, leather tanner, head of the house of Traugott Schmidt, was besieged by questions about why he continued his business trips to Germany until America entered the war. He defended himself by endowing an entire field hospital unit in France for Harper Hospital. Schmidt's choice of a humanitarian cause could have been no coincidence. He was, after all, a Socialist and a pacifist as well. He continued to attend meetings in aid of the Socialist presidential candidate Eugene Debs, and it was during this period that he bought a retirement home for his old friend Jo Labadie. It was a time when lesser Schmidts changed their names to Smith. There was little *gemütlichkeit* among Detroit's very large German-American community as they dutifully bought Liberty bonds.[1]

Twenty-five thousand blacks came to Detroit to find work. They slept on the floor of the railroad station and, till rousted by the police, in parks. They stretched five to a bed in the rooming houses of the east side. Luckiest of all were those met by friends or relatives. They might be just as crowded, of course, but the fear of a strange town, with strange customs, would be less.

The Urban League, to its everlasting credit, tried to meet the need. It was considerably misunderstood at times, by whites and blacks alike. The early Urban League was a benevolent creation of industrialists and social leaders, mainly white. They hired a young man fresh from Harvard as executive-secretary, then questioned his phone bills and the cost of office supplies. Despite this lack of trust, Forrester Washington went on with the job. He instituted a questionnaire for employers in an effort to find factory openings for blacks. Instead, he found any number of managers who felt they should be thanked for hiring a "colored night man" or a janitor among a work force of several hundred. The future dean of the Atlanta University School of Social Work got his basic training in heartbreak and disappointment in wartime Detroit.

Washington left for a federal post in 1918 and was replaced by John Dancy. Dancy continued Washington's efforts to get the newcomers to conform to urban habits. Women were told not to appear in public wearing housedresses and dustcaps or bandanas, men not to gather in large groups talking loudly at street corners. All were urged to cultivate the white man's definition of good manners to gain his respect. These warnings naturally caused annoyance among some local blacks.[2]

For a first look at the changes brought about during this period of concentrated industry before and during the first world war, we return to the river and use it as a measure for what was happening. This time we look at a particular spot on the Detroit River, Sam Zug's old island, sold by him long ago, which industry was distorting beyond recognition.[3]

By 1914 people were coming to Detroit from all over the country. One reason was Henry Ford's widely advertised Five Dollar Day. A news account from the *Detroit Journal* indicates that the start of the Five Dollar Day was not Ford's greatest moment.

Later workers would learn that for a variety of reasons the five dollar day often did not amount to five dollars. Also, strings attached to the money repelled many workers not used to personal intrusion in their lives.[4]

Then in "Detroit—A City Awake," we take a first look at what the influx of workers was already doing to the shape of the city as early as 1911. The need of housing for workers' families was already acute. Yet Myron Adams, writing for *Survey*, found there were still green trees, fresh air, and open space in much of the city. Adams also saw factories creating a ring of blight at the city's edge, and a sad lack of planning to prevent further troubles.[5]

There were crosscurrents, of course, amid the general conformity demanded by industry. Businessmen began to welcome some women workers during World War I, but with a startling lack of response to their needs. In a report of the state labor inspectors, Mary Girardin and her colleagues recorded again and again, "Immediately provide a separate lavatory for your women workers," or "Readjust the working hours of your female employees to conform to state law," as well as serious safety violations.

Editor's Notes

1. Carl Schmidt's war years are described in a scrapbook of clippings and miscellany (Schmidt Collection, Bentley Library, University of Michigan).

    Another person who suffered from ties to Germany was Rebecca Shelley, a young pacifist who spent some time in Detroit as one of a group persuading Henry Ford to finance a peace ship in an effort to ward off war in Europe. Shelley lost her U.S. citizenship upon marrying a German citizen because of a restrictive wartime law. Though she spent much of her life in the Battle Creek area, her Detroit ties at the time of World War I have been documented in a recent monograph by Beverly Fish of Wayne State University. Shelley lived to be an active pacifist during the Vietnam War.

2. Detroit Urban League Papers, Bentley Library, Box 1. See also *Sand against the Wind: The Memoirs of John C. Dancy* (Detroit: Wayne State University Press, 1966). Dancy made a determined effort to befriend

all who could help his people and served for many years as executive secretary of the Detroit Urban League, following Forrester Washington.

3. Sam Zug has been blamed too often for downriver industrial pollution. Zug was a furniture maker, businessman, and philanthropist He was also an abolitionist and spent large sums to buy farmland in Canada for those who came by the Underground Railway. It is entirely possible, though not proven, that Zug Island, at the narrowest point of the Detroit River, was a way station on the route to Amherstburg—and freedom.

4. The beer and wine served as a matter of course in the homes of many ethnic groups had investigators from Ford's "Sociological Department" opening the doors of the workingman's icebox to check his habits.

5. Myron Adams's 1911 article was followed by another look at housing in Detroit published by *Survey* just five years later. John Ihlders, writing in 1916, was shocked at the preventable troubles that had come to the city's working poor. No one had cared enough to prevent inflationary high rents, the progressive dilapidation of homes, and even homelessness itself.

1. Industry and the River: The Fate of Zug Island

Detroit Free Press

On July 14, 1891, the business pages of the Free Press *carried the headline, "SALE OF ZUG ISLAND." This was news indeed, and just the beginning. The next fifteen years of rapid growth in Detroit heavy industry, especially automotive, would bring many changes to the marshy bog that thrust out into the Detroit River at the mouth of the Rouge.*

The sale mentioned here was of property that had been known as Brady Island since Sam Zug had sold it to George Brady and Charles Noble. In detailing the current sale, the writer gives us much island history and captures the ongoing process of change.

Brady Island can hardly be called an island at all, it being that peninsula of Ecorse Township that fronts on the Detroit River just below the Exposition Building, while a bend of the Rouge affords water frontage to one side and the rear. A swale known as Mud Run cuts it off from the mainland, but as Mud Run is only five feet deep, it doesn't count as an island maker.

The property includes 4,000 feet of Detroit River frontage from the mouth of the Rouge to the big coaling trestle of S. B. Smith & Co. and 8,000 feet of River Rouge frontage. . . .

[The island] was orginally the property of Lewis Cass, who sold it to the late Samuel Zug, who in turn sold undivided inter-

"Sale of Zug Island," *Detroit Free Press* (14 July 1891): 7.

Zug Island in later days: Ford works and shipping at the mouth of the Rouge River, 1970. (From UAW International. Used with permission of Reuther Archives.)

ests to George N. Brady and the late Charles W. Noble. . . . Messrs. Russell and Bourke will proceed at once to the improvement of the property by dyking the island, dredging slips for factory frontages into the interior of the island and the construction of railroad side tracks. The whole property will be made available for manufacturing purposes as soon as possible. It is altogether likely that in 1892 a railroad trestle, and a coal dock, similar to that of S. B. Smith & Co., will be constructed at the mouth of the Rouge River. A sulphur spring on the island that bubbles up 1,200 barrels of mineral water per day may be put to earning its living by the new owners.

This deal insures the completion of the work of reclamation of the marshes that formerly extended from Fort Wayne down to

Ecorse. The exposition property is a piece of reclaimed marsh. The Rouge River Improvement Company, composed of Michigan Central Railway people, has reclaimed 500 acres with a mile of frontage on the Detroit river.[1] Another mile of frontage, including 245 acres, is in process of reclamation, by Messrs. Russell and Dee, adjoining the Rouge River property, and the remaining three-fourths of a mile, the property of George A. Dupuis and William Blay, will be attacked just as soon as Mr. Dupuis' dredges are disengaged from work already contracted for in the same district. The home of the duck, the muskrat, and the mud hen seems to be doomed to destruction.

Editor's Note

1. At the time of these transactions, the "Michigan Central Railway people" were headed by president and general manager Henry Brockholst Ledyard, eldest grandson of Lewis Cass. Cass was not only the original owner of Zug Island but of much of the other area property—that is, of course, if we disregard the Indians, for whom the mouth of the Rouge had been a traditional gathering place.

2.   The Five Dollar Day

Detroit Journal

ICY FIRE-HOSE DELUGE
STOPS 1,200 IN RIOTOUS
RUSH FOR FORD'S JOBS

Five Men Arrested and Three Thousand Soaked With
Water in Zero Cold When Crowd
Tries to Enter Works.
SMASH WINDOWS; WRECK STANDS
Crowd Irritated at Douche Hurls Stones at Factory
Then Angrily Attacks Street Venders' Places—
14,000 Applications By Mail.

A deluge of ice cold water, playing from two fire hoses in the hands of Highland Park policemen, stopped the rush of 12,000 men for jobs at the Ford Motor Co. plant Monday morning and caused a near-riot in Manchester avenue, on which the factory entrances to the Ford shops are located.

Three thousand men were soaked with water, it is estimated. With the temperature hovering close to the zero mark, and a biting blast coming across the fields from the northwest, they were an unenviable lot as they hurried away to find some place in which to thaw out. Their clothing froze a moment after they encountered the business end of the hose.

"Icy Fire-Hose Deluge Stops 1,200 in Riotous Rush for Ford's Jobs," *Detroit Journal* (13 December 1913): 1.

Five of the job-seekers were arrested. Chief of Police Seymour, of the Highland Park department, was inclined to blame the slowness of Ford factory heads for the necessity of turning the hose on the crowd.

Only One Door

"Only one door into the factory was open at 8 o'clock," said Chief Seymour. "Had several been open, the Ford employes could have entered without trouble. But they all were heading for the single door and the job-seekers were mingled with them inextricably. We could not reason with the Ford employes or with the others. The Ford men were going to work later than usual, owing to the new eight-hour shift going into effect today, and were afraid they might lose their jobs if they were late. So they kept pressing forward. Had there been several doors open, we could have kept the crowd back while they went in, as we did afterwards when some of the officials arrived and threw the other entrances open."

As early as 10 o'clock Sunday night, when a gale was blowing and the mercury steadily falling, with a promise of zero weather in the air, men began to congregate about the Ford plant. Monday was the day when the $5 minimum for laborers went into effect, and the thought of it was sufficient incentive to the gathering men to brave the elements by an all-night vigil. By midnight a line of the job-seekers was extended to Oakland Avenue from near Woodward. As the hours passed, the shivering, stamping crowd increased little by little until at daybreak records of last week for men seeking jobs went by the boards.

Crowd Angry

The crowd was not as good-natured as last week's gatherings. The weather had its effect, of course, but hope of success was not as great Monday as before. The temper of some in the crowd was shown late Sunday evening, when some men attacked Patrolman Smith and tore his uniform, snatched away his revolver, club and handcuffs, and were fighting hard when help arrived for Smith.

Chief Seymour said Monday that the officer's assailants were Turks, and that they did not belong in the job-seeking crowd.

Disorders have been feared daily and Chief Seymour each day has detailed his entire forces to the Ford district. Up to Monday, however, inconsequential battles between men seeking vantage points in the crowd were the only disturbances.

Monday morning the scene appeared to be about as normal as any day last week until close to 8 o'clock. Then the Ford employes began to appear in large numbers to go to work. They found the street so congested that entrance was difficult. The police were holding back the job-seekers so as to leave a lane for employes, but the latter arrived so rapidly that they soon filled all the space left and soon the job-holders and job-seekers were thoroughly mingled.

The Ford employes wore little badges, but as the dense crowd jammed toward the single door that was open the police found it difficult to see just who got in. Soon there was such a congestion that no one could move. The police shouted orders until they were hoarse, but without effect. Then they threatened the crowd with the fire hose, but the crowd would not listen. The job-holders kept pressing forward and the job-seekers clung to them. Many could not do otherwise because of the enormous pressure on them from behind.

Then the police turned on the water, and employes, job-seekers and police officers themselves were drenched in short order. Scrambling backward, the mob overturned the "hot dog" lunch, cigar, and other stands across Manchester avenue. Some men, drenched and angry, picked up bricks, stones and bottles and hurled them at the hose users. Many of these missiles went through the factory windows.

When the crowd had backed off to a safe distance the Ford workers were permitted to come up again and other doors to the factories were opened, so that they soon were at work. Then the jobless ones began to move away. By 10 o'clock there were only a few hundred left walking about in the cold, wind-swept streets.

3. Detroit—A City Awake

Myron E. Adams

During the Progressive period, many cities took a fresh look at the homes of their newcomers and poor. Detroit was experiencing unprecedented growth in 1911 when the magazine Survey, *a guidebook for the profession of social work, published a series on housing. Writer Myron Adams was perhaps too hopeful of positive action in Detroit. Devastated by wartime in-migration, the city lacked homes for thirty thousand families by 1920.*

The completion of a comprehensive building code, the reorganization of the department of buildings, and the establishment of a housing commission under the direction of the Board of Commerce are indications of an awakened interest in protecting the city of Detroit from the evils attending its constantly increasing housing problem.

The census shows one of the causes of a housing problem in Detroit. In 1870 the population was 77,599; in 1880, 116,340; in 1900, 285,754, and by 1910, it had increased to 465,766, without unusual gain by annexation. Through all these years Detroit has ranked among the first cities in the number of houses owned by residents. Its position at the crossroads of interstate and international commerce, its varied industries, the conditions under

Myron E. Adams, "Detroit—A City Awake," Survey (5 August 1911): 666–71.

which men have labored, as well as the unusual recreational opportunities on river and lake, have made a strong appeal to the home-builder and have been among the most obvious causes of its growth.

The city was well planned. From the civic center, the Campus Martius, which is located some blocks from the river front, radiate a series of avenues, while the streets run parallel and perpendicular to the river. Thus Detroit resembles an open fan with the river for outer edge. Three miles to the east and the west, the Grand Boulevard Parkway commences at the river and extends around the city, enclosing the most thickly built part in a square. Outside this parkway are the best residential and an increasing number of factory districts.

Congestion has been retarded, notwithstanding the rapid growth of the population, in a number of ways. The land is without hills or valleys to raise natural obstacles to normal expansion, and there have been many open spaces, some of them large farms held for a rise in value. Of late, however, improved transportation facilities and the tendency to build farther out have forced the sale of these lands, and they are fast building up. Other obstacles to congestion were the diffusion of population in special industrial districts along the river front, with its twelve miles of factories, the Parkway and its factory districts, and the routes by which the railroads have entered and completely encircled the city. Not only are foreign groups separated from one another, but the groups themselves are divided, and we have two Polish, two Hungarian, and two Italian settlements.

To these hindrances to congestion must be added the possibility of almost unlimited expansion, with easy access to places of labor. It is significant that practically all the automobile factories, which have been built within the last five years, are located in the outskirts, where before there were great tracts of vacant land.

The census shows that the population of Detroit increased by 180,000 during the last ten years. The question immediately suggests itself as to what provision has been made for housing these people. The answer is unsatisfactory because of insufficient statistics, except for the last three years . . . .

Thus in three years 63,493 people were housed in new buildings, independent of alterations and additions. . . . Despite all this Detroit has felt the pressure of incoming population, and shows evidences of overcrowding. There are two chief causes of this in two distinct classes of districts.

The first is the steady exodus to the suburbs of people whose homes once formed the downtown portion of the city, and whose places are taken by renters and roomers with little interest in the property they occupy and still less in the neighborhood. On the east side, and within a radius of three-quarters of a mile from the center of the city, this old district with its cheap boarding houses, many in bad repair, and its men's lodging houses, combined with the infrequent homes of long-time property holders, forms the border of the dreary district of houses of prostitution and their kind. On the west side is a similar district where these conditions are being duplicated. The disintegration goes on, without perceptible opposition. The number of people who crowd into smaller quarters constantly increases.

The second cause is the rapid growth of foreign-born colonies. Ten years ago the first evidences of congestion became evident in the Jewish quarter. Practically every family lived then in its own house, with grass and flowers in the yard. But with rapid growth, rents increased, and the occupation of the same house by two families began. The demand for more rooms continued; landlords raised the roofs of their cottages to admit another story and extended the buildings so that they covered the whole lot; some moved the house to the rear and put another in front of it, others attached it to the barn by a connecting apartment, or remodeled the barn to house more than one family.

If the process of remodelling which has been going on for the last five years is to continue without interference, the whole Jewish quarter will become one great district of overcrowded tenements, some of a very bad type. In the center of the district is the largest public school in Michigan. . . . The city has appropriated $65,000 for a recreation park, which will in some measure compensate for the loss of open spaces for children, who are found here in great numbers. But it will not change housing conditions nor prevent congestion.

The Hungarian colony lies in the Delray district, an industrial section some four miles from the center of the city. The Hungarian has a racial magnetism that attracts all friends and relatives from the other side. Admission is denied to none who can crowd in. Cottages built for four or five people house thirty and thirty-five. Every corner is used, and there is little furniture but beds and kitchen utensils. Sometimes the cellar or back yard is made into a primitive refuge for boarders.

The Polish district on the west side is by far the best of the sections inhabited by foreign-born residents. Industrial advantages have divided the Poles into two distinct communities. They are thrifty homemakers, owning 90 percent of the houses in the district. They seem to prefer the one or two-story dwelling with a yard, and seldom occupy the two-family flat or the tenement, as their Jewish and Servian neighbors do.

The Italians, rapidly increasing in number to 15,000 or 20,000, occupy a large district within the inner mile circle. There are few homemakers among them, and the boarders roam from city to city and from section to section. Many live in houses once among the most desirable in the city. These bring high rents, with consequent overcrowding. Repairs are lacking and disorder prevails.

The Servians, the Dalmatians, and the Bulgarians form a colony of about 5,000 near the car shops. Here under the "boarding boss" system familiar in most industrial cities, there are few houses with fewer than six boarders, besides the boss and his family. When the shops are busy this number is doubled, and the beds are used day and night. In one tenement on a rear lot, which had four separate flats with twelve rooms, were seven women, five boarding bosses, and fifty-two boarders—and that in a slack season. Inspectors of the Board of Health, who have power to prevent overcrowding, have cut down the number of boarders and improved the general sanitary condition of the neighborhood. One of the serious problems is the number of dark rooms created by the building of new houses and tenements on the lot line. These shut off all light from one side of the building. In addition to positive causes of concentration of population and increasing congestion, there was a lack of proper building legislation for prevention, regulation, and inspection. It is fair to say that until last February there were no ordinances which could keep conditions from growing more serious. Methods of building were practically unrestricted. Tenements could be built to cover the entire lot. A building could be so erected as to shut off the light and air, and even to prevent access to another building on an adjoining lot. Practically the only restrictive provisions were within limited fire districts, and they covered only the construction of side walls and roofs. In certain respects, where the condition of the house actually created a public nuisance, the Board of Health had authority to bring the matter before the courts, and from time to time some of the most unsightly and unsanitary places were reached in this way. The Board of Building Inspectors created in 1885 and the fire marshal's office created in 1887 lacked jurisdiction over dwellings.

But in 1907 the Legislature empowered the mayor to appoint a building commission of five men, which was instructed by the Common Council to formulate a building code. The commission completed the code in the spring of 1910, and for almost a year the Common Council gave it serious consideration. . . . [The code enacted for the construction of dwellings and tenement houses seems] adequate to remedy defects already apparent and to prevent prospective building operations which might lead to congestion. . . .

. . . [The cooperation of] the Board of Commerce and the Central Council of Charities resulted in the organization of the Detroit Housing commission, composed of representative men who intend to reinforce and supplement at every point the work of the Department of Buildings. . . .

There is every reason to believe that this commission will eventually approach the problem on the constructive side, and lead the movement to increase the number of houses that can be secured at small rents, or be purchased by men earning moderate wages. This combination of public administration reinforced by private support and approval will do much to keep the problem of congestion out of the increasing list of conditions that prevent natural and healthy living in a city which has always been a city of homes.[1]

Editor's Note

1. The Adams study is valuable for its clear descriptions of the shape of the city's growth and the special nature of its housing. Most material on housing needs of that period refers to "tenements" and "walk-up apartments." This was never the Detroit pattern, and the problems of New York were not those here. Detroit had its own.

4. Women Workers: A Surprise to Industry

Michigan Department of Labor

In every American war, women and minorities have been drawn into performing new sorts of work. World War I was no exception. Detroit employers had some problems in getting used to women workers. Some of these are revealed in the introduction to the Thirty-Fifth Annual Report of the Michigan Department of Labor, followed by a few typical citations made by labor inspectors of Detroit companies where women were part of the 1917 work force.

The most important question that the Labor Department has to deal with is that to do with women wage earners. The world war has brought about a revolution in women's work. Woman's tendency to venture more and more into traditional occupations of men received an enormous acceleration when the first soldiers were called to the colors abroad. Thousands of women are now working in occupations that not even the most advanced suffragist asked to be thrown open to them. There is literally not a thing that man has done that women are not now doing. This is not only true of manufacturing work and the

Michigan Department of Labor, "Women Wage Earners" and "Factory Orders Issued, 1917," in *Michigan Department of Labor, Thirty-Fifth Annual Report* (Lansing: Michigan Department of Labor, 1918), 9–10, 365–93.

professional and business occupations, but it is also true of the hardest kind of mechanical and laboring work.

So there has arisen the most vital problem that has ever faced the Department and the State. Women have been employed in some occupations in which men only were formerly employed, and for which little or no protection was provided by law. Again in some cases new dangers have developed for which former laws made no specific provisions.

In 1916 there was employed in the work shops and factories in Michigan 72,613 women, 14 years of age and over pursuing gainful occupations, of whom 72,063 were over 16 years of age.

In all groups of occupations the number of women to each man has increased, or the number of men to the number of women has decreased since the beginning of the war. The change in some instances has been remarkably abrupt, and must continue to be increasingly so.

The specific question asked: What will be the reactions between the excessive and abrupt employment of women, the diminuation in the number of working men, and the effect upon labor conditions generally throughout the State?

A great number of industries throughout the State have sought to break down the standards regarding the hours of labor women and children are permitted to work in gainful occupations. . . .

The engagement of women in the manufacturing of war materials . . . presents many features of outstanding interest. There, workers include dressmakers, laundry workers, textile workers, domestic servants, electrical workers, shop assistants, women and girls of every social grade and of no previous wage earning experiences. The danger of industrial employment to these workers include not only the risk of injury from accident but also the risk to health arising from the conditions under which an industry may be conducted. . . .

Factory Orders Issued, 1917 [Detroit] September 17, 1917

DODGE BROTHERS MOTOR CAR CO.—At once guard pulleys on machines 5871–5872, Dept. 17. Guard all lower pulleys. Guard wheel running machine 5022, Dept. 40. . . . Place signs opposite all stairways where women are working on third floor, and also on fourth floor directing way to fire escape.

September 6, 1917

HUPP MOTOR CAR CO.—At once box all lower belts and pulleys throughout plant. Box belt and wheel on machines 147–148–149. Box large belt machine 143. Guard all electric switches lower than 6 feet from floor. Guard emery wheel, Dept. XX. Put fire escape on fourth floor where women are employed.

September 4, 1917

JONES-REGAN CO.—At once place a higher hood on meat chopper machine to prevent one operating the machine from getting their hand in knife while machine is in operation. Do not permit males under eighteen years of age to operate dangerous machinery.

December 6, 1917

KROGER GROCERY AND BAKING CO.—At once provide separate toilets for use of your men and women employes at 394 Grand River Ave. Provide stools for use of women in their leisure time. Keep store heated to at least 70 degrees. Drain and keep basement in a sanitary condition.

August 28–29–30–31, 1917

PACKARD MOTOR CAR CO.—[among some sixty-five citations] . . . At once in Department C cover gears on lathe 2668. Box lower pulley on machine 4118. Put hood on all enameling tanks. . . . Guard all belts and pulleys where women are working. . . .

March 21, 1917

POSTAL TELEGRAPH CO.—At once arrange the hours of your female employes to conform to the 54–hour law and procure and keep on file permits for all employees under 16 years of age.

November 2, 1917

WABASH RAILWAY COMPANY—At once provide at least two or three additional toilets for female employes, and about three more for male employes. Provide another door or exit in rear of offices, second floor, leading to freight house, as a means of exit in case of fire.

December 28, 1917

WOLVERINE CREAMERY PRODUCTS CO.—At once provide a sanitary, properly designated toilet for the use of your female employes.

Part X

The Twenties: Decade of Contradictions

The Twenties: Decade of Contradictions

On New Year's Day, 1920, the new Federal Bureau of Investigation, under the direction of Attorney General A. Mitchell Palmer, who was rumored to have presidential ambitions, arrested several thousand persons in cities across the country, more than three hundred of them in Detroit. All were suspected of being "Bolsheviks."

The drive for Americanism did not stop at the war's end. Like other aspects of American life in the twenties, it carried with it its own contradiction or crosscurrent. There was an anti-Bolshevik drive, but there were also dissenters and fighters for civil liberties. The twenties have often been portrayed as carefree and prosperous, the happy-go-lucky days of the flapper. But Detroit, which had seen sharp rises in employment and inflation during the war years, now suffered sharp depression. Many small businesses failed during the postwar slump. Merciless layoffs occurred at the larger ones.

Never were the twenties as prosperous for all as the myth would have us believe. In part this was because the continuing Americanism drive was accompanied by a drive against labor unions. Industrial Detroit was proud of its strong "open shop" policy. Even the craft unions of skilled tradesmen were on the defensive. Still there remained throughout the decade a sharp discrepancy in pay between the organized worker and his more numerous unorganized brothers and sisters. The thousands of autoworkers, the best known and most conspicuous part of Detroit's work force, were almost completely unorganized. They were subject to extremes of seasonsal unemployment, often working only five or six months a year. Since this situation caused many to leave town, the city was subject to a constantly shifting population.

As for clerical employees, these, usually female, were consistently and notoriously underpaid during that period of high living costs. Even before the depression years, both embezzlement and suicide were known among Detroit's middle class. Meanwhile, the drive for Americanism was tied in with an increasing social pressure for conformity that, perhaps for the first time, was clearly beamed at the consumer as well as the worker.

Nowhere were contradictions more apparent than in civic and moral questions. Huge churches were built and filled with worshippers, yet many claimed liquor was surpassing automobiles as the town's largest industry. There was no real proof of this, but it sounded well, and certainly the demand for alcohol increased, and the industry was resourceful and inventive. The river traffic between Detroit, Walkerville, Sandwich, Ecorse, and Amherstburg was phenomenal.

Detroit's geographic location on the Canadian border certainly helped organized crime to get a foothold. There was the Purple Gang, involved in labor racketeering and extortion, targeting small businessmen. There was the Sugar Hill gang. There were gamblers galore, though the widespread policy, or "numbers," racket did not become a growth industry until the end of Prohibition in the early thirties. The Detroit Police Department had established what it called its "Italian Squad" well before the twenties. Now it was said to be needed because of the Mafia. Certainly Detroit had its own coalition of definable Italian families believed to be affiliated with organized crime. The situation was a great embarrassment to autoworkers, small storekeepers, and fine craftsmen of Italian heritage. The names of the families suspected by the community, sometimes unjustly, of being unduly rich may still be read on the gravestones of the downtown Church of the Holy Family. It is less certain whether the "Italian Squad" of the Detroit Police Department was at all effective in pinning down this sector of organized crime.

Sometimes it seemed as if everyone wanted the glamor of being part of the "liquor racket," and certainly many of the town's journalists, politicians, and, unfortunately, police were. Even in the relatively arid stretches of northwest Detroit, there was a legend that a fern or other large plant in the window of any small business meant "booze served here."

The first urgent problem Detroiters acknowledged was the housing shortage. The war years had brought uncontrolled inflation of rents and an acute shortage of physical space. The postwar years led to the creation of new "subdivisions" at the edge of town. These new fringe areas for workers were distinctly segregated. An example was Brightmoor, developed by B. E. Taylor for a working-class clientele. Brightmoor was strictly white and in its early days a focal point for Ku Klux Klan agitation.[1]

In the mid-twenties the Eight Mile-Wyoming area was opened to blacks—some said in part because of the anger of a white developer against a former colleague who owned adjacent land. Brightmoor, Eight Mile-Wyoming, and a number of other subdivisions catered to the poorest workingman's wish to own a little place in the country where he could sustain himself and his family during layoffs with a few chickens and a garden. Just a few years later, as Detroit's city limits would stretch out to engulf those new communities, those chickens and the occasional pig would come to seem inappropriate.

The housing crisis came to a head with the Ossian Sweet case. A young, black doctor who had lived through the bloody wartime riots in East St. Louis, Sweet was faced with the hostility of new neighbors on Detroit's east side. He made the decision to barricade himself, his family, and several friends in his new home. The evening ended with the besieged firing guns over the heads of rock throwers who had clustered around the house; one man across the street died in the gunfire, and Dr. Sweet and his companions were tried for murder. The Sweet trial forced at least some Detroiters to recognize that there were factors here that they did not understand and led to open acknowledgment that the Ku Klux Klan was a force in the city. It also led to the first official attempt to examine race relations in Detroit.

The selections for the twenties begin with the Red Scare, as it was viewed in U.S. Senate Judiciary Committee hearings held in 1921, two years after the Detroit arrests. There was another crosscurrent here in the events of the winter of 1920. A number of local business and government leaders, including the former Ford executive, Mayor James Couzens, were repelled by the outside invasion by the fledgling FBI. Whatever they had bargained for, to their credit, it wasn't this. The Red Scare story itself, as it appears in testimony given by a local reporter to the Senate committee, is self-explanatory.

Several documents follow that are related to the Ossian Sweet case, beginning with the news story itself with its revealing headlines. John Smith was mayor at the time and tried manfully to work through his own confusions on race problems to a realization that the Klan was active and that injustices were occurring. His open letter to his police chief immediately after the shooting is revealing social history of the times.

A far more sophisticated view than the mayor's is that taken by a young observer at the trial, David E. Lilienthal, later to be appointed director of the Tennessee Valley Authority (TVA) by Franklin Roosevelt. Lilienthal's praise for the fairness of Judge Frank Murphy sharpens one's perception of the state of justice received by blacks in other courtrooms across the country.

An important view of another major problem in the city of the twenties—police brutality—is revealed in a report by an interracial commission appointed by Mayor Smith. The report was prepared under the auspices of the Detroit Bureau of Governmental Research, now the Citizens' Research Council, and the director of the study was the same Forrester Washington who had been the first executive secretary of the Detroit Urban League in 1917. The material that appears here is a segment dealing with the killings of black civilians by Detroit police within a period of less than one year. It is important to remember that this entire study was a by-product of the mayor's concern and bewilderment over the Sweet case. There is no reason to suppose that official Detroit would have taken any notice of police brutality directed against blacks, or their housing, employment, recreation, and other problems if the city had not been upset by the actions of Dr. Sweet.

The murder of a crusading radio journalist in the lobby of his downtown hotel ties together various threads of gangsterism, civic corruption, and the Ku Klux Klan. Cyril A. Player, a local journalist aiming at a nationwide liberal audience through the

New Republic in 1930, did his best to show the pattern of an increasingly troubled Detroit.

Detroit of the twenties was suffering simultaneously from organized crime, the Klan, bitter racial and ethnic prejudice, auto layoffs every summer, and constant hardship among its respectable poor. Yet all of it was played against a backdrop of reported wealth, glamor, and excitement.

No one can fault that backdrop. The stage setting of the twenties has left magnificent architectural remainders: the Union Guardian Building, the Fisher Theater, the gilded movie palaces of downtown, and a string of mammoth churches along Woodward Avenue. Carrara marble, Tiffany windows, and Detroit's own irridescent Pewabic tiles: those were the glittering hallmarks of the twenties. Today the Pewabic formula is gone and no one can find the gilded frogs that once served as ashtrays in the ladies' rest room of the Fisher Theater. Too bad the reality never matched the backdrop.

Editor's Note

1. John W. Carey, "The Growth of Brightmoor," *Brightmoor: A Community in Action* (Detroit: Brightmoor Community Center, 1940), 1–2.

1. The Red Scare of 1919

U.S. Senate Judiciary Committee

The pattern of "Americanization" and its identification with a distrust of organized labor was firmly set by Detroit employers by the war's end. When Attorney General A. Mitchell Palmer ordered the mass arrest and possible deportation of "enemy aliens" in Detroit, the effort was massive, overextended, and, in all, sloppy.

In a town where the business community was committed to the open shop, Palmer had clearly gone too far. Mayor James Couzens, (later a United States senator) was among the city's leaders shocked into protest. Detroit leaders would be among those to appear later at the hearings of the Senate Judiciary Committee when it investigated the conduct of the Justice Department.[1]

The most substantive Detroit testimony was given on March 20, 1921, by a Detroit News reporter, Frederick Barkley, whose employers had apparently given him a free hand in investigation and reporting.

Statement of Mr. Frederick R. Barkley

Senator STERLING. Will you state your full name and your occupation?

Mr. BARKLEY. Frederick R. Barkley. I am a writer on the Detroit News, and I have lived in Detroit the last four years.

Senator STERLING. Have you been connected with the Detroit News during that period?

Senate Judiciary Committee, *Hearings on Charges of Illegal Practices of Department of Justice*, 66th Cong., 1 March 1921, U.S. Cong. Hearings, 41st–73d Cong., 1869–1934, 169: 709–23.

Mr. BARKLEY. I have been connected with the Detroit Free Press during the first year of those four years and with the Detroit News the other three years.

Senator STERLING. What do you know, if anything, about these arrests?

Mr. BARKLEY. . . . On January 3 I was sent by my paper to the Federal Building to write a story or make a report—to find out what the conditions were there, which we had heard of indirectly.

I went up there and found great confusion among the department agents. . . . It was very difficult to get any information from them. . . . I think the figures show, as they have been collected, and as they have been published from time to time, that they made around 1,000 arrests altogether, so that that would account for the fact that they only reached 800, because they had been able to release some by the time they had made the last raid.

As I said, they did not have the names; they had no name lists available of the men. Their women, of course, having missed them and having heard about this, came in and went into the lower corridors and tried to get information about whether their husbands were there or not, and it was difficult to get up to the top of the stairs, and, even if they did, it would be very difficult to find them. Sometimes, as a man would be rushing back and forth attending to his work, one of these women would get hold of him and ask if such and such a man was there, and then he would shout the name up, and these officers would shout through and ask if Mike So-and-so was there.

Senator STERLING. Do you know of any instances where an answer to the question as to whether a certain man was there or not was denied to those who went there?

Mr. BARKLEY. Not deliberately; but on account of the general circumstances it was apparently impossible to pay any attention to these friends and relatives. They had too big a crowd to take care of the men themselves.

Senator WALSH of Montana. [Senator Walsh will be referred to hereafter as Senator Walsh.] You spoke about when these raids were made in dance houses, and study halls, and restaurants.

Mr. BARKLEY. Yes. Of course, I did not witness the raids myself, but at the House of the Masses or Shore Hall [*sic*, Schiller

Hall] was, I understood, where they got the most. That was the headquarters of the Socialist Party. It was a big, 3-story building, and they had a restaurant on the ground floor, which I understand, they ran cooperatively by an association, I think, with the Workers' Educational Society.

Senator STERLING. They had rooms there where the Socialist Party came and held their meetings?

Mr. BARKLEY. Yes, the whole building had been owned by the Socialist Party. When they were thrown out by the Socialist Party at the convention, they joined the Communist Party as a body, and the same group just transferred their membership, and the hall went over to the Communist Party; and it has been the subject of litigation ever since. And as I have been informed, they were having a dance in this hall the night of January 2, when the raid occurred. We were told that they arrested all the members of the orchestra that was playing there, which plays at all the high-class entertainments in Detroit.

They also arrested all the men who were eating in the restaurant on the ground floor, which, so far as I could tell from the outside, resembles any short-order restaurant. There is nothing to indicate that it is different from any other restaurant.

Senator STERLING. Do you know whether they cater to anybody except their own members?

Mr. BARKLEY. . . . . I know that a girl I talked to down in a lower corridor said that her brother had belonged to the Socialist Party, and when the switch to the Communist Party was made he did not join the Communist Party because he did not believe in force; but he continued to patronize the restaurant, and he was eating his dinner there that day; and he had been confined there for three days because he was caught in the restaurant getting his dinner. She seemed an intelligent girl, more Americanized than most of those who were arrested.

Senator WALSH. They found both men and women in the place?

Mr. BARKLEY. Yes.

Senator WALSH. Did they arrest women also?

Mr. BARKLEY. No, they did not arrest the women. This girl was at dance this night in the hall. She said they were holding classes in the anterooms and the side rooms there, and they broke up the classes.

Senator STERLING. Do you know whether or not, aside from the dance hall, there are rooms or halls which are used for the purposes of societies, socialist and communist?

Mr. BARKLEY. Oh, yes; I assume the whole building was owned by the Communist Party at that time and operated by them.

Senator WALSH. Was it your understanding that the members of that orchestra were identified with those societies?

Mr. BARKLEY. No, it was just a professional orchestra, which played for balls and dances and all sorts of affairs.

Senator WALSH. Did you say they were arrested?

Mr. BARKLEY. I was so informed. I would not say that at first hand, but I was informed that they were arrested, the whole thing; that they took in every man they found.

What I started to say was that these women would come up there looking for their husbands. As they transferred the men to the various precinct police stations and other places, they had no record kept of where the men went. A woman might come up there, looking for her husband, and he might have been transferred by that time to a police precinct station. Some of the women told me that it was five or six days before they found where their husbands were. In one case in particular I remember the woman had no money, and she had to beg her food from the neighbors, and it was five or six days before she found her husband. I think she got some cash from him then. . . .

There were nine precinct police stations in Detroit, and so far as I know they were sent to all of those. In the outlying sections it would be difficult, if a person did not know which one of them a relative was at, to find him. They might have to make the whole round.

Senator WALSH. Some reference was made to some of them going to the Municipal Court Building.

Mr. BARKLEY. Yes; I will go into that now. I have some figures on that here. In the first place, about 400 men were released out of this group as soon as they could get to them, possibly within a day, and sometimes two, or three or four or five days, as they came along, and were examined. Some of them were found to be citizens who had been picked up accidentally. I was told of one man who was going past this building when the raid took place, and he just got swept along with the crowd.

They took 128 of them to what is known as the "bull pen" at the municipal court. That is a room that is designed to hold prisoners awaiting trial for petty offenses—to hold people for two or three hours. They bring people up from the jail and hold them there until their cases are called. It is a room 24 feet by 30 in size, I was informed by officials in the building. They had 128 men in there. That had a stone floor, with some flat benches with no backs—just room for perhaps 20 men to sit on those benches. In that room they were held for seven days. This was a cellar room with one window. It had a little toilet off it, and one door, a grated door; and that was the condition that led the health commissioner upon the complaint of the municipal court judges, and the threat of the employees in the restaurant in that building to strike if those men were not removed, to make recommendations and recommend again to the mayor, and that led to the action that was read to you that the council later took. I went down there and looked in. They were packed in there just about as close as you could get them. One man had an infected hand and he had not had any treatment for it, that was the second day, and his hand was all swelled up and purple; and I think that was one of the conditions that led these men, the employees in the restaurant, to threaten to strike.

They told me they had been fed one cup of coffee and two biscuits twice a day. That was the only food they had had.

Senator WALSH. Did you try to verify that?

Mr. BARKLEY. . . . I was not able at that time to verify it. . . . It was similar to the action that had taken place in the Federal building where Barkey [Arthur Barkey, chief agent for the Justice Department at Detroit] said that they had brought in coffee and doughnuts.

Senator WALSH. Was there any systematic effort on the part of the officials to feed them?

Mr. BARKLEY. No. Barkey said, "We brought them in coffee and doughnuts; but," he said, "they have all got good food from their homes, and boxes of oranges, and," he said, "we did not have time to bother with it; and they are being fed now anyway. Their friends are bringing in food." . . . Of course, I assume probably their friends did furnish them with food. This is what they told me they got from the Government.

The Twenties—Detroit's Golden Age of architecture. Facade of the Metropolitan Building, John R. Street. (Courtesy of Bob McKeown, 1987.)

Senator STERLING. You do not understand that they were limited to that?

Mr. BARKLEY. No, I do not; but the conditions were such that Mayor Couzens said, in his report to the city council: "These conditions are intolerable in a civilized city." . . .

Senator WALSH. . . . What publicity was given to this condition of things?

Mr. BARKLEY. On the day I made the inquiries and the investigation in the Federal building I wrote a story which was printed on the front page of the News, about a column and a half—it was given rather striking publicity—just outlining conditions there as stated by Mr. Barkey. When that story appeared, The Detroit Free Press, which was friendly to Mr. Barkey and never criticized his actions or appeared to criticize him, quoted Mr. Barkey as follows:

"The public should bear in mind that this is not a picnic, and the Department of Justice is not providing settees for criminals."

Three hundred and fifty of them were later released for lack of evidence.

"They have to sleep on the floor. That is right. But a stone bed in the post office probably isn't any harder than a board bed in the jail. The majority of them are getting better than in their five-sleep-in-a-bed homes, and they have more food than they can eat. Relatives and friends have brought in whole boiled hams, boxes of oranges, and other delicacies."

Senator WALSH. Was the Detroit Free Press quoting Mr. Barkey there?

Mr. BARKLEY. They were quoting Mr. Barkey to that effect.

I believe that covers pretty nearly the situation, as far as the detention is concerned. Of course of these 800 that were held for varying periods from a day up to three or four days, many of them were released. I am told that many of them were former servicemen, who had gone to a dance at the House of the Masses, and that they had managed to get in a body early next morning and announce who they were, and they were let out right away. . . .

. . .They brought one man in to me on April 12. . . . I wrote down the story he told me. . . . this man's name was Walter B. Reps. I do not know what the final outcome of his case was. . . . He was born in Poland 34 years ago, and married there and came

310

to the United States in 1913. He was a small man, neatly dressed and sturdy, with work-calloused hands and an intelligent, kindly expression. He had been an industrious workman. He had learned his trade as a cabinetmaker in Poland, and when he reached the United States he came to Detroit and went to work at once in a furniture factory. Later [Reps] left this factory to work for the Ford Motor Company, where he was employed at the time of his arrest. In order to become more expert in mechanics and English, he attended a school conducted four nights a week in a Polish educational society's hall.

In 1917 he bought a little house, paying $1,000 down and $75 every two months. He continued to go to night school and placed his children, now 5 and 7 years old, respectively, in the public schools. He had been a member of the Socialist Party in Poland, and as all his associates in Detroit were members of the Detroit Polish branch of the same party in this country he also joined here.

When the Detroit Polish branch switched its allegiance from the Socialist Party to the Communist Party last fall, he believed, as did his fellow members, that the switch meant merely a change in name, inasmuch as the membership group remained the same. That was the basis or ground for his arrest. He told me that he was arrested on the evening of January 2 when he and a dozen others were studying an English lesson at their hall, No. 1648 Central Avenue.

Senator WALSH. Is that the House of the Masses?

Mr. BARKLEY. No; this hall is the social center for the Polish workmen of the neighborhood, where they held their dances, their classes, and political meetings. He said that was all there was going on that night; they were studying an English lesson when the Department of Justice agents broke in. He said that as far as he could understand there was no presentation of warrants. They did not tell them what they were wanted for, but just took them out and bundled them into the automobiles and took them down and put them in this Federal building cage. . . .

Senator STERLING. You do not know just what he meant by "political meetings?"

Mr. BARKLEY. No, I do not know. I remember he said he wanted to live in this country and wanted to pay for his home; and he seemed to be inoffensive and have no idea of violence.

Senator STERLING. I do not know whether or not you stated when he came to this country.

Mr. BARKLEY. In 1913. Reps's wife did not find him until Monday. I think January 2 was Friday. She was allowed to talk to him through the bars long enough for him to tell her to bring him some food. Soon after she left, his turn to appear before the examiners came. This was when they asked him, according to what Reps said, his name, age, and nativity, whether he was a citizen or an alien, and whether he belonged to the Communist Party; and on his assertion that he did, and without any questions to learn whether he knew what the party platform was or whether he believed in it, he was set down presumably as a "dangerous alien" and was taken with others to a cell in police headquarters. He was there two days, he said, in very crowded conditions. When his wife again sought him at the Federal Building where he had been, she was unable to find out where he was. . . .

Two days later Reps and others were again transferred, this time to the "bull pen" of the Municipal Court Building, and later he was taken to Fort Wayne. He was kept at Fort Wayne until February 1.

On January 26th he was subjected to a second examination, which was a duplicate of the first. In neither instance was he informed of the charge against him. He had had no counsel, nor had he had an opportunity to be judged by a jury.

At the time of his second examination, he was told to make ready for deportation in two or three days. . . .

Three days later, when desperate pleas from his wife had induced Dr. P. L. Prentis, the chief immigration officer, to reduce his bail from $10,000 to $1,000, Reps was released on bail, which his wife had been able to borrow in various small amounts from neighbors and acquaintances. In the month he had been held, Mrs. Reps had only $25 from his last pay at Ford's on which to live.

He expected deportation orders at any hour, and he sold his house, getting $200 less than he had paid for it. He also sold his furniture, for $170, and he spent considerable money buying heavy winter clothing for the expected trip to Russia.

He waited two weeks for the deportation order. It did not come. The purchasers of his house demanded occupancy and moved in, leaving Reps and his family one room in which to live.

Then he got another job with the Cadillac Motor Car Co., and was working there in April.

On April 10 he received from Dr. Prentis a second order, telling him, "The order of deportation in your case has issued, You are directed to have all your affairs straightened up so that you will be ready for conveyance to port of departure within a short period." On inquiry of Dr. Prentis, Reps was told that his wife and children could not accompany him; that the "Government had no money to deport wives and children," and that inasmuch as his orders from Washington directed deportation of men only Reps would have to go alone.

That was the status of this poor man at the time I questioned him. He had lost considerable money selling his home and his wife had been under a period of uncertainty and was at that time.

Senator WALSH. What I was really desirous of getting was what impression they made upon you as a body.

Mr. BARKLEY. They seemed simple men, not perhaps very highly educated. They were clean. Most of them were fairly well dressed for workingmen, not dirty-looking fellows. They did not look like what we have been led to believe bolsheviks look like— that is, when they were taken in there. After four or five days, of course, they had all grown a pretty good crop of beard. They were not permitted to shave, and they slept in their clothes.

Senator WALSH. Did they look like good, decent, reputable dressed workingmen, or did they look like what you might call tramps or general rounders?

Mr. BARKLEY. No; they were reputable workingmen. Their families were very well clothed. In fact, one of the papers stated about some well dressed women who had incited these men. It was their wives and families who had come in there. Some of them were making good money, up to $10 and $12 a day. They were skilled workmen. . . .

Senator WALSH. Were you permitted to talk to any of them?

Mr. BARKLEY. No; not while they were in the Federal building corridor. It was impossible to talk to them. There were police at this one door where you could go up there.

When I went to the municipal building I talked to them there through the gates.

Senator WALSH. Were they allowed to see their attorneys?

Mr. BARKLEY. They were not allowed to see any attorneys, as I was told, while they were in the Federal building. Whether they were after that, I do not know. . . .

Editor's Note

1. Mayor Couzen's actions included calling on the common council for a resolution of protest to the federal government for the manner in which the arrests were made and the prisoners confined. He insisted that the Department of Justice remove its prisoners from any city-owned facilities. He had his health commissioner protest the fact that men were held in buildings with hopelessly inadequate sanitary facilities, little food, and no medical care. He was joined in his efforts by attorney Fred Butzel, chemical company president Frederick Stearns, and Sebastian S. Kresge. These men secured bail, attorneys, and funds for the men's families.

Two young lawyers, who were less known in 1920–21 than they would become later, involved themselves in the defense efforts. One was Walter Nelson, who was active in the Sweet trial as one of the attorneys assisting Clarence Darrow. Nelson became a widely respected lawyer, specializing in labor and civil rights issues.

The other was Solomon Paperno, who courageously wrote the Justice Department in Washington with questions on behalf of arrested clients. Perhaps it shows something of the nature of the new FBI that Paperno, who had been born in Russia, became an immediate suspect because of his immigrant status in spite of his American citizenship.

2. Dr. Ossian Sweet Defends His Home

Detroit Free Press

ONE SLAIN AND 1 SHOT BY NEGROES
VICTIM'S WIFE IN COLLAPSE, IS NEAR DEATH. . . .
Home at 2905 Garland Avenue, In White Neighborhood, Is Scene;
12 Jailed

At 3:30 o'clock this morning, it was announced that Assistant Prosecutor Edward H. Kennedy, Jr. would recommend warrants charging murder against the 11 negroes now under arrest in connection with the outbreak last night at 2905 Garland Avenue. . . .

Shots poured without warning and seemingly without provocation last night at 8:30 o'clock from the second story windows of 2905 Garland Avenue, into which Dr. and Mrs. Ossian M. Sweet, a Negro couple, had moved Tuesday, cost one man's life, put another in the hospital with a bullet in his leg, and called out 200 heavily armed police reserves, detectives, and regular policemen from every precinct, as well as an armored car.

"One Slain and 1 Shot by Negroes," *Detroit Free Press* (10 September 1925): 1.

A police Inspector, a Lieutenant, and a patrolman had been standing within 25 feet of the house which was lighted only in the upper windows. They had been talking over the potential trouble that might emerge from Negroes moving into the white neighborhood.

A rain of bullets ended the conversation. As if the triggers of a dozen guns were being pulled simultaneously, the firing started. It stopped with the same suddenness that it began. While the police ran up the steps and hammered at the door of the house, the gathering throng counted the casualties.

Father Killed Instantly

Leon Breiner, 3063 Garland avenue, father of two children, who was walking on the east side of Garland, across the street from the house, was killed instantly, a bullet entering his head. Erik Hofberg 52 years old, 2918 Garland avenue, ran out of his house when he heard the shooting and was just in time to receive one of the last bullets fired. He was taken to Receiving Hospital, shot in the leg. . . .

Thousands of angry residents surged down the streets, and these were joined by hundreds of other people. . . . It was estimated 5,000 persons gathered.

When inspector Norton M. Schuknecht, of the McClellan avenue station, leaped to the veranda, and hammered in the door, Dr. Sweet, an interne at Dunbar Hospital, a Negro institution, answered at once.

Weapons Are Seized

People outside were throwing stones through the windows, Sweet asserted.

The house was sparsely furnished. There were so many Negroes in it that there were not enough chairs for them to sit on. All apparently had gathered on the upper floor, and all, according to the police, were armed. The police seized six revolvers, two rifles and a shotgun. The kitchen was well stocked with provisions, however, and there were several trunks in the place.

In a corner of the front upstairs room there was a black traveling bag. It was tagged with a card which read "Madame O. H. Sweet, Paris", and there were various other labels of transatlantic travel. Inside were several varieties of ammunition, shells, and cartridges.

12 Taken To Headquarters

Sweet, his wife, and their 10 guests were taken to police headquarters. Then the police began the difficult task of maintaining order.

About an hour after police had quieted the crowd, a car filled with Negroes drove up two blocks away from the scene of the shooting and stopped. When a score of persons started toward it, police fliers escorted the Negroes out of danger.

In describing the start of the shooting, Inspector Schuknecht said there had been no demonstration previously. . . .

Residents of the district today will ask why the neighborhood was not informed by police that a special police guard had been stationed in the vicinity of 2905 Garland avenue and a riot squad maintained at the McClellan avenue station. . . .

3. Mayor John Smith Accuses the Ku Klux Klan

John W. Smith

The gunfire in front of Dr. Sweet's home had hardly died away before the city's mayor laid the blame for this and other incidents on the Ku Klux Klan. The Detroit Free Press, *on the morning of September 13, headlined an open letter from Mayor John W. Smith to Police Commissioner Frank Croul.*

Dear Commissioner:

The outrage of Wednesday evening, in which one man was killed and another seriously injured, deals with the province of government under the direct jurisdiction of the department of police. . . .

[It has been] the custom, not only in this city, but in all communities of the northern part of this country,—to treat for political purposes—jealousies and prejudices existing between different races as non-existent. I believe that the present crisis in Detroit must put an end to such criminal delicacy.

My duty, which is your duty and your officers' duty, is laid down by law. The constitution of the United States, the constitution of Michigan, the charter of the city of Detroit, and the laws

John W. Smith, "Mayor's Open Letter," *Detroit Free Press* (13 September 1925): 1–2.

of all those governmental agencies fix clearly the legal relation-
ships which may exist regarding life and property. And they affect all races the same.

When any person moves into a new neighborhood, it becomes
by law the duty of the police agencies to protect that man or
woman in his life and property. . . . A mayor, police commissioner, or police officer, who fails in any particular in extending
legal protection to all persons, regardless of creed or color, would
be subject to removal from office. . . .

But the duties which are ours legally, differ materially from
what we, as sensible men, know are the causes which resulted in
the recent murder, and which, if they are unchecked, may cause
equally shameful incidents in Detroit's future history.

In that connection I must say that I deprecate most strongly
the moving of Negroes or other persons into districts in which
they know their presence may cause riot or bloodshed. I express
this personal feeling, which is perhaps beyond the proper province of an executive officer, sworn to enforce legal policies which
are different, but I do it in the hope that some official expression
can prevent a recurrence of the tragedy of Wednesday evening.

. . . In all these years there was no such incident as that which has
blackened our city's name within the past few days. These colored men and women who were long residents of this city, decided their own problems, with the realizations of their legal
rights, modified by their own common sense. It does not always
do for any man to demand, to its fullest, the right which the law
gives him. Sometimes by doing so he works irremediable harm
to himself and his fellows.

The first sign of a feeling, which resulted fatally Wednesday,
came with the revival of the Ku Klux Klan. The evidence is clear
that the unfortunate incidents which recently happened in the
northwest section of the city and the tragedy on Garland avenue
came from the activities of that organization. . . . for months, the
men and women of whom I have spoken before, have been going
from house to house conducting a cowardly campaign which
they would not dare suggest in public. These men and women
have gone to homes where resentment is strongest against members of the Negro race and have whispered their criminal propa-
ganda. They have stated that the mayor of the city, who happens
to be me, has placed 500 Negroes in the fire department. They

have reported that the mayor of the city has filled the police department with Negroes. They have stated that every department of the city government is overrun with Negroes. They have stated further that it was I who inspired and fostered the movement of colored citizens into districts inhabited previously entirely by white persons. . . . Every one of these charges is untrue.

And on the other hand, a similar campaign by the same people was conducted to arouse the resentment of the Negro population against the present government. There the story told was exactly the opposite to that told to the white persons. It was that no Negroes were being employed in the city government; that no police protection required by law was being given to Negro residents. . . .

For months, during the course of this criminal campaign, a constant procession of colored persons has been moving in and out of the headquarters of a candidate for Mayor [Charles Bowles] favored by the Ku Klux Klan. I have evidence that certain colored persons are on the payroll of the Ku Klux Klan, with the aim of influencing members of their race against the present government. . . .

I have said that I deprecate the moving by colored persons into districts in which their presence would cause disturbances. I shall go further. I believe that any colored person who endangers life and property, simply to gratify his personal pride, is an enemy of his race as well as an incitant of riot and murder. These men who have permitted themselves to be the tools of the Ku Klux Klan in its efforts to fan the flames of racial hatred into murderous fire, have hurt the cause of their race in a degree that cannot be measured. I feel that it lies with the real leaders of the colored race in Detroit to dissipate their murderous pride. This seems to exist chiefly in a very few colored persons who are unwilling to live in sections of the city where members of their race predominate, but who are willing to rely on the natural racial pride of the rest of their people to protect them when they move into districts where their presence may be resented. . . .

It lies with you and members of your department to protect fully life and property of all persons without regard to creed or color. And in addition to those laws, there are laws against inciting to riot. There are those in this community—some who think themselves in positions of security, who have been deliberately and maliciously arousing the people of both races against each other, driving [the] less cowardly to defy the law, and as we have seen, to murder and death. . . . [1]

Editor's Note

1. Mayor Smith won reelection two months later, after a bitter campaign against Klan-endorsed Charles Bowles. Though more open-minded than many other politicians of his time, he was not able to divest himself of the confusions shown in this letter. Like most white Detroiters then and for some years later, he did not comprehend the extent of the need for housing for Negroes. He conceded that the law was clearly on the side of the Negro who wished freedom to choose his neighborhood, yet appealed to him to forgo his legal rights.

4.   Has the Negro the Right of Self-Defense?

David E. Lilienthal

Few criminal cases have combined the dramatic intensity, the forensic brilliance, and the deep social significance present in the trial just concluded at Detroit of Dr. Ossian Sweet and ten other Negroes charged with the murder of a white man. For more than a month all the efforts of the prosecutor and the police were bent towards securing a verdict of life imprisonment from the white jury. Fighting for the right of the defendants and all other Negroes to defend themselves against assault was the ablest criminal advocate who ever faced an American jury, Clarence Darrow, and with him Arthur Garfield Hays of New York, Walter M. Nelson of Detroit, and Herbert Friedman of Chicago. The jury, after deliberating for forty-six hours, was unable to

David E. Lilienthal, "Has the Negro the Right of Self-Defense?" *The Nation* (23 December 1925): 724–25. Reprinted by permission of The Nation Company, Inc.

agree, and on November 27 was discharged. Perhaps it was only to be expected that there would be no agreement among twelve men selected at random from a community—or a nation for that matter—in which there is so little agreement upon the difficult problem really at the bottom of the case.

For this was no ordinary murder trial. Back of it all was the whole sensitive problem of race relations, intensified a thousand-fold by the recent Northern migration of the Negro; hovering over and touching the whole proceeding was the somber cloud of race prejudice.

. . .It is a tribute to the capacity of Clarence Darrow to rouse the best in common men, and to the fairness of the extraordinary young judge [Frank Murphy] who presided, that seven jurors held out for two days for acquittal and thus prevented their fellows from sending the defendants to the penitentiary.

The theory upon which the prosecution sought to send these eleven Negroes to prison for life—the extreme penalty in Michigan—is an interesting phase of this memorable case. No evidence of who fired the shot which killed Leon Breiner was available; he was struck by one bullet, whereas eight or ten were fired from within the house. It was therefore impossible to charge one defendant as the murderer and the others as co-principals, aiding and abetting. The charge of a conspiracy to kill would have been less severe than first-degree murder. The state accordingly charged each of the eleven with murder, alleging that all eleven acted under an *agreement* to kill anyone committing even the slightest trespass, regardless of the necessity for defense, so that each was equally responsible for the shooting done by one. No effort to prove such an agreement was made either by words or conduct, but the killing itself was regarded both as the crime and proof of the murderous agreement! Trade unionists who have suffered for generations by reason of the legal sleight-of-hand known as "conspiracy" will do well to keep their eyes open upon this latest refinement upon that doctrine of oppression.

Proceeding upon this ingenious theory, the state, after proving that there was a killing, sought to anticipate and defeat the defendants' plea of self-defense. Witness after witness, chiefly white residents of the neighborhood, took the stand and insisted that the crowds which gathered about Dr. Sweet's home were

small, orderly, and even "neighborly." Some were sorry specta-
cles under Darrow's pitiless cross-questioning and biting sarcasm, but for the most part they clung to the story that although
it was necessary to have on duty sixteen policemen, in charge of
a deputy chief, the neighborhood was a veritable vale of peace.
One witness, asked by the prosecutor how many people he saw
about the Sweet house, replied: "There was a great crowd . . .
no, I won't say a great crowd . . . a large crowd . . . well, there
were a few people there and the officers were keeping them moving." The cross-examination was illuminating:

> Q. Have you talked to anyone about the case?
> A. Lieutenant Johnson (the police detective in charge).
> Q. And when you started to answer the question you forgot to
>   say "a few people," didn't you?
> A. Yes, sir.

Those state witnesses who could be induced to admit that
stones had been thrown amused the courtroom by referring to
them as "pebbles," the "pebbles" introduced into evidence being
chunks of cement, some of them the size of one's fist. The testimony of the police detailed to guard the house corroborated that
of the residents of the vicinity in every respect.

The defense first produced witnesses, most of them Negroes,
who gave a wholly different picture of conditions just before the
shooting—a picture of an angry, threatening crowd, determined
"to run the niggers out." It was further established that shortly
after Dr. Sweet's purchase of a house in this white neighborhood,
some seven hundred residents of the community held an over-
flow mass meeting, and organized an "Improvement Association." That the "improvement" intended was keeping Negroes
out of the district was clear.

The principal defendant, Dr. Sweet, was put on the stand and
stated the circumstances surrounding the shooting, as they appeared from within the beleaguered house. He told of the crowds
on September 8 when he moved in, of the police detailed because
of the known temper of the vicinity, of the threats and the stoning, of the massing of the crowd, and of the shooting. Then followed one of the most remarkable direct examinations to be
found in all the records of criminal cases: a vivid picture of the

324

fear-ridden mind of a black man, terrified by a hostile crowd of whites outside his home. The testimony was particularly effective because it came from the lips of a highly educated man, a graduate of two universities, just returned from research in Vienna, and a highly skilled physician. To show that Dr. Sweet believed his life was in danger Mr. Hays questioned him upon his mental life and emotional experience in so far as they touched upon his fear of mob violence. The examination brought out that the witness had seen the brutalities of the Washington race riots, had read accounts of the Chicago cruelties, of those at East St. Louis, Tulsa, and Omaha. He had talked with Detroit Negroes who had been driven from their new homes by white neighbors: in one case a fellow-physician whose house but three months before had been sacked by a mob, and who had been forced to convey away his newly-purchased home while policemen looked on approvingly. Much of his information concerning the way his people had been abused and tyrannized by whites came from a reading of *The Nation*, and a number of issues were introduced into evidence. Thus the whole sordid panorama of bestiality was unrolled before the jury, in an effort to convey to the white men an understanding of the fear that gripped those eleven barricaded blacks. When finally the witness was asked his state of mind at the time of the shooting, he answered: "When I opened the door I saw the mob and I realized I was facing that same mob that has hounded my people throughout its entire history. . . . "

The climax of the trial was reached when Clarence Darrow walked slowly to the jury box and began his closing argument. A deep silence fell over the crowded noisy courtroom. The old man with the unutterably sad face and the great stooped shoulders seemed no mere lawyer pleading for hire. He seemed, instead, a patriarch out of another age. . . . Quietly and sadly he besought these twelve men to inflict no further hatred and injustice upon a race that has known nothing but hatred and injustice. He seemed to be pleading more that the white man might be just than that the black be free, more for the spirit of the master than the body of the slave. . . .

And then suddenly the voice of the lawyer rang out like a brass gong, his eyes became hard and grim, every muscle of his huge body was tense and strained. Darrow was no longer the patriarch, the philosopher. Now he had become the warrior, the

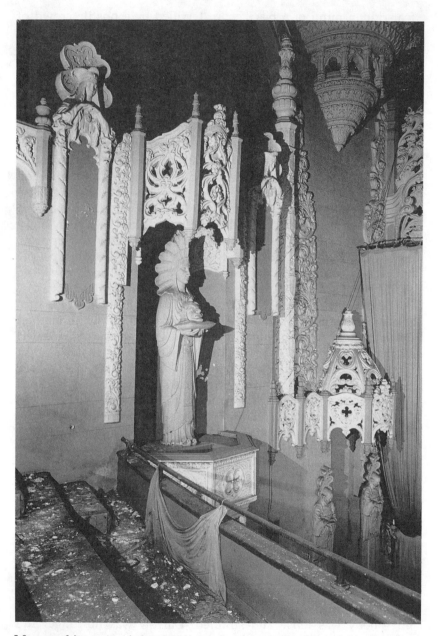

More architecture of the 1920s, much of it neglected and in disarray.
United Artists Theater. (Courtesy of Bob McKeown, 1987.)

veteran of a hundred battles for human freedom—battles against the greed of the strong, the cruelty of the many, the bigotry of the ignorant. . . . his head lowered like a fighter coming out of his corner, he turned upon the prosecutors, his arms swinging, eyes narrowed and pitiless, the brass gong clanging an alarm and a challenge. . . . John Brown before the Arsenal at Harper's Ferry. Owen Lovejoy defying the mob at Alton.

. . .There are no more underground railroads or fugitive-slave laws or whipping-posts. But there are mobs and torches and trees hideous with swinging black shapes, and there is suspicion, prejudice, hatred. And on the new battlefield, fighting a subtler foe, and one that perhaps may never be wholly defeated, is Clarence Darrow, son of the Abolitionists.

The story told in that courtroom was undoubtedly a sordid and disheartening one, but not wholly so. Has the white man of today advanced beyond his brother of two hundred years ago who traded slaves for rum? No one can answer with any assurance. But that the black man is making headway is clear beyond doubt. Of this, the young defendants themselves are striking evidence. Most of them are either graduates or students of colleges and professional schools; their grandparents were slaves who could neither read nor write! At the press table sat two colored newspapermen the match of any correspondent there. The factories seen from the courtroom windows are employing more and more Negroes every week. And there is encouragment, too, in the fact that Negroes can command so fair a trial in a land where most trials of Negroes have been mob-dominated travesties. For this trial was probably the fairest ever accorded a Negro in this country; had it been otherwise the defendants would now be on their way to a life in prison.

5.   Police Brutality

Forrester Washington

Mayor Smith's almost immediate reaction to what he and the police saw as the September, 1925, murder of a presumably innocent white bystander by violent blacks was to appoint a committee to discover what had gone wrong in the city's race relations. To head the staff he brought back to Detroit the sociologist Forrester Washington, who had been executive secretary of the Detroit Urban League during its opening days.

The study itself was in twelve parts. Among them were included sections on housing, police brutality, employment opportunities, discrimination, the refusal of some labor unions to accept Negro members, and comparable health conditions for Negro and white families. I have reproduced here several of the cases from the police brutality section of the report.

Each of the cases presented here ends in the death of a civilian.

Negroes Killed by the Police

The homicide reports show that during the period from Jany. 1, 1925 to June 30, 1926, 25 Negroes, as compared with 24 whites were killed by the police. The following are case studies of samples of these killings, beginning with June 30, 1926 and working back through 1925. The names were selected according to date. Only those cases whose families could be located are included. The method followed is to submit for each case 1) the

Forrester Washington, "Police Brutality," in *The Negro in Detroit, 1926*, report of the Mayor's Interracial Commission (Detroit: Bureau of Governmental Research, 1926).

findings of the Survey Staff 2) the verbatim police reports 3) Negro Newspaper Reports and Comment.

Henry Noble

Survey Findings

Henry Noble was born in Fort Valley, Georgia in 1898. When he was around fifteen years old his family migrated to Steubenville, Ohio. . . .

Because of the high wages which can be obtained in Detroit, Henry and his brother came here for the purpose of accumulating sufficient money to purchase their mother a home. When they first arrived he and his brother resided in the same home, but in October, 1925, he moved to 972 Lafayette Avenue, because of his continual connections with petty theft charges. Here his landlady informed him on the first of December that he would have to vacate his room. While there he did not work but spent a great deal of his time in pool rooms and gambling joints.

He was absolutely illiterate. His landlady had to read and write his letters.

He was married, but separated before coming to Detroit.

At the time of his death Henry did not own any property nor did he have a bank account. He was insured, however, in the Metropolitan and National Benefit. These policies provided enough money for his burial and left a surplus for the family.

The Police Report

"About 3:25 A.M., March 31, 1926, Henry Noble, Frank Foster and Jack Griskell were breaking into the Congress Pharmacy at 901 E. Congress Street. Frank Foster and Jack Griskell were arrested by Patrolmen W. Burkuhl and H. Bartlett. Henry Noble was inside the Drug Store, and when he saw the officers he ran out of the side door. The officers commanded him to stop, but he kept running, so they fired several shots, which struck him in the head and chest. He was taken to Receiving Hospital in subconscious condition in #1 Auto where he died shortly after arrival. Patrolmen Burkuhl and Bartlett were exonerated by Assistant Prosecutor Oscar Kaufman. Inquest pending."

The Detroit Independent (Negro Newspaper)

"Henry Noble, 22 years old, who resides at 972 E. Lafayette was shot and killed by Patrolman Burkuhl of the Central Station. The killing took place at the Congress pharmacy, 901 E. Congress Street, where Patrolmen Burkuhl and Harry Bartlett went in response to an alarm that the store was being robbed. On reaching the scene the officers are said to have found and arrested two colored lookouts stationed outside the building. After handcuffing the two men to their automobile wheels, they returned to the store, where it is reported they saw a third man on the inside busily engaged in plundering the place. Burkuhl then fired at the man through the window, at the same time calling him to halt, and as the latter fled through the door, Patrolman Burkuhl fired four shots in his body. Noble died before he reached the Receiving Hospital. Officer Burkuhl has the reputation of being one of the crack shooters of the local police department, having to his record the killing of three other alleged bandits."

Bertram Johnson

Survey Findings

Bertram Johnson . . . came to Detroit about eleven years ago and was married six months after his arrival. Since coming to Detroit the family has resided at 4179 Beaubien Street for the last seven years.

Johnson has worked steadily since his arrival in Detroit. For the last four years he had been operating a tailor shop at 4181 Beaubien. He worked with the D&C Navigation Company for five years and for three years as captain of waiters at the Charlevoix Hotel.

His chief recreation outside of home was race horses. The greater part of his spare time was spent attending the race tracks. He was not especially interested in any other sport.

Johnson was an intelligent man. He took advantage of the educational opportunities offered in New York and completed three years of high school work there.

His educational training enabled him to take part in much of the Negro community life of Detroit. He was a member of the Catholic Church and was associated with a number of fraternal organizations, among which were the Elks and Moose. Johnson was a voter and was interested in political issues.

The Police Report

"Bert Johnson, colored, age 25, 4181 Beaubien Street, about 6:15 P.M. February 17, 1926. Bert Johnson, colored, while resisting arrest for violating the prohibition law and attempting to attack Patrolmen Cornelius Everdyke, Harold McNinch, and Paul Perdew with a large knife in his blind pig at 3725 St. Antoine Street. He was shot in the neck by Patrolman Everdyke. Bert Johnson was taken to Receiving Hospital in #1 auto where he died shortly after arrival. February 23, 1926, Patrolman Everdyke exonerated by coroner's jury in charge of Coroner Albert L. French."

The Owl (Negro Newspaper)

"Bertram Johnson was murdered when he tried to compel Patrolmen Everdyke and Perdew to respect the legal rights of another Negro, Roland Hicks. These Patrolmen were invading Mr. Hick's place of business without search warrant, and without any other right under the law, to proceed. Johnson demanded that they leave—this so wrought up these policemen who were acting, seemingly, under the old adage of the South, that the black man had no rights that needed to be respected—that they began to assault Bertram Johnson and when he resisted Patrolman Everdyke shot at him.

"Investigation discloses that on the first shot Johnson stopped dead still with his hands down, and his head erect, looking at the policeman, at which time, Patrolman Perdew grabbed Johnson from the back, held him, while Everdyke, taking aim, shot Johnson through the neck—murdering him in cold blood."

331

Gertrude Russian

Survey Findings

Gertrude Russian was born in Arkansas in 1892. Because of the poor educational opportunities offered, she was unable to go any further than the third grade.

She spent her childhood and practically her entire womanhood in Arkansas. It was not until the fall of 1924 that she and her husband migrated to Detroit. While in Detroit she was not engaged in any work outside of the home. Mrs. Russian had not taken much part in the community life of Detroit. . . .

Police Report

"Gertrude Russian (colored) age 31 years, 2494 Beaubien Street. About 11:40 P.M. November 25, 1925, Patrolmen Joseph MacManus, James Dooley and John Nee, while walking in plain clothes and when in front of 2494 Beaubien Street Joseph Mac-Manus was accosted by Gertrude Russian (colored). The patrolman placed her under arrest for accosting men on the street. They placed her in a Ford police car near by and Patrolman Mac-Manus sat alongside her, while Patrolman James Dooley and John Nee were taking care of a disturbance across the street. Gertrude Russian drew a knife and stabbed Patrolman MacManus in the abdomen and right side of back. Patrolman MacManus drew his gun and shot Gertrude Russian in the neck, killing her instantly. Patrolman MacManus was taken to Receiving Hospital. Inquest pending."

Detroit Independent (Negro Newspaper)

"Gertrude Russian was shot and killed on Thanksgiving Eve, November 25, 1925 at the corner of Beaubien and Winder. She was arrested for soliciting and thrown into scout car No. 320–015 by three policemen. There was a disturbance a few yards away on Beaubien Street and two of the officers who made the arrest were called away from the car. The officer remaining got into a heated dispute with his arrested victim and was seen in the act of striking her with his blackjack.

332

"The woman made desperate by the blows pulled out her knife and began slashing the officer across the stomach; the officer fired, the bullet making a gunshot wound in the leg. As the two officers who were called away approached the car, the wounded officer in charge of the woman yelled to them, 'She cut me'. 'He shot me', the woman answered.

"The other two officers jumped into the car and drove away, but when only a few yards, two other shots were heard fired into the body of the woman, and she died instantly."

Marcus Lawhorn

Survey Findings

Marcus Lawhorn was recognized by neighbors as an outstanding character in [the] Negro Underworld. It was said that he was both a user and peddler of narcotics.

Because of the absence of relatives there is not very much known about his early life. It is said, however, that he had only a meagre amount of education.

He was not lawfully married, but at various intervals, had several women in his apartment.

Lawhorn was not a member of a church nor was he associated with any of the constructive forces of the city. He was buried by the Welfare Department.

Police Report

"Marcus Lawhorn, alias George Williams, alias Wilson, alias Markus de Horn, colored, 45 years, of 550 Watson, about 12:50 P.M. January 20, 1926, Patrolman Alfred Letourneau, Roy Rollyson and Clarence Mayo of the 13th Precinct, went to 550 Watson Street to serve a warrant for assault and battery on a Mrs. W. Smith. Patrolman Letourneau was searching the house for Mrs. W. Smith when he found Marcus Lawhorn, alias Marcus De Horn, alias George Williams, alias Wilson, lying on a bed in the house smoking an opium pipe. Marcus Lawhorn, alias De Horn, offered Patrolman Letourneau some money if he would not arrest him on a dope charge. The officer upset the money, Marcus Lawhorn then ran out of the house. Patrolman Roy Rollyson chased him and commanded Lawhorn to stop. He refused and when in the rear of 534 Erskine Street, Lawhorn reached for his hip pocket and Patrolman Rollyson drew his gun and shot, striking Lawhorn in the left side of the back, killing him instantly, January 26, [sic] 1926. Patrolman Roy Rollyson was exonerated by coroner's jury in charge of Coroner J. E. Burgess."

The Detroit Independent (Negro Newspaper)

"Marcus Lawhorn, 550 Watson Street, was shot in the back and killed here, January 20, 1926 by Patrolman Roy Rollyson.

"It is reported that a squad of officers, of which Rollyson was a member, went to the Watson Street house in answer to a telephone call informing them that there was a disturbance in the house. They found Lawhorn in his apartment where it is said a quantity of narcotics was thought to be concealed. It is alleged that when the officers attempted to arrest Lawhorn, he ran from the house. He was followed by Patrolman Rollyson through the back door and out into the alley at the rear of 534 Erskine, where Lawhorn and the officer stopped. The officer shot him in the chest. Death came instantaneously. Rollyson was brought before the police trial board and exonerated. Lawhorn did not have any weapons on his body."

Steve Tompkins

Survey Findings

Steven Tompkins was born May 25, 1885 at Parsville, S.C. Tompkins attended the public school at Parsville until he reached the fourth grade. He and his wife came to Detroit in 1917 to answer the great demands for Negro labor. During the eight years he spent here, he was employed as a laborer at Ford Motor Company. He was not a member of a church here nor did he take an active part in the community life of Detroit. Tompkins was not associated with any of the fraternal organizations, but held several policies in insurance companies.

Police Report

"Steve Tompkins (colored) age 42 years, 7727 Russell Street, about 12:20 P.M. August 20, 1925, Patrolman Proctor Pruitt was serving a summons on Steve Tompkins at his home at 7727 Russell Street for violating the Prohibition Law. Steve Tompkins is the colored man that shot Patrolman Proctor Pruitt back in April, 1923 and Judge Jeffries discharged Tompkins. When Patrolman Pruitt tried to serve Steve Tompkins with the summons he recognized the officer and ran to his bedroom. Patrolman Pruitt followed Tompkins into the bedroom and, when the officer saw Tompkins reaching into the dresser drawer and drawing a gun, Patrolman Pruitt shot Steve Tompkins in the left temple, killing him instantly. Inquest pending."

The Owl (Negro Newspaper)

"Steven Tompkins, colored, was peacefully residing in his home at 7727 Russell Street when Patrolman Proctor Pruitt knocked on his door. He was admitted by his wife. The officer served a summons on Steven Tompkins, and investigation disclosed the fact that while Tompkins was reading the summons Patrolman Pruitt pulled out his gun and deliberately, in cold blood with malice aforethought, killed and murdered Tompkins in his own home on the pretext that Tompkins, a few years before had shot him."

Mrs. Lillie Smith

Survey Findings

Mrs. Lillie Smith was born in 1900 in Charleston, S.C. The meagre amount of education she had was received in the public schools of that city. She completed the third grade.

Mrs. Smith was a church member but was not allied with any of the fraternal organizations of Detroit. She was insured with several insurance companies.

Police Report

"Lillie Smith, colored, age 25 years, 1545 Alger Avenue. About 7:25 P.M., February 1, 1925, Patrolman Fred Williams, while walking his beat at Russell near Brewster Street, heard two shots fired in rapid succession and then saw an International Truck, No. 95–485, driving at a rapid speed north on Russell near Brewster Street with James Smith driving and Lillie Smith, his wife, beside him. The Patrolman went out into the street, flashed his light and called to them to stop. They refused and the patrolman fired two shots, one bullet striking Lillie Smith in the left jaw. She was taken to Receiving Hospital in No. 3 Auto where she died February 8, 1925 at 5:00 P.M. Patrolman Fred Williams arrested and now awaiting trial (February 28, 1926)."

The Detroit Independent's Report
(Negro Newspaper)

"Fred Williams, a policeman, deliberately murdered Mrs. Lillie Smith, expectant mother, by shooting at the truck driven by her husband, February 1, 1925, near the corner of Alfred and Russell Streets, striking her directly in the neck, was freed in five minutes by a jury. Mrs. Smith was taken to the Receiving Hospital after the shooting, where she died a double death, by giving birth to an infant who still lives. Mrs. Smith died as a result of the wound."

George Sims

Survey Findings

George Sims was born in Knoxville, Tennessee in 1893. . . . he successfully completed three years of high school work.

In 1915 he married and the following year he and his wife migrated to Detroit in response to the great demand for Negro labor. At the time he was killed, he was employed at Ford's River Rouge Plant. He supplemented his payroll by peddling coal because at this time Ford's plants were only working four days a week. Sims was a member of the St. John's Methodist Church.

The Police Report

"George Sims, colored, age 38, 1985 Mullett Street. About 1:10 A.M. February 25, 1926, Patrolman Peter Scalley and Kenneth Lawrence while patrolling in a scout car, they saw a man in the alley between Hastings and Rivard, Clinton and Macomb Streets. The officers approached this man and ordered him to throw up his hands. He immediately reached for his pocket. Patrolman Scalley, thinking the man was reaching for a gun, shot him in the chest and below the heart. He was taken to Receiving Hospital, where he died shortly after arrival. This man was later identified as George Sims, colored, and has the reputation of being a strong-arm man. Inquest pending."

The Owl's Report (Negro Newspaper)

"Last Thursday morning about one A.M. George Sims, a Ford worker, was killed by Patrolman Peter Scalley, in cold blood.

"Sims, a Ford worker working four days a week, has a wife and two daughters and lived at 1985 Mullett Street, called at a friend's house who lives in the alley off Russell between Clinton and Macomb Streets, to borrow his wagon, to peddle coal with, in order to make extra money for his family, due to the loss of two days in the factory.

"He was standing in the alley talking with this friend from the window, with a thermos bottle under his arm, when officers Scalley and Kennedy drove up. Scalley ordered Sims to 'throw up his hands' which he did. The thermos bottle he was carrying under his arm fell on the pavement and Scalley fired and killed Sims in cold blood. Sims had no weapons on his body."

. . .The explanation given rather generally by the police especially by the inspector of the homicide and Italian squads as to why there are so many killings of Negroes is that the Negro is a desperate criminal and officers have to shoot first. The Inspector of the Italian Squad and others have spoken of the number of brutal killings of police by Negroes. The reports of the homicide squad, however, show that during the eighteen months from January 1, 1925 to June 30, 1926, policemen were killed by four Negroes. In one case, that of Edward Jordon, the policeman received a bullet which was intended for another Negro with whom Jordon had been fighting. This other Negro ran out of the hotel and Jordon firing after him killed the officer who was standing on the corner. In the other two [*sic*] cases the officers were killed by men whom they had cornered.

During the same period seven white men killed officers and in six of these cases the murder was committed by a hold-up man who turned on the officer when he interfered. In other words, as far as killings are concerned, the records do not show the Negroes to be hunters of policemen.

As an example of what may be done by a different method of handling there is a case of a lieutenant of the Italian Squad who is in general charge of that Department dealing with Negroes. He has not shot a man in fifteen years yet the Inspector of the Squad says that he can go into a den and arrest any man he chooses with perfect impunity. The general situation may be inferred from a comparison with the statistics for New York, which has the largest Negro population in the country (183,248). The Secretary of the Police Department of New York City says that in 1925 there were three Negroes killed by policemen. In the same year 14 Negroes were killed by policemen in Detroit with its Negro population of 82,000 in 1925.

As a complication of the situation it is commonly believed among colored people that a large number of Southern policemen are employed in Negro districts, having been recruited for the specific purpose and that they come with deep-seated prejudices against the Negroes which make it impossible for them to give them fair treatment. At any rate Detroit has not followed to any great extent the policy adopted by some cities of using colored policemen and on the local force there are only 14 colored men out of 3000. . . . [1]

Editor's Note

1. Minor errors and inconsistencies in the staff or police reports have not been corrected or noted unless they raise questions as to content. It might also be mentioned that the victims included all sorts of men and women, not only the innocent or well-behaved.

   There were many areas of police administration and performance targeted for criticism in the report; among these was the bland assumption of the police that the Negro district and the "vice" district shared the same boundaries. Given police willingness to believe that any black neighborhood was at best a potential crime area, the net result was that one group of Detroiters—about eight percent of all citizens at that time—was essentially powerless to determine its own life-style.

6. Gangsters and Politicians in Detroit: The Buckley Murder

Cyril Arthur Player

Radio was still new in 1930, and the election night murder of popular radio announcer Jerry Buckley stunned the city. Buckley had been stalwart in his opposition to both the Klan and organized crime. His large popular audience included many who had not responded to the tragedy of the Sweet case. The Buckley mystery is recounted here from an article by journalist Cyril Arthur Player written for the New Republic.

Detroit is paying the penalty for its negligence. The tomb of Gerald E. Buckley, whither tens of thousands have tramped to share their conviction of his martyrdom, is the melancholy monument to a citizenship that fell asleep.

The obvious facts are these: In November, 1929, Detroit elected a mayor, Charles Bowles. On July 22 last, Detroit recalled Mr. Bowles from that office. Within an hour or so after the last returns had been announced—in fact, at half past one in the morning—Jerry Buckley, "political commentator" for a local radio station, a champion of the recall and foe of the underworld, was shot to death as he sat in the lobby of a hotel.

Cyril Arthur Player, "Gangsters and Politicians in Detroit: The Buckley Murder," *The New Republic* (13 August 1930): 361–63.

The Buckley murder was the eleventh so-called gangster killing in Detroit within two weeks, but he was also the first "white man" to be "put on the spot." Previous murders, excepting the attempt last January on the life of a police inspector, have been confined to an Italian group and may have been due to an imported Sicilian domestic feud. Buckley's murder marked the added and anticipated step of the paid-killer era, which troubles the land, and proved also the unsoundness of the "dog eat dog" policy which police authorities say spells eventual self-extermination of the gangster.

Probably 100,000 persons passed through the modest Buckley home to view the slain man. Almost as many attended the funeral, which was the largest seen in Detroit since that [of] the celebrated mayor and governor, Hazen Pingree. The newspapers have not columns enough to express the popular horror and indignation . . . in tribute to a man who fought energetically for old-age pensions, for jobs for needy families, and for every form of humanitarian relief. . . .

But the significant fact is that the Buckley slaying was the logical climax of preceding events, although it arrived after the tide of Detroit's political fortune had turned. The shots of the slayers were almost a dramatic necessity as the "curtain" for the campaign that was waged here, and for such a piece of lawlessness as had been read into local history. But the tremendous demoralization of city government caused by looseness, ignorance, incapacity and selfishness had already been recognized by an alarmed citizenship. The offending regime, so young in months, already was doomed.

Charles Bowles is one of those inadequate men whom destiny occasionally chooses for tragi-comic relief. He . . . came into local politics from nowhere. Twice defeated for mayor, though ardently supported by the Ku Klux Klan, he obtained a place on the bench of the recorder's [criminal] court. He was reelected to this position but resigned it to make the race for mayor in a three-sided primary. The incumbent, John C. Lodge, was eliminated, and Bowles defeated a former mayor, John W. Smith.

As soon as he became mayor it became apparent that Mr. Bowles, sipping at the sweets of power, was cradling large ambitions. Under the charter, the mayor's office is non-partisan. Mr. Bowles began to build up a branch Republican machine, and in that process the well integrated units of public service began to fall apart. He made his chief blunder at the very start. He chose for commissioner of public works a man whose previous activity in public office had left him thoroughly distrusted by the public, a man who had been obliged to resign the police commissionership in a former administration to save his chief, the mayor, from defeat in a reelection.

This man who, meanwhile, had built up a substantial fortune in business, was John Gillespie. From the very day he took office until the day he abruptly resigned, following the recall, Gillespie was known as "commissioner of the works." He was the administration, and all those who knew their way around waited at his door.

The town, moreover, was running pretty much as it liked. Mayor Bowles had campaigned on the platform that the police department needed a shaking up. . . . A well-known lawyer, Harold H. Emmons, was named commissioner. The Emmons appointment was the only one made by Bowles which really commanded public respect. It was made at the request of an informal committee of citizens and before the advent of "the Gillespie" to power.

Police Commissioner Emmons returned from a business trip to meet the rising anger of a community that was fast preparing to take drastic measures. Mayor Bowles went to the Kentucky derby with a party organized by "the Gillespie". Emmons promptly launched his raids on the gamblers, and the familiar haunts began to "go dark." But when Bowles and Mr. Gillespie returned from the races, the mayor promptly fired Commissioner Emmons, replacing him with Thomas C. Wilcox, as futile a man as was Bowles himself.

Mr. Wilcox . . . was prompt to warn the gangster world that "Detroit is going to get the best blankety blank cleaning of its life."

Nevertheless, things went on as before. The News and The Free Press continued to call attention to open law violations and unsavoury conditions. Former supporters of Mr. Bowles drew away, non-political well-wishers became shocked and the voice of indignant criticism became a loud and swelling chorus. But somewhere out of that chorus, at first vague and shifting, then suddenly firm and positive, there emerged the word "Recall."

. . .The [recall] campaign itself set a record, probably nationwide, not only for its bitterness, but for the lavish employment of
the radio, and for the mud two of the opposing speakers slung at
each other over the air. . . . Mr. Gillespie [acting as Bowles' campaign manager] hired an army of workers and a squadron of automobiles was marshalled to carry voters. When Mr. Gillespie
came to pay up, after the battle was lost, the amount of the bill
for defending Mayor Bowles and himself, nearly reached, it is
said, the sum of $100,000. He then suddenly resigned, with the
words that he was "sick and tired of the whole mess." . . .

But the news of the recall count, exciting though it was,
was drowned out by the noise of the shots that killed Jerry Buckley, who had just finished his night's work of announcing the
returns.

Buckley was born in Detroit. He was the son of a horseshoer,
who became editor of the *Horseshoers' Journal.* He worked his way
through college . . . and in time graduated from a law school. He
sold real estate, became interested in government work and was
engaged by the bureau of intelligence of the Internal Revenue
Department. At one time he did social service work for the Ford
Motor Company, and often told friends that the knowledge he
gained in that work made him the relentless enemy of racketeers
and gamblers.

He certainly went after them when his radio announcing developed into editorial comment on affairs. During the recall campaign his speeches were the most pungent and devastating of
any that were on the air. Several times his life was threatened,
and on election night it is said that he had three bodyguards
standing near him while he was at work.

His work done, he returned to the lobby of the hotel where he
was staying, and took his seat in one of two chairs placed pecu-
liarly and conspicuously together. The other chair was occupied.
He chatted a few minutes and then began to read a paper. Three
men entered. One stood aside while the other two went behind
Buckley and pumped a stream of lead into him.

This dramatic climax to a notorious situation brought the Governor of the State and the Adjutant-General hurrying by airplane
to Detroit. Commissioner Wilcox, when he was offered state aid,
reported to the newspapermen that he told the Governor:

"We are doing very nicely."

Then happened one of the most inscrutable things in the whole queer story. The Hearst-owned *Times*, which had stood on the fence during the campaign, took occasion to say in its issue reporting the tragedy:

"Buckley also was known as an associate of underworld racketeers and had been accused many times of using the radio for blackmail."

Doubtless *The Times* has since regretted this unjustified attack on a dead man, for the public rose in wrath and pilloried Buckley's defamers. But Commissioner Wilcox obviously was impressed, and had an idea. He announced that he was the fortunate possessor of an affidavit declaring Buckley had shaken down a man in the whiskey racket. Closely pressed by a News reporter, and asked to submit the affidavit to a judge to establish its validity, Wilcox admitted that the document had no signature as yet. The following day he proclaimed he had obtained a signature. And the next day the signer, a self-confessed bootlegger, made a second affidavit in which he declared that he could not read English, except very slowly, that he did not know the contents of the first affidavit, that he had signed it at the instigation of the commissioner, and at a time when he, the signer, thought he would be imprisoned if he did not sign. He added that personally he thought very highly of Buckley.

The evil genius which had accompanied Mr. Bowles all through his administration, managed to stay with him to the end. Arrests have been made. The centralized vice squad has been abolished and, as a consequence, hundreds of blind pigs were raided—proving, of course, that they had been in existence all the time and that the police knew where to find them. But neither the affidavit which Commissioner Wilcox worked so hard to obtain in order to destroy Buckley's character, nor the raiding of the blind pigs, has any relationship whatever to the capture of Buckley's slayers who, presumably, were imported killers and promptly disappeared. . . .

The reasons for Buckley's slaying still remain as much a mystery as the identity of the man or men who hired the killers. . . . Buckley's character scarcely is the issue, however, and the majority of Detroit's citizens believe profoundly in his integrity. . . .

Detroit seeks today a big man to take up the burden. . . .

Part XI

Hunger Comes Early to Detroit: A Decade of Depression

Hunger Comes Early to Detroit: A Decade of Depression

The depression of the 1930s has been the remembered war of older Americans for some years now. Its memories were ground into later generations as an unattainable standard of human suffering. Now only older grandparents have the dubious privilege of passing on the oral traditions of the depression. Among blacks with family roots in Paradise Valley, there are tales of rent parties. The music v·as never better than when "the man" would serve a final eviction notice in the morning, unless friends could raise the money tonight. In one west side Polish neighborhood there is a memory of lard sandwiches in the lunch bucket.

During the forties and fifties, Mary West Jorgenson, social worker at the Brightmoor Community Center, heard from several families the story of "the roast that went around the block." Half a dozen families on one street had worked out an ingenious method to preserve the tradition of beef on the table. One family, chosen by lot the first time, was obligated to buy the first roast on Saturday and enjoy their own Sunday dinner—but no more—from it. The remainder went next door to be reheated on Monday, to another house on Tuesday, and then on down the street, becoming progressively stew, then hash, until there was a final bare bone at the home of the last family for a watery soup at the end of the week. That family then scraped up the funds for a good twelve-cents-a-pound roast on the following day, which in turn began its own wanderings down the block.

The legend was wonderful. It included the self-discipline needed not to steal for your own child, and the housewifely resourcefulness of gravy on day-old bread, or the stew that was almost totally carrot and onion, with lots of water. The heartbreaking end of the story for Mary Jorgenson, teller of the folktale, came some years later when she spoke of the story in front of some of the women who had told it to her, thinking of it as a proud recollection for those who had lived it. One woman in the room abruptly began to scream, "We never did anything like that at all on X Street. We were never, ever that poor. Someone just made that up! It's a filthy, disgusting lie!" The other women, including several original narrators, kept shamefaced silence.

But that, too, was part of Detroit's depression. Lots of pride and a constant self-questioning stalked all adults who lived through those years. It was hard on those with middle-class beliefs and habits. Depression legends were filled with tales of the wealthy who were reported to have jumped out of office building windows or off the decks of cruise ships. There were also clerks and small businessmen and unemployed autoworkers who had hunting rifles. But most people survived as best they could.

The women stayed at home, confined by poverty to bitter loneliness and isolation. Detroit was a tradition-oriented society as far as men's and women's roles went—a "lunch-bucket town," some said. It was hard for the nonworking woman to comprehend the size of the problem destroying her life, or the new ways of perceiving it. Lucky were the men whom tradition allowed to play catch, or horseshoes, or even kick-the-can in the alleys, and who filled the public libraries to bursting, reading till closing time.

There were several legacies of the depression. Even before the full impact of the New Deal and its message of hope, there was a joining of issues over that very basic question of blame and self-blame. The Ford Hunger March demonstrated openly to many that Big Business didn't care. To some, the depression began to point the way to radical solutions as surely as had the bank failures that had preceded President Roosevelt's bank holiday. Honorable men went into chain groceries (this was before the supermarket) and stripped the food from the shelves for their families. Solemn, hard-faced men asked the librarian to find them a copy of this Karl Marx they had heard so much about. Both Mayor Frank Murphy and the president proclaimed that there was a right not to go hungry—and both made enemies who came to be seen as the people's enemies. Could the poor be blamed for poverty when it was so universal and openly acknowledged? Some did blame them, of course. When a bureaucrat in the welfare department embezzled, there were those to whom it proved only that the welfare clients themselves were cheaters who created an atmosphere that infected the respectable persons who dealt with them.

For most Detroiters the mutual acknowledgment of poverty led to a belief in the need for changes in society. One of these was the rapid growth of cooperative associations. A rural idea brought into town, it spread into many fields: buying clubs which expanded into grocery stores, a dairy with milk delivery routes, several housing efforts, and an optometrist's clinic. The expanding cooperative movement faded with the later transitions brought about by World War II, but while it lasted it provided exciting alternatives.

If some of the depression perceptions did not last long, the union movement, growing at first in secret, had at last come to stay. There came with it, for some, a lively interest in radical solutions of many sorts. It was an interest bred in those crowded libraries, but also in church halls, in "penny restaurants," in bars, on park benches, and in back alleys where grown men played kick-the-can.

Against this grim backdrop I reprint several articles portraying Detroit in the thirties. The first demonstrates that the depression really did begin early in Detroit. No one waited for the October, 1929 stock market crash. When Ford discarded the Model T for a new Model A, thousands were out of work. Paul U. Kellogg described the times for *Survey* magazine in October, 1928.

Next, "Detroit in Black and White," a wide-ranging account of the condition of blacks during the years before and during the depression, from a unpublished manuscript on the Michigan Civil Rights Federation by Norman McRae.

"Labor Spies and the Black Legion," by Forrest Davis, appeared in the *New Republic*. It can be regarded as a fairly accurate account of some horrible events, and shows some evidence that Davis probably talked with attorney Maurice Sugar during its preparation. There is considerable documentation for both its facts and its analysis of them in the Maurice Sugar Collection at the Reuther Library.

A significant crosscurrent was beginning as unorganized, unskilled workers began to fight back. One chapter from Steve Babson's *Working Detroit*, "The Tide Turns," tells of the moment when the UAW sit-down strikes created a new order of things.

The Reuther brothers knew to their sorrow that life was dangerous for union leaders. I include Victor Reuther's account of intruders at a family birthday party to illustrate this.

At the end of the decade, there came another political upheaval. Mayor Reading, the apparently innocuous choice of the outer sections of the city, was revealed as guilty of large-scale corruption and went to jail. Other changes were on the way. Mayor Reading was almost crowded off the front pages by the outbreak of war in Europe.

1. Ford Motor Company's Changeover from the Model T

Paul U. Kellogg

Acres of modern glass and steel construction, huge cement works, high lines and ore bins, blast furnace stacks and towering ovens form the matrix of the ocean-going port Henry Ford has dug out of the River Rouge. This is his Fordson plant at Detroit—"home" to Model A; and in one of the swift new Fords I was swung along a concrete road that led into it. . . . But the broken hopes, the plans gone wrong, the households wrenched apart, the children [removed] from schooling, as results of such a lay-off as that of the Ford plants in 1927 are not so easily visualized. They are there, nonetheless, as Detroit knows to its cost. . . .

Statistics given me by the company show 82,890 on the payroll last June as against 99,739 for June, 1926—a spread of 17,000; but

Paul U. Kellogg, "When Mass Production Stalls," *Survey* (1 March 1928): 683–728.

as against 120,275 for January, 1926—a spread of 37,000. These totals take no account of local companies supplying Ford parts, some of which shut down entirely. A social worker put the figure between maximum and minimum production at the Ford plants and those serving them at 60,000. A lay-off of 25,000 people at $6 a day, means a loss in wages for one month of $3,750,000, a lay-off of 60,000 means $9,000,000 a month less income for men and families.

The situation was mitigated by the fact that several other cars manufactured in Detroit, with Ford getting off the market, had a boom year in 1927—Hudson, Essex, Chrysler, Cadillac. There were no signals of panic. Bank deposits were up. New skyscrapers were going up. Merchandising in the big downtown stores was satisfactory. But that of the outlying stores that serve the residence neighborhoods of factory people was poor. Home buyers and real-estate operators were in trouble all down the line. The leniency of banks in tiding people over was not alone due to considerateness; it would have been disastrous to foreclose. Doctors were hard hit, and there was scarcely a trade or profession that did not feel the pinch. The municipality was confronted with a pyramiding load of relief. In its money-raising campaign last fall, the Community Fund appealed to well-to-do Detroiters for $600,000 more than the year before (and they responded)— $300,000 to make good the loss in collections from wage-earning families, $300,000 to carry on the greater burden of work thrown upon the private medical and charitable agencies of the city.

The Ford family was one of those to respond, giving $175,000 in all. Yet I do not gather that Mr. Ford thought through his relations to his employes in a way that would altogether distinguish between their households and his idle coal seams and his timber reserves or the unused water that ran over his spillways. Since his comparatively short-lived foray in paternalism, he has hewn to the line of paying high for work and letting the workers take care of themselves. "Put it all in the pay envelope." Ford dealers had lean months after the fat of the years also; and I imagine Ford lumped dealers and workers together in his mind. . . .

$72,539 was given in relief [by the Detroit Department of Welfare] in December, 1925; $150,950 in December, 1926; $248,187 in December, 1927. By November, 1926, the department was giving relief to 8,000 individuals as against 5,523 in November, 1925; by January, 1927, the figure had gone up to 21,750 as against 8,559 twelve months before; by March it had reached 24,117, continued around 15,000 throughout last spring and summer, and stood at 19,245 November last.

In these comparisons it should be borne in mind that 1925 was a fairly normal year. In 1926, employment, . . . was at its peak during the first half year, but by December twice as many families were on the books of the department as the year before; throughout the winter months of 1927 they were treble. . . . As time went on, the plants of the Detroit firms making screws, springs, cushions, bodies, etc., of whom Ford was the biggest customer, closed down. Their employes were out entirely, as were many of Ford's production men, after last May.

In the earlier period, Ford men were laid off and on in shifts, but Commissioner Dolan [Thomas A. Dolan, of the Detroit Welfare Department] told me that for over a year the department had found it necessary to supplement the wages of men thus staggered by the Ford Motor Company. Among them were men who had worked there for ten and twelve years, but could not support their families on the part-time pay. . . . The Ford commissary, which sells at cost, on a cash basis, offered no credit to help them along. The city department strengthened the hands of the little neighborhood merchants who were carrying them, by giving out (food) orders on these stores. The emptying of shops on the main thoroughfares of the west side of town was illuminating as to the failure of the pay envelopes. Meat markets closed, drug stores, moving picture houses. In a thousand ways the lay-off ravelled the fortunes of households. Help was needed to keep children in school. . . .

The crowded waiting rooms of free clinics registered the inability of people to meet their ordinary doctor's bills. The numbers coming to Harper Hospital's clinic last October were a third more than in October, 1925; to the Children's Hospital, a half more; to the North End Clinic, double; to Grace Hospital treble. . . .

Of all the sufferers, perhaps the Negroes, as the newest comers to Detroit, were hardest hit. A social worker in a Negro district told me of their predicament, but it was set down in cold figures at the City Department. Of the 4,029 families given relief

353

last November, 1,118 were colored, or 28 per cent. These included 5,137 persons out of the 86,000 colored population in the city. More than one out of twenty, in the old hard phrase, were "on the town". . . .

What the Ford Company did tallies pretty well with what the manufacturers attending the President's Unemployment Conference thought other manufacturers could do in the depression of 1921. It employed men, turn about, two or three weeks at a stretch so as to spread out its reduced payroll into as many pay envelopes as possible. It kept up production on Model T till June and thereafter continued to manufacture parts (as well as trucks and airplanes). It employed large numbers in overhauling the plant, designing and rebuilding machinery. It cut the working week to five days, and some of the time and for some of the departments to two and three days a week. It had reason to believe there was a large margin of floating workers, single men—the suitcase crowd—who could shift for themselves, here today, there tomorrow. And another margin of men from small towns and farms, who had home places to go to, and might welcome a vacation. For the rest, it hoped . . . to keep the cut in its labor force down to 25,000, and with part-time work and the savings which people had had a chance to lay by at the high wages, it assumed that they would make out all right. . . .

[Paul Kellogg compared lay-off programs in other companies, some of which met the 1921 depression with joint worker-management committees to plan the necessary cutbacks; in others, mainly in the Chicago garment industry, the committees were actually *union* management committees, and the company assisted in setting up emergency unemployment funds.]

. . . In contrast at Ford's, while there may have been lively considerateness, man to man, as employes were laid off or taken on during the emergency, they had no participation whatever in dealing with a situation they were in up to their necks. In workshop slang, decisions came down "through the roof." Responsibility was single, and divorced from those who most sorely felt its consequences. Through the roof came the intention to keep discarges down to 25,000; but that did not hold by 10,000 between the maximum for 1926 and the minimum for 1927.

Through the roof came the well-intentioned plan of staggering shifts. . . . Meanwhile, they could not meet expenses at home on the part-time pay. Through the roof came the assumption that high wages in the past had given Ford employes fat they could live on over the lean months. . . . Men who had taken Ford employment in earnest as a means of earning permanent livelihood, who had responded to the Ford policy of encouraging high standards of home life, were among those who were squeezed hardest when the bottom fell out of their earnings and they could not keep up payments on their houses.

If automobile manufacturers or tool makers elsewhere invent anything that plays into the making or the running of a car, the management "on the roof" at Ford's are quick to know of it. But there was nothing to indicate that they had heard of what Hills Brothers or the Dennison Manufacturing Company have done in tackling the problems of broken employment, what has been attempted by pioneers in glass and machinery, what any one of a dozen firms in textiles, clothing, or novelties has tried out. . . . Ford cars have invaded Europe from Ireland to Russia. It is to be doubted if his overseas salesmen have sent back anything on the systems of employment insurance abroad, which are national inventions after their kind. . . .

The baseball diamond outside the employment office at Fordson had been thronged on Monday morning, the week of my visit, with men who wanted to work for Ford. Six or seven thousand men applied for work that week in December, and they were hiring three or four hundred a day. . . . They were picking men for the assembly line, and here it was that the sifting process . . . was at work. They were after intelligence, activity, auto experience if possible; young fellows for the most part, American, Canadian, British; Scandinavians as well and Americanized Poles and Russians. "Everyone wants to work on the new car" said the superintendent.

There was something simple and direct in these hiring and firing negotiations, contrasting as they did with the more elaborate functionings of the employment departments of some of our big industries. Certainly the whole situation, the lure of the pay, the pressure for jobs, tended to create a picture of labor as a foot-loose commodity, welling in like a tide. . . . under such circumstances, many an industrial executive comes to regard the employment reservoir as something to tap today and empty into tomorrow, without thought of its human entourage. That indeed was the crux of the situation when they laid off men at Ford's no less than when they were taking them on.

Then the burden of household support was being lifted from the payroll to some hypothetical base outside the realm of Ford concern. As a Detroit business man put it, the Ford Motor Company is a business not a philanthropy; with sales off, the only source from which wages could have been drawn was past profits. Yet that is the source from which an industrial corporation meets payments on its bonds during a depression. And a whole trade insured against unemployment could shift much of the load from profits to prices.

Meanwhile to cut down a working force is all but like lifting a mortgage and transferring the interest charges by magic to other shoulders. There was a saving, a bonus, if you will, on every man put on part time or lopped off Ford's payroll. The discontinued earnings of Ford employes did not coalesce into any obligation which had to be reckoned with in company plans, any pressure to shorten the lay-off and overlap the two productions; anything even to compare with the administrative concern over throwing out old machines which as tools were worth a dollar a pound and as scrap $9 or $10 a ton. The pressure was all the other way round. And in the general view, it was just the men's hard luck.

With such tenuous security from above, what chances are there of the automobile workers bestirring themselves from below, other than individually, for their protection? . . . . The old craft organizations were long since ironed out of the mechanized industries of Detroit. The United Automobile, Aircraft and Vehicle Workers' Union of America, described to me as an embodiment of the One Big Union Idea, pulled a strike among the body workers at the Fisher plant some years ago which lasted thirty days. A strike last fall at the Briggs' plant was over in a week.

Among the old-line unions in the metal trades, the last strike of any consequence was that of 1920 in the Timken works, engineered by the machinists. Today, an employer told me there are scarcely 300 men in the machinists' local. A trade unionist put the figure at 700. At any rate, in this great center of machine production, it is inconsequential and President Martel of the city labor federation was frank to say that to unionize the 150,000 workers in the machine trades was too large a mouthful for organized labor in Detroit to bite off by itself. . . .

I attended a meeting of the central body in Detroit. . . . The picture I came away with was that of small groups of unionists, who had contrived to build dikes against the undermining tides of non-union workers, employed and unemployed, which surrounded them. Indeed, I could not help but feel that they regarded the semi-skilled workers of the machine shops more as a threat to their security than as a field for missionary effort.

In talking with me, President Martel blasted the employers in the mechanical trades for firing out the unions, cutting wages, installing prison labor methods and what not. He was equally outspoken as to the Communists, a lot of hare-brained people whom it was wise to let talk their heads off. "But if Weisbord can crack open the situation and give the employers the hell they've given us, it's coming to them. They won't get any consolation from us—either way."

His reference was to Albert Weisbord, the young Communist who effectively organized the long drawn-out textile strike in Passaic. There is nothing gumshoe about his presence in Detroit. He has opened an office downtown. . . .

To Weisbord's mind unemployment in Detroit has been due not merely to changes in models but to such mechanization and speeding up of work that men are chronically jobless. And to him the change in models is but a curtain-raiser for the "most intensified competition that has ever taken place" (with the home market saturated, foreign makes and tariff walls abroad) between Ford's vertical trust and General Motors aligned with DuPont and U.S. Steel. He sees business headed for a slump within a year, further and violent market changes, increased competition, greater speeding up, longer hours, more unemployment, attempts to beat down wages—"and this in turn means opportunity to organize and revolutionize the working class. . . ."

Therefore the urgings of party members to join their respective trade unions and bore from within. Therefore the missionary work among clubs, sick and death benefit organizations, fraternal bodies, and what they call "language fragments." Even now Weisbord claims they are the only group strong enough "to jam 3,500 to 4,000 people into some of the largest halls in Detroit—

almost entirely auto-workers." Today, his soap-boxers are unmolested, the penny sheets sold at factory gates. This he regards as temporary, due to "the arrogance of Detroit employers," but—

> To organize here means jail and clubbing. We are organizing for struggle. When once the workers begin to move, this city will be the center of revolutionary activity. Any large strike here means a general strike. Any large strike means a revolutionary situation— here at the heart of American capitalism and Ford worshipped all over the world. With hundreds of thousands of workmen out, 2,500 police are not going to stand in their way. That means the militia, the regular army. That means men shot down in the streets, and when a government shoots down men, events shape themselves.

In other words, if Weisbord is a prophet, Detroit will have more than an unemployment situation on its hands in case of a general depression. . . . The general wage-cuts he anticipated were discounted to me by Detroiters familiar with the industrial situation; but there was no blinking the maladjustments in employment, for which the big employing corporations are ultimately responsible. . . .

The general front of the Employers' Association is indicated by a paragraph at the top of one of its folders: " . . . 97 per cent of Detroit's work people pursue their various callings without let or hindrance from organized labor domination."

The association stands for the "American plan," which in local practice in the building trades means that the strongest organized unions work closed shop on the same buildings on which the weaker trades work open shop. There was a sympathetic strike to unionize them all on a large theater under construction last fall. It was met by a muster of builders, owners and bankers involved in the other great structures going up (one of them announced as the biggest office building in the world). A war chest of $100,000 was said to have been quickly subscribed, one maverick contractor was made to toe the line and the strike was nipped in the bud. It was a foretaste of what might happen if the dominant motor industry were confronted with a serious labor conflict.

In the Detroit factories there is no such hybrid situation. I was assured at the offices of the Employers' Association that men are not discharged because of union membership or activity; but was told that there has not been a unionized metal trades plant since the war. And to their minds, Detroit "would never have produced the automobiles it has if the unions were in the saddle". . . .

The complete dominance of the employers must exaggerate the tendency on the part of all to follow the line of least resistance, the tendency on the part of the least scrupulous to disregard the human element utterly, and thus to drag the rest down to their level. . . .

After all, Ford with his initiative and power merely exhibits in advance and on a large drafting board, dynamic trends in modern industry. My feeling is that there is something instinctive and fundamental underlying his ruthless dismissal of executives, his near-sightedness when it came to social by-products while he laid off men and overhauled his tools. What I have in mind is something different from the customary charge of autocracy lodged against him. He has had to buck tradition, business opinion, shop practices; he wants orders obeyed, or his insurgency is short-circuited. There is always the danger that his course will degenerate into the whims of a narrow dictatorship. But on its constructive side, his is an intense desire to have his establishment free to experiment. His is the genius of foraging. . . .

If modern industrial operations are themselves to be kept free from the drag of human commitments, then the men who work at them must find security outside the day's job. Security against such hazards as unemployment. My best guess is that if Ford dropped $100,000,000 of his surplus in 1927, his employers dropped a sum very nearly equaling it in lost wages; but his hundred million was in a sense investment; theirs, in every sense, waste. If Ford, with his abhorrence of waste, should put his mind to work on the problem, something as revolutionary as his scheme of financing might come out of it. If he could visualize the junk of household goods and chattels, of smashed hopes and wrecked endeavors, thrown up by his lay-off, see it as he sees that great pile of war scrap at Fordson, and set his bent for salvaging at work . . . what might not issue?

Much has been written of the monotony of mass production. I have dealt here with its insecurity. . . . Workers have tendrils that have struck roots in the households and schools of a city's

life. Of the cases receiving relief from the Detroit Department of
Public Welfare in 1926, there were considerable numbers born in
Austria, Germany, Italy, Poland, Rumania, Russia, but together
they did not make up a third of the total. They were not new
immigrants. They averaged five to the family. And more than
two-thirds of the total were born in the United States and Canada; over one-third were native white Americans averaging over
four to the family. . . .

[The production men's] specialized aptitudes give them no
equivalent foothold in other industries; their habit-sets even
stood in the way of some of them getting back into the new assembly lines at Ford's. Theirs had been dead-end occupations.
They had no equity in their work; no say as to the manner in
which they were staggered or laid off. They might have been red
iron ore or limestone or coal in the big bins at Fordson. And their
footing as members of society was equally shaky. Thrift is a good
thing; but is it social thrift for tremendous corporate industries to
count on individual savings as the sole protection against their
own hazards? A year's savings go under rapidly before the fixed
charges in a city where the cost of living is notoriously high.
Modern business has developed all manner of credit schemes by
which workers mortgage their incomes over long periods of time
for equipment for urban living, but little as yet to give security
for that income—or any part of it.

Ford has done more than any living man to strengthen the position of the man who would work his livelihood out on the soil.
He has helped him master isolation and distance. He has put
power at his elbow. But when it comes to the production men
who build his cars, the net result of his hiring and firing is the
other way round. High pay, fear, the urge of the machine and of
the boss have been relied on at Ford's, like a four cylinder engine
to keep them at work, and when the gas was shut off they
stopped. They were no longer production men and their livelihood was a flat tire.

The security of a city rests on the security of its citizens. Detroit needs to re-examine the underpinnings of democracy in this
day of untrammeled industrial enterprises which have drawn
such huge accretions to her urban mass—so piled up wealth and
tall buildings, but so weakened the normal rootholds of domestic
well-being.[1]

Editor's Note

1. The magazine *Survey* (which Paul Kellogg edited for many years) and its partner, *Survey Graphic*, failed to survive the thirties depression and therefore missed the times of modern expansion in the field of social work. Old issues of *Survey* represent an unparalleled source of American social history for the years of the magazine's existence.

2. Detroit in Black and White

Norman McRae

*In a study dealing primarily with the Michigan Civil Rights Feder-
ation, a radical activist group that reached its peak strength between the late
thirties and 1950, historian Norman McRae sketched a background of events and
emotional overtones that spans years before 1935 and the early years of the automotive unions.*

Although the C.R.F. [Civil Rights Federation] techni-
cally serviced all of Michigan, most of its activities took place in
Detroit and Detroit was where the action was. . . .

In the 1920's Detroit's corporate area increased to 137.9 square
miles through annexation. In 1920, its population was 993,687
and a decade later it had grown to 1,568,662 and became America's fourth largest city in terms of population.

In order to provide adequate educational and municipal services for an additional half million citizens, the city fathers increased the bonded debt from $26,682,325 to $255,432,020. The
total municipal debt soared to $378.000,000 . . . and hampered

Norman McRae, "The Michigan Civil Rights Congress and Its Involvement in the
Struggle for Negro Rights, 1935–1945" (Unpublished MS, n.d.): 27–37.

the city's efforts to provide welfare services for their destitute citizens early in the depression.

The city tried to obtain some financial assistance from the automobile giants for their pauperized auto workers, but the automobile industry invoked the Protestant ethic, social Darwinism and their various corollaries to justify their refusal. The relief rolls reached their peak in 1931 when 192,000 people were on welfare.

During the period of 1935 to 1945, there was some hope. . . . From 1935 to its demise, the WPA [Works Progress Administration] supported at least 2,000,000 persons in Michigan. The CCC [Civilian Conservation Corps] was a boon to thousands of young men, seventeen to twenty-eight. When it was discontinued in 1942, there were 103 segregated CCC camps in the state that had given young black and white males work and a sense of dignity. The NYA [National Youth Administration] was another New Deal program that was a bulwark against poverty and anomie.

Some Detroiters were employed and they guarded their jobs just as a lioness guarded its cub. A great deal of energy was expended trying to secure work; men left home at midnight and stood in line all night . . . to see the straw boss who might let them into the plant. It was a *rara avis* who got the worm. Another strategy was the practice of leaving home before dawn and systematically canvassing every business and factory within a given area. This saturation technique was predicated upon luck, but men had to have something to believe in.

Those men who had unskilled jobs in the automobile industry endured all kinds of indignities and privations because they knew they could be fired at any moment and there would be 100 men waiting outside to take their places. They knew that the system was stacked against them, but they endured the dehumanizing aspects of the assembly line, the physical torture of the foundry, the monotony on the speed-ups because they knew that their jobs meant survival.

Detroit had a history of being an open-shop town. . . . A man could be on the job for as long as eighteen hours and get paid for only three or four hours, but he had to be on the job to keep it.

The average automobile worker made seventy-six cents an hour. The average annual wage was $1,150, but forty-five per cent of the auto workers made less than $1,000. During this period, auto workers in Michigan made seventy-five per cent of the motor vehicles in the world and eighty-three per cent of those sold in America.

Production figures did not tell the world how difficult life was for these workers. . . .

On August 26, 1935, the United Automobile Workers of America was organized. It was not the colossus that it is today. It was a "blue baby" that needed great care because it was in danger of dying momentarily.

During this period, Walt Disney produced one of his first full-length extravaganzas, "Snow White and the Seven Dwarfs". In this film the dwarfs sang a rousing song called "Heigh Ho". Some wag changed its lyrics to be sung as follows:

Heigh, Ho, Heigh Ho!
I joined the CIO
Now I get my pay from WPA
Heigh, Ho, Heigh Ho![1]

In many cases this was the fate of those who were brave enough to join the UAW. Large companies spent large sums of money on arms, espionage, and the placing of *agents provocateurs* in positions of leadership within the unions. Large companies also practised the rule of *divide et impera*. . . . This was how they maintained the industrial status quo. . . .

By trying to pull . . . diverse [ethnic] groups together under the banner of fair play and civil rights, the C.R.F. made a noteworthy attempt to develop a *modus operandi* that might have helped to improve race relations in Detroit. During the period upon which we have focused, there was an ethnic, class, and racial pecking order that operated in the following manner: Protestant, nativist, middle class and working class, whites and the foreign born, disparaged each other. All of the above groups vilified Jews, but tended to have a pathological fear and hatred of Negroes. Jews did not ignore these attacks nor did they turn the other cheek. They used their organizations to counter attack. They also managed to manifest some compassion for Negroes, but thanked their God that they were not "Swartzers" because that would have been too much of a burden to bear.

Black was not beautiful to the black people of that era, and they did not see themselves as being black. In those days, one was either colored or Negro. Black was a term of derogation and they rejected the idea of being an ethnic group. Most black Detroiters had laughed at Marcus Garvey's U.N.I.A. [Universal Negro Improvement Association] movement and declared that those initials stood for the "Ugliest Niggers in America". The average black and white southerner had more in common than they dared admit. They were created in the same cultural matrix and nourished from the same umbilical cord. And in more cases than either would dare to admit, they were related by blood, but they were diametrically opposed to one another. . . .

The black community was divided. The colored people who were "old Detroiters", those colored people who lived in Detroit prior to the great northern Negro migration of 1915, had little to do with the newcomers. They were content to withdraw into their elitist enclaves and bemoan the passing of the "cherry orchard". The Afro-American power elite might have prevented . . . erosion of their civil rights if it had used its organizations and institutions as an irrigation system to assist this outpouring of black humanity from the rural south. Instead, they used them as dams and many of their rights were washed away along with their complacency. . . . [2]

Everybody suffered during the depression, but some suffered more than others and blacks in Detroit suffered more than anyone. . . . [The black community] needed more housing, jobs, and better education for its young. Blacks with college degrees found it extremely difficult to obtain jobs commensurate with their education. Many lucky and educated blacks found jobs in the post office, and the post office became the cesspool for Negro talent. During the 1935–1945 period, jobs and housing were the key to their Jim Crow kingdom because a person needed a job to secure the limited, over-priced, and inadequate housing.

The automobile industry in general and the Ford Motor company in particular were the magnets that drew black workers to Detroit. This great migration caused a "backlash". Northern whites became alarmed when Negroes were no longer occasional visitors but had instead become part of the community. . . . Hotels and restaurants started to refuse black patronage. Even some theatres began to segregate their Negro customers.

In the auto plants, racial antagonism increased as competition for jobs increased. Management came up with the idea that pro-

ductivity of Negro workers depended upon the selection of foremen who understood "Negro psychology". Although southern
whites resented working with blacks as equals, many of them
jumped at the opportunity to secure positions as foremen and to
reinforce management's conviction that they understood "the
Negro" and could make him produce. This same argument was
advanced to justify the hiring of white southerners as policemen
in Detroit. Blacks were "the last hired and the first fired." They
were not hired at all in some plants. The relationship of blacks to
white workers was that of a sparrow to a horse. [McRae supplies
an example of the truth of this rural saying in his following quotation from Lloyd Bailer, one of the first black economists, and
one who studied the auto industry:]

> I asked if Negroes were not employed anywhere in the plant.
> He said, 'yes, some jobs white folks will not do; so they have to
> take niggers in, particularly in duco work, spraying paint on car
> bodies. This soon kills a white man.' I inquired if it ever killed
> Negroes. 'Oh, yes,' he replied. 'It shortens their lives, it cuts them
> down, but they're just niggers.'[3]

Black workers were short-lived. They had a shorter life expect-
ancy than their white counterparts. Pneumonia, tuberculosis and
other respiratory diseases were their chif killers. These illnesses
caused black workers to drop like flies after an attack of pesticide.
In those harsh days before the advent of penicillin and sulfa,
whenever a black factory worker caught pneumonia his friends
came by to bid him adieu.

The Ford Motor Company hired the largest number of blacks.
Although most of them worked in the foundry and foundry machine shop, some were in other departments as well. In other
auto plants the foundry was called the "black department". A
black man either worked in the foundry or he worked as a janitor. At the Ford Motor Company, there were Negroes in key positions. Willis Ward and Donald Marshall worked in the
Sociological Department and were junior executives with some
power. There were also several black foremen, white collar employees and star men.[4] The Ford Motor Company was the exception, but it did not establish any trends. And furthermore, Henry

Ford's liberalism was really tokenism motivated by his paternalistic approach to black workers.

During the dog days of the depression, many black families were held together by the wife. Long before white women joined the work force as the glamorized "Rosie the Riveter", black women were working in laundries and in the homes of the well-to-do as maids and cooks for two dollars a day plus carfare. Early in the morning, one could see them at transfer points waiting for streetcars and buses to carry them to Northwest Detroit, Highland Park, and Grosse Pointe. Many carried the badge of their profession—a large brown paper bag.

The Detroit Housing Commission inventoried housing in 1938. Its findings revealed that 85 per cent of all housing was closed to blacks. Moreover, 50 percent of all housing inhabited by Negroes was substandard, whereas only 14 per cent of that occupied by whites was in that category. . . .

Throughout the city there were a number of invisible lines over which it was not safe for blacks to move even if they could. In Paradise Valley, it was Woodward Avenue on the west, Russell or Chene Streets on the east, the Detroit River was on the south, and in the north the line of demarcation was flexible, in that it moved a block or two every year. On the west side, Grand Boulevard, Tireman, Epworth and Warren Avenue were the outer breastworks. . . .

Officially, the police department did not defend these boundary lines, but they were sympathetic to whites in the area. Reverend Charles Hill reported that when he protested to the police at McGraw Station on the west side of Detroit about the lack of police protection when blacks moved into a previously all-white neighborhood, the police inspector exploded, "Don't you know we could hire somebody to kill you for going on this way?"[5] Reverend Hill was not killed, but neither did the police department protect blacks who dared to move into white neighborhoods. Mob violence also caused a number of Jewish families to retreat from gentile areas.

Indifferent police protection was a major flaw in the relation between the black community and city hall. This aberration illustrated the fact that blacks had some influence, but no power. Municipal reform and a revision of the city charter that changed the representation on the common council stripped black Republicans of what little power they had had. This loss of power happened before World War I.

During the years of 1935–45, a new sycophantic practice was developed. Mock elections were held to elect mayors from certain black neighborhoods such as Sugar Hill and Brownsville. . . . These pseudo mayors had their pictures taken with the mayors of Detroit, but they had no real influence. The real influence wielders during Mayor Richard Readings's administration were Charles Roxborough, one of Joe Louis' managers, and Ulysses Boykin, editor of the *Detroit Tribune*.[6] Some ministers, doctors, and lawyers had influence with various mayors and public officials in Detroit.

There were a number of feeble attempts to establish a political power base such as the attempt to build the United District Congressional Organization, Inc. This organization tried to organize every precinct where Negroes lived. Its efforts were unsuccessful and its organization was short-lived. The resurgence of black political power in Detroit did not come about until it coalesced with the Democratic Party and the CIO [Committee for Industrial Organization].

Notes

1. A reminiscence from the author's boyhood.
2. Norman McRae, review of John M. Green's *Negroes in Michigan History;* Reprint of Francis H. Warren's *Michigan Manual of Freedmen's Progress, 1915,* in *Michigan History,* LIII (1969), 163–64.
3. Lloyd H. Bailer, "Negro Labor in the Automobile Industry" (unpublished PhD. dissertation, Department of Economics, University of Michigan, 1948), 34.
4. Bailer, 32–117. J. C. Price was a star man in the abrasive stock section. He was the supervisor of an all-white crew. E. J. Collins was a general foreman in the die casting department. He supervised 147 men. This group was racially mixed. C. Mimms supervised 24 men in the tank link section. Mr. Jarvis was a foreman in the steel construction division. There were 30 men in this group. R. Hearst was a foreman in the magnesium foundry. P. Norwood, A. D. Boon, T. Shelton, and Linsey Sheffield were foremen in the foundry. . . . A star man was someone who could only be fired with the consent of

Henry Ford. [In an interview with this editor shortly before his death in 1987, Charles Mimms, one of the star men listed by Bailer, spoke of the importance of this role in his own life.]

5. Oral interview with Reverend Charles Hill, May 8, 1967, Charles Hill Papers, Walter Reuther Archives of Labor History and Urban Affairs, Wayne State University, Detroit, Mich.

6. Letters to Mayor Richard Reading in the Mayor's Papers, 1938, BHC, DPL, Box 6. Correspondents with Mayor Reading include: Reuben J. Patton, Rev. William H. Peck, William Sherrill, M. J. Morrison. The latter was the mayor of "Sugar Hill".

3.   Labor Spies and the Black Legion

Forrest Davis

The Black Legion Murders have exposed the existence of an atavistic Detroit under the smooth, modern hood of the motor metropolis. But the human exhibits lined up in Common Pleas Court for the oathbound murder of a W.P.A. worker declined to look the part of throwbacks. Instead, the row of manacled Black Knights, minus skull-and-crossbones regalia, seemed strikingly familiar as they lounged in the jury box—as if you had seen them somewhere else a little while before, perhaps in the bleachers at Navin Field, where the Tigers play. Excessively typical, if that is possible, the twelve might have been trying Dayton Dean, their compeer, who was on the witness stand, as he reviewed the midnight execution of Charles A. Poole for the ethical

Forrest Davis, "Labor Spies and the Black Legion," *The New Republic* (17 June 1936): 169–71.

deviation of wife-beating. Typical working-class, native Americans, frightened and childlike.

Dean, a pudgy pipe-coverer by day, a degenerated romantic by night with a mania for guns and homicide, discussed in emotionless phrases the last moments of Charles Poole. The Detroit press unanimously dubs him the "trigger man," chief of the "killer band." He behaved more like a small boy who has been called before the faculty for shooting paper wads at teacher. The prosecutor, Duncan C. McCrea, asked Dean what he did after Davis—"Colonel" Harvey Davis yonder in the jury box—stopped upbraiding Poole for his supposed mayhem on Mrs. Poole. Said Dean:

"Well, I—Davis stopped talking—I looked around—I knew I was supposed to shoot him, so I started firing."

The execution of Poole, which awakened Detroit to knowledge that a pathological body of assassins operated just under its day-by-day pattern, was performed as casually as that. Nothing in the witness's tone or demeanor suggested that he understood the unprovoked wantonness of his act. The faces of the twelve reflected no revulsion as . . . they stared reproachfully at the "boy" who was tattling. A row of dreadful children they seemed, too young to realize the enormity of their dream world of guns, dire oaths, midnight powwows and group vengeance.

The defendants, from a beardless youth in the center to two gray-headed men at the ends, had unlined faces. The discipline of thought had not furrowed them. A man on one end, nicknamed "the deacon," might have been listening to a hell-and-damnation sermon in a cabin church in Tennessee; at the other extreme, a dark-skinned defendant of sixty-odd, with rapt, deep-set eyes, looked equally capable of playing the fiddle or prophesying for his mountain neighbors. Native stock Americans from the Midlands, they seemed to be as young as the Detroit in which their fumadiddles came to light.

The city of Detroit was not in the jury box with the Black Knights. It should have been.

Detroit is a new city.[1] Here the utmost in technology, or applied science, has been put magnificently to work. A city where nothing in sight existed yesterday; the last word among twentieth-century communities, in which, one might suppose, the scientific spirit had swept aside such anachronisms as night riders. Detroit is bounded on the west by Fordissimus—by Ford's Rouge plant, where 70,000 workers quickstep to the cadence of the conveyor belt; by Ford's Greenfield Village, . . . by Ford's company town, Dearborn, and by Ford's presence as a disguised feudal monarch. Henry the First, radical newspapers call him, in token of the absolute power he wields. On the north, Detroit is bounded by the Reverend Charles E. Coughlin's pulpit—a triumph of that other modern engine, the microphone. In between these points of interest, Detroit's million and a half souls go through the gestures of moderns.

Yet this brittle new town harbored the Black Legion. The punishing assembly line left enough vigor in native workers transplanted to Detroit for them to take bullet-sealed oaths, swear a pox on Catholics, Jews, Communists and Negroes, drape themselves in black robes and conduct punitive expeditions at all hours of the night. Moreover, the social climate was so unscientifically intolerant that the Legion—patched together out of the broken Ku Klux Klan—thrived, making converts, until it acquired political power. Until, indeed, unnoticed by the majority of citizens, the courts, the police force, the street-car and lighting services were infected with men vowed to murder—no less.

The truth, it would appear, is that there are at least two Detroits—Fordissimus and night riders, side by side. The marvels of industrial production on one hand; on the other, reactionary night skulkers, carrying on an American tradition running from the Know-Nothings of the 1840's through Knights of the Golden Circle, barn-burners and whitecaps to the Klan. Two Detroits apparently far apart but not total strangers. At times, as a closer investigation discloses, they meet. They meet at the contact point of labor strife. The night rider, 1936 style, in Ford's Detroit is likely to be a labor spy as well as a Catholic-baiter. The lash that peaks his dark will may as well be hatred of Communists, *i.e.*, union organizers, as distrust of Jews.

A pair of questions troubles any inquirer who looks into the Black Legion phenomenon in the Michigan automobile towns. Who organized and who directs this disciplined body, so secret that its strength is not yet known; so assured that it continues, by informed reports, to grow during the Poole case hullabaloo? That is number one. The leaders of record will not do. Virgil F. (Bert) Effinger, of Lima, Ohio, Dr. William J. (Shotgun) Shepard, of Bellaire, Ohio, and Arthur F. Lupp, the only revealed Michigan "brigadier general" won't answer. They haven't the iron or the intelligence. So rigid, however is the Legion's obligation that the Detroit authorities are still unaware—or so they profess—of the identity of higher-ups. The second question ties in with the first. How nearly does the Legion's behavior approach fascism?

Henry Ford has acquired fame on two counts at least. In the world at large he receives credit for making the most profitable use of the assembly line. Labor regards his factory spy system, euphemized under the title Service Department, as the tops. The motor car industry is open-shop. Other employers do not lag far behind Ford in opposing unionization, by means secret and open. In such a community one would naturally look for a possible link between an anti-social band of night riders and the extensive anti-union forces of dominant employers. Especially as one remembers that the Detroit area lives, breathes and makes motor cars. Economically, Detroit has no other concern.

The link in not concealed.

George Marchuk, treasurer of the Communist Auto Workers' Union, was found murdered in a ditch in Lincoln Park on December 22, 1933. Lincoln Park, a suburb adjoining Dearborn, is predominantly populated with Ford workers, and is a one-time Ku Klux stronghold. There is reason to believe that the Legion has enrolled Lincoln Park officials there. In March, 1934, the body of John A. Bielak, a member of the Hudson Motor Company local of the A.F. of L. United Automobile Workers, was discovered by a roadside near Monroe, Michigan. He had been beaten. Under Bielak's head. his assassins significantly had placed a stack of applications from other workers for union membership. Bielak hadn't had a chance to turn them in.

The murders were unsolved. Labor leaders vainly besought action. Evidence was clamorously offered by the Communists in the Marchuk case; offered with no takers. But, as an outgrowth of the Legion inquiry, it appears that both homicides may be traced. The name of Isaac (Peg Leg) White, ex-policeman in Detroit, later a "brigadier general" of the Legion and now living on a farm near Lansing, Michigan, recurs through the investigations.

White, although he now denies having led the Legion, came into dubious prominence in the months that followed the fatal Ford "hunger march" of March, 1932. The emotional shock administered to Detroit by the deaths of five hunger marchers, the wounding of others, brought on anti-radical, anti-labor hysteria. White found employment for his talents. . . . The ex-policeman was in the employ of the Citizen's Committee at that time . . . the open-shop, vigilante agency of the Detroit Board of Commerce. . . .

White, in company with two other men, came to [a grand jury witness's] office at the Hudson Motor Company to reveal gratuitously, that Bielak and four other men in the paint shop were agitating for the union; were sabotaging the work, and were Communists. The three visitors disclosed that they belonged to a secret order which had as one of its objectives the suppression of Communists. The witness . . . joined the Legion. He attended a number of meetings, including one at which Lupp was elected to succeed White as "brigadier general." . . .

This witness relates White to Bielak's murder. White, as a matter of record, warned Marchuk twice to mind his business and lay off the "union stuff." Bielak, incidentally, was not a Communist.

All this tends to show—a deduction supported by the State Police—that the brotherhood began its life as a labor-spy organization with skull-and-crossbones trimmings. The Legion continues to figure, by report, in subsequent labor disputes. In the Motor Products strike of last fall, the strike headquarters and the homes of five strikers were bombed with black, smokeless powder—indicating expert work. The United Auto Workers and the Farmer-Labor Party in Detroit attribute the bombings to the Legion. . . . William Green of the A.F. of L. demanded from Attorney General Cummings an investigation into the anti-union aspects of the Legion. . . .

Searchers for the fascistic formula in the Legion must find first that the industrialists of Detroit—specifically Ford, General Motors, and Chrysler—,the "big three"—have consciously backed the movement. An occasional relationship between strike-breaking agencies and Legionnaires is not enough. It is possible that manufacturers, large or small, have paid into the coffers of the Legion. No one in authority seems to know where the money has come from. But, so far as my inquiry goes, the motor magnates have not subsidized the Legion. We shall be clearer on that point if and when the leadership stands exposed.

What then? . . . Is [the Legion] merely a survival of the Klan? Michigan, it may be recalled, had the largest Klan membership of any state—875,000. . . . Do we find in Detroit, and Michigan, the sprouts of a new fascistic enterprise that may sweep the country?

The characteristically open behavior of Hitler and Mussolini's movements is lacking in the Legion. Black Knights are sworn to die before revealing the body's existence. We do have here the catering to innate prejudices, the underdog desire for power, the rallying around a symbol—in the case of the Legion, the bullet. We have a private army, this one, indeed, organized under military terms.

But the Legion has no political program. . . . Its desires appear to be parochial and selfish—acquiring jobs and police immunity. The Legion has expended itself in antagonism toward Catholics and, as an afterthought, Communists. The energies of the Legion, a reading of the record shows, have been diffused in the punishment of private offenses. Did a father mistreat his family?—the Legion, made up of indifferent husbands and fathers, galloped to the rescue. . . .

I would say, if called upon, that the Black Legion was a sort of depraved Ku Klux Klan. The Poole execution unmasked it prematurely, so far as its own welfare was concerned. One may suppose that the reverberations of that senseless murder caught the Legion in an early stage. If that is the case, the whole American public may be grateful, while extending condolences to the widow.

Life in Detroit, according to competent authority, is empty as a dried gourd for the creatures of the assembly line. Empty and insecure. One feels that about Detroit. It is a city of strangers; two-thirds of the residents came here after 1914. The town is not devoid of ferment. An isolated, beleaguered minority holds out. . . . The Methodist communion may preen itself on the presence of Bishop Edgar Blake . . . and the Reverend Frederick Fisher as pastor of a downtown church. Both hate fascism, war and injustice and make no bones about saying so. Maurice Sugar, another of the elect, polled 55,000 votes—one-third of all cast—when he ran for the City Council as a Farmer-Laborite last year. . . .

But the working-class norm is in too large a part represented by the defendants in the jury box. Typical 100-percenters, they detest alike Communists, liberals and labor organizers as well as Catholics and Jews. Let no one make the mistake of thinking that the incarceration of Dean and Davis, the displacing and reprimanding of minor office-holders and the public scorn heaped upon the Black Legion will expunge from this community the backward sentiments dramatized by the Legion. . . .

Editor's Note

1. If it seems unlikely to term one of oldest cities in the Midwest "new," we must note that Davis is quite correct in referring to the massive turnover of population during the twenty years of industrial growth before 1936. We cannot quarrel with his appellation, "city of strangers."

4.   The Tide Turns

Steve Babson, with Ron Alpern, Dave Elsila, and John Revitte

The prospects of a union breakthrough against Detroit's Open Shop seemed impossibly remote the morning of November 25, 1935.

Several thousand workers had gone on strike ten days earlier at the Motor Products Corporation, a manufacturer of automobile frames and body parts on the city's East Side. Demanding higher wages and the removal of company-paid detectives from the plant, the strikers had initially won the backing of all the unions competing for members at Motor Products—MESA [Mechanics' Educational Society of America], AIWA [Automotive Industrial Workers' Association], and the AFL's federal local.

Steve Babson, with Ron Alpern, Dave Elsila, and John Revitte, "The Tide Turns," in *Working Detroit: The Making of a Union Town* (Detroit: Wayne State University Press, 1986), 68–75.

But AFL support was grudging. Both AIWA and MESA were winning new members in the plant at the federal local's expense, and AFL leaders called the AIWA-led strike "irresponsible" from the outset. It took only a company promise (never kept) of future union-representation elections to persuade AFL members to break ranks and lead their members back to work.

On November 25, the police escorted hundreds of AFL members and leaders past jeering picket lines on Mack Avenue. AIWA and MESA leaders called the AFL capitulation "the most disgraceful scene ever enacted in Detroit." The company called it the beginning of the end for the remaining strikers. They were right.

Detroit's union movement seemed as fragmented and weak as ever. But even as the AFL's strikebreakers crossed MESA and AIWA picket lines that November morning, the elements of a unified and broad-based union movement were beginning to fall in place. That very month, the AFL's national leadership had split into two openly warring camps—a majority still committed to the Federation's traditional craft unionism, but a growing minority now committed to new forms of industry-wide organization.

The tremors that opened this rift in the AFL's leadership began shaking the organization in 1934. Strikes by dockworkers on the West Coast, truck drivers in Minneapolis, autoworkers in Toledo, and textile workers in New England and the South grew into passionate crusades after police gunfire killed 21 strikers in these four conflicts. Rather than surrender to the fatal violence, tens of thousands of workers joined mass picket lines and general strikes, shutting down San Francisco, Minneapolis, and Toledo. Such tactics won at least partial victories in all but the textile strike.

This groundswell of militancy led to the final breach between craft-union leaders who repudiated the strikers and industrial unionists who saw them as the wave of the future. In November, 1935, a half-dozen of these rebellious leaders formed the Committee for Industrial Organization (CIO) within the AFL. Their chief spokesman was John L. Lewis, President of the United Mine Workers.

Industrial unionism had finally found its voice. "Let him who will, be he economic tyrant or sordid mercenary," Lewis declared over NBC radio in 1936, "pit his strength against this mighty upsurge of human sentiment now being crystallized in the hearts of 30 million workers. . . . He is a madman or a fool who believes that this river of human sentiment can be dammed by the erection of arbitrary barriers of restraint." Lewis, in fact, knew better than most that anti-union employers would not surrender to mere "human sentiment." The CIO needed organizers: hundreds of organizers prepared to take on the biggest corporations in the world in a no-holds-barred campaign. To secure these leaders, Lewis turned to the militants he had expelled from his own union in the 1920's—Adolph Germer, Powers Hapgood—and veteran organizers like Rose Pesotta from the Ladies Garment Workers Union, and Leo Krzycki from the Amalgamated Clothing Workers. Brookwood Labor College, founded in New York in the 1920's by A. J. Muste, also provided CIO unions with organizers, including Roy Reuther, Sophia Goodlavich, Merlin Bishop, and Frank Winn.

These men and women were Socialists, a fact the politically conservative Lewis (he'd endorsed Coolidge and Hoover in the 1920's) certainly was aware of. But he needed industrial organizers of proven ability, and despite the fact that he barred Communists from his own union, he was also willing to work with radicals like Wyndham Mortimer, Bill McKie, and "Big" John Anderson to build the CIO. "In a battle, I make arrows from any wood," Lewis responded when asked about his collaboration with Communists. "Who gets the bird?" he later added, "the hunter or the dog?" There was little doubt which role Lewis saw himself in.

The Communists, for their part, had stopped attacking their Socialist and liberal rivals as "Social Fascists." Such carping had isolated Party members from the labor movement at precisely the point when many workers were joining unions and fighting for recognition. To participate in this upsurge, the Party dissolved the Auto Workers Union late in December, 1934, and proposed a Popular Front with moderates and liberals. Individual Communists thereafter muted their radical politics and harnessed their considerable organizing skills to the CIO bandwagon.

The AFL's top leaders also compromised their views in an effort to salvage some control over events. Local leaders and members of the Federation's federal autoworker unions had long demanded their own national organization—coordinating the unionization of a large corporation's scattered operations was otherwise impossible. In August, 1935, the AFL grudgingly responded to this pressure by chartering the United Automobile Workers (UAW) as an international union within the AFL. But the Federation's cautious leaders initially muzzled the new organization by postponing elections and appointing conservative officers.

When delegates to the UAW's next convention, in April, 1936, finally won the right to elect their leaders, they settled on Homer Martin, a former Baptist minister and one-time autoworker from Kansas. The fledgling organization immediately allied itself with Lewis' Committee for Industrial Organization and invited the independent unions in the industry to join its ranks. MESA's two Detroit locals, led by fellow Scotsmen Bill Stevenson and "Big" John Anderson, split off from their parent organization and merged with the UAW in July. The AIWA and a third independent union, the Associated Automobile Workers of America, joined that same month.

The emergence of the UAW as a unified and democratic union gave a tremendous boost to organizing efforts in Detroit's auto industry. There were signs of new life in other sectors of Detroit's labor movement as well. Rebellious truck drivers in the AFL's Teamster Local 299, a small union of general freight drivers, ousted the local's corrupt leaders and began a recruiting drive with three new organizers—one of them Jimmy Hoffa, former Kroger warehouseman. Waiters and Waitresses Local 705 of the AFL's Hotel and Restaurant Workers also expanded its staff and began an organizing drive in the opening months of 1936.

While many workers opposed joining these unions, or, fearful of losing their jobs, chose to remain neutral, a growing number, particularly among the young, were eager to risk joining a militant union movement for change. Their confidence was buoyed by a growing sense of common interests bonding workers together. That emerging "solidarity" had many long- and short-term causes. Americanization campaigns and steep declines in immigration after the 1921 Immigration Act had diluted the "alien" stigma that isolated many unskilled workers from the rest of the population. The city's workforce had also been sifted through a prolonged process of deskilling and mechanization that blurred the old hierarchy of industrial trades. Craft distinctions had not disappeared, but they had become more fluid and unstable. The Depression narrowed the gap between skilled and unskilled still further, for floundering companies usually found more to cut from the above-average wage of their skilled craftsmen.

Indeed, the Depression had been a relentless leveler. Workers who had defined themselves in terms of their trade, their race, their nationality group, or their ambitions, had been merged, at least temporarily, into a single group: the unemployed. . . .

Unemployment had also partially merged the working worlds of men and women. The steep lay-offs in Detroit's heavy industries idled many men whose wives and daughters still worked in service or retail trades. Unemployment among Michigan's wage-earning women was 30 percent lower in 1935 than among men, and in Detroit, the number of working women actually rose by 10,000 during the 1930's—even as the number of employed men fell 74,000. . . .

By 1936, these Depression experiences had transformed peoples' sense of the future. Storybook tales of upward mobility seemed a little ludicrous in the midst of widespread unemployment and poverty.

. . . In November, 1936, politicians pledging to uphold [the] "Wagner Act" won sweeping victories over conservative and right-wing candidates, paced by President Roosevelt's landslide re-election. "If I worked for a wage," announced Frank Murphy, the former Mayor of Detroit who became, that November, the Governor-Elect of Michigan, "I'd join my union."

On November 27, 1936—one year after [a] fiasco at Motor Products and just three weeks after Murphy's election—the first wave of a flood tide of worker unrest washed over Detroit's Open Shop. At 11:30 a.m., 1200 workers at Detroit's Midland Steel plant sat down and occupied their workplace. . . . the Midland workers refused to budge until management met their key demands: recognition of the UAW as their sole bargaining agent, and a 10¢ an hour wage increase for all departments.

Their "sitdown strike" foreshadowed a dramatic shift in the balance of power between Detroit's employers and workers. In the past, management had always relied on the police to forcibly break through union picket lines and convoy strikebreakers into the plant; once inside, the strikebreakers could then be housed in makeshift dormitories and put to work on the machines left idle by the strikers. But Midland's sitdowners had decisively turned the tables. Now they were on the inside, protecting their jobs and machines, while bewildered policemen trudged the plant in the snow and rain. . . .

Morale among the sitdowners remained unusually high throughout the eight-day occupation. Instead of only periodic and often lonely picket duty, the sitdowners now lived together in a tightly knit, 24-hour strike community. The once alien and dingy plant became the scene of a continuous round of pinochle and poker, calisthenics and even football, played in the plant yard. By the time the occupation ended, most of the sitdowners had also memorized the first verse and chorus of *Solidarity Forever:*

> When the Union's inspiration through the workers' blood shall run,
> There can be no power greater anywhere beneath the sun.
> Yet what force on earth is weaker than the feeble strength of one?
> But the Union makes us strong.
>> Solidarity forever!
>> Solidarity forever!
> For the union makes us strong.

The words were not mere rhetoric. In a city with a long and dismal record of racial conflict, the Midland sitdown stood out as an unprecedented example of racial unity. Scores of black and white workers participated jointly in the occupation, and Oscar Oden, a black assembler, was elected to the strike committee. Unity also prevailed between the Detroit AFL and the UAW-CIO, despite the fact that CIO unions had been expelled from the national AFL that same month. . . .

The 200 women workers who joined the sitdown on its first day were not, however, asked to "Hold Fast." Fearing a scandal if the women stayed overnight in the factory with the men, the UAW asked them to evacuate the plant—but the women did not return to their homes. Under the direction of Dorothy Kraus, they established a strike kitchen in the nearby Slovak Hall on Strong Avenue and organized committees to visit and reassure the wives of men still occupying the plant.

382

When a shortage of body frames forced Chrysler and Ford to lay off 100,000 workers in early December, the pressure on Midland to settle finally grew irresistible. On December 4, the UAW's chief negotiators, Wyndham Mortimer and Richard Frankensteen, announced the terms of a tentative agreement: abolition of piecework wages as soon as possible; a 10¢ per hour pay raise for all but the higher classifications; and recognition for the UAW's elected grievance committee.

For the first time in the city's history, a major auto company had been forced to come to terms with a union representing all its workers. The example was not lost on UAW organizers centered in Flint and Detroit's West Side.

Flint, less than 60 miles north of Detroit, was the homebase of General Motors, the auto industry's undisputed leader. If the UAW was to organize the industry, it would eventually have to win the allegiance of that city's 50,000 GM workers, concentrated in more than a dozen major engine, body and assembly plants. Detroit's West Side was equally crucial. GM had three major factories on the West Side, and dozens of independent parts suppliers also produced everything from brakes to body trim for Ford's huge River Rouge plant in neighboring Dearborn.

Ranged against these corporate giants was the UAW's West Side Local 174. By all appearances, the companies had little to fear: when the local formed in September, 1936, it had only 78 members, a handful of organizers, and a treasury that frequently dipped below $10. With these meager resources, Local 174's President, a 29-year-old toolmaker named Walter Reuther, set out to organize the more than 150,000 autoworkers in West Detroit and Dearborn.

The first target was the Kelsey-Hayes Wheel Company, a West Side employer of 5,000 that made brakes for Ford. After UAW organizers Victor Reuther (Walter's brother), George Edwards, and Merlin Bishop hired on at the firm's McGraw Avenue plant, the UAW asked the company for a bargaining conference and began building its membership. The chief tactic was to call "quickie" strikes in one department after another. These brief sitdowns gave the union visibility, attracted new members, and put the company on notice that it could not fulfill its supply contract with Ford unless it improved working conditions and bargained with the union.

On December 10, 1936, Victor Reuther called one such strike in Department 49, where foremen were "riding herd" on the men and women in the hub and brake-drum section. "Twenty minutes before the shift was to end, I ran and pulled the main switch and shouted 'Strike! We've had enough of this speed-up!' The call for strike action spread through our whole department . . . , and we soon had an enormous crowd gathering around us." When Reuther explained to the company's personnel director that only his brother could get the workers to return to their jobs, the production-conscious manager agreed to allow Walter inside the plant.

What happened next typified the brashness that became the UAW's trademark. Victor, speaking from atop a large crate, continued to "talk union" to a crowd of 500 workers until company officials returned with his brother. "I stepped off the box," Victor remembered, "and Walter stepped on and continued with the same speech. Danzig [the manager] grabbed his trouser leg: 'What the hell is this? You're supposed to tell them to go back to work.'

'I can't tell them to do anything,' Walter replied, 'until I first get them organized' ". . . .

[Kelsey-Hayes] did not want to negotiate the issues of production speed and overtime pay that won the union such support. After several more quickie strikes brought these issues to the fore, company managers finally retaliated, barring the UAW negotiating committee from the plant and threatening to fire anyone who stayed on company premises after quitting time. Some 300 union supporters defied the company's ultimatum and, following the example of Midland Steel, barricaded themselves inside the plant.

Removing them proved to be more difficult than the company had anticipated. In these opening episodes of Detroit's sitdown wave, no one had yet determined the legality of the sitdown tactic. The company claimed the occupiers were guilty of criminal trespass, but the city and county officials refused to evict the peaceful protesters, particularly since the strikers had originally been invited onto company property by Kelsey-Hayes employees.

While public officials debated the point, the company tried to force the issues by infiltrating twelve professional strikebreakers into the McGraw Avenue complex. Entering on the fourth night of the occupation, their apparent goal was to provoke a violent incident as a pretext for calling in the police. But before the intruders could make their first move, UAW lookouts trapped the men in the plant's infirmary.

"This was a Friday and there were a half-dozen union meetings in town," Sophia Goodlavich Reuther, Local 174's secretary later wrote. "We called all the unions and asked them to come in a body to enforce the picket line. When they did, here were a few thousand strong, yelling, 'Throw the scabs out, throw the scabs out!'" . . .

Five days later, with Ford threatening to find another brake supplier, Kelsey-Hayes signed a truce agreement and the plants were evacuated. As the sitdowners marched out the night before Christmas Eve, 2,000 supporters and a union band helped them celebrate the new 75¢-an-hour minimum wage the company had agreed to for both men and women. . . . Kelsey-Hayes also agreed to premium pay for overtime, seniority rules to protect job security, and a 20 per cent reduction in the speed of the assembly line.

Hours after the strike's settlement, organizers Victor Reuther and Merlin Bishop left for Flint, where both played pivotal roles in the upcoming GM sitdown strike. That historic 44-day occupation, lasting from December 30, 1936 to February 11, 1937, riveted world attention on the UAW and elevated John L. Lewis to national prominence. When Governor Frank Murphy sent 3,000 National Guardsmen into Flint and deployed them between the sitdowners and the Flint police, GM abandoned all hope of forcibly evicting the strikers and eventually conceded victory to the UAW.

The world's largest corporation could be challenged and defeated by unarmed workers. The victory had an electrifying effect in Detroit. "Somebody would call the office," recalled Robert Kantor, an organizer for Local 174, "and say, 'Look, we are sitting down. Send us over some food.'" Local 174 grew at a rapid clip, with sitdowns at Cadillac and Fleetwood during the GM strike, and with sitdowns in dozens of smaller places afterwards. Within ten days of the victory at Kelsey-Hayes, Local 174's membership had jumped to 3,000; by the end of 1937, it had reached 35,000.

5. Dangerous Living for Unionists: The Spoiled Birthday Dinner

Victor G. Reuther

By 1938, Walter and Victor Reuther were trying to organize the Ford workers. This was an effort as unsafe for the organizers as it was for the employees because of the bitter resistance of old Henry Ford and Harry Bennett, whom he had hired especially to keep the UAW out.

[Walter Reuther] was a stubborn fighter, and it was no secret that he was a marked man. This was, unfortunately, proved true in the spring of 1938.

April 9 was Sophie's birthday, and we were celebrating it at Walter and May's apartment instead of our own, because Walter had come down with a cold that day. Roy was there, and Ben Fisher, a steel worker organizer, his wife, Hannah, Lewis Steiger, our old friend Tucker Smith from Brookwood, Frank Marquardt, active unionist at the Briggs plant, and Al King, a rank-and-file member of the UAW. No one was aware that for some weeks the apartment had been under constant surveillance by two of Bennett's hirelings, who had rented an apartment close by. Walter

From *The Brothers Reuther* by Victor Reuther. Copyright © 1976 by Victor G. Reuther. Reprinted by permission of Houghton Mifflin Company.

phoned a Chinese restaurant to send up dinner. About an hour after he had called, there was a knock on the door, and Sophie and I, who were the closest, opened it. Instead of the delivery boy, there stood two toughs with drawn revolvers. They pushed their way into the room, shouting, "Okay, back against the wall!" At first it was as unreal as a clip from an old silent movie. The shorter gunman wore a dark hat with the brim turned down to conceal his eyes; he was obviously the trigger man. The other gangster spotted Walter immediately, put his gun in its holster, and drew out of his rear pocket an enormous blackjack with a leather strap, which he twined around his wrist.

"Okay, Red, you're coming with us," he said.

Only gradually did we realize this was no joke. George Edwards muttered, "You're not getting out of here. You may shoot some of us, but you won't get out yourselves."

The attackers were obviously surprised by the presence of so large a group; they would have known, by watching the house, that Walter seldom had meetings in his own home. The shorter gunman kept his .38 pointed at us and toyed with the trigger. Walter, who happened to be standing somewhat apart, slowly maneuvered himself into a corner, where he could best fend off the blows. The bigger of the two hoods broke a glass floor lamp over Walter's head, trying to get him off balance so that he would come within striking distance. That failed to put Walter out of commission, so the thug threw a glass-topped coffee table at him. Walter was then on the floor in the corner, using both feet and arms to keep off the swinging blows of the blackjack, and at some point he managed to grasp the end of the weapon and wrench it loose from its leather thong. He tossed it over the man's head in our direction, yelling, "Catch, George!" Comparing notes later, many of us confessed to a sensation of hot lead going through our guts when that happened, and no one made the slightest motion to catch the blackjack before it fell to the floor with a thud.

"Kill the son of a bitch," the larger bruiser shouted to his companion.

Four or five of us moved a few inches toward the man with the gun; it was the slightest of movements, but it gave meaning to George's earlier threat that they could kill some of us but wouldn't themselves get out alive.

During the commotion, little Al King, who had been standing near the kitchen door, slouched down, backed into the breakfast nook, jumped out an open window into the concrete alleyway two flights below, and started to shout for help. This brave action woke up the neighborhood and broke the deadlock. Sophie, at about the same time, decided to distract the killer; she reached her hand into the kitchen and as Al jumped out the window, a pickle bottle came sailing in the direction of the trigger man. We all felt there would surely be shooting now, but after Al's "Help! Help!" had gathered a group in the street, the two professional hoods decided they had better retreat before they got caught, and abruptly fled the apartment.

May and Roy rushed to Walter to see how seriously he was injured. There were some cuts on his face from the broken glass but he had avoided any direct blow from the blackjack. We all collapsed into giddy hysterical laughter. There was an eerie un-reality about that attempt to take Walter on what would have been his last ride. I can't even remember if the Chinese food ever came. I know we bolted the door and propped furniture against it, and immediately called the police. They took an hour to arrive and we let them in only after they had passed identification cards under the door. As they came in, whom should we see in the doorway but three men dressed in civilian clothes wearing dark hats with wide brims pulled down over their eyes! We told them what had happened, and I shall never forget Sophie's wonder-fully blunt response when they asked for a description of the two thugs. She looked the officers straight in their faces, and said, "They looked very much like you."

That birthday party made a change in our way of life that was to last for years—until Detroit's criminal element, backed by cor-poration money, was removed from power, and the workers could win a measure of security and protection. Walter and I got per-mits to carry revolvers and bought .38s. Neither of us had ever fired a revolver in our lives, though we had hunted a little with rifles in the west Virginia hills. We went for target practice to a firing range operated by the Sheriff of Macomb county; we had no confidence in the Detroit police. The idea of carrying a gun in order to fire at another human being was alien and uncomfortable, and I don't think that Walter wore his every day; I certainly did not carry mine. But the guns gave us some security at home. For quite a while after the birthday party, Sophie carried the revolver under her apron when she took the garbage out to the alley.

The police were not overly anxious to find our attackers, but in the underworld there are always individuals who will squeal for a fee. Within two days, Walter received an anonymous call, met the informer in a bar—filled with husky union men in case the call was a trap—and bought the names of the gunmen: Eddie Percelli, alias Eddie Tall, and Willard "Bud" Holt. Percelli was a former rumrunner who had been held as a suspect in the Harry Millman slaying. Bud Holt had once been a Ford Serviceman, and had recently been employed by John Gillespie.[1] Each one of us who had been at the birthday party, brought in separately to view a police line-up, recognized both men at once.

The trial in September of 1938 was a farce. Over eighty prospective jurors were rejected for one reason or another, and the jury, it was reported, was composed of people chosen at random off the street. From the final verdict, one might surmise that many members of this jury were waiting on certain street corners to be picked "at random." Sherman, the defense lawyer, who had championed many other underworld characters, told the jurors, "We contend that Reuther arranged with Holt to come to his apartment at 13233 La Salle Boulevard and stage a sham battle before witnesses to embarrass Homer Martin, president of the UAW, with whom Reuther was at war." An attorney for the Ford Company, working with Sherman, repeatedly spoke of the "radical background" of all the guests at the birthday party, and implied that Walter and I were sinister revolutionists undermining the American way of life. After all, we had lived and worked in Russia for a year. The state prosecutor mentioned nothing about possible motives for an attack on Walter, though everyone knew he was on Ford's blacklist and that until two weeks before the event Holt had been employed as bodyguard for Ford's Gillespie. I strongly suspect that Judge George B. Murphy was as shocked as we were when the jury acquitted Holt and Percelli.[2]

Editor's Notes

1. The Reuthers and many UAW members believed that some Ford Motor executives had been involved in this scheme to eliminate a major

labor leader. But Harry Bennett, responsible only to Henry Ford the elder, had at that time almost total power over personnel and security matters. Gillespie, whom Ford had hired for duties that overlapped confusedly with Bennett's, was a former Detroit Police Commissioner. Homer Martin, then president of the UAW, was a rival of the Reuthers. Martin allegedly contrived a secret agreement with Bennett to control Ford-UAW negotiations. Martin was removed from office by the UAW Executive Board, and charges against him were filed with the National Labor Relations Board. As Victor Reuther muses, "How was it possible that one of the world's largest industrial firms could have had such a barbaric labor relations policy? Certainly the elder Ford must be held responsible for giving Bennett carte blanche and never questioning his methods. . . . " Approximately three years after the birthday party, Ford Motor at last signed a contract with the UAW. It was the last of the auto giants to do so.

2. The Reuther brothers later faced more serious injuries when each of them was wounded in his own home by gunmen. Victor lost an eye, Walter the partial use of one arm. Once again, the would-be assassins were not punished, and there were strong indications that organized crime was involved. By contrast, the affair of the Chinese carry-out dinner, as retold by Victor Reuther, seems a series of absurdities, though for some there it must have been the first real foreboding of fear. Everyone at the birthday party was young, with a world to be changed just ahead of him.

6. Political Corruption: The Time the Mayor Went to Jail

Detroit Times

Mayor Richard Reading, an affable, well-liked man backed by the Civic Searchlight, *filed for reelection on Monday, August 7, 1939. On the same day, page one headlines of the* Detroit Times *shouted, "MAYOR HUNTS PO-LICE GRAFT IN SUICIDE MOTHER'S EXPOSÉ." On Sunday Mrs. Janet McDonald had dressed her eleven-year-old daughter, Pearl, in a pink taffeta party dress, then killed the child and herself.*

Mrs. MacDonald left a number of suicide notes to the newspapers and public officials, and one to her estranged lover, William McBride, a low-ranking employee of the gambling interests. She provided photos and a copy of her letter to McBride for the press, and eventually succeeded in overturning local government.

Keep Not Your Kisses
Janet MacDonald to William McBride

. . . In spirit I'll return and curse any woman that you make a friend of. Until the day you die I'll keep returning, then we'll go together, and you'll know we should have been together here.

You couldn't fathom the loneliness and sorrow I've had these last few weeks. Some day you may have a glimpse of it, too.

I must go now. My time is up and I'm just a little frightened.

Janet MacDonald, "Keep Not Your Kisses" and "There is a Good Deal of Vice Going On in Detroit," *Detroit Times* (7 August 1939): 1, 2. Permission given by Robert Giles, publisher of the *Detroit News*, holder of *Times* files.

391

"Keep not your kisses for my cold, dead brow;
The way is lonely, let me feel them now. . . . "

There is a Good Deal of Vice Going On in Detroit
Janet MacDonald to John Bugas, of the FBI

Dear Sirs:

It seems there is a good deal of vice going on in Detroit, and as long as the police are a part of it, it seems perhaps the government should know something about it in order to do a bit of cleanup work.

I am privileged to know that the so-called G-Men are watching a certain Wm. McBride.

This McBride was a partner in the Great Lakes Number house in Oakland Avenue, which closed down July 1st. While the Great Lakes was in operation, McBride took care of the bribe end. He paid (here she named a Detroit police lieutenant) a neat sum monthly, also a large number of sergeants and officers got their portion each month. As long as a number house or handbook paid off, it was allowed to run.

At present McBride's position is that of a go-between man for the lieutenant and the racketeers. The houses pay the lieutenant through McBride and are therefore permitted to run. In the event a house has to be raided of course the lieutenant leads the raid and makes a beautiful bluff of it. However, before the raid, the lieutenant gets in touch with McBride and consequently McBride informs the house to be raided and the headmen clear out before the raid and take any important evidence with them. This is quite a profitable business for both the police officer and Racketeer McBride.

Occasionally they run across an officer or detective who refuses to accept the money, in a case of this kind the detective or officer promptly gets moved to another district or put down in rank.

For a number of years, although McBride always made a large salary, he evaded paying his income tax, however having to pay social security this year he got frightened and had a certain lawyer (whose name I shall omit), fix up his tax returns as though it had been paid properly for the last three years.

McBride had a bad record during prohibition days for smuggling liquor over from Canada. There was a warrant against him for a length of time, but he now claims witnesses are dead and nothing could be done about it. Until very recently he was afraid to cross the Canadian border.

I am mentioning these facts just to let you know how bad a character McBride is. It seems people of his sort should be clamped down on.

McBride has been arrested many times for owning and operating the wrong type of places, but with the majority of the police working with the racketeers nothing has ever been done to convict the wrong ones.

I trust this information is of value and that it will be put to use.[1]

Editor's Note

1. The purple prose and fury of Janet MacDonald scorned had their political effect. In November, 1939, Reading lost the election to Council President Edward Jeffries, Jr., son of a humanitarian turn-of-the-century judge, the Edward Jeffries for whom some west side public housing apartments were later named. Reading lost two to one to Jeffries, after basing his campaign on charges that Jeffries, who was mildly liberal on union matters, was a Communist, or a "fellow-traveler." Charges of major involvement in gambling and protection rackets came later from the one-man grand jury led by Homer Ferguson. Reading would go to federal prison in broken health. Homer Ferguson would go to the U.S. Senate.

Part XII

Arsenal of Democracy

Arsenal of Democracy

World War II brought Detroit the distinction of being called the "arsenal of democracy," a phrase that was easily and often corrupted to "arsehole" by tired people waiting in lines everywhere—at bus stops, at grocery stores, at newsstands for the first chance at the "home for rent" or even "room for rent" ads.

It was a city of absolutely full employment, with all the discomforts that supposedly good state can bring. The last to be hired were being hired. Qualified blacks were suddenly discovered, with the diplomas and certificates they had held all along. A black R.N. appeared as night supervisor at one of the better hospitals. She would have preferred days, she said, but it had been explained to her that her night shift would give her less contact with the public, to whom her presence might give offense. Home care for the elderly or children was all but impossible to obtain on any terms. Wartime child care programs were discouragingly slow to develop and often inadequate when they arrived. Grandma was still the best choice—if she wasn't already working at the bomber plant at Willow Run.

Jobs in Detroit were tied in with the needs of war. For men they were a substitute for, or an adjunct to, military service. If you were here at all, it was because somebody higher up thought you should be. If civilians became tired of living the war effort a minimum of forty-eight hours a week as part of that total concentration of defense industry, government was also troubled by the concentration. Some aircraft were being manufactured in California, and the FBI rushed to head off a suspected plot to blow up the locks at the Soo. Never again, military planners vowed, would all the eggs be in one basket. "Hitler will come here first," people told each other, only half believing it. One thing everyone agreed on was that nobody, but nobody, knew what was going on at the war front. Another was that money— the best money ever— was little fun when you had no time to spend it, or everything you wanted was cancelled out by shortages.

Movies, restaurants, bowling alleys, union halls, tried to meet the upside down, multishift schedules of the war-workers. If your time for hilarious recreation began at 6:30 A.M. or your time for grocery shopping was 10 P.M., someone would make efforts to accommodate.

The city was unbelievably overcrowded. There was rent control, but large, spacious flats were everywhere being divided into tiny apartments, or "housekeeping rooms," for which the owner might charge the rent that had gone with quarters several times as large a few months earlier.

There was price control, but the quality and availability of twenty-six-cents-a-pound hamburger varied tremendously. Complaint about these persistent but minor league hardships was self-defeating and absurd. "Don't you know there's a war on?" was the ready response. Of course Detroit knew. Detroit was part of it. Besides, everyone had a friend or relative in those frightening and glamorous places in the news. Emotions ran high for those in the "real" war.

Selections include Victor Reuther's "'500 Planes a Day,' " in which he tells of the early rejection by both business and government—short of FDR—of his brother's creative plan for conversion of the auto plants to defense.

During the war years there was a crosscurrent of unreadiness. There were the pacifist conscientious objectors, including a group of young ministerial students from Union Theological Seminary. After a year or two living openly in Detroit, they would be sent to various federal prisons as draft resisters. Other Detroit pacifists served as volunteers in army medical units or tried the camps for conscientious objectors. The "Brooklyn House" group of young ministerial students found the camps too oriented to military life. (They did not object to physical labor or danger; several volunteered as human guinea pigs for medical experimentation while serving in federal prison.) During their time in Detroit, the pacifists supported themselves by the nonwar jobs no one else wanted—driving coal and ice trucks, for instance.

Temporary allegiance to pacifism was found among the small but vigorous group of Communist party members during the time when Germany and Russia were allies. This broke apart abruptly when Hitler invaded the Soviet Union, but while it lasted, many of Detroit's Polish were horrified that their native land had been abandoned by the ideologues. Continuing throughout the war years there were also local Bundists, America Firsters, and respectable isolationists who regarded the war as one of Franklin Roosevelt's stunts of self-promotion.

A few of the war critics took the ugly path of stirring up race hatred. Their traces are to be seen in the Sojourner Truth riots of 1942 described by Bette Smith Jenkins. Bigotry was here aided by government vacillation.

Racism shows again in the scenes of June, 1943, described to us by Walter White and Thurgood Marshall in a report for the NAACP. Their report searched out basic causes for this major riot and found lack of housing, official ineptitude, and the actions of would-be saboteurs to be among them. They did *not* find violence within the auto plants, where the UAW-CIO worked constantly to build a sense of brotherhood among its members. This did not prevent nay-sayers who lived outside of Detroit from telling each other that the rioting was started by "union radicals."

For many, survival came to depend more and more on daydreams of the future. These often centered around a postwar dream house. The red-white- and blue-covered women's magazines were filled with them. Among Detroit's young labor union and professional workers, there came to be a dream book of another sort. A mimeographed pamphlet, "What about Housing Cooperatives?", the spare time work of two young city planners interested in Scandinavian housing, circulated widely. The dream grew into a project that almost became a reality. Part XIII will tell of its demise in the early fifties, but here I reprint selections from the text itself, written by Merle Henrickson. It was accompanied by talented and imaginative architectural drawings by Donald Monson, which are not reproduced here.

As the war years went on, most Detroiters were loyal, patriotic—and bone-tired. They showed their customary lack of curiousity about those whom—rightly or wrongly—they characterized as "kooks." They joked about WAVES and WACS, questioning their motives. They honored, the fighting men, however, and endowed them with glamor.

One night at Orchestra Hall (then the Paradise Music Hall), at a meeting of the Wayne County Council of the AFL-CIO, a group that had a considerable importance of its own, the chairman paused as a young man in uniform—a Tuskegee airman home on leave—ran onstage from the wings. "This young man is one of ours, a union brother—he will be back with us and will go far. Watch him, and remember—Brother Coleman Young!" The crowd leaped to its feet, cheering the unknown young man.

1. "500 Planes a Day"

Victor G. Reuther

Months before Hitler's armies marched east into Poland, Walter and I had a conversation with Ben Blackwood, a trusted aide in the General Motors Department [of the UAW] and himself a skilled toolmaker, about Roosevelt's call for aid to Britain and the kind of help America was best equipped to give. Because of the unremitting Luftwaffe offensive, it was obvious that England needed planes, not only guns and tanks, for her defense. As toolmakers we knew it would be many years before American industries turning out civilian goods could be tooled to produce weapons in any quantity. But, as Walter said, we should not romanticize about the nature of the airplane, though the aircraft industry had for so long made a fetish of the highly specialized expertise involved. A plane was made of steel and aluminum, like other vehicles, and its component parts could be manufactured by essentially the same kind of machines and machine tools that stamp and turn out the parts of an automobile. We had seen the conversion of peacetime tools—and helped make it—in the Gorky plant, when Russia was arming itself against the inevitable German invasion.[1]

Of course, the automobile manufacturers, asked to take on enormous defense contracts, assumed that they would gradually close down their automobile plants, keeping them on a standby basis, while the government proceeded to build and put at their disposal spanking new factories, equipped with millions of dollars worth of machine tools, most of which would be duplications of the tools sitting idle, or about to sit idle, in the automobile plants as we moved into an all-out war effort.

A careful survey taken by Ben Blackwood and me in GM plants all over the country corroborated Walter's hypothesis and became the basis of his proposal for a "500 planes a day" program, to be undertaken by the automotive industry. He had informal meetings with R. J. Thomas and Philip Murray about his plan.[2] They were both enthusiastic, and Murray submitted it to President Roosevelt on December 20, 1940. . . .

Roosevelt responded with interest, and sent a memo to Knudsen, co-director with Sidney Hillman of the Office of Production Management. . . .

William Knudsen, though deeply devoted to FDR and to the defense effort, must nevertheless have felt put out that Walter Reuther, the "red-headed upstart" who had so often clashed with him across the General Motors bargaining table, should presume to tell the nation what the automobile industry could do about mass tooling for aircraft production. Yet an editorial in Knudsen's home town newspaper, the Detroit *News*, stated on January 6, 1941, that "no industrial leader has paralleled Reuther's initiative and ingenuity in presenting such a plan for consideration."

There was a meeting of top officials of the OPM [Office of Production Management], the Air Force and the Navy, Knudsen, Hillman, R. J. Thomas and Walter. A courtesy call was paid on the President after the discussion. . . .

Walter had made a public appeal on the radio the week before. It was a long speech and an emotional one. Some of it is well worth remembering:

> In London they are huddled in the subways praying for aid from America. In America we are huddled over blueprints praying that Hitler will be obliging enough to postpone an all-out attack on England for another two years until new plants begin to turn out engines and aircraft.
>
> Packard has just finished pouring the concrete for its new engine factory and Ford may soon be ready to begin digging ditches in which to sink the foundations for his. Not until the fall of nineteen forty-two, almost two years hence, will these bright, shiny new factories actually begin to turn out the engines. This is snail's pace production in the age of lightning war. . . .
>
> We believe that without disturbing present aircraft plant production schedules we can supplement them by turning out five hundred planes a day of a single standard fighting model by the use of idle automotive capacity. We believe that this can be done after six months of preparation as compared to the eighteen months or two years required to get new plane and engine factories into production. . . .
>
> Fortunately, despite the headlines which tell us of unfillable orders and labor shortages, we have a huge reservoir of unused machinery, unused plants, unused skill, and unused labor to fall back upon. . . . The tool and die workers . . . are also partially idle. . . .
>
> The plane, from certain points of view, is only an automobile with wings. Our greatest need is for plane engines. . . . The plane engine is the more delicate and compact combustion engine but it is still a combustion engine, containing the same parts. . . . There stand idle in the Cleveland Fisher Body plant toggle presses huge enough to hold and operate a draw or flange die weighing seventy to eighty tons. Such a machine can stamp out airplane parts as well as automobile parts. . . .
>
> It would take years to install in new aircraft plants the same type of presses which now stand idle fifty percent of the time. . . .
>
> Equipment at the Chevrolet Drop Forge plant in Detroit operates at sixty percent of capacity even at this time, which is a peak period for the automobile industry. The machines and hammers in this plant could produce all the drop forgings required for five hundred planes a day and still supply the Chevrolet Company with sufficient forgings for one million cars during the coming

year. Labor asks: Why not use this equipment instead of duplicating it?

Labor's plan springs from the pooled experience and knowledge of skilled workers in all the automotive plants, the same skilled workers who are called upon year by year in the industry to produce new machine marvels. Each manufacturer has the benefit of his skilled workers. We of the United Automobile workers, CIO, have the benefit of the skilled manpower in all the automotive plants, not just in one of them.

Labor asks only in return that its hard-won rights be preserved . . . only that it be allowed to contribute its own creative experience and knowledge and that it be given a voice in the execution of its program. . . .

No question of policy needs to be settled. The President has laid down the policy. We must have more planes. . . .

Quantity production was achieved in the Reich and is being achieved in England by methods labor now proposes to apply to the automotive industry.

The difference and our opportunity is that we have in the automotive industry the greatest mass-production machine the world has ever seen. Treated as one great production unit, it can in half a year's time turn out planes in unheard-of numbers and swamp the Luftwaffe. This is labor's answer to Hitler aggression, American labor's reply to the cries of its enslaved brothers under the Nazi yoke in Europe.

England's battles, it used to be said, were won on the playing fields of Eton. America's battles can be won on the assembly lines of Detroit.

The swollen wartime bureaucracy, with its myriads of dollar-a-year men jammed into Washington, consigned many proposals to limbo, Walter's among them. It was not, of course, attractive to the automobile manufacturers, but it was both imaginative and timely, and was finally given serious consideration by the War Department. It stirred up debate in the press and even inspired Charles E. Wilson, Knudsen's successor as president of General Motors, to challenge Walter to a face-to-face verbal duel in Detroit. . . .

No one was more outspoken against Walter's plan than the chairman of General Motors, Alfred P. Sloan, who declared categorically on November 20, 1940, that automobile plants were not adaptable to the manufacture of any other products. "Only about ten or fifteen percent of the machinery and equipment in an automobile factory can be utilized for the production of special defense material." He was in effect saying: Leave our plants alone on a standby basis, and build new plants for aircraft and tanks and gun carriages; tool them completely for that sort of specialized work though it may take two years to get them into real production.

The tragedy of this two-year delay was compounded by the insanity of saddling American taxpayers with the enormous cost of building new plants, which the corporations would later argue were "special purpose defense plants unsuited for civilian production" and ask that they be turned over to them, for a token fee, to be converted to their own purposes. The auto industry seemed ready to sacrifice the very life of the nation to its profit interests.

Many American workers paid dearly for this intransigence, which, of course, enriched the owners of industry. Corporate profits and the incomes of auto, steel, and other executives went up considerably during 1941. Eugene Grace of Bethlehem Steel, for instance, enjoyed a salary increase that year, boosting his remuneration from $478,000 in 1940 to $537,000 in 1941. Even the small Willys Overland Corporation provided for its president a 71 percent salary increase. Tom Girdler of Republic Steel had his salary raised by 56 percent, bringing it up to $275,000. When these men advocated business as usual, they knew what they were defending—and it wasn't the nation's survival.

Our UAW survey had indicated that at least 50 percent of auto-producing machinery was suitable for defense production. The refusal of General Motors to put at the disposal of the defense effort even its idle machine tools meant that in the urgent first six months of 1941, a crucial period, GM, out of a total production of $1,350,000,000 worth of goods, delivered only $131,000,000 worth of defense products.

Most American industrialists were trying at that point to make money from civilian *and* military sales. Their continued production of civilian cars and other consumer goods brought them huge profits, to which they intended to add the lucrative cost-plus defense contracts. With all their patriotic protestations and "victory councils," they had, in fact, to be shoved, against their will, into a maximum defense effort.

The final assessment of the merits of the Reuther plan came much later. It could be found in the reports of the auto executives themselves when, at the war's end, they boasted, as did K. T. Keller, Chrysler's head, that 89 percent of their machine tools had been converted to war production and could now be easily reconverted into making civilian cars. . . .

Finally, in December, 1941, there was a decree to cut back by 51.5 percent the passenger car production of the "big three" auto producers and the quotas of the smaller firms like Studebaker, Hudson and Nash, by 15.3 percent. A month before, I had challenged automobile executives to concentrate on fewer models in order to eliminate waste of materials and machinery. When the cutback was made an official order, serious pockets of unemployment appeared, as we had anticipated, lasting for six to eight months, and this at a time when the nation was calling for the labor of every person is a combined defense effort.

Within hours after the Japanese air attack on Pearl Harbor and before declaration of war by Germany against the U.S., I reported to the press: "The President's appeal for increase of production seven days a week in defense industries has received the unanimous support of the UAW-CIO. . . . This will not only speed defense production, but will also provide immediate defense employment for additional thousands of workers displaced by auto curtailment and whose skilled labor would otherwise be unused."

Needless to say, the automobile industry went on dragging its feet and it was urged that the cut-off date for passenger cars should be extended to the middle of February.

The CIO and the UAW began to carry their case to the public by writing an open letter to the OPM:

> Half of the nation's auto plants are today closed down. Virtually all of them will be down by the end of January. Blacked out not by Hitler and Japan. Approximately 25,000 automobile workers, men trained in precision, mass production methods, and highly skilled tool and die workers are now idle. Fully 400,000 will be idle by the end of January. The nation has lost two million man days every week in war production. . . . Only a few plants are turning out the vital materials of war. . . .
>
> The program drafted by Walter P. Reuther and other members of the UAW-CIO was referred to you for study and recommendation.

You did nothing about it. Similar plans for increasing production of steel, aluminum, copper and other materials vital to the war program were proposed. You did nothing about them. Labor is ready and determined to do its part . . . willing to accept the bitter necessities of a righteous war. Labor had the right to expect industry to do its part.

Editor's Notes

1. Victor and Walter Reuther spent a year and a half working in the Soviet Union, commencing in November, 1933. Their very understandable wish to see Soviet life at first hand was misunderstood by conservatives, even though the Reuthers were disillusioned with the Soviet government.
2. R. J. Thomas was then president of the UAW, having succeeded Homer Martin; Philip Murray was national president of the CIO.

2.   Sojourner Truth Housing Riots

Bette Smith Jenkins

Early in 1941—months before Pearl Harbor—the Federal government was becoming increasingly concerned about the necessity for providing housing for workers who were to pour into defense areas in very great numbers. As early as May 28, 1941, mention is made of the defense housing program in the Detroit Housing Commission minutes. . . .

On June 4, 1941 the Detroit Housing Commission approved two sites for defense housing projects, one for Negro occupancy and one for white occupancy. The Negro site, in accordance with local policy prohibiting the change, through construction of public housing, of the racial characteristics of a neighborhood, was located on the northwest corner of the intersection of Dequindre

Bette Smith Jenkins, "The Racial Policies of the Detroit Housing Commission and Their Administration" (master's thesis, Wayne University, 1950), 3: 73–130.

and Modern streets in an area predominantly Negro. The site selected for the white project of from three hundred to five hundred units was located on the northwest corner of Mound Road and Outer Drive. . . .

However, the first in a series of stumbling blocks which was to delay the defense housing program developed at the June 16th meeting. The site for the Negro project selected by Washington authorities was at Nevada and Fenelon Streets adjacent to the Atkinson School. . . . [It was previously considered by the Housing Commission to be a white area.]

The minutes of June 19 show dissatisfaction on the part of Commission members with the action of the Federal government. Commissioner Ed Thal objected to the United States Housing Authority's disregard of Housing Commission recommendations. However Commissioner White [the Reverend Horace White, only black member of the commission] stated that, "As much as I disagree with the site selected for the two hundred unit project, the housing shortage in Detroit is so acute, particularly among Negroes, that I feel we should cooperate." . . .

On September 29, 1941 the project was named Sojourner Truth in memory of the leader and poet of Civil War days.

Construction proceeded but by mid-November the ensuing storm of protest came to the attention of Congress under the leadership of Representative Rudolph G. Tenerowicz, Michigan Democratic Congressman from the First Congressional District, in which Sojourner Truth is located. Congressman Tenerowicz carried on an active campaign to bring about a change from Negro to white occupancy. . . . [On November 17, 1941, the housing commission] entered in its minutes a report from Reverend Horace White that Mr. Tenerowicz was attempting to bring about a change to white occupancy. This was the Commission's first official cognizance of "the brewing storm of neighborhood objections."

The project was completed on December 15, 1941, but was still untenanted on January 20, 1942 in spite of the fact that there was a serious housing shortage in the Detroit area, particularly for Negro war workers. On January 20 the Detroit Housing Commission was informed that Washington had designated Sojourner Truth for white occupancy and that a new site for a project for Negro defense workers would be selected. Later Federal officials reported that there was no site available in Detroit. They therefore recommended that the project be located outside the city limits. . . .

But, as other records show, the matter was not closed. [LeRoi] Ottley describes a day-and-night vigil by white people before Detroit's City Hall.[1] He states that when the Ku Klux Klan entered the picture, the picket lines were shifted to the project—and the racial explosion occurred when the Negroes sought to move into the buildings. He further points out that without government protection, Negroes were blocked from entering the project for months. Meantime, he says, F.B.I. investigation turned up links with Axis agents among the agitators. Soon a large section of the liberal white public took up the issue and supported the Negro's right to live at Sojourner Truth. Pressure by Negroes was again applied to make the Washington officials stand firmly by their decision, and the Sojourner Truth Homes were finally turned over to Negroes. . . .

On the night of February 27, 1942 a fiery cross was burned in a field close to Sojourner Truth Homes. . . . That same night one hundred fifty white pickets patrolled the project with the avowed purpose of preventing occupancy by Negro tenants assigned to the first twenty-eight units. By dawn the crowd of picketers had grown to twelve hundred, many of whom were armed.

The first of the tenants, having already paid his rent and signed a lease, arrived at the project about 9:00 A.M. on the morning of February 28, but left without attempting to move in after viewing the mob. A few minutes later two cars and a moving van tried to enter the project grounds but were stopped by the pickets.

Fighting began around 9:30 A.M. when two Negroes endeavored to run through the picket line in their car. At 10:15 A.M. the first heavy flare-up occurred when bricks began to fly between white and Negro groups lined up on opposite sides of Ryan Road, a street near the project. This clash was brought to an end by sixteen mounted police who drove into the ranks.

The most heated battle of the day occurred shortly after 12:15 P.M. when a truckload of Negro men carrying pipes crossed Ryan Road on the west into Nevada Avenue. White pickets bombarded the truck with bricks. The police brought this incident to an end by placing the Negroes under protective custody. Within

410

fifteen minutes, following a decision of authorities to postpone the moving, street battles began, with Negroes lined up west of Ryan road opposite to four hundred fifty white persons who greatly outnumbered them.

The *New York Times* as well as local Detroit papers carried stories on March 1, 1942 indicating that scores of both Negroes and whites were injured before the fighting quieted down.

Two hundred police were stationed in the area by Mayor Edward J. Jeffries Jr. They tried three different times to disperse the crowd with tear gas. Shots were fired, several passing through the windows of Mrs. Mary Williams, a Negro living near the project. Several persons were slashed. Three policemen and fifteen others, both Negroes and whites, were hospitalized.

The *Detroit News* story of March 1, 1942, states that the disorder resulted from the "determination of a crowd of five hundred whites to prevent fourteen Negro families from moving into Sojourner Truth, one half mile east of the riot scene." The same story indicates that "at 3:30 P.M. three Negroes passed police lines and walked east on Nevada toward the project. At Justine Street, one half block from the project, a crowd of whites halted them and fighting ensued."

In general the *Detroit Free Press* story of March 1 confirms the details of the rioting. It reports that knives and guns were detected among the rioters who were disarmed by the police whenever possible. It had been hoped earlier in the day when police sent the moving vans away on order of Mayor Jeffries that the crowds would dwindle.

According to the *Free Press* version rioting finally was halted when the police forced the factions about two blocks apart and Superintendent Alfred Siska issued an order to "clear the streets in the entire area."

The *New York Times* of March 2, 1942, reports that one hundred four persons were arrested on charges of rioting and carrying concealed weapons as a result of the clash. To prevent further violence after the initial disturbance of February 28, one hundred policemen were stationed in the area on March 1 to keep everyone but residents from entering. Boundaries marked off a section one mile square and traffic was detoured around it. On the second day the trouble was confined to minor skirmishes. The *New York Times* story indicates that of the one hundred four arrests,

411

six were for felonious assault, twenty-three for carrying concealed weapons, and seventy-five for inciting to riot.[2]

The *Detroit News* story confirms this report, adding disturbing the peace to the list of charges. Of the persons arrested, all but two were Negroes.

Aftermath of the Riot

On March 2, two days after the major disturbances had taken place, Judge George Murphy began to hear inciting to riot charges against seventy-eight persons who were said to have participated in the skirmishes of February 28. According to the *Detroit Times* of March 2, 1942, the courtroom was jammed with Negro sympathizers. The first four defendants brought before Judge Murphy, all Negroes, were found to be innocent, it being Judge Murphy's contention that there was insufficient evidence to prove that they had disturbed the peace by inciting to riot.

Attorneys for Negroes held for disturbing the peace testified before Judge Murphy in Recorders Court that white persons were illegally picketing the controversial area at the time the incidents were said to have occurred and that no peace existed for Negroes to disturb. The *Detroit News*, March 2, 1942, reported that picket lines had been maintained intact by whites in the Fenelon-Nevada area for three weeks preceding the riot. They made a point of the fact that all of the defendants but two were Negroes.

Felony warrants based on carrying concealed weapons were sworn out against seventeen Negroes. A felonious assault warrant named a white man.

A *Detroit Times* story of March 2 states that police handling of the disturbance was roundly criticized by twenty Negro and white leaders who "voiced particular resentment against Davison precinct Station." The police were accused of bias and of "siding with an organized conspiracy of the Ku Klux Klan." Although picket lines were resumed on the days immediately following the moving-day clashes which marked February 28, further violence was prevented. When fifty white persons assembled for picketing on March 3, they were dispersed by Inspector Cox of the Davison Station. . . . It is interesting to note the terminology used in the *Detroit News* account of that date. It asserted that police *refused* to permit Negro groups to gather at the project; that Inspector Cox *requested* a picket line of fifty people to disperse and that the whites then set up a "headquarters" on Conley Avenue, one block away.

It was the opinion of police and housing officials that the only thing which could prevent continuation of violence in the Sojourner Truth area was postponement of the move-in date for the Negro families and there was, of course, much discussion as to whether or not they would be permitted to occupy the project at all.

The *Detroit Free Press* of March 2, 1942 reports that: "Ever since high-ranking police officials assayed the temper of the crowds around the project, they have agreed that only a small standing army could get Negro families moved into the project peacefully and they wouldn't try to estimate how many it would take to keep peace after the project was in use."

. . . Although sixty-five units of the project had been ready for occupancy since February 6 and one hundred sixty-five were completed by the time the rioting occurred; although they were seriously needed to house Detroit's war workers, Charles Edgecomb, as the Housing Commission's director-secretary, requested and obtained Common council approval to return $1055 in advance rent payments made by prospective tenants who had already signed leases for their dwellings.

Meanwhile the families, having given up whatever shelter they had in anticipation of their new homes, were left with no place to go and were being temporarily housed at Brewster Homes and in buildings located on the site acquired for a future Housing Commission development, Douglas Homes.

On March 2, 1942, word was received by Mayor Jeffries from Washington that occupancy of Sojourner Truth had been postponed indefinitely.

There were those who continued to point out that, had the police acted differently, postponement might not have been necessary. Commissioner Horace White, who had spent considerable time at the scene of the disturbance, informed the mayor that the police, prior to the fighting, had made no effort to disperse the crowds of whites gathering there. He pointed out that the police had permitted both sides, that is whites and Negroes, to line up along Ryan Road across from each other in what he called "an open invitation to fight." This was the culmination of months of protests against Negro occupancy.

Reverend White and Reverend Charles Hill, a Detroit Negro minister, were leaders of a Citizen's Committee which was working to get adequate police protection for families so that they could move to their homes. . . . The committee demanded the removal from his position of Charles Edgecomb whom they accused of cooperating with those advocating white occupancy of Sojourner Truth. It appears that State Police protection might have been available for the task of achieving Negro occupancy but Governor Murray van Wagoner stated that his troops would be sent only upon official request from City of Detroit officials and no such request was made.

Because Mayor Jeffries estimated that the services of three thousand policemen would be required to move Negro tenants to their units at Sojourner Truth, he issued orders that the project be left vacant until the issue could be settled. Police protection to supplement the city force was available, as Detroit police were asked in a telephone conversation whether Federal troops were wanted. However, Detective Inspector Edward Graff turned down the offer, stating that "the situation was in hand."

As Charles Edgecomb, in his capacity as director-secretary of the Detroit housing commission, made his announcement that money for rent advanced by twenty-four Negro tenants would be returned and their leases cancelled, he also assured members of white groups that there would be "no sneak moves" and that they would be notified in advance of any future attempts to move in Negro families.

. . . Serious charges regarding the handling of the emergency were made by John R. Williams, 1926 St. Antoine, Detroit representative of the *Pittsburgh Courier*, (a national Negro weekly with a Detroit edition), who claimed that "real estate interests" were back of the picketing. Williams' statements were quoted in a *Detroit News* story on March 1, 1942. He said,

This is not a sincere movement by white citizens. These pickets were introduced by real estate interests.

Seemingly, a deal has been made whereby there is picketing and mob atmosphere. The mob atmosphere has given Edgecomb an excuse for postponing Negro occupancy. Edgecomb is playing ball with the real estate interests. White citizens as a whole are not opposed to Negro occupancy of the project.

In response to the charge, Mr. Edgecomb said that it was "obviously ridiculous. . . . "

One of the encouraging developments during the riot period was that a number of organizations and individuals whose only interest was an unofficial one, a sincere desire to see the controversy settled equitably and fairly and with a minimum of damage, came forward to offer constructive suggestions and to assist in whatever ways were possible.

. . . John Blandford [National Housing Administrator], in an announcement published in the *Detroit Free Press* of March 7, 1942, designated Sojourner Truth for Negro tenancy. In doing so he made "a patriotic appeal" to white residents in the area. . . .

Although Mr. Blandford expressed the fear that the Detroit situation might set off riots in other cities, there is nothing in later records to show that his fears were substantiated. The most serious and tragic aftermath of the Sojourner Truth affair was the race riot which occurred in Detroit in 1943. It is the opinion of Detroit experts in race relations that there are very definite connections between activities of the Detroit Housing Commission and the riot which occurred on June 20, 1943. . . .

Meanwhile sixty-five policeman were assigned to guard the project . . . white protesters were still not ready to accept the determination that Negro war workers were to live at Sojourner Truth, and a crowd of five hundred of them were again picketing on March 10. Tear gas bombs were used to disperse them. The crowd had been stimulated by Joseph Buffa, described as a real estate dealer, and the man who had been their declared leader all along. . . .

Picketing was resumed the following day, March 11, and [the *Free Press*] . . . stated that there were one thousand white men, women and children on hand to picket Sojourner Truth for two hours in the evening despite cold and rain. There was no disturbance as police were on duty on a twenty-four hour schedule and kept the picketers a distance of two blocks from the project in all directions. Joseph Buffa, who, throughout the controversy, was acting in his capacity as president of the Seven Mile-Fenelon Improvement Association, at no time seemed to feel that he was not acting in the best interest of the community. . . .

When it was announced that [two] special assistants to Attorney General Francis Biddle, were arriving in Detroit on March 10 to initiate a Federal grand jury investigation, Mr. Buffa welcomed the news, stating, "We have done nothing but protect our property rights. I don't think there is any law yet against protesting an action. . . . I welcome the investigation. . . . Maybe they will bring into the open some of the 'pinks' on the other side."

There were some differing opinions, however, as to whether Mr. Buffa and his group had been acting within their rights. District Attorney John C. Lehr announced, as plans were carried out for the investigation, the Federal Grand Jury would look into charges that there was a conspiracy to prevent Negroes from occupying Sojourner Truth. . . . Attorney General Biddle announced simultaneously that if it were found that a conspiracy *had* existed to prevent tenants from occupying a Federal project, prosecution might be brought under the civil rights section of the criminal code.

This investigation continued for some time after the immediate situation was cleared up and no study of it has been made. Inquiries were directed to former government employees who worked on the investigation and it is their opinion that it would be impossible to obtain any detailed information from records of the case. There seems to be no indication that charges were brought against anyone connected with the riot as a result of the investigation and Mr. Buffa and his group are still found to be on hand whenever what they consider their right to maintain an untainted neighborhood defined by their standards of racial purity seems to be threatened.

As the Federal investigation got under way, days passed and still Sojourner Truth stood untenanted. . . . The National Housing Agency finally acted, when on April 17, it sent a wire: "Please proceed as soon as feasible with established program for occupancy of Sojourner Truth. . . . "[On April 30] the first Negro families moved to the project and now, eight years later, many of the tenants are still living there peaceably, having proven that they make good neighbors and do not cause a neighborhood to deteriorate. . . . There is, however, evidence that people living in the area were still being stimulated by an organized pressure group, the Seven Mile-Fenelon Association. At the meeting held by the Housing Commission on July 2, 1942, the director read a letter from this organization requesting that a fence be constructed at the project to prevent children living there from playing on privately-owned property.

Notes

1. LeRoi Ottley, *New World A-Coming*, Boston, Houghton Mifflin, 1943, pp. 219 ff.
2. A study of newspaper accounts of the riot reveals that in most instances the *New York Times* refrained from Negro and white designations while the three metropolitan Detroit papers, *The Detroit Times*, *The Detroit Free Press* and *The Detroit News* used them.

Editor's Note

Jenkins notes that the groups who worked on behalf of Negro occupancy of Sojourner Truth covered a wide spectrum: labor unions, particularly Local 600 of the UAW, the NAACP and the Detroit Urban League, and many Protestant churches, both black and white as to membership. In spite of the hostility to Negro occupancy shown by several Catholic parishes in the Sojourner Truth area, many liberal Catholics from across the city were drawn in to protest the violence. One civic leader, the Reverend Henry Hitt Crane, pastor of the downtown Central Methodist Church, urged Mayor Jeffries to appoint an interracial committee, a proposal that failed at the time. However, the mayor did appoint such a committee only a little over a year later, following the riot of 1943.

Major sources used by Jenkins were local newspaper accounts. She was an employee of the Tenant Selection Office of the Detroit Housing Commission, and so was daily aware of the events described. As this editor, who was a coworker at the time, remembers, Jenkins (now Mrs. Thomas Downs) showed a quick grasp of the realities and compassionate concern.

3. June, 1943: A City Split in Two

Walter White and Thurgood Marshall

The riot of June 20, 1943, left most Detroiters as surprised as they had been in 1833, 1863, and at the racial incidents in between. It was first assumed, and the media agreed, that this was a "Negro riot," and that a large part of the violence was being committed by Negroes upon whites. A more reliable source of truth was the analysis circulated from the national office of the NAACP.

The NAACP report was in two parts: the first, by Walter White, national Executive Secretary, set forth the background, including demographics and employment, with some factual material on labor unions, which non-Detroiters found hard to believe. The second section, by Thurgood Marshall, then counsel for the organization, later to become Justice Marshall of the U.S. Supreme Court, detailed the events of the riot, focusing on the actions of the Detroit Police Department.

What Caused the Detroit Riots?

In 1916 there were 8,000 Negroes in Detroit's population of 536,650. In 1925 the number of Negroes in Detroit had been multiplied by ten to a total of 85,000. In 1940, the total had jumped to 149,119. In June, 1943, between 190,000 and 200,000 lived in the Motor City.

According to the War Manpower Commission, approximately 500,000 in-migrants moved to Detroit between June, 1940 and

Walter White and Thurgood Marshall, *What Caused the Detroit Riots? An Analysis* (New York: National Association for the Advancement of Colored People, 1943), 5–37.

June, 1943. . . . The War Manpower Commission failed almost completely to enforce its edict that no in-migration be permitted into any industrial area until all available local labor was utilized. Thus a huge reservoir of Negro labor existed in Detroit, crowded into highly congested slum areas. But they did have housing of a sort and this labor was already in Detroit. The coming of white workers recruited chiefly in the South not only gravely complicated the housing, transportation, educational and recreation facilities of Detroit, but they brought with them the traditional prejudices of Mississippi, Arkansas, Louisiana, and other Deep South states against the Negro. . . .

Here and there among these Southern whites were members of the UAW-CIO and other labor union, churchmen and others who sloughed off whatever racial prejudice they had brought with them from the South. But the overwhelming majority maintained and even increased their hostility to Negroes. . . . During July, 1941, there had been an epidemic of riots allegedly by Polish youths which had terrorized colored residents in Detroit, Hamtramck, and other sections in and about Detroit. Homes of Negroes on Horton, Chippewa, West Grand Boulevard and other streets close to but outside of the so-called Negro areas were attacked by mobs with no police interference.

Detroit's 200,000 Negroes are today largely packed into two segregated areas. The larger of these is on the East Side bounded by Jefferson on the South, John R on the West, East Grand Boulevard on the North, and Russell on the East . . . —approximately 60 square blocks. A somewhat smaller Negro area is on the West Side . . . —an area of approximately 30 square blocks. In addition to these two wholly Negro areas, there are scattered locations throughout Detroit of mixed occupancy in which, significantly, there was during the riot less friction than in any other area. . . .

Meantime, but little public housing was created to meet the tragic need for housing for both whites and Negroes in Detroit. Even this was characterized by shameful vacillation and weakness in Washington which only added fuel to the flames of racial tension in Detroit. The notorious riots revolving about the question of who should occupy the Sojourner Truth Housing project in February, 1942, are an example of this. . . .

From all other public housing projects [except Sojourner Truth and Brewster] erected in Detroit, Negroes were totally excluded,

419

although Negroes and whites had lived in complete amity in some of the areas on which these public housing projects, erected through the taxation of Negro as well as white Americans, were built.

Equally contributory to the explosion which was to come has been the attitude of the Detroit Real Estate Association. . . . meantime, every train, bus, or other public conveyance entering Detroit disgorged an ever increasing torrent of men, women and children demanding places to live while they earned the war wages Detroit factories were paying. . . .

Jobs

Early in June, 1943, 25,000 employees of the Packard Plant, which was making Rolls-Royce engines for American bombers and marine engines for the famous PT boats, ceased work in protest against the upgrading of three Negroes. Subsequent investigation indicated that only a relatively small percentage of the Packard workers actually wanted go on strike. The UAW-CIO bitterly fought the strike. But a handful of agitators charged by R. J. Thomas, president of the UAW-CIO, with being members of the Ku Klux Klan, had whipped up sentiment, particularly among the Southern whites employed by Packard, against the promotion of Negro workers. During the short-lived strike, a thick Southern voice outside the plant harangued a crowd shouting, "I'd rather see Hitler and Hirohito win than work beside a nigger on the assembly line." The strike was broken by the resolute attitude of the union and of Col. George E. Strong, of the United States Aircraft Procurement Division, who refused to yield to the demand that the three Negroes be downgraded. Certain officials of the Packard Company were clearly responsible in part for the strike. . . .

There had been innumerable instances, unpublicized, of work stoppages and slow downs by white workers, chiefly from the South, and of Polish and Italian extraction. Trivial reasons for these stoppages had been given by the workers when in reality they were in protest against employment or promotion of Negroes. A vast number of man hours and of production had been irretrievably lost. . . . John Bugas in charge of the Detroit office of the FBI, states that his investigations prove that the Ku Klux

Klan at no time has had more than 3,000 members in Detroit. Other investigations by officials and private agencies corroborate this fact. But the Klan did not need to be a large organization to cause serious disruption of war production in Detroit, because of . . . the increasing percentage of Southern whites who went to Detroit to work in 1942 and 1943. . . .

Gerald L. K. Smith, former assistant and protege of the late Huey Long, has long been active in stirring up discord and dissension in the Detroit area. His activities in America First, anti-union, and other similar groups have been greatly increased in effectiveness by his also being a Southerner trained in the art of demagoguery by Huey Long. . . . Active also have been the followers of Father Coughlin. . . . Ingrained or stimulated prejudice against the Negro has been used as much against organized labor as it has against the Negro. . . .

Detroit Labor Unions and the Negro

One of the most extraordinary phenomena of the riot was the fact that while mobs attacked Negro victims outside some of the industrial plants of Detroit, there was not only no physical clash inside any plant in Detroit but not as far as could be learned even any verbal clash between white and Negro workers. This can be attributed to two factors: first a firm stand against discrimination and segregation of Negro workers by the UAW-CIO, particularly since the Ford strike of 1941. The second factor is that when the military took over, the armed guards in the plants were ordered by the Army to maintain order at all costs. . . .

The Detroit riot brought into sharp focus one of the most extraordinary labor situations in the United States. Prior to the Ford strike of 1941 many Negroes in Detroit considered Ford their "great white father" because the Detroit plant almost alone of Detroit industries employed Negroes. When the UAW-CIO and the UAW-AFL sought to organize Ford workers, their approach at the beginning was a surreptitious one. The unions felt that the very high percentage of Southern whites in Detroit would refuse to join the Union if Negroes were too obviously participating. But when the strike broke, far-sighted Negro leaders in Detroit took an unequivocal position in behalf of the organization of workers. . . .

During the recent riot, R. J. Thomas, president of the UAW-CIO, proposed an eight-point program which was widely published, and helped to emphasize the basic causes of the riot. These points included: 1) creation of a special grand jury to investigate the causes of the riot and to return justifiable indictments with a competent Negro attorney appointed as an assistant prosecutor to work with the grand jury; 2) immediate construction and opening of adequate park and recreation facilities. Thomas called it "disgraceful that the City's normal, inadequate park space was permitted to be overtaxed further by the influx of hundreds of thousands of new war workers;" 3) immediate and practical plans for rehousing Negro slum dwellers in decent Government-financed housing developments; 4) insistence that plant managements as well as workers recognize the right of Negroes to jobs in line with their skill and seniority; 5) a full investigation by the special grand jury of the conduct of the Police Department during the riots; 6) special care by the courts in dealing with the many persons arrested. Those found guilty should be severely punished, and there must be no discrimination between white and Negro rioters; 7) the loss of homes and small businesses, as well as personal injuries, is the responsibility of the community and the city should create a fund to make good these losses; 8) creation by the Mayor of a special biracial committee of ten persons to make further recommendations looking toward the elimination of racial differences and frictions, this committee to have a special job in connection with high schools "where racial hatred has been permitted to grow and thrive within recent years. . . . "

[White cited several other factors that caused the riot, or affected its timing—among them the ineptness of Mayor Edward J. Jeffries, Jr., though he absolved him from personal racial prejudice. He criticized the role of the major newspapers. (He found the Hearst-controlled *Times* actively racist, the *News* apathetic, and gave only the *Free Press*, under the new ownership of John Knight, a clean bill of health.)

Section II of the report, which follows, relates to the activities of the Detroit police force, and includes charges of both malfeasance and corruption. The demand by the NAACP for a grand jury investigation was never heeded.]

Activities of the Police during the Riots June 21 and 22, 1943

From June 24 to July 9, 1943, we maintained an emergency office at the St. Antoine Branch of the YMCA. In addition to myself, we used the services of two private investigators from New York City, one white and one Negro. During this period we received all complaints that were brought to us and made several independent investigations. All of the material in the following report is supported by affidavits. . . .

One of the important factors in any race riot is the local police. Very often disturbances reach riot proportions as a result of inefficiency on the part of the local police. The affidavits we have taken are more than sufficient to justify the calling of a special grand jury to investigate the nonfeasance and malfeasance of the police as a contributing factor in the Detroit riots. . . .

In the June riots of this year, the Detroit police ran true to form. The trouble reached riot proportions because the Detroit police once again enforced the law under an unequal hand. They used "persuasion" rather than firm action with white rioters while against Negroes they used the ultimate in force: night sticks, revolvers, riot guns, sub-machine guns and deer guns. As a result, 25 of the 34 persons killed were Negroes. Of the 25 Negroes killed, 17 were killed by police. The excuse of the Police Department for the disproportionate number of Negroes killed is that the majority of them were killed while committing felonies: namely, the looting of stores on Hastings Street. On the other hand, the crimes of arson and felonious assault are also felonies. It is true that some Negroes were looting stores on Hastings Street, and were shot while committing these crimes. It is equally true that white persons were turning over and burning automobiles on Woodward Avenue. This is arson. Others were beating Negroes with iron pipes, clubs, and rocks. This is felonious assault. Several Negroes were stabbed. This is assault with intent to murder.

All of these crimes are matters of record; many were committed in the presence of police officers, several on the pavement around the City Hall. Yet, the record remains, Negroes killed by police—17; white persons killed by police—none. Eighty-five percent of the persons arrested were Negroes.

Evidence of tension in Detroit has been apparent for months. The *Detroit Free Press* sent a reporter to the police department. When Commissioner Witherspoon was asked how he was handling the situation, he told the reporter: "We have given orders to handle it with kid gloves. The policemen have taken insults in order to keep trouble from breaking out. I doubt if you or I could put up with it." This weak-kneed policy of the police commissioner coupled with the anti-Negro attitude of many members of the force helped to make a riot inevitable.

Sunday Night on Belle Isle

Belle Isle is a municipally owned recreation park where thousands of white and Negro defense workers and their families go on Sunday for their outings. There had been isolated instances of racial friction in the past. On Sunday night, June 20th, there was trouble between a group of white and Negro people. The disturbance was under control by midnight. During the time of disturbance and after it was under control, the police searched the automobiles of all Negroes and searched the Negroes as well. They did not search the white people. One Negro who was to be inducted into the Army the following week was arrested because another person in the car had a small pen knife. This youth was later sentenced to 90 days in jail before his family could locate him. Many Negroes were arrested during this period and rushed to local police stations. At the very beginning the police demonstrated that they would continue to handle racial disorders by searching, beating and arresting Negroes while using mere persuasion on white people.

The Riot Spreads to Detroit Proper

A short time after midnight disorder broke out in a white neighborhood near the Roxy Theatre on Woodward Avenue. The Roxy is an all night theatre attended by white and Negro patrons. Several Negroes were beaten and others were forced to remain in the theatre for lack of police protection. The rumor spread among the white people that a Negro had raped a white woman on Belle Isle and that the Negroes were rioting.

At about the same time a rumor spread around Hastings and Adams Streets in the Negro area that white sailors had thrown a

Negro woman and her baby into the lake at Belle Isle and that the police were beating Negroes. This rumor was also repeated by an unidentified Negro at one of the Negro night spots. Some Negroes began to attack white persons in the area. The police immediately began to use their sticks and revolvers against these Negroes. The Negroes began to beat out the windows of stores of white merchants on Hastings Street.

The interesting thing is that when the windows in the stores on Hastings Street were first broken, there was no looting. An officer of the Merchants' Association walked the length of Hastings Street starting at 7 o'clock Monday morning and noticed that none of the stores with broken windows had been looted. It is thus clear that the original breaking of windows was not for the purpose of looting. Throughout Monday the Detroit police instead of placing policemen in front of the stores to protect them from looting, contented themselves with driving up and down Hastings Street from time to time and stopping in front of the stores. The usual procedure was to jump out of the squad cars with drawn revolvers and riot guns to shoot whoever might be in the store. The police would then tell the Negro bystanders to "run and not look back." On several occasions, persons running were shot in the back. In other instances, bystanders were clubbed by police. To the Detroit police, all Negroes on Hastings Street were "looters." This included Negroes returning from work. There is no question that some Negroes were guilty of looting. . . .

[On Monday] small groups of white people began to rove up and down Woodward Avenue beating Negroes, stoning cars containing Negroes, stopping street cars and yanking Negroes from them, and stabbing and shooting Negroes. In no case did the police do more than try to "reason" with these mobs, many of which were at this stage quite small. The police did not draw their revolvers or riot guns, and never used any force to disperse these mobs. As a result of this, the mobs got larger and bolder and even attacked Negroes on the pavement of the City Hall in demonstration not only of their contempt for Negroes, but of their contempt for law and order as represented by the municipal government. The use of night sticks or the drawing of revolvers would have dispersed these white groups and saved the lives of many Negroes. It would not have been necessary to shoot, but it would have been sufficient to threaten to shoot into the white mobs. The use of a fire hose would have dispersed many of the groups. None of these things were done, and the disorder took on the proportions of a major riot. The responsibility of this rests with the Detroit police.

At the height of the disorder on Woodward Avenue, Negroes driving north on Brush Street (a Negro street) were stopped at Vernor Highway by a policeman who forced them to detour to Woodard Avenue. Many of these cars are automobiles which appeared in the pictures by several newspapers showing them overturned and burned on Woodward Avenue. While investigating the riot, we obtained many affidavits from Negroes concerning police brutality during the riot. It is impossible to include the facts of all these affidavits. . . .

One Negro, who has been an employee of a bank for the last eighteen years, was on his way to work on a Woodward Avenue streetcar when he was seized by one of the white mobs. In the presence of at least four policemen, he was beaten and stabbed in the side. He also heard several shots fired from the back of the mob. He managed to run to two of the policemen, who proceeded to "protect" him from the mob. The two policemen, followed by two mounted policemen, proceeded down Woodward Avenue. While he was being escorted by these policemen, the Negro was struck in the face by at least eight of the mob, and at no time was any effort made to prevent him from being struck. After a short distance this man noticed a squad car parked on the other side of the street. In sheer desperation, he broke away from the two policemen who claimed to be protecting him and ran to the squad car, begging for protection. The officer in the squad car put him in the back seat and drove off, thereby saving this man's life. During all this time . . . blood was spurting from his side. Despite this obvious felony, committed in the presence of at least four policemen, no effort was made at that time either to protect the victim, or since to arrest the persons guilty of the felony. . . .

Vernor Apartments

On the night of June 21st at about eight o'clock, a Detroit policeman was shot on the two hundred block of Vernor Highway, and his assailant, who was in a vacant lot, was in turn, killed by another policeman. State and city policemen then began to attack the apartment building at 290 E. Vernor Highway, which was fully occupied by tenants. . . . Tenants of the building were forced to fall to the floor and remain there in order to save their lives. Later slugs from machine guns, revolvers, rifles, and deer-guns were dug from the inside walls. Tear gas was shot into the building. . . . The tenants were lined up in the street, the apartments were forcibly entered; locks and doors were broken. All of the apartments were ransacked. . . . Most of the tenants reported that money, jewelry, whisky, and items of personal property were missing when they were permitted to return to their apartments after midnight. State and City police had been in possession of the building during the meantime. . . .

After the raid on the Vernor Apartments, the police used as their excuse the statement that policeman Lawrence A. Adams had been shot by a sniper from the Vernor Apartments, and that for that reason, they attacked the building and its occupants. However, in a story released by the Police Department on July 2, . . . it was reported that "The shot that felled Adams was fired by Homer Edison, 28 years old, of 502 Montcalm from the shadows of a parking lot. . . ."

One member of the white mobs, whose face appeared in at least four violent action pictures which have appeared several times in the daily papers of Detroit, is well known to police and has a police record, yet he was never arrested for his part in the Detroit riots. He has since left town after having seen two of his photographs placed again in the *Detroit Free Press*. This type of deliberate non-action is typical of the Detroit Police Force. . . .

Y.M.C.A.

On the night of June 22nd at about 10 o'clock, some of the residents of the St. Antoine Branch of the Y.M.C.A. were returning to the dormitory. Several were on their way home from the Y.W.C.A. across the street. State Police were searching some other Negroes . . . when two of the Y.M.C.A. residents were stopped and searched for weapons. After none were found they were allowed to proceed to the building. Just as the last of the Y.M.C.A. men was about to enter the building, he heard someone behind him yell what sounded to him like "Hi, Ridley." (Ridley is also a resident of the Y.) Another resident said he heard someone yell what sounded to him like "Heil, Hitler."

A State policeman, Ted Anders, jumped from his car with his revolver out, . . . and fired through the outside door. . . . Julian Witherspoon, who had just entered the building, was shot in the side by the bullet that was fired through the outside door and fell to the floor. There had been no show of violence or weapons of any kind by anyone in or around the Y.M.C.A.

The officers with drawn revolvers ordered all the residents of the Y.M.C.A. who were in the lobby of their building, to raise their hands in the air and line up against the wall like criminals. During all of this time these men were called "black bastards, monkeys" and other vile names by the officers. At least one man was struck, another was forced to throw his lunch on the floor. All of the men in the lobby were searched. . . . Witherspoon was later removed to the hospital and has subsequently been released. . . .

4.   What about Housing Cooperatives?

Merle E. Henrickson

The real estate pages are in reaction against modern technology. They have become frightened because people are taking "Postwar Houses" seriously. There are probably two reasons for this campaign: fear that little builders can't turn them out, and fear that if anyone does produce them, people will refuse to pay for the stuff they have now.

When the real estate pages say that the postwar house will have a little more glass and many more gadgets, but will otherwise by much the same, they mean that builders cannot or will not produce a better house. Architects and financing agencies are both frank to admit that the system of home financing has done

Merle E. Henrickson, "What about Housing Cooperatives?" plans and drawings by Donald Monson, 1945, Halbeisen Collection, Reuther Archives, Wayne State University.

much to curb experimental work. There must be not hint of deviation from the mortgage bankers' notion of the average taste, "The mortgage risks a banker will assume must necessarily, for the protection of bank depositors, be predicated on the preference of most of the people in housing."

But unfortunately not most of the people looked at one at a time to see who has children, who has dogs, and who has phonograph records. No! It's most of the people tossed in a hat and come out "average American", with 1.8 children, 0.3 dogs. For a million of these average Americans the mortgage bankers will be happy to build about 50,000 five-room Cape Cod cottages on forty foot lots, with petunias and a white picket fence in the front yard and a garage and bird bath in the back. . . . They will point out that in the interest of individuality they have put one-third of the front doors on the left side, one-third on the right, and one-third square in the middle.

The pressure to keep the house a liquid commodity limits the size and type of all homes, even though the family recognizes that it needs four bedrooms or a special feature to accommodate a hobby; it must eliminate what is unique to its own needs because it would make the house harder to sell. . . .

If people are to get better houses, they must decide what needs improving and organize their own cooperatives to get what they want.

A house is intended first of all for shelter. It must have floors, walls, and a roof suitable for the climate in which it is built, and a heating system capable of maintaining a temperature of 68 degrees in winter. Better heating systems are necessary both to reduce pulmonary diseases, and to cut down the amount of housework. Housekeeping is becoming an increasing ritual of washing, dusting, and vacuum cleaning. As the number of labor-saving devices increases, the amount of time spent in performing the basic cleaning operations is also increased. The first technical job to be done in the home is to make surfaces which are easier to keep clean rather than more powerful machines to get dust out of the deeper rugs. For our bathrooms and kitchens we now try to have walls and floors that can be watered down—if ever so gently. But we have other points of heavy traffic in the house where washable surfaces would be a great improvement. Where are small children to play? Must we continue to build houses in which floors are so cold that they must be covered with dust-catching rugs for children to play on? Recent experiments have studied the adaptability of two ancient heating principles to the home. Radiant heat, extensively used by the Romans, employs the principle of heating surfaces with which people come in contact, rather than heating the air and leaving surfaces cold. Solar heating—that is, proper orientation—exposes rooms to the maximum of winter sun by increasing south window exposure while giving greater protection from prevailing winds.

Whatever heating system may prove most practical for installation in group housing, one factor to be considered is elimination of dirt-producing fuel-burning devices. . . .

Whether the things that all families need are to be secured in the homes of low and middle-income families is now a practical problem of standardizing construction methods and organizing a large-scale market to demand a sound product. . . . There is no reason for the house building industry to go farther in the direction of [the] artificial style obsolescence of the automobile industry. . . .

The cooperative neighborhood is not a utopia, but neither does it need to have those limitations of bourgeois individualism which find fullest expression in the suburban home [which] tries to buy everything of the good life for itself, then surrounds it by four walls, a tight fence and a privet hedge, and finds its security in a bill of sale limiting ownership to "white Caucasians"—whatever they may be. The fences around the back yards which chop up the only open space large enough for a ball diamond and cut off the suburban child from social intercourse in his street, are only symbolic of the fuller isolation of the whole suburban family. These families arranged in nice neat rows don't know their neighbors, and seemingly they don't care how high the hedge grows between them.

Part XIII

The Fifties: The Look of Togetherness

The Fifties: The Look of Togetherness

A leading women's journal used the slogan "the magazine of togetherness." It wasn't far off the mark in describing its own goals or those of the times. Yet a young historian said recently, "It must have been terrible to live through the fifties." He was thinking of McCarthyism. But for many Detroiters the fifties seemed an arrival of the promised land: a single family home of one's own, children, and usually with a mother at home to care for them. Auto production was up, the pay the best ever, and the UAW was removing the seasonal layoffs with guaranteed annual wage clauses in the new contracts.

The city expanded. The Northland shopping mall was one of the earliest in the country, designed by Victor Gruen. It was a place to sit in the gardens under flowering crab trees and treat the children to Sanders ice cream. From its opening year the J. L. Hudson anchor store in the mall outdid the expectations of its owners, and in very few years it surpassed the sales of its parent store downtown. Soon Hudson's took the lead in developing other new malls. Meanwhile Northland performed a second function—it proved the need for a second family car.

Other changes in the social structure of the fifties also pinpointed that need. It is well known that American church membership reached its peak during the fifties. It was been less noted that membership in everything else skyrocketed as well. Girl

435

Scouts, Boy Scouts, Cub Scouts, Little League baseball, American Legion, Veterans of Foreign Wars, Masonic groups—all grew. The organizations that commanded the most time and energy from their membership did the best. All of them reached out for ever younger members, and mothers became chauffeurs.

With the baby boom, pediatrics caught on. The sick child was driven to the office for the new wonder drug penicillin. Then there were music lessons, dance and baton-twirling lessons, plus the parenting organizations of school and church, with their weekend family get-togethers and camp-outs. In an ultimate effort at organization, there was the "family council" for making democratic choices in the home. It took a lot of time to discuss allowances, chores, and maternal frustration with the food budget. Fathers rarely found time to attend a second meeting, and mothers took grim reports of failure back to the Child Study Club.

Some women had more options, but no more time. Improved washers, then driers, supposedly saved many hours per week. So where did the new time go? It was absorbed into increasingly complex routines and skills. There was more clothing to be washed as upscale diversification set in: sportswear; "coffee coats" replacing housedresses; not just bathing suits, but "beach cover-ups"; sharper differentiations in childrens' clothing; and the introduction of the whole range of separate "teenage" styles. The net result was that the traditional Monday wash day ended up being spread through the entire week.

Women's magazines sponsored an endless variety of needle-crafts and recipes. In all of this there were distinct social gradations. Nancy Williams, the governor's lady, did fine needlepoint work; many other women knitted and sewed. Possibly at the bottom of the social and aesthetic heap was the conversion of plastic bleach bottles to sequin-covered containers for the toilet brush.

On top of it all was added television. "We are destroying childhood—the only time left in our world for imagination and reflection," said a perceptive social worker.

Women were everywhere discouraged from working outside the home, except in minor part-time jobs, assumed to be temporary. A report from a young wife and mother of the fifties who did not think of work as temporary is included here in our interview with Benita Mullins. A peace activist then, as she is today,

Benita Mullins represents one of the many crosscurrents in the world of the fifties, when the norm was conformity. An interview with her is included for its insights into the world of the women who did work.

Other changes came about through the rising strength of labor unions. Their growing political strength was shown first by the UAW. There were also changes in the scope of labor's interests. The UAW reflected the family orientation of the fifties with a new excitement about health, recreation, child welfare, and schools. This shift in emphasis began with a few determined women. The role of certain UAW wives and women staff members has never received enough credit. The thinking and drive of May Wolf Reuther, for one, was minimized by her husband Walter's notable role.

A meaningful accomplishment in which labor and parents of the general community joined was the Serve Our Schools Committee. Their joint efforts rescued a moribund school system. We include an early program and membership leaflet of the Serve Our Schools Committee.

Liberal reformers were gradually drawn into concern for civil rights. The most profound contradiction of the good life of the fifties lay in the life of the black community. Nowhere was trouble more sharply revealed than in the nature of the Detroit Police Department in its dealings with blacks. This real world of false arrest and midnight beatings was largely avoided by white Detroiters. It was easy to neither know or understand.

The section "White Police in Black Communities" consists of a factual report by the Detroit chapter of the NAACP in 1956. The survey points the way to the years just ahead when a mayor (Jerome Cavanagh) would be elected principally on his promise to combat police brutality.

To capture the dark side of the conformity that came to represent the decade, we must realize that in Detroit the fifties began in 1949.

A major turning point in Detroit history came with the election of Albert Cobo over George Edwards for mayor. Cobo's victory in the primary came as a surprise to many area politicos and opinion-makers, since Edwards had been the high vote-getter for the council in the previous election and was serving as council president. Both the *Free Press* and the *News* favored

Cobo in the primary, the *News* more actively. When Cobo won the primary the *News* took a more aggressive stance in his favor. The editors assigned one of their top reporters, a man who personally liked and respected Edwards, to write an article stressing the location of black precincts that had voted overwhelmingly for Edwards. It was widely believed that the article had an impact in switching blue-collar worker votes to Cobo in the final election. Few noticed the disappearance of the incumbent mayor, Eugene van Antwerp, in the primary. Probably a critical error of van Antwerp's had been favoring the creation of a dozen public housing sites in the city's outlying areas. This raised the possibility that the city's blacks might have a fair choice in housing location.

Included in the campaign literature prepared for Edwards in 1949 and distributed by COPE (Committee of Political Education), the political action arm of the UAW, was a flyer summarizing the differences in outlook between Edwards and Cobo. It is reproduced here, and it sets out clearly several strong directional choices to be made by citizens.

At the same primary election, the voters agreed to create a Loyalty Commission to investigate the presumed dangerous and Communist ideas of city employees. The body operated for many years, providing a few jobs at taxpayers' expense but failing to uncover any Communists. It did, of course, serve as a constant threat to free expression of opinion.

Liberal groups and individuals who made it through the fifties were hurt by the remnants of divisive factionalism that had split the UAW in the late forties, as much or more than they were by the forays into Detroit of outside investigators, such as HUAC, the House UnAmerican Activities Committee. Few "left-wingers" remained in the UAW hierarchy, and the UAW was still the power source of social and political movements in Detroit and the surrounding area. The controlling Reuther group still included many Socialists and former Socialists. Only its opposition on the left could possibly refer to it as "right-wing," yet the factions were unforgiving. Liberals fell into sad, laughable descriptions of themselves and their fellows as "non-Communist, but not *anti*-Communist," "a non-red-baiting authentic Socialist," or "an Addes fellow-traveler—how un-American can you get?" These varied definitions covered lost friendships and much personal pain. Distrust was contagious and not reached by the new anti-biotics. Both sides added considerably to the distortions of labor history for which younger generations would pay in false perceptions of unionism.

On the surface, labor in Michigan was never healthier than in the fifties. Noticeable political gains were made by workers to accompany the economic ones. Union political leadership became more sophisticated after 1949. No longer did labor's top leaders run for elective office themselves. The days of the forties when several members of the UAW Executive Board ran for city council or mayor—and lost—were gone. Like the leaders of industry, these men were now too busy. New methods worked better anyway. Rank and file union members ran for precinct delegates in the Democratic party, rang doorbells, and passed out literature in their neighborhoods—a "worked precinct" was said to increase its margin of victory by an average of thirty percent. Men and women who might have no direct connection with the labor movement but who did have the skills and background needed for a particular elective office were sought out and put on labor-endorsed slates that carried with them an almost certain victory.

Unions had no monopoly on organizational skills. The campaigns of Congresswoman Martha Griffiths made the most of women staying at home. A house trailer took the candidate through far northwest neighborhoods each weekday. Women volunteers, often in yellow skirts embellished with "Martha" in green stitchery, rang doorbells and begged the housewife to drop her duties for "just a few minutes" to come out to meet Mrs. Griffiths. Fresh coffee, tea, or lemonade and homemade cookies helped to establish rapport with the direct-speaking candidate.

Griffiths served Michigan and her country well. She was the first woman to serve on the House Ways and Means Committee and the author of much substantive legislation.[1] At this moment she continues to speak her mind as Michigan's lieutenant governor.

Labor continued to extend its scope of operation into such fresh areas as recreation, education, and housing, from desegregated bowling leagues to school board elections.[2]

In addition to much lobbying for low- and middle-income housing and better landlord and tenant relations, labor found time to assist with two specific cooperative housing developments. There was the small Schoolcraft Gardens Cooperative, which failed, and the giant Gratiot Redevelopment Project, which did not. In the latter case labor stepped in after years of inaction by the city administration had left a large tract of downtown land unused. A coalition was formed between business and labor that at last got the project in operation.

I include documents relating to both Schoolcraft Gardens and Gratiot Redevelopment, as well as Harold Norris's significant statement on the important failure of the Cobo administration to deal with the problem of finding homes for the previous dwellers in the downtown area.

Although I have attempted to show that in the perception of many Detroiters the fifties were more tiring than terrible, there *were* witch hunts. If the Loyalty Investigating Commission was unsuccessful in its efforts to locate and fire any dangerous subversive among city employees, the Detroit Board of Education did remove—and later rehire—one teacher. She was also compelled to go through a rather absurd session of questioning by the Dies Committee when it visited Detroit in 1951. So, too, was a young dry cleaner whose previous job as a union organizer had come to an end when the State County and Municipal Workers were expelled from the CIO for alleged Communism. Coleman A. Young refused to reveal membership lists of the local chapter of the National Negro Congress to the House UnAmerican Activities Committee. It did not hurt him several years later in his election to the state senate, and certainly not in his subsequent election as mayor of the city of Detroit.

Although New York was the venue rather than Detroit, George Crockett also stood firmly on the Fifth Amendment in defending clients accused of conspiracy against the United States. Again, there were some years of semi-obscurity, but after a distinguished career as judge in the local courts, Crockett is now congressman of the Thirteenth District, and represents Detroit's most inner inner city.[3]

There are other examples: "Edie" Van Horne, an effective union steward at Dodge Main, was run out of the factory one day by a group of men who accused her of Communism. She was promptly welcomed back—with flowers—by the rest of her fellow workers.

Editor's Notes

1. Besides sponsoring the original proposed Equal Rights Amendment, Griffiths until her retirement from Congress was a major figure in exposing cost overruns and other absurdities in military spending.
2. Desegregated bowling was won over the protests of a chain of community newspapers who hinted at orgies at which white women would be "forced to have Negro male bowling partners."
3. Like Coleman Young, George Crockett lost some employment due to labor union struggles. He had served with Maurice Sugar as an attorney for the UAW before Reuther's presidency. It would seem that the right to choose counsel would be a prerogative of a new executive, but the bitterness of the times did not permit Crockett's friends and associates to see the matter in that light.

1. Women Workers in the Fifties: Interview with Benita Mullins

Wilma Wood Henrickson

At the war's end the country expected women to return home from their jobs, and many did. However, many women still had to work, and wanted the better pay that had come with the war years.[1] Benita Mullins, who worked at the now-closed Dodge Main automotive plant in Hamtramck during the late forties and early fifties, recalled this and other working experiences of the period during a March, 1988, interview.

[Let's talk about] Dodge Main. This was during the late forties—early fifties?

It was soon after World War II—the late forties. I was hired into the trim shop, and had several different jobs there. I remember one was on the paste line; I think that was the first one—where the seats are made and there's a carousel goes around. Marianna [a friend of Mullins and a fellow Socialist in those years] was working there then as a tack spitter. It was all women who were doing that paste job and all the tack spitters except Marianna were men. I think it's the tacky little jobs, it's the sticky little jobs, more detailed work, that they would want to have all women doing the job.

Benita Mullins, interview with Wilma Wood Henrickson, March, 1988.

442

On the paste line we had a bucket like a paint bucket and a brush like a paint brush. We worked on a car seat as it came by us on the carousel. We put a paste on the iron frame of the seat and then we had pieces of felt that we put on the back of the frame—that came before the upholstery was put on.

What did they pay an hour back then? I know that earlier, during the war itself, the standard rate was $1.03 an hour for practically every job in town.

At some point there—I guess it was when I had gone through the ninety-day probationary period—I know that it was a great day when I was taking home fifty dollars a week. That would be about $1.25 an hour or a little more than that, by the time you figured out the deductions, but I took home fifty dollars.

You told me a little bit the other day about maternity leave, and I gathered that the company didn't really enjoy [giving] maternity leave, and didn't feel much inclined to go along with it.

No, they expected women to take their leave by three months. I did get a letter from my doctor that was worded in such a way that it didn't say exactly when I had to leave so that I could stay as long as I felt okay. Since it was my first pregnancy and I was still very slender, I was able to go on working until really my sixth month. . . . The last several months I was working in a section—this was afternoons, the afternoon shift—in a section where the women made the arm rests and the headlining. I was on a sewing machine making the armrests for a while, and then when it was getting nearer the time—I was farther along—and I don't know whether she [the floor lady] knew that I was pregnant or not, but she probably did—she put me on the headlining. The headlining was on a very wide belt. The ceiling of the inside of the car is what the headlining is. It was felt with channels sewn into it and into those channels long rods are put, different ones in different channels. There were about six in each—four anyway, and maybe six, depending on the length of the car. They are sewn in each piece, in each single headlining. So you have to pick up these rods and get them in there. According to how many women there were working on it you might have to cover more.

Changing shifts at Dodge Main, Hamtramck, c. 1950. (From UAW International. Used with permission of Reuther Archives.)

Did you have to lift these rods over your head or waist-high or what?

Oh, yeah. The table was up above your waist and you had to lift them above the table. The thing was that you'd be eight hours working, lifting these long rods way above your waist.

How did the rods come to you? Were they on a belt line?

No. They were in stacks, in some sort of bin. I don't remember whether they were on the floor. You have to lift them and slide them in and get the beginning of the rod into this little channel and maybe the smallest ones would be the size of your little finger and the other ones like your other fingers, because they were different thicknesses—and slide them all the way in. . . .

Do you know what sort of metal these rods were?

Oh, iron and steel; in those days they weren't using any light metals.

Well, after Rachel was born I was still nursing her and I had a four month leave of absence. When I was ready to come back, the company doctor was giving a physical to see what condition I was in—if I was okay to be rehired. She was using the stethoscope and so on, and when she came to the part where she's sitting in front of me and I'm standing, she says, "So you're still nursing the baby?" Then she says, "Are you pregnant?" and at the same time when she says the word "pregnant," she takes her fist and whams it right into where there would be a baby if I *were* pregnant, before I could say yes or no. I thought this was a pretty horrible thing to do to anybody who might be pregnant. I hadn't even said "yes" or I hadn't even said "no" before she did that.

It was terrible. It sort of confirms your feeling that the company didn't want the women to have maternity leave.

There must have been a lot of pressure on her as a doctor to keep the women's work force within certain bounds. Her reason for not giving me permission to go back to work was that I was still nursing. So I never did go back.

After that I went to the unemployment office, and I guess there must not have been an opening, but later when I had finished nursing at six or seven months, I went back and they made me take a job and by then I *was* pregnant. . . . The early part of my pregnancy I was over at an automobile supply place. It was at Antoinette on Woodward.

Right then they were making plastic seat covers for Oldsmobiles. It was a seat cover that was only used from the time the car left the assembly line until it got to the new owner. It was to protect those beautiful seats until the new owner got them, so that maximizing the output was the main goal. They had a woman who had been working there seventeen years and she set the pace, and it was piecework, the only time I was on piecework.

The thing I remember about that [job] was that in the same building they were repairing cars on the first floor. They did something or others to cars—but a different crew. Where I was

445

sitting at my sewing machine, the back of my chair was within two or three feet from where they were working on a car, and this was inside a building. The exhaust fumes, when they had the motor running, would be coming right on me and I did not like that at all—breathing these car fumes when I was pregnant. And I went to them and said, "This is a great big building, and can't you move that away?" And they said, "No, that's his work station and that's where he is."

Tell me about how you happened to want to work in the auto industry in the first place? I remember that you wanted to. I know that you didn't particularly want a war-related job during the war, and that you were working in the cooperative movement.[2]

That's right. Well, I had a feeling that I really wanted to know—I wanted to know all the different kinds of working situations, the situations that working people have, and I didn't work in the factory during the war. I worked at other jobs that had nothing to do with the war. I worked places like drugstores, bookshops, selling records, for a number of years. One time I had a job processing unemployment claims at MESC [Michigan Employment Service Commission] and MUCC [Michigan Unemployment Claims Commission].

After the war there were people needed for almost every automobile job in town. That was [because of] the postwar auto production. At the factories you got paid more than at the other places—bookstores, dime stores, selling records. As long as you felt young and healthy, it was a fun thing to do, but any time you weren't young and healthy, or had problems of your own, the forced pace, the exhaustion would all make a difference.

And the attitudes of the men in the union?

Well, there were several units where they had just women working—the job on the paste line where I started out—there was a man running it, and I do remember when we went out to lunch he would take the key and turn the line up. There was a key to the carousel and he would turn it up so it went faster. I thought that was a terrible thing to do. You had a half hour for lunch and you run out and get it and you run back in. That's the time you least feel like working faster than usual, but that's when he would turn it up.

Another [woman's job] was the wire room and only women worked in that place. In both cases there was a woman in charge of that unit, a floor lady. They were there because they were able to get the production out.

The women were accepted when Marianna first started working there during the war. . . . As the war ended the men didn't really want women working. They wanted more of their buddies there. But Dodge Main is in Hamtramck, and the Polish women had been working there for a long time, and you kind of had an ethnic community there. In the union the women were just a very small minority. The men controlled the union. It took a very unusual person to make progress in the union—like Edie van Horne.

During the Chrysler strike—I remember that the union was very glad to have people come in and help. I worked at the union hall for a while, processing requests for assistance, I think. They paid fifteen dollars a week, which was just about enough to pay my rent and get enough food to live on; but you did get a meal while you were working there in the union hall. In many ways women got equal treatment with the men when the war ended, but still certain kinds of jobs were reserved for women.

What were some of the things you hoped the union would accomplish for Detroit workers in general, and did it fail you in any way?

There really was never enough chance to improve working conditions. The Chrysler strike, that went on for more than a hundred days. The demands were always for the money conditions, the amount of money you made, and never for the working conditions. The pay scale was sort of a common denominator. There never was any chance to improve working conditions. The working people never had any control. Of course, all the fringe benefits did not exist at all in the forties or early fifties.

In union meetings there was less participation by women, but there were less women employed of the thousands of people employed. . . .

So that would automatically be a smaller minority?

447

And women who would attend union meetings, that was a minority too. They had less time to spend in the politicking that would go on in a union hall. They had to maintain the home even if they did work. That's where I first saw parliamentary procedure used as a way of gaining political power,—the uses and abuses of it. . . .

Editor's Notes

1. Of women's work in the auto plants at the war's end, Nancy Gabin, labor historian, says: "Despite efforts of the Fair Practices Department and the Women's Bureau [of the UAW] to challenge prejudice against women on the part of management and the union, there was rampant discrimination against women on the local union level. The discrimination took the form of local union toleration of inequitable hiring practices, layoffs of women workers, discriminatory pay scales and transfers by management. . . ." ("Women Workers and the UAW, 1945–1954," in The Labor History Reader, ed. Daniel J. Leab (Urbana: University of Illinois Press, 1985), 407–32.

2. Mullins was actively involved in the Socialist party and the union movement and was then, as she is today, a peace activist. This accounts for her not seeking work in war-related industries, but rather joining the automotive work force during the postwar auto boom.

2. Our Principles, Purpose and Program

Serve Our Schools Committee

In the postwar housing boom—and baby boom—all schools were overcrowded. Serve Our Schools was a coalition of religious, labor, and ethnic groups as well as a number of individuals representing only themselves and their children, formed to meet the pressures. Labor played an important role throughout the group's life, though never the dominant one sometimes attributed to it.

The political strength of the group made it possible to elect first board members, then a majority of the board of education. The board recruited as superintendent of schools Dr. Samuel Miller Brownell, former commissioner of education under President Eisenhower. A copy of the program and platform of Serve Our Schools follows.

Our Principles

To offer each child, each citizen, who goes to our schools the best chance for personal growth, for self-realization, and for a full, good life.

To prepare each child and citizen for a constructive life in the community, in the democratic American tradition.

"Our Principles, Purpose and Program," Serve Our Schools Committee, Mildred Jeffrey Collection, Box 17, folder 11, Reuther Library, Wayne State University.

Our Purpose

—To determine
the real needs of the public schools in Detroit.
—To secure
public understanding of those needs.
public support for a program to meet those needs.
—To find
good candidates for membership on the Board of Education.
—To work
for their election.
and at the same time
—To cooperate
with other groups in Detroit who want similar goals.
with the Board of Education, interpreting school problems to
the public, and public views on education to the Board.

3.   White Police in Black Communities

National Association for the Advancement of Colored People, Detroit Chapter

Thirty years after Forrester Washington's 1926 study of the Detroit Police Department, the Detroit branch of the NAACP found it necessary to study once again the matter of police brutality. The complaints studied occur in the terms of Mayors Cobo and Miriani.

The study is entitled, An Analysis of Police Brutality Complaints Reported to the Detroit Branch National Association for the Advancement of Colored People in the Period from January 1, 1956 to July 30, 1957.

In August of 1957 the Detroit Branch NAACP began an analysis of police brutality complaints which were reported to the Branch office in the period January 1, 1956 to July 30, 1957. The analysis covered a total of 103 cases and was completed in October, 1957.[1]

The principal objective of the NAACP in making this study was to illuminate some of the basic problems in the area of police-community relations and to find the common factors that might emerge. The results, it was felt, could be used in a further

National Association for the Advancement of Colored People, *An Analysis of Police Brutality Complaints Reported to the Detroit Branch National Association for the Advancement of Colored People in the Period from January 1, 1956 to July 30, 1957* (Detroit: National Association for the Advancement of Colored People, 1957).

effort to inform the public and the appropriate public officials on the extent of the problem of police brutality in the community and some of the factors contributing to it. Such information should also be helpful in bringing about some of the desired corrective measures in police methods and a better climate of goodwill between law enforcement officials and the community. . . .

Our records show that anywhere from 1 to 9 complaints are filed with the NAACP during the period of a month, with the largest number of complaints being recorded in July of each year. . . .

The most frequent type of police misconduct involved in these complaints is physical assault, followed by insulting epithets:

a) The common use of profanity and a reference to the complainant's race in a derogatory manner.

b) The indiscriminate searching of citizens' pockets and wallets on public streets.

c) When citizens question the violation of their rights the officers resort to physical assault, followed by arrest.

Rank order of the various types of police misconduct involved in these complaints.

Our reports show that out of 103 cases, 33 were physical assault, and 23 were cases of both physical and verbal assault. Our reports show 12 cases of insulting epithets used by arresting officers, and 12 cases of illegal search of home or car, and 4 cases of false arrest.

a) In 19 of these assault cases, victims were held without charge (usually overnight) and released. 3 were dismissed in court for lack of evidence.

b) Women were the victims of 18 of these assault cases.

c) One case involved a 16 year old boy.

d) Our files show an additional 8 cases of threats and intimidation on the part of police officers.

The central problem . . . seems to be the unprovoked attack by the police while questioning them. This, followed by false charges of "resisting arrest" has created distrust and bitter resentment of the police department on the part of the complainants.

Do the attitudes of the complainants toward the police reflect any common factors or prejudices of interest to this inquiry?

Our reports show that 90% of the complainants are working people without a previous record, who believe they are subjected

452

to unwarranted abuse because of their race. They feel that their freedom and well-being is in constant jeopardy since they are exposed to the sadist whims of race-baiting police officers. This is evident because of the similarity in the complaints where the officer is quoted as demanding that the complainant say "yes sir and no sir when answering a white man," or "I can see that you are one of those smart niggers."

Do the attitudes of policemen toward complainants reflect any common factors or prejudices of interest to this inquiry?

Our reports show a total disregard, on the part of the policemen, for the complainant's rights as a citizen in every case recorded. Example:

1) Searching of citizens in public streets for minor traffic violations.

2) Physical assault.

3) The common use of racial slurs.

4) The common practice of assault and arrest of those friends or relatives who attempt to intervene on behalf of the person being attacked by the police.

5) Abuse of complainants in police precincts.

6) The search and destruction of property, without a warrant, in citizen's homes.

7) The use of profanity in the presence of women.

8) The prevalent indication that the complainant has no rights that he (the police officer) has to respect.

9) The intimidation and abuse of interracial couples, while expressing their opposition to mixed personal associations.

10) Assumption that complainants are guilty of some crime, if not, they should be, without any evidence.

11) Hostile references to the NAACP in an effort to intimidate complainants.

12) The indiscriminate and common practice of stopping women on the street and accusing them of prostitution or of writing numbers.

Do the complaints show that any particular police precinct stations are involved more often than others?

Our records show that out of 98 complaints, 23 were made against officers from the Woodward Station; 15 against officers from the Vernor Station; 13 against officers from the Petoskey Station and 12 against officers from the Hunt Street Station. This shows a total of 63 complaints against the officers of these four precincts, which is 64% of the complaints of the entire 15 precincts.

What conclusions can be drawn from the Branch records regarding the official attitude of the police department to the complaints reported by the NAACP?

The most significant official attitude of the police department is the reluctance to take stern disciplinary measures in dealing with officers who have exceeded their authority.

1) The attempt, by the Department, to defend the behavior of police officers even when there is reasonable doubt of their innocence.

2) The failure of the Department to curtail the practice of strong-arm methods in making arrests.

3) The failure to replace those officers who bully underprivileged and unpopular elements of the community; who think their badge gives them authority to judge and punish a suspect, and who do not hesitate to enforce not only the "law" but their own prejudices as well.

4) Criticism of the NAACP and other community leadership, by the Department, for not being "cooperative" when they point out existing police brutality, and the danger of this practice if it is not corrected. An example of this is the statement made by the Police Commissioner in defense of police officers who were unduly violent in dispersing a crowd of people who had gathered on the street to hear a group of speakers from the Muhammad Temple. In a statement to the press the commissioner said: "The officers are to be highly commended for their alertness and patience in preventing what might have been a much more serious incident. A minimum of force was used and only the perpetrators were apprehended. The assembly was not only unlawful, but constituted a breach of the peace."

This statement was made after receiving a protest from Arthur L. Johnson, Executive Secretary of the Detroit Branch NAACP, who arrived on the scene along with Congressman Charles C. Diggs, Jr., a few minutes after it began. Another example of the official attitude of the police department was the failure to acknowledge a complaint where the complainant, a Mr. Marvin Petit of 3529 Nottingham, reported that an officer requested his signature on a petition for Mayor Orville Hubbard [of Dearborn] on the basis that Mayor Hubbard "is against Colored People." Despite the fact that a letter urging that this matter be looked into and the offending Officer be dealt with accordingly, no disposition of this case was reported to the Branch.

[The report then details the methods used by the branch to follow up on complaints and gain cooperation from the department by letter writing and requests for reports. As shown in the following, these efforts had little success.]

What are the weak points as indicated by the records in Branch approach to the police-community relations problem?
The weak points indicated by the records are:
1) The lack of an opportunity to examine the claims of both sides in complaints made to the police department, including:
    a) The record of police officers accused by the complainants.
    b) The number of complaints made by Negro citizens against these officers.
    c) The number of complaints made by white citizens against these officers.
    d) The common reasons for arrest of the complainants by these officers?
    e) The common reasons for arrest of white persons by these officers?
In summarizing . . . the victims of these assaults, for the most part, are working people without any previous police record. The records also show that the complainants live in various sections of the city rather than in supposedly "crime" areas! This seems to suggest that the manhandling and 3rd degree methods revealed in these cases [are] unnecessary and reflect the need for a thorough and impartial investigation of police methods in this city, if the Department is to have the confidence and respect of law-abiding citizens. . . .
The following suggestions might help to establish good police-community relations:
1) Increase the number of Negro policemen at all levels in one department by a completely "open" hiring policy.
2) Integrate the police. (mixed details)
3) Conduct human relations programs in neighborhoods surrounding each precinct. This program should place special em-

phasis on courtesy by the police and respect for the police by the citizen.

4) Organizing of a representative interracial citizens group to make a survey of the police department and recommend improvements based on their findings. This survey should be as much in the interest of favorable working conditions for the police as in the civil rights of the citizens. This group should publicize the achievements of the police department in an effort to establish pride in their work and at the same time build respect for intelligent law enforcement.

5) Investigation of police brutality complaints by an independent representative committee, so as to avoid the hazards and pitfalls of the Department investigating itself—an inherently wrong procedure.

Editor's Note

1. I was given a copy of this report at the time of its issue by Charles Wartman, then editor of the *Michigan Chronicle*. As a white "liberal," I am still grateful to him for an embarrassing encounter with reality.

4.   The Cobo-Edwards Choice

Wayne County Democratic Political Action Committee

This ad and similar campaign material was sharply criticized by Edwards's opponents for injecting party politics into a "nonpartisan" election. In retrospect, it provided a rather accurate assessment of the issues of the day.

YOU Decide Who Ought to be Mayor
Then Vote Next Tuesday

EDWARDS is for lower taxes on homes—higher taxes on downtown office buildings.

REPUBLICAN COBO is for higher taxes on houses and for lowering the tax "burden" of corporations and owners of downtown property.

EDWARDS will use federal funds for a slum clearance and housing program already OK'd by the federal government.

REPUBLICAN COBO is for a private real estate deal to provide profits to private real estate companies. (Cobo is a real estate man himself—Cobo Realty Co.)

EDWARDS would reorganize the DSR to serve the people and make downtown business pay its share of the costs through taxes.

Wayne County Democratic Political Action Committee (1949), Mildred Jeffrey Collection, Box 9, folder 9, Reuther Library, Wayne State University.

REPUBLICAN COBO plans curtailed DSR service—higher fares "if necessary."

EDWARDS would fire police boss "Headline Harry" Toy.

REPUBLICAN COBO would "conduct a survey" of the police department.

EDWARDS has a plan under way for more playfields and public swimming pools for your kids. A playground within leg reach of every child.

REPUBLICAN COBO'S main support comes from Ohio, California and Grosse Pointe. Why should he want more playfields in Detroit? There is no profit in playfields.

EDWARDS is for development of a City-operated Detroit River Front (as in Chicago and Milwaukee) to beautify the city and use profit from the commercial property to reduce taxes.

REPUBLICAN COBO is for turning the river front over to private real estate owners for private profit.

EDWARDS comes from the ranks of labor.

REPUBLICAN COBO comes from an anti-union open shop company—Burroughs Adding Machine.

EDWARDS is against the payroll tax. Fair assessment and taxing of big real estate holdings would pay for his city improvement plan.

REPUBLICAN COBO is backed by those who would raise taxes the "easy way" by direct deductions from your pay—the payroll tax.

EDWARDS is supported by the people of Detroit—the homeowners, the small business men, THE PEOPLE WHO LIVE AND WORK IN DETROIT. Edwards has 8 years experience in the Detroit Common Council, 4 years as Council President.

THE REPUBLICAN candidate represents owners of downtown office buildings, the real estate interests, the automobile manufacturers, the Republican newspapers—the gang that fought against the interests of Detroit workers year after year. THE PEOPLE WHO LIVE OFF OF DETROIT BUT NOT IN IT.

Don't let the newspapers tell you how to vote—

MAKE UP YOUR OWN MIND—AND VOTE NOV. 8

5. History of Schoolcraft Gardens

Schoolcraft Gardens Cooperative Association

In July 1950, the cooperative dissolved. A press release prepared at the request of some church leaders who urged clarification for their parishioners actually was a last-ditch effort to build the homes. It records the months of disaster that followed the euphoria of 1947–48, when everyone from Governor Mennen Williams on down had seemed enthusiastic.

Date: March 7, 1950

Schoolcraft Gardens Housing Cooperative is a non-profit corporation organized to provide its members with adequate-sized, well built homes at the lowest possible cost. It was started three years ago when a small group of families bought a 70-acre tract of land at the northwest corner of Schoolcraft and Lamphere and started making plans for a neighborhood of 400 to 500 homes, complete with playgrounds, shopping center and community facilities.

The site bought for the development was one of some twenty vacant tracts later studied by a Committee of the Common Council for possible development with rental-type or multiple housing

Schoolcraft Gardens Cooperative Association, "Statement on Schoolcraft Gardens Co-operative Prepared for the Presbytery and Presbyterial of Detroit," Halbeisen Collection, Reuther Archives, Wayne State University.

(row houses or apartments). The Committee, which consisted of Councilmen Oakman, Rogell and McNamara, recommended the site for re-zoning from R-1 (single free-standing houses).

Nothing further happened on the matter, until, shortly after an article appeared in the *Michigan Worker* indicating the "bi-racial" character of the group, the Tel-Craft Association [a neighborhood group of homeowners south of Schoolcraft at Telegraph Road] on December 13, 1949 petitioned the Common Council for a hearing to change the zoning of the site back to R-1, charging that there had been irregularity in the zoning procedure in 1947. The matter was referred to the City Planning Commission, which held a hearing and unanimously voted to deny the petition. The Commission's recommendation was given to the Common Council, which on December 29, 1949 voted unanimously to deny the petition, Messrs. Kronk, Garlick, Miriani, Edgecomb [former housing director, by then on the council] and Smith voting.

On December 22, 1949 and each week thereafter, a series of inflammatory articles appeared in the *Redford Record* and Floyd McGriff's other newspapers in which various appeals to racial prejudice were made under such banner headlines as "Cooperatives Seeking Conflict? Move to Bring Racial Housing into Area. Will Start with 500 Units for Unrestricted Tenancy" (December 22); "Socialists Force Multiple Housing Clash. More Details on Plan to Build Biracial Flats Here" (December 29); "Tel-Craft Group Demands Hearing on Multiple Flats" (January 5); "Bi-Racial Group Seeks Tax-Payer's Cash" (January 19).[1]

With the approval of Council President Miriani, the Tel-Craft Association secured another hearing before Common Council on January 18, 1950. . . .

At about this time the Council began to be flooded with printed post cards and letters urging the re-zoning of the land. It has been said that as many as 7,000 pieces of mail were received by each Councilman. In spite of this, members of the Cooperative were repeatedly assured by at least six members of Council that they would support the Cooperative. As a three-quarters majority (seven votes) is needed to re-zone property over the owner's protests, it did not appear as if the campaign would be successful.

Meanwhile, the Cooperative had been perfecting its building plans and completing its membership lists for the first group of

460

fifty-four homes to be built. In order to secure a building permit, it has submitted to the Common Council a site plan calling for acceptance by the City of dedication of land for streets. . . . Although normally a routine matter, the motion to approve the site plan was on February 8, 1950 recommitted to the Council's Committee of the Whole, Councilmen Garlick, Kronk, Oakman, Rogell, and Smith voting to recommit while Councilmen Beck, Connor, Jeffries and Miriani voted no.

At the same meeting, Councilman Kronk introduced a resolution to re-zone the site back to R-1 and a public hearing was set for March 10th. . . .

The issue here is plain: Shall a group of Detroit citizens be deprived, by improper use of the zoning ordinance, of their legal rights to use their property, when the admitted real reason for the opposition to the development is the fact that the group, in accordance with the laws of the land, refuses to bar from membership an otherwise qualified family solely for reasons of race, color, creed, or national origin? Will the responsible elected officials of the City Government bow to the demands of a small group of bigoted citizens who have stooped to a campaign of lies, misrepresentation and appeals to religious and racial prejudice in their determination to keep other citizens from building their homes on land they own, and according to a plan which meets every legal requirement?[2]

Editor's Notes

1. Floyd McGriff was the flamboyant, Hearst-trained editor of a chain of widely read community newspapers that were the bane of Detroit liberals for years. McGriff had been in Paris during the latter part of World War I and had been the original bureau chief of what eventually became United Press International. Detroit's outer fringes must have seemed dull in contrast. Certainly McGriff did his best to add the spice of excitement to local politics.

   It was, in fact, the *Brightmoor Journal*, serving the community adjacent to the cooperative, that had first followed the *CIO News* with its own form of investigative reporting. One of the Fall, 1949, stories suggested that the cooperative site had been deliberately chosen because it was on the route to the new race track in Livonia. "Race mixing," sex, and gambling were injected as items to be feared. The young cooperative members were slow to discover the existence of the *Brightmoor Journal*, however. McGriff's *Redford Record*, serving a middle-class neighborhood, was more widely known. Many of the cooperative members did not understand blue-collar Brightmoor; they assumed that since it was a neighborhood of unionized workers, they would follow union policies of racial equality. Those who had themselves been labor organizers knew better. Sophie Reuther and Mildred Jeffrey, for instance, expected no miracles of instant understanding.

2. The public appeal to churches and other liberal organizations for help staved off disaster for a few weeks. On March 15 a majority of those present at a council meeting supported the Cooperative's multiple zoning label; on March 17 Mayor Cobo vetoed it. Among the shifting supporters, there were no longer enough votes to override a veto.

6.   History of Lafayette Park

Robert J. Mowitz and
Deil S. Wright

> It would never have happened without Walter Reuther. Lafayette Park would still be under rocks and weeds without him. People forget that the land lay there a wasteland and a dump for six years after Cobo was elected . . . until we got CRDC [Citizens' Redevelopment Corporation] going, and Walter started pushing people to get together and get it done. . . .
>
> His leadership was also responsible for putting to rest an all-too-prevalent idea that this land was to become a "containment area" for the Negro people. At the time this concept was promoted by both the city Administration and the Private-Builder-Real Estate community.
>
> —James W. Bell, coordinator for CRDC
> (Oral interview, August, 1987)

During and following World War II, the city of Detroit was beset by a number of problems that stemmed in part from the prewar depression and in part from wartime conditions. The depression had brought the construction of private dwellings to a virtual standstill, and the wartime influx of workers plus an increase in the number of births created a serious housing shortage. The results followed the pattern familiar in American urban centers: a high concentration of low-income families in the older residential setions near the entral business district of the core city. At the same time, middle- and upper-income families had begun the exodus to the suburbs as fast as available housing would permit. The "Detroit Plan" was designed to deal with these two conditions, urban slum and suburban flight.

The Detroit Plan was made public on November 18, 1946, by Mayor Edward J. Jeffries, Jr. The substance of his proposal was that the city acquire approximately one hundred acres of land a few blocks northeast of the central business district, . . . demolish the slum residences and other buildings, and prepare the land for resale to private developers for residential use. . . . The city would recapture its $2,000,000 investment through a net annual gain in tax revenue amounting to $134,200 from the same hundred acres once redevelopment had been accomplished. Thus, the argument went, the city would recover its investment in fifteen years. . . .

In February, 1947, condemnation proceedings were begun on the first ten of the site's forty-three blocks. . . . A taxpayer's suit was filed in November, . . . and halted further action until the legality of the condemnation was clarified by the court. Land acquisition for slum clearance and eventual resale to a private developer was an innovation. . . . In October of 1948 . . . the Michigan Supreme Court handed down a decision upholding the right of the city to proceed with condemnation. . . .

[The 1949 election of Mayor Cobo intervened, creating vital shifts in housing policy.] Late in 1951, labor leaders were convinced that Mayor Cobo and his new housing director, former builder and real-estate developer Harry J. Durbin, were involved in a plan to turn over the Gratiot site to private developers eager to exploit the land as soon as it became available. It was feared that this pattern would be followed in the future to the detriment of public housing projects. The mayor's opposition to public housing was no secret and had been an issue in his successful election campaign. Soon after he took office in January, 1950, not only was a new housing director [Durbin] named, but also three new commissioners were appointed by the mayor to the five-man Housing Commission.[1] During the previous year the Housing Commission had submitted a plan to the Detroit Common Council for public housing on twelve new sites, eight of which were vacant land. Before 1950 was over, the "Cobo Commission" had recommended that the council abandon the eight vacant sites and two of the slum sites from further consideration. The council obligingly complied, leaving only two slum sites. . . .

It had taken almost five years to acquire 129 acres, but in the process clear legal precedents had been established which would facilitate further projects. . . . The long-pending federal legislation finally emerged from Congress as the Housing Act of 1949 and was signed by President Harry S. Truman on July 15, 1949. . . .

The election of Mayor Cobo in the fall of 1949 had a direct bearing upon the future of urban redevelopment in the city. . . . It meant that public housing programs were to be deemphasized and that slum clearance leading to private development of cleared land would receive the major emphasis. . . .

The deletion of the vacant sites for public housing, all of which were located in the outlying areas of the city, meant that low-income families would continue to be concentrated in the city's core area, and the elimination of the projects slated for slum sites meant that public housing would not be used as a vehicle for slum clearance. Thus, these decisions meant that projects such as Gratiot would have to bear the brunt of urban redevelopment to accommodate low-income families. . . . The two conditions that were to prove most demanding to city officials were the requirement that a local development plan be prepared that would require local approval, meet federal standards, and at the same time [be] attractive to private capital, and the requirement that adequate provision be made for the relocation of families displaced through the demolition. . . .[2]

That the Gratiot site should be redeveloped for residential use was never seriously questioned. The persistent question was, For whom?. . .

Mayor Cobo had his own ideas about how the site should be developed, and he was quick to voice them after learning of the commission's decision. The mayor immediately met with the commission and expressed his disapproval of their failure to include single-residence units in the plan. The builders reacted to this suggestion by arguing that the site was too small to permit inclusion of single residences. For that matter, they felt that the

465

present plan calling for practically all row housing on small lots was a waste of land. . . .

With the beginning of demolition and relocation in the fall of 1950, Negro housing problems had to be faced. Was the Gratiot site to be redeveloped for the former residents who could not qualify for public housing [mainly those with incomes above the poverty level]? All available evidence up to the end of 1950 indicated that providing housing for former Gratiot residents was a major goal of the project. This goal was clearly stated in the informational letter sent to families to be relocated. If facilities were to be built for this clientele, density standards had to be relatively high in order to make the building of low-rent units a profitable investment. Many of the local builders and real-estate men believed that low-cost housing, or at least Negro housing, was the only possible residential use for the site. They felt that since the site was almost completely surrounded by slum housing occupied by Negroes, only Negroes would live in the area, regardless of the type or quality of housing construction. Thus construction had to be for the Negro market, which was predominantly low-income. These businessmen felt that site planning had to recognize these circumstances in setting density and other restrictions in order to attract private investment.

The professional planners on the Plan Commission staff recognized the goal of rehousing former residents, but they wanted to accomplish this in a way which would maintain "good planning" standards. These standards seem to defy explicit articulation, but they include population-density criteria as well as engineering and aesthetic considerations. The commission itself, which included by law an architect, civil engineer, structural engineer, real-estate dealer, builder, attorney, and physician, did not share all the professional planners' values, but they tended to defend them. . . .

[Plans were drawn and redrawn in the months ahead to satisfy Washington's concern as to relocations as well as the local divisions over land use and density, phrases that became inextricably tied in with housing for blacks. At last a compromise was reached that seemed to offer something for everybody, and much more park space. This plan was approved by Washington in April, 1952. "A little over two years," state the authors, "had been consumed in the planning and approval process."]

A prospectus was prepared, and the council approved the holding of an auction at 2:00 P.M., July 30, 1952 in the council chambers of City Hall. The auction came off on schedule. Some fifty builders and brokers appeared, but all sat in silence when the call came for bids. No bids were offered, and no property was sold.

Density standards were the main reason publicly cited for failure to offer bids. . . . Privately, doubt was expressed over the likelihood that middle-income whites would not move into the project area; therefore to be realistic, construction had to be for the Negro market. . . . None of the builders who were interviewed were optimistic about the chances of selling or renting to both Negroes and whites in the same area. . . .

[A second auction was scheduled for May 6, 1953. Compromises were tried. In December, 1952, the *Detroit News* claimed the "idealists" at the plan commission had given into the "realists" of the housing commission. Durbin this time tried to line up at least one bidder in advance of the auction. Not only was the New York-based company he contacted on hand to bid, but also a local group, headed by a builder of goodwill, Bert L. Smokler. The New York firm captured the bid, but both sides soon became disenchanted, and the agreement was revoked. The whole operation was once again on hold, and seemed doomed to remain there. In 1954 a market survey, paid for by the housing commission, was made of people employed in the downtown area, who were considered the best potential prospects. It brought the discouraging news that seventy-six percent of the whites surveyed did not want mixed occupancy. At about this time there arrived a "white knight," the Citizens Redevelopment Committee (later Corporation).]

The Citizens Redevelopment Corporation traces its origin to the spring of 1953, when, in anticipation of the second auction, a brochure was prepared by Walter J. Gesell, mortgage broker and consultant, entitled, "Constructive Housing Program for Detroit's Gratiot Redevelopment Area." The key person behind the brochure, however, was James W. Bell. Bell had become interested in urban redevelopment some time earlier when he served on the staff of the Plan Commission. Bell was not a professionally

467

trained planner. In fact, his formal education ended when he graduated from Cass Technical High School in 1932, but in addition to his job on the Plan Commission staff, his experience included work with a firm of architects and employment with one of Detroit's largest builders. The brochure prepared by Bell and Gesell, who was at the time a member of the Housing Commission, proposed that a non-profit corporation be formed for the purpose of acquiring and retaining control of the entire redevelopment area in order to "promote its redevelopment under highest standards of design and construction." The specific plan, illustrated with a map and photographs, called for a number of multi-story apartment buildings which would provide "high density without crowding the land." It was pointed out that high construction costs made cooperative ownership the best possible financing method.

The authors took their plan to Mayor Cobo, but he urged them to forget about it, since negotiations had cleared the way for a firm bid from the Housing Corporation of America. When this agreement fell through a year later, the time was ripe to revive the non-profit corporation plan. This time, instead of going to the mayor, Bell contacted *The Detroit News*, with the result that the plan . . . was a feature story in the Sunday, June 27, 1954 edition of the *News*. The next day the mayor and the council received a long telegram from Walter Reuther, president of the United Auto Workers. Reuther urged that action be taken to set up a citizen's committee to deal with the Gratiot project. "It is economically and morally wrong for an industrial community with the wealth and power and the know-how of Detroit to tolerate the social cess-pools of our slums, which breed crime and disease," he wrote. . . . Reuther backed his interest with an offer of $10,000 from the UAW to help finance the work of a citizen's committee. . . .

Mayor Cobo found himself in a difficult position. Any endorsement of a citizens' committee authorized to dispose of the Gratiot site was public acknowledgment of lack of confidence in his housing director, Durbin. . . . Added to this was the Cobo distaste for being pressured into anything, compounded by the fact that the pressure was being applied by Walter Reuther, for whom Cobo had little liking. Nevertheless, the Gratiot site was now being referred to in the press as "Ragweed Acres" and privately as "Cobo's Acres," so something had to be done.

On July 12, Housing Director Durbin recommended that the mayor and council jointly appoint a citizen's committee to study site layout, consider the creation of a non-profit corporation, and work out a redevelopment program for the Gratiot area as a whole, which would include the area to the east that had been designated for public housing and the area directly south that had been earmarked for an extension of the original project. The following day the council passed a resolution authorizing the mayor and president of the council to appoint jointly a Citizens Redevelopment Committee of twelve members. . . . the committee [was to] include one *ex officio* member of the city government to maintain liaison with the various governmental agencies. This post went to Harry Durbin, who was also made committee chairman. The four key citizen appointees were Gesell, Reuther, Walter Gehrke, chairman of the board, First Federal Saving and Loan Association of Detroit, and Foster K. Winter, vice-president, the J. L. Hudson Company. These four made up the executive committee. . . . James Bell was appointed full-time coordinator.

By September 13, the Citizens Redevelopment Committee. . . . reported that a working agreement had been reached with two Detroit architectural firms (Victor Gruen Associates and Leinweber, Yamasaki, and Hellmuth) along with the Philadelphia architect, Oskar Stonorov to prepare a comprehensive plan for the Gratiot area. The committee requested an additional ninety days . . . and asked that during this period the council refrain from selling "or otherwise disposing of said land". . . . The council granted the request.

[After publicly blaming the committee for delays, Durbin resigned his chairmanship. On December 20, 1954, the committee formally presented its plan, and in a report to the council said:]

> Our committee is convinced that a successful program—for now and in the future—is completely dependent upon the city obtaining an integrated residential community of the most advanced design, of the highest possible standards; a community that, on a completely competitive basis, can attract back to the heart of the city people who are finding their housing in the outlying sections of the city and its suburbs. Anything short of attaining that objective would be of dubious value from both an economic and social point of view. . . .

On April 6, 1955, the Citizens Redevelopment Corporation of Detroit was incorporated as a Michigan non-profit corporation, and James Bell was hired as its full-time coordinator. . . . The corporation soon decided that they would prefer to work with only a single developer for the whole site, if one could be found. The proposals made by Cities Redevelopment Inc., owned by Herbert S. Greenwald and Samuel N. Katzin . . . so impressed the trustees that early in November 1955 they decided that this firm would be the exclusive co-developer of the site, with Architect Luwig Mies van der Rohe as the chief designer of the redevelopment construction. . . .

When the Citizens Redevelopment Committee first took over the Gratiot project, it was intent on preventing the area from becoming a low-income ghetto. In its various pronouncements it stressed the need for what it called an "integrated" community with a range of income levels. The award-winning plan of the committee's architects [a casualty of the CRDC's decision to go with Greenwald and the plans of the eminent Mies van der Rohe] stressed low-cost housing, including public housing, integrated with more expensive housing. . . .

The area due east, the St. Aubin extension, had been earmarked for public housing since 1949. Some 3,800 units were planned for this area. This prospect now disturbed the committee's planners, for it would guarantee that one boundary of the Gratiot site would consist of a large, Negro public housing project. (It was taken for granted that the project would be Negro, since Negroes substantially outnumbered eligible white applicants for public housing, and since the area had been occupied by Negroes.) This large Negro housing project was considered a threat to the development of the desired integrated neighborhood, and the committee prevailed upon the council to reduce the number of authorized units for St. Aubin to about twelve hundred. By 1960, plans for a public housing project had been dropped. . . .

The first unit of Lafayette Park-University City [the name given the development by CRDC], a twenty-two story apartment building, began receiving tenants in the fall of 1958. . . . By early 1959, construction had begun on an expressway [the Chrysler] which would give the western side of the site a new and secure physical boundary. Just east of the expressway, the new buildings of the

Wayne State University Medical School and Lafayette Clinic (a research unit of the Michigan Department of Mental Health) gave the site an institutional tone, the reason for the "University City" part of the site's new name. Construction had also begun on ten two-story "Townhouse" apartments, and the developer had filed an FHA application for another twenty-two-story apartment and was preparing to apply for an FHA approved mortgage for three twenty-seven-story apartments. There was still a long way to go before the eighteen hundred to two thousand families contemplated for the area could move in, but the repopulation of the Gratiot site had begun. . . .

The role of James Bell, promoter of Citizens Redevelopment Committee, is worthy of special note. It is rather extraordinary for a private citizen to move in and take over control of a project from two major city agencies, the Housing and Plan Commissions, but Bell's excellent contacts at the operating level of the community decision-making system permitted him to literally play the role of coordinator. The interest of the department store executive, the mortgage consultant, and the banker in urban redevelopment was obvious, whereas labor's interest was less obvious. . . .

They welcomed the opportunity to aid in taking the initiative from Durbin and Cobo, in whom they had little confidence. Reuther was interested in the prospects of an integrated neighborhood which would include all income groups as well as racial groups. He felt that cooperative ownership arrangements would help achieve this. With the support of Reuther, combined with that of Winter, representing Detroit's largest department store, the J. L. Hudson Company, [now Dayton-Hudson, headquartered in Minneapolis], plus support from mortgage and banking circles through Gesell and Gehrke, Bell was able to put together a formidable combination, which, in fact, took over the Gratiot project.

There were other reasons for the Citizens Committee's success. Bell was careful to avoid stacking the committee with members who played the role of official ambassadors of various interests whenever citizens' committees were organized. The mayor's Detroit Tomorrow Committee, with over a hundred members, was filled with this kind of talent. Bell's committee was composed of decision-makers. . . . The original Detroit Plan was hopefully designed to cope with the problem of housing low-income families. Although racial attitudes conditioned the various plans for the Gratiot site, in the long run economic values prevailed. It proved economically impossible to obtain private development of housing for low-income families, regardless of their race. Even the "integrated" plan of the Citizens Committee had to give way to the development of units for middle- and upper-income families. There is no evidence that Negroes will find difficulty in obtaining units on the rebuilt site, if they can afford the rents; eight of the first two hundred tenants of Lafayette Park-University City were Negro.[3] But the problem of decent housing for the former residents remains unsolved.

Editor's Notes

1. Mayor Cobo, on taking office, appointed realtor Harry Durbin to head the housing commission and quickly replaced the highly respected commissioner, the Reverend Bradby. Both actions were certainly within the mayor's powers, but the replacement of the Reverend Bradby sent unexpected shock waves through the defeated liberal and black communities. Some who had welcomed Cobo's self-proclaimed businessman's approach to government suddenly realized the new mayor was playing for keeps. Years later, in Coleman Young's administration, a drive winding through Elmwood Park on the city's near east side was given the name Bradby Drive. It serves as a memorial to the man who had fought, not only against slum housing, but for integrated housing and equality of access to the city's most attractive land.

2. The effort to relocate families was perhaps the least successful of any part of the work as, Harold Norris indicates in a following section. The Mowitz account makes clear that once the decision to abandon outlying housing sites was made, the options of inner city residents disappeared.

3. Of the eight families mentioned, several were among those who once hoped to live in Schoolcraft Gardens. Eleanor Wolf and Mel Ravitz, Wayne State University sociologists, did studies of the first dwellers in Lafayette Park and those who were there three years later. [See Eleanor P. Wolf and Mel J. Ravitz, "Lafayette Park: New Residents in the Core City," *Journal of the American Institute of Planners* (August 1964): 234–39. On the whole, they found a singularly happy neighborhood, whose residents for the most part had deliberately

chosen to live in a community that had among its other qualities racial integration. For once, time had outrun many of the barriers created by prejudice.

Wolf and Ravitz prophesied that the weak spot of the area would be its schools, specifically at the middle school level. Lafayette Park remains one of the city's good neighborhoods, though the glamour of the "urban pioneers" has faded, but its children are usually enrolled in private schools, regardless of rising costs.

7. Dislocation without Relocation

Harold Norris

Harold Norris, attorney, professor, and longtime activist in civil right causes, delivered a speech in the fifties that summarized the failure of the city to come to grips with the problem of relocating the people who lived in the Gratiot Redevelopment Area.

The Cobo Administration is proceeding to evict some 6000 people from the Gratiot-Orleans area. The ostensible purpose for this removal program is to clear the land and permit the private development of housing. Mayor Cobo states that some of the housing to be built will be available at rents that some of the displaced people can afford. We must remember that these 6000 people are being added to some 17,000 people being displaced by the expressways. We have seen very little done to assist the relocation of the people displaced by the expressways. If past is prologue, it can be reasonably predicted that very little will be done to assist the relocation of the 6000 people in the Gratiot-Orleans

Harold Norris,"Dislocation without Relocation, Excerpts from Talk Opposing Mayor Cobo's Urban Renewal Policy; to the Greater Detroit Public Housing Tenants Council, 1952," in *Some Reflections on Law, Lawyers, and the Bill of Rights: A Collection of Writings, 1944 to 1984* (Detroit: Michigan Law Book Society, 1983), 813–15.

area. What is really happening is that poor people, mostly Negro people, are being removed from what little housing they have. This really amounts to Negro removal, not urban renewal. . . .

I have been representing many of the evicted families in proceeding before the Wayne County Circuit Court Commissioners. This is the court with jurisdiction over landlord-tenant matters; this court is the forum for non-payment of rent and eviction cases. I have been able to get some additional time for many of those being evicted. We've held up the city's ill-designed plan for some months now. But the tragic and pervasive impact of this inhuman policy of what I call "dislocation without relocation" is overwhelming. Mothers testify in court, in response to my questioning, that faced with eviction and dislocation their families are being split up. "I've had to send my son to live with my sister in Alabama, and my daughter to my mother in Chicago. . . . I don't have any place to move to now. . . ."

I believe this policy of "dislocation without relocation" is terribly wrong and ought to be opposed, opposed vigorously. . . . it is a policy that is wrong, wrong legally, wrong pragmatically, and it is dangerous. There must be a price to pay down the line sometime in some way for something that is so wrong.

Dislocation without relocation is wrong legally. I submit that the Federal Housing Act of 1948 squarely places a duty upon the city to find accommodations for renters before evicting them. The city is just going through the motions of complying with this law. After our protests the city has established a store front office and placed one brand new lawyer in that office . . . to get some qualifying displaced renters into limited public housing. But this is no remedy for the great mass of displaced people. And most of this audience knows of all the income-determination problems associated with public housing. The city is just not making a good faith effort to comply with the relocation requirements of the Housing Act of 1948. The city's policy is plainly illegal.

Second,. . . [it] is clearly immoral. It places the prodigious burden of change in our city disproportionately upon the backs of those people least able to bear it. . . . What is really being done is kicking people out. The city is creating refugees. Mayor Cobo has been quoted as saying to those protesting these evictions. . . "we don't want them here." This crude, heartless, and inequitable policy is just plain wrong, just plain immoral.

Third, this policy of dislocation without relocation is pragmatically wrong. It simply won't work. The city will either meet the problem now with a plan, or meet a crisis later without a plan. . . . There will be a price to pay. For every choice there is a price. And for every bad choice there will be a bad price. Where are the 17,000 people displaced by the expressways to go without adequate assistance? Where are the 6000 people displaced by "urban renewal" in the Gratiot-Orleans area to go without adequate assistance? They must live, they must survive. They will split-up and double-up. They will find attics and basements. They will move in with others—relatives and friends. There will be increased density of use elsewhere. And any housing, no matter how good, will deteriorate with density of use. Hence, all that will be accomplished will be the transfer of one area of relatively poor housing to the making of another area of relatively poor housing. This is not slum clearance. This is slum creation. I do not want to be misunderstood. I do not disparage the people forced out. I am merely saying this, that no matter how good the housing, if you put a lot more people in that good housing than that housing can accommodate, the good housing becomes bad housing. The costs of maintenance go up and revenues are not proportionate. Needed repairs will not be made. Bad housing will breed other problems. There is the danger of unrest. The situation has the potential for strife and combustibility. Prediction is not desire. But danger can be predicted. There will be a price for this inhumane eviction policy.

In short, Mayor Cobo's policy of dislocation without relocation, of urban renewal, of what is factually Negro removal should be opposed and changed. That policy is illegal, immoral and dangerous. . . .

Part XIV

Camelot, Riot, and Renaissance: The Sixties and Seventies

Camelot, Riot, and Renaissance: The Sixties and Seventies

Detroit during the sixties seemed more open to revolution than it had been at any point since the depression. It is, on the whole, not surprising that the Black Manifesto, made famous at Riverside Church in New York, was first presented at the National Black Economic Development Conference held at Wayne State University some five months earlier, or that its details were worked out in sessions at St. Joseph's Episcopal Church.

For some time there had been unease in labor unions, symbolized in the UAW by the split between the rank and file membership and its salaried executives. The city's neighborhoods, too, were restless, especially within the inner three-mile circle of Grand Boulevard. There was talk of getting a grip on the "establishment," of having more to say about planning decisions, police actions, zoning. The phrase "Urban renewal means Negro removal," frequently used by the Reverend Albert Cleage, caught on. It serves as an indicator of the wide distrust of local government, even though these were supposed to be the Camelot years.

A wave of new acronyms began to spread around the town. There was WCO, the West Central Organization; GOAL, Group on Advanced Leadership; PAR, People against Racism; WRO, the Welfare Rights Organization. In the auto plants there were DRUM, the Dodge Revolutionary Movement, and ELDRUM, its chapter formed at the Mt. Elliot Avenue Dodge plant. Then there were the Black Panthers, with rhetoric, but also with a program. In 1970 a dozen young people affiliated with the Panthers barricaded themselves in a house on the near west side; a confrontation with the police brought about a charge of first-degree murder. On that day Councilman Mel Ravitz, among others, intervened to secure their safe-conduct out of the house. Months later when all the evidence came in, the murder charge was dismissed. If some of the police seemed somewhat trigger-happy in those years, it is no less true that revolt had become to them just a middle-class act. No doubt the police felt harassed when some of the nicest people in town, including many clergy, insisted on bringing a broken toilet seat to the office of the head of the Detroit Housing Commission as a demonstration of the ills of Hobart Street, a neighborhood taken over by the city.[1]

Some successes for citizens grew out of the turmoil. The Cavanagh programs were built around community demands: defense lawyers available to the poor,[2] consumer watch programs and nutrition agencies in housing projects, field trips in the schools, exploring the city's Cultural Center (often seen only by suburban students in the past).[3]

Government response to demands for radical reform eventually included a new city charter, the rebuilding of the general city hospital in the medical center, useful redefinition of some functions of county and metropolitan government, and the reorganization of city welfare services under the new state Department of Social Services, in the hope of delivering more efficient and more humane services. If the social service reorganization accomplished nothing else, it enabled the very poor to leave neighborhoods that had long disenchanted them for the cheapest of the green fields beyond the city limits. Sadly, during the years of demand for change there *was* a great deal of outward flight—both white and black—that served to diminish the gains that might have been made by a focused effort on reform.

One change that occurred and lasted was a general opening to African-Americans of jobs at every level of employment in government, and an authentic but more limited integration of the corporate world, stopping somewhat short of top management.

Revolutionary moods do end in time. Members of the League of Revolutionary Workers viewed some of their colleagues' absorption into middle-class jobs as a "sell-out," condemning even

480

those who took jobs with the new mayor, Coleman Young, in 1974.[4]

In this study of the sixties I have included B. J. Widick's "Mayor Cavanagh and the Limits of Reform," a chapter from his *Detroit: City of Race and Class Violence.* That selection ends in 1967, when the Camelot years ended sharply.

I continue with a statement of radical prophecy that I term "Eyewitness to Disaster," by the Reverend David Gracie, whose church east of the riot scene ministered to many black and white Detroiters in the area. He was healing and comforting, trying to prevent the spread of violence, but his statement here is a plea for understanding of the root causes of rebellion. This is followed by a section of a Pulitzer Prize-winning account, published in the *Detroit Free Press,* of the meaningless deaths of July, 1967.

Risking some repetition, I include a play-by-play account of three of those deaths, which startled the nation as well as the city. It has been my experience that many Detroiters, then and later, chose to block the deaths at the Algiers Motel from their minds. I thank John Hersey, author of *The Algiers Motel Incident,* for making it harder to forget, with "The Death Game" and "The Death Game Played Out."

The years after 1967 were noted for the politics of "participatory democracy" and still more efforts at radical reform. However, the federal funds of the Cavanagh years that had made possible the major experiments of the Model Cities program ended abruptly, with disillusionment for many Detroiters who had taken part.[5]

In May, 1970, came another major turning point when May and Walter Reuther died in a plane accident in northern Michigan. Some revolutionists, convinced that Reuther had lived beyond his time, felt little reason to mourn, but the courage and common sense he brought to both labor and civic problems have been missing from many crises ever since, and the loss cannot be adequately measured. The limitations and strengths of both May and Walter Reuther deserve the best of historical study.

Both participatory democracy and rebellion hit the schools in 1969–70. More than was generally realized at the time, student unrest was closely tied to some of the radical factions of the UAW. Unlike the demands of the mid and late sixties for higher standards (as at Northern High's "Freedom School"), the violence was directed at language laboratories, study carrels, and science equipment considered to be part of the white man's elitist learning systems. The enablers of this wave of unrest were young adults, including a few teachers.

In April, 1970, the labor-liberal coalition that had worked for some seventeen years came to an end in a bitter struggle over educational integration. William Grant, at that time education writer for the *Detroit Free Press*, tells the story succinctly in "Integration's Last Hurrah," first published in the *New Republic*.

Meanwhile, "black schools for black students" became the cry of many urban students of 1969–70. Out in the larger metropolitan area, candidates for public office had to convince their constituents that they were absolutely opposed to cross-district integration.

As the struggle over school integration escalated, the NAACP brought a law suit, *Bradley v. Milliken*,[6] charging the state of Michigan of condoning and prolonging the racist practices in the public schools. After NAACP victories in both the court of federal judge Stephen Roth and the U.S. District Court of Appeals at Cincinnati, the case was lost in the United States Supreme Court. Published here is an abridgment of the dissenting opinion of Justice Thurgood Marshall, with its grim prophecy for the schools of metropolitan Detroit.

Editor's Notes

1. Detroit planned to locate a "research park" on Hobart Street near the site of the Burroughs Corporation (now Unisys). The idea created instant anger among neighbors, who resented the city's condemnation of their homes. There were long delays during which they were allowed to rent their homes on a temporary basis, but the houses received little maintenance or repairs. A number of groups from across the city kept vigil in organized protest for months.
2. Among the young, radical defense lawyers who found time to offer free and constructive legal advice to high school students in the spring and fall of 1967 were attorneys Justin Ravitz (later a Recorder's Court Judge), Dennis Archer, (later Chief Justice of the Michigan Supreme Court), and the late Kenneth Cockrel.
3. MCHRD, the Mayor's Commission on Human Rights Development; arranged field trips for students of both public and parochial schools,

perhaps the concept skirted close to the wind on the doctrine of separation of church and state, but teachers welcomed the imaginative flair of Rosemary Dolan, (later Mrs. Judd Arnett) in suggesting outings, and the free buses. A bus is the last item to be included in any school budget, but provides access to the world.

4. See Georgakas Collection, Reuther Library, Wayne State University.
5. The Model City/Model Neighborhood programs suffered not only from the loss of federal funding after the Johnson years, but from a stylized jargon of bureaucracy that was little understood among the poor who were being helped, or by anyone else.
6. After the first courtroom victory by the NAACP, the state joined the Detroit Board of Education in the appeal. At that time the case became titled *Milliken v. Bradley.*

1. Mayor Cavanagh and the Limits of Reform

B. J. Widick

Widick, an astute observer of Detroit's political scene, is a labor economist and writer who for some years watched local politics as a reporter and factory worker before looking back at Detroit from academia. In 1972 he undertook to describe the Camelot years of Mayor Jerome Cavanagh.

At the beginning of the 1960's, "public opinion" in Detroit was excited by newspaper headlines about a "crime wave." According to newspaper accounts, the number one problem was crime on the streets. . . . What Detroit needed, Mayor Louis C. Miriani insisted, was more vigorous law enforcement to curb the criminal elements roaming the streets, and he ordered a police crackdown. The police responded zealously.

Frisks and searches, mass arrests, and "holding on suspicion" became the standard practice of police operations, which were concentrated in the black community. Soon feelings of fear, humiliation, and then anger developed among the Negro people—feelings to which the white community was largely insensitive. . . .

B. J. Widick, *Detroit: City of Race and Class Violence* (Chicago: Quadrangle, 1972), 154–65.

484

Mayor Miriani (who was later convicted on criminal charges of income tax evasion) disregarded the protests and maintained his assertion of police "impartiality." Yet City Hall received reports of incidents involving prominent black leaders. . . . Many white policemen had learned not to call blacks "niggers," for there were now influential black municipal judges, a federal judge, and some business and union leaders. Instead they would be called "boy". . . .

. . . The persistence with which the racial issue permeated local politics, long before the issue of "white backlash" became widespread, was reflected in every mayoral campaign. In 1947 the CIO endorsed incumbent Mayor Jeffries against Eugene Van Antwerp, a conservative councilman. Van Antwerp won. In 1949 the racial issue caused the UAW to suffer its most important defeat, when George Edwards was beaten by Albert Cobo, the city treasurer, in the contest for mayor. Edwards was the most attractive candidate to appear on the Detroit scene since Mayor Frank Murphy in the 1930's. A former UAW organizer and close friend of Walter Reuther, he had returned from army service to win the presidency of the Common Council by the highest vote of any candidate. He was a law school graduate, articulate, and capable. Cobo swamped him primarily because he had stood for open housing. At dozens of property owners' meetings Edwards was denounced as pro-Negro. The AFL endorsed Cobo. To the astonishment of secondary UAW leaders, the new homeowners in Detroit among the autoworkers spoke openly in the shops against "labor's man". . . .

When the time came to face reelection in 1961, Mayor Miriani was the picture of self-confidence, if not smugness. He was the unanimous choice of the entire power structure in Detroit: the UAW, the Teamsters, the AFL-CIO council, the Chamber of Commerce, the auto companies, the newspapers. Moreover his opponent was a comparatively unknown young lawyer, a newcomer in city politics. No one in the Establishment took Jerome P. Cavanagh seriously.

Perhaps the most significant aspect of the 1961 mayoralty campaign was not the fact that the 33-year-old Cavanagh beat Miriani by over 40,000 votes, or that it was the biggest political upset in Michigan politics in 32 years, but rather its disclosure of a growing gap in attitudes between institutions, such as unions, and the people they ostensibly represent—in particular the split between white liberals and the black community.

Considerable credit for Cavanagh's victory went to TULC [Trade Union Leadership Council] which mobilized the black community against Miriani, protesting his support of discriminatory police practices.[1] The long-neglected city employees, particularly the firemen, worked hard for Cavanagh. In a postmortem, the *Detroit Free Press*, which opposed Cavanagh, stated that he "owes his victory to Detroit's Negroes, blue-collar workers and the unemployed." Five liberal councilmen also won in this tide of protest. The growing division between labor leaders and the ranks was indicated by the campaign [by UAW executives] to fire Horace Sheffield, the head of TULC. The victory of Cavanagh gave TULC too much prestige for that kind of bureaucratic stupidity.

Suddenly it appeared as if a new day had dawned for Detroit. Almost overnight the city gained a new image under the direction of the talented, articulate, and personable mayor, who soon became a favorite of the nation's press and television. It seemed that Detroit had also found the road to racial peace in the programs and policies instituted by Cavanagh, with assistance from the Democratic administrations in Washington.

As a first act in office Cavanagh persuaded Alfred Pelham, an acknowledged and successful Negro expert on municipal finance, to leave Wayne State University and the county auditor's office and direct city finances. Cavanagh made another shrewd political move in persuading George Edwards, the one-time mayoral candidate who had become a justice of the Michigan Supreme Court, to accept the tough post of police commissioner. Both the police and the black community knew this meant the end of the overt police harassment of blacks. As Edwards told a TULC audience one night, "My first job was to teach the police they didn't have a constitutional right to automatically beat up Negroes on arrest."

Soon Henry Ford, Walter Reuther, and the press were praising Cavanagh's administration, and the beginning of $360,000,000 in federal assistance started pouring into the city.

Filled with euphoria at the national economic growth and prosperity, the nation came to see the formerly distressed city as a model of social progress—the harbinger of the future for solving urban problems. This was the illusion of the early 1960's. . . .

486

This rosy outlook extended to the area of racial relations. While outrages against blacks in Selma and Birmingham shocked many people, and Rev. Martin Luther King, Jr., aroused the conscience of the nation to begin the mass civil rights movement, Detroit felt it was an exception because it had what it assumed to be an effective program for racial progress. Detroiters were fond of contrasting the calm in the auto city with the turbulence elsewhere.

Any doubts on this score were dispelled on July 23, 1963, when a massive civil rights demonstration led by Reverend King took place in Detroit. Between 150,000 and 200,000 people participated, about 90 per cent of them black. . . . Mayor Cavanagh, Governor George Romney, and Walter Reuther were among the prominent whites marching with Reverend King. The size of the march surprised everybody. About 50,000 were expected, and at least triple that number showed up. . . .

Social reform seemed to be working. . . . The Institute of Labor and Industrial Relations, of Wayne State and the U. of M. recalled that Michigan's Civil Rights Act had predated that of the federal government and praised the "broad community leadership". *Fortune* magazine included the UAW in its praise of local leadership, and pointed out that more than 40% of the Negro population were homeowners, and Michigan alone among states, had two Negroes in its congressional delegation. . . .

The role played by TULC in Detroit's comeback was a major one. In the 1960–1967 period its membership rose at one point to over 9,000, and its achievements led Bayard Rustin, the civil rights leader, to comment, "I wish there was a TULC in every industrial city in the country." The concept of a labor-liberal-Negro coalition seemed to be working. Mayor Cavanagh appointed Negroes to prominent positions. Industry consulted TULC for assistance in hiring people. Even the building trades found it expeditious to talk with TULC about Negro apprentices. When UAW opponents of Sheffield tried to have him removed from the Detroit scene or ousted from his UAW staff job, the daily press and many black and white leaders insisted that Reuther allow him to remain active in the city.

But nothing fails like success, and TULC was soon divided and fragmented by new issues. A congressional seat opened in the predominantly Negro first district, and John Conyers, Jr., the legal counsel of TULC, wanted it. His father, John Conyers, Sr., a long-time UAW activist and staff member, argued in TULC for an endorsement. Sheffield and Battle, [Robert or "Buddy" Battle, co-founder of TULC] however, had their own choice: Richard Austin, an outstanding businessman and civic leader. Conyers won the primary by 32 votes, but the election split TULC deeply.

A rival organization was set up to further fragment the power of black unionists. The Negro church leaders who had sponsored the June 1963 Freedom March in Detroit began exerting independent political pressure, vying with the NAACP, TULC, and other organizations for a dominant role in the city. Meanwhile a dynamic black nationalist spokesman, Rev. Albert Cleage, was drawing larger and larger audiences with his scornful attacks on TULC's "Uncle Tomism." Most white community leaders treated the struggles within the black community as a case of "too many black Napoleons." But this superficial analysis ignored the conflicting pressures building up behind the various black leaders. Whites underestimated the impact of national events on Detroit's black community.

TULC didn't win its fight with the building trades. George Edwards, the police commissioner and a member of TULC, resigned in 1963, and his successor, Ray Girardin, never established the firm control over the police that Edwards had, even though he was well liked in the Negro community and was a "Cavanagh man". . . .

In 1965 Mayor Cavanagh won reelection, but on the issue of "law and order." Councilman Mary Beck had attacked Cavanagh for being too friendly with the Negro community. Thomas Poindexter, whom all Negroes considered a racist, defeated a Negro for the council in a special election.

These local events were partly a reflection of the national turmoil. Newspaper reports, TV coverage, and personal accounts of friends and relatives throughout the country kept the Detroit black community in a constant state of agitation. Who could forget the ordeal of James Meredith, or the figure of Bull Connor of Birmingham, Alabama, with his police dogs, fire hoses, and cattle prods? Or the murder of four children in a Negro church by a bomb explosion, the burning of the freedom buses, and the near-murder of Detroiter Walter Bergman because he had joined the Negroes on the bus? Or the murder of Mrs. Viola Liuzzo, the idealistic Detroit housewife, and the humiliations of Rev. Martin

Luther King, Jr., who insisted that Christians practice their religion? Or the riots that kept breaking out in the Eastern cities, in Cleveland and Chicago, and then, like a grand finale, in Watts, California?

Detroit was not an island unto itself. For the black community it was a time of memorial meetings and protest rallies, of shame and anger and despair. In this atmosphere the gains of Detroit blacks—and there were some gains—seemed more like mere tokenism than true social progress.

For closer examination showed that most of the gains benefited the Negro middle class. Economic progress was reflected in the enrollment of more than 2,500 Negro students at Wayne State University—more than in the Big Ten and the Ivy League combined. Ownership of homes rose to over 60 percent among black dwellers. Yet a survey showed that 90 per cent of the graduates of a Negro high school were unemployed, as compared with only 50 per cent of the dropouts.

The deterioration of the Detroit public school system was another sore point in the Negro community. The increase in the black population from 30 to 40 per cent of the total population created de facto segregation in the schools. The number of children rose by 50,000, adding to the already overcrowded conditions. And the 50 per cent drop-out rate among black youth is hardly surprising when one considers that the white teachers and principals were totally unprepared—either by education or experience—to handle black students. "Baby sitting" rather than education, and discipline rather than influence over youth, became the frequent pattern of work for the frightened or helpless school teachers. The contrast with the suburban school system was obvious. In one case, students at the all-Negro Northern High School struck in a demand for a better education.[2]

No significant attention was paid to the new mood of dissatisfaction among the black youth. No organization had attracted them in real numbers. No program really involved them as full participants.

The disparity between the poor blacks and the whites increased in this period of prosperity. With all the publicity about housing programs and model cities, only 758 low-income units were built in Detroit in the decade beginning in 1956. Unemployment averaged about 30 per cent for Negro youth. In 1960 the median income in the ghetto was $2,640 for a household, compared to the median family income in Michigan of over $6,000. This was the period when everybody but the poor seemed to make money on the poverty programs.

New programs and massive federal assistance may have changed certain trends in Detroit, but the escalation of the war in Vietnam reduced the federal aid at a time when it was most needed. No man knew this better than Mayor Cavanagh. Unless a drastic shift in national priorities took place, Detroit and other urban centers were doomed to failure. Cavanagh decided to run for Senator on a peace and social reform program, but he was ahead of his time. His opponent in the Democratic primary, [former Governor] G. Mennen Williams, proved too strong, with the backing of labor hierarchy, and he defeated Cavanagh in the primary only to lose to Robert Griffin in the fall of 1965.

The black community was upset by Cavanagh's decision to seek a higher office so soon after his reelection as mayor. They had a fondness for "Soapy" Williams, and they were concerned over a possible successor to Cavanagh. The frank dialogue and rapport between the mayor and the black community were somewhat strained at the time when each needed the other the most.

In the fall of 1966, Detroit barely avoided a race riot. A handful of black nationalists clashed with police on the east side, but the populace didn't join with the youths. Neighborhood and community leaders convinced the blacks to stay at home, and the scuffle was confined to a minor incident.

However, the storm signals appeared in the spring of 1966, and no one recognized them more clearly than Mayor Cavanagh. The killing of a young Negro war veteran by a gang of white youths infuriated the Negroes. The police arrested only one of the gang. . . . A prostitute was killed by a pimp, according to police; by the police, according to Negroes. Friction between the police and the blacks was visible everywhere.

In private sessions Cavanagh met with both Negro and white leaders to find ways of alleviating the tension, but their efforts were fruitless. In May 1967, the mayor and I discussed the situation and concluded that it would be a miracle if Detroit escaped what already appeared inevitable in other cities: a major riot.

The disintegration of cohesive social and political forces suggested events were getting out of hand.

490

In June the Detroit Police Officers Association, led by Carl Parsell, staged a blue-flu strike in which hundreds of Detroit policemen, for the first time since the Boston police strike in 1919, walked off their jobs for five days to support demands for higher pay.

The city was a keg of social dynamite. Yet a public warning by Cavanagh that Detroit had not eliminated any of the causes of a potential riot was not taken seriously. The people were too busy with business-as-usual, politics-as-usual, and unionism-as-usual, to listen. The illusion that Detroit was different was too strong to dispel.

Only two days before disaster struck Detroit, the highly respected Negro councilman, Rev. Nicholas Hood, reflected the views of most Detroiters when he denounced the "long hot summer mongers." Reassuring the white community, he added, "I haven't heard any Negroes talk about the possible violence this summer—only white people are talking about it."

And this is not the least of the reasons why the riot in July 1967 shattered Detroit like a terrible earthquake. The shock was to prove painful indeed.

Editor's Notes

1. The TULC grew largely out of the UAW Ford Local 600 and was organized by black leadership within the factory at the time of the Ford strike of 1940. Leaders included Horace Sheffield and the late Robert "Buddy" Battles. Both men remained active in politics.
2. Even so, a "revolution of rising expectations" might be a reason for the perceived deterioration of the Detroit Public Schools during the fifties and early sixties. Certainly the black community began to have more active participation in the schools following the election of labor-endorsed candidates.

   Black teachers and administrators made up an increasing proportion of the staff, for the most part leaning toward "basic education" rather than the wider curriculum favored by the labor-reform group. There was a new emphasis on testing, with demonstrable competence as a goal.

   For another view of the schools during this period, see the article by William Grant, "Integration's Last Hurrah ," later in this section.

2. Eyewitness to Disaster

Reverend David Gracie

David Gracie, rector of St. Joseph's Episcopal Church, was no new convert to radicalism in July of 1967. A year earlier he had offered the church for use by a "Freedom School" for student protesters from nearby Northern High. There were other radical churches in Detroit, of many faiths, with leaders trying to be in step with the new times. What is notable about the Reverend Gracie was his skill in defining the terms, the frame of reference for blacks and whites in what he saw as the revolution immediately ahead.

During the week which began on Sunday, July 23, Father Gracie lived on the tense streets near his church and in the homes of his distressed people. This sermon was preached on July 30, one week after the outbreak.

A Final Call to Repentance

We must sense the judgment in what has happened to us in Detroit. I believe the events of this week are in themselves a call to repentance, perhaps a final call to this nation.

We are called to repent from consumerism. The looting teaches us that. We have devised an economy which has as its aim consumption, an economy which will only remain stable if consumer desires are continually pumped up by advertising. This constant barrage of advertising teaches people that they are nothing without the products, that to possess the products is the goal of life. This anxiety to possess makes looters of us all. I sat

Reverend David Gracie, sermon at St. Joseph's Episcopal Church, 30 July 1967, St. Matthew's and St. Joseph's Church Archives, Detroit.

and watched from my office window the continual stream of people going through the broken windows of the drug store across Woodward helping themselves to all the products they could carry. I went home then and happened to see an afternoon TV show. There was a studio full of white housewives, screaming and quite hysterical with delight and anticipation, because some of them might win the gleaming washers and dryers and other appliances hidden behind a curtain on the stage. This was white middle-class looting and the atmosphere was not a "carnival atmosphere", it was one of hysteria.[1] And so our consumer-oriented economy tends to destroy us all. It puts tremendous strain on every class, but mostly on the lowest classes, and the marginal workers, who have to listen to the advertising day in and day out but cannot buy. . . .

We are called upon to repent from violence, which has become in so many ways an accepted part of our nation's life. I spent a night in the Church House, trying to sleep, but listening all night long to the shooting down Woodward Avenue, then closer, then finally at the A&P around the corner. I heard that shooting out of one ear and with the other heard the shooting from the TV western in the next room. We spend a good part of every day listening to gun fire and we accept the fact that our sons are going to be taught to shoot and kill anywhere in the world our government orders them to do so. When President Johnson came on TV to address us in our hour of need, we had to condemn him as a hypocrite for his words. "We oppose violence under any slogan", he said. The slogan he meant was "Black Power", but the slogans he forgot were the ones he and his staff invent every week to justify continuing violence in Vietnam. . . . Let us oppose the violence of our armies, of our police, and the "frozen violence" of our institutions which crushes the lives of the poor in our land.

How many of us had guns in our hands this past week? A State Representative had a gun in his hand and used it to kill to protect his store. A group of white snipers had an arsenal on a roof and excused themselves by saying they were just trying to help the National Guard. By way of contrast . . . I shall never forget our neighbor at the Standard gas station on Holbrook. I asked him if he had spent the nights at his station trying to protect it. He said he didn't. "I know all the kids in this neighborhood. How could I shoot one of *them* if he came at my place?

We must repent of our neglect of the poor. The relief center which ran so well at St. Joseph's did not just supply food and clothing to those who had been burned out. We also met the needs of ADC mothers who missed their checks by a day or two because the mails were disrupted, or who couldn't cash their checks because the banks were closed. People on ADC and other forms of relief are apt to be kept at such a subsistence level that a day's delay in the check can work a terrible hardship. Our welfare system keeps the poor alive, but barely, with their chins just above water all the time. So an emergency relief center would be welcome anytime. It is important, too, that we recognize that the slums did not just start to burn last week. They are smoldering and burning always. The rate of burning accelerated last week, that's all. When I drove down Oakland [Avenue] after the worst night there, it was as if I were seeing an apocalyptic vision. The flames seemed to be worst where I had known conditions to be worst. It was as if an artist had drawn a symbolic painting of the way Oakland always is, with its broken homes, broken dreams, its tendency toward self-destruction in crime and dope and aimless violence. . . . A nation and a city which consigns people to live under the conditions which prevail on 12th and on Oakland must repent.

Finally, we must repent of the domination of the poor by the wealthy, of blacks by whites, which prevails in our land. The explosion was kicked off by a police raid on a blind pig on 12th street. Now, the police are perceived by the poor black communities as agents of domination. They are not the police of that community, but rather the police of the white community sent there to control the lives of black people. When they pull something as blatant as that raid, . . . an explosion of resentment is likely to occur. It is my understanding that that kind of raid was not supposed to occur anymore. The Commissioner had realized that hauling great numbers of people into the paddywagon like that could be provocative action. But it did occur, and the trouble started. . . . It is only with a sense of identity that a police force of a few thousand men could hope to be effective in a city of many thousands. When this identity breaks down, as it has in the ghettos, there is little to be gained in discussing police techniques in dealing with troubled situations. Prior to that discussion must come a realization that the police force must once

494

again belong to the people. A man will not fight his own police department.

Nor will a man smash his own store or the stores of his own people. The exceptions to the inviolability of the stores marked "soul brother" just proved the rule. If they are ours we are going to protect them. If they belong to "the man', he can try to protect them with his own police force. In rebuilding the city the number one priority should be given to efforts to turn control of the communities over to the residents of those communities. This will mean allowing the growth of strong community organizations and their sponsorship of community controlled shops and housing. Can we do this? Will a blue ribbon committee headed up by J. L. Hudson be likely to relinquish our grip of power and domination in the economic area?[2]

Our choice is between real economic and political power by the ghetto dwellers or firepower. . . . Community organization efforts in Detroit have been maligned, misunderstood and undercut, but there is real hope.

Political reorganization is called for as well. Here is a voice from Jackson Prison commenting on the meaning of what has happened: ". . .riots are a necessary evil, showing that the present form of representative government is unjust. It fails to represent properly the lower and lower-middle classes of people."

Will we heed or will this city become "a curse for all the nations of the earth", with "not one stone standing on another"?

Editor's Notes

1. The phrase "carnival atmosphere" had been used by the media early in the week to describe the looting.
2. As it turned out, few individuals in Detroit would pay a higher price for social commitment than Joseph L. Hudson, Jr. His leadership on the New Detroit Committee was backed by a very thorough program of equal opportunity in the stores, which he then served as president and chief executive officer. Hudson's reforms did not please all his colleagues, nor could he hold off the forces that led to Hudson's merger with Dayton's of Minneapolis and his own withdrawal from the business.

3. Newsgathering during Turmoil

Detroit Free Press

During the weeks following July 23, 1967, though both major newspapers and the airwaves were filled with accounts of rioting, looting, snipers, and the arrivals of or delays in getting help from outside the city, there was still an urgent need for trustworthy news. Rumors and contradictions took on new outlines by the hour. For a time, the News followed a conspiracy theory, while the Free Press was practicing investigative journalism on riot deaths, learning that they had been preventable. On Sunday morning, September 3, 1967, this article—written by reporters Barbara Stanton, William Serrin, and Gene Goltz—appeared in the Detroit Free Press. The newspaper would later receive a Pulitzer Prize for the story.

The 43 Who Died; An Investigation into How and Why Detroit's Riot Victims Were Slain

William Dalton

William N. Dalton, a 19-year-old ex-Job Corps trainee, was killed by a police shotgun blast.

A number of witnesses claim Dalton was goaded by into making a break, then shot when he ran. Investigators from the Detroit homicide Bureau say the case is hardly that simple.

They say they have no doubt that Dalton was an arsonist, along with several of his companions that night. They also say

"The 43 Who Died," *Detroit Free Press* (3 September 1967): 1–5B.

that Dalton may well have been attempting to escape arrest, although this theory seems riddled when it is noted that no police report was ever filed on the shooting. Nevertheless, if Dalton was attempting to evade apprehension, the officer had every right to fire, the officers point out.

The investigators also note that of the number of persons who say they witnessed the incident, not one has been able to provide information that might help identify the officer they say fired the shot.

. . . The incident took place shortly after midnight on July 28, the fourth day of the riot.

According to witnesses, Dalton had been sitting on the porch of a Fernwood Street home until shortly after midnight, when he left, perhaps to go to the home of his girlfriend, Marcia Kitchen, 15, daughter of Mrs. Martha Kitchen, of 4871 Fernwood. The homes are just two doors apart.

As he walked between the homes, witnesses say, he was arrested by three policemen, probably as a curfew violator.

Philip Hyde, 23, of 4852 Fernwood, who says he observed the arrest from his porch across the street, claims that the officers put Dalton against a tree and searched him. He says they "tried to make him run, but he said he wasn't going to do it."

Hyde and another witness, Willie Arnold, 26, say the officers then walked Dalton towards Grand River, and forced him to turn down an alley which runs on the south side of Grand River between Fernwood and Edmonton. He and other witnesses say they later heard a single shot.

Other witnesses say Dalton was marched to the intersection of the Fernwood-Edmonton alley with the Grand River alley, where he was forced against the wall of a warehouse, his hands on his head.

From the warehouse, witnesses say, Dalton was marched across Edmonton to the vicinity of a parking lot, just west of Wild's Cleaners, at 8687 Grand River.

Picking up the story here is Mrs. Alberta Jones, who lives at Grand River and Arcadia, directly across from where Dalton was shot.

She claims she saw officers take Dalton into an alley on the west side of Edmonton. There, she says, she heard Dalton cry: "I didn't set no fires. You didn't see no fires."

497

She says Dalton was then brought into the parking lot, where a police officer pushed him against a wall, shoving him with a shotgun.

Then, they say, officers ordered Dalton to run. They say he ran along the building and vaulted over the hood of a car. As he did, a policeman raised his shotgun and fired one shot, felling Dalton on the sidewalk in front of a cleaners.

Mrs. Jones says the officer then yelled, "Let's get out of here." She says. "Everyone jumped in their cars and went off in every direction. . . . "

[In the case of George Talbert, which follows, one of the witnesses is Julian Witherspoon, the same Julian Witherspoon who was wounded by police gunfire at the St. Antoine Y.M.C.A. in the 1943 riot, and whose story appeared in the NAACP report by Walter White and Thurgood Marshall included in Part XII.]

George Talbert

George Talbert was shot and mortally wounded by a National guardsman as he walked down a West Side street in broad daylight, unarmed and innocent.

The shooting occurred about 5 p.m. on Wednesday, July 26, as Talbert, 20, of 4451 Thirtieth Street, walked east on La Salle Gardens South, a residential street near the devastated Twelfth Street area.

One of the witnesses is Julian F. Witherspoon, 47, 1978 La Salle Gardens South, an area chairman for the Mayor's Committee on Human Resources Development. Witherspoon calls himself an "eyewitness to murder."

At about 4:30 p.m., Witherspoon says, he heard shouting and shooting and went to his porch to investigate. He says he saw two Guardsmen proceeding up the street, waving back cars that were trying to go east to 12th St. When cars failed to stop, the Guardsmen squeezed off rounds over the cars from their M-1 rifles.

"You could see the drivers duck," Witherspoon says. "One minute you'd see their heads. The next minute you wouldn't."

Witherspoon says the two Guardsmen also yelled at residents on porches to get back in their houses.

The Guard's procedure that day is confirmed by a Free Press reporter assigned to that area. He says that several of the streets approaching 12th Street were closed by the Guard. He says the technique of closing them consisted of "standing in the middle of the street, shouting obscenities at whoever they were trying to move. If they didn't instantly obey, they'd fire over the car or over people's heads as they stood on their lawns."

At about 5 p.m., Witherspoon says, he saw a man—Talbert— walking east on La Salle Gardens South. His companion, Lance Smith, 28, of 3010 Gladstone, walked several paces behind. Talbert had just left his car, a 1965 Chevrolet, on Dunedin.

Witherspoon says he was frightened for Talbert but had no chance to wave him back. A moment later, one of the Guardsmen raised his rifle, aimed directly at Talbert and shot.

Talbert fell hard on the sidewalk, bleeding profusely. "Help me, I'm dying," he cried. He died 10 days later, on Aug. 5, in Henry Ford Hospital. An autopsy attributed death to pneumonia caused by the wound.

Witherspoon's version is corroborated by numerous La Salle Gardens residents. One of them is Frank Morrow, 34, of 1974 La Salle Gardens South, a combat veteran of Korea who disobeyed a Guard order to go to Talbert's aid.

By the time he got there, Morrow said, five other Guardsmen had arrived. He says he asked a Guard captain to take Talbert to the hospital, but the captain said that he was "not authorized."

Two priests from St. Agnes Catholic Church, Father John Markhan and Father Norman Thomas, came up, administered the last rites to Talbert and took him and Smith to the hospital in Smith's car. Smith had been struck by the same bullet that hit Talbert, but his wound was less serious.

Why Talbert was shot is a mystery. He had broken no law and carried no weapon. He was no curfew violator; the time was 5 p.m. He could not be mistaken for a looter; he carried nothing with him, and there are no stores in the immediate area where he was shot.

According to the Guard, Talbert was shot for refusing to heed a command to halt. The Guardsman who fired the shot told police that his guard companion had repeatedly ordered these men (Talbert and Smith) off the street. He says that one of the men, either Talbert or Smith had earlier told him, "I'm going to cut your throat, you sonofabitch." He says that "his man (Talbert) continued to come forward" so he aimed and fired at him.

Even if one accepts the National Guard's story, and none of the witnesses do, Talbert's death must be called inexcusable.

Talbert had a legal right to be where he was and to do what he was doing. Martial law had not been declared; the Guard had no arrest power whatever and its authority to give orders to anyone was sharply limited.

The Guardsman himself disobeyed a standing order—a court-martial offense—when he fired the shot that killed Talbert. Lt. Gen. John Throckmorton, commander of the Federal troops during the riot, had ordered the Guard to unload its weapons and told Guardsmen to fire only on command of an officer. This order was not followed.

Prosecutor William Cahalan has not yet ruled on Talbert's death.

Tonia Blanding

Tonia Blanding, a four-year-old Negro girl, paid for the crimes and mistakes others.

The corner of Euclid and Twelfth was like a battlefield the night of July 25.

National Guardsmen said there was sniper fire originating from the second floor of the apartment building at 1756 W. Euclid. A part-time employe of Bowman Private Police, John W. Bryant, said in a sworn statement that he had been fired on from the building a half hour before Tonia was killed and also the night before.

Guardsmen said one of their 2½-ton trucks was under fire by a sniper who was apparently shooting from the second floor apartment where Tonia was killed. The Guardsmen said they returned the fire.

During this time Cpl. Danny Kwieczinski reported to a tank commander, Sgt. Mortimer J. LeBlanc, 41, that he had seen a flash in the apartment window.

Huddled on the living room floor of a second-floor apartment were June Blanding, Valerie and William Hood, William Hood, Jr., James Matthew Blanding and several other children, including Tonia.

LeBlanc, while moving his tank to a position on Euclid directly opposite the apartment building, said the vehicle was under fire from the apartment. Once in position, LeBlanc fired short bursts from his 50-caliber machine gun into the windows he believed the sniper fire had come from.

Occupants of the apartment said later that they were not fired on until William Hood lighted a match for a cigarette.

Detective David Mason of the Detroit Police Department investigated later and decided that the Guard's firing had been directed only at the apartment from which they believed they were fired on.

Tonia died from bullets believed fired from the machine gun.

Mason said he later found one spent .38 caliber hull next to one of the windows in the apartment and a box of .38 caliber shells with some rounds missing. Police said Hood testified he owned a .38 caliber revolver.

Mason said he found in the apartment 20 men's coats, 35 pairs of men's trousers, 40 shirts, four overcoats, 23 paint brushes, two portable record players, a tape recorder, a portable television set, three portable radios and a movie camera.

There are discrepancies between the version given by the occupants of the apartment and the National Guard investigation.

The occupants said they were not fired on until after the match was lighted, yet the guardsmen from the 2½-ton truck were reported to have fired at the apartment also. Nowhere is it explained why the private guard, Bryant, did not report being fired on the day before from the apartment which he said he had pinpointed.

Finally, the wisdom of turning a .50 caliber machine gun, which fires a slug that will cut through a quarter-inch steel, on a frame dwelling is questionable. Certainly, the men in the tank did not require protection from snipers, and no sniper was found in the building.

Police procedure calls for tear gas to be used on snipers wherever possible, a technique used on sniper Sydnor. If that fails or is impossible, officers are directed to rush the building, armed with shotguns, as long as other citizens will not be endangered by their doing so.

The police were never involved in the death of Tonia Blanding. No one asked them for help.

Auburey Pollard, Carl Cooper, Fred Temple

At midnight Tuesday, July 25 three Negro youths were shooting craps on the second floor of the three-story annex of the Algiers Motel.

Two white girls who had run out on a $308.17 bill at the Ponchartrain Hotel were in the Algiers Annex, and seven or eight other persons were mingling and visiting between floors.

A little more than an hour later the three crap shooters were dead from shotgun blasts.

Carl Cooper, 17, was lying face down in a pool of blood in Room A2. Fred Temple, 18, and Auburey Pollard, 19, were lying dead in Room A3.

The girls were crying, one had a cut on her head, and both they and other guests claimed they had been beaten and threatened by officers in blue uniforms.

It had been a night of horror and bloodshed, with rioting and gunfire in all areas outside, and shotgun blasts along with reports of sniping—and worse—from inside.

The motel guests said that half a dozen uniformed men broke open the front door with gun butts, spread through the building and rounded up the occupants.

The guests said they were lined up against the wall, threatened and beaten. They heard gunshots, but none said they saw any of the youths get killed, and when the police told them to leave, they all fled into the night.

A pre-trial examination was begun Aug. 14 in Recorder's Court to determine whether Detroit Patrolmen Ronald W. August, 28, and Robert N. Paille, 31, should be held for trial in the killings of Pollard and Temple.

A youth who was in the motel, Michael Clark, testified that Paille and August had taken him into a room where Paille put a cocked pistol against his head and threatened to kill him.

Clark testified he later saw August take a youth into another room and that he heard a shot and someone fell to the floor.

August, charged with killing Pollard, submitted a statement that said he shot the youth in self-defense when the youth tried to wrest the gun away.

August was ordered to stand trial for first degree murder. No trial date has been set.

A National Guard warrant officer, Theodore J. Thomas, testified that he saw a policeman lead a man into a room and make him lie on the floor. Then the policeman fired a shot into the air, Thomas said. He could not identify the policeman.

He also said he saw August lead a man into a room and then heard a body fall. He said he had seen one body in room A-2 and one in A-3 but did not see the other body in A-3.

Days later, when confused testimony from witnesses was pieced together, one Detroit policeman was charged with first degree murder in the death of one Negro youth.

Another policeman was freed after a pre-trial examination failed to turn up enough evidence to hold him for trial.

Two policemen and a private guard were charged with conspiracy in connection with alleged beating, intimidation and abuse of persons in the motel.

The Algiers Motel had a shadowy reputation even before the events of that awful night. The police had made arrests for prostitution, and narcotics users were known to frequent the place.

An investigation was begun by the Free Press the day after the shootings when stories began to circulate among the Negroes, stories containing allegations of brutality and unwarranted killings.

A pathologist hired by the Free Press, Dr. Warren Sillery, examined the bodies of the three dead youths with the consent of relatives.

Dr. Sillery concluded that all three men were shot from inside the building from a range of 15 feet or less by 12-gauge double-0 buckshot. All the men were shot more than once. None could have been killed while engaged in a sniper battle with authorities outside the building.

Two of them, Temple and Pollard, were shot while lying or kneeling. The county medical examiner's autopsy reports agreed substantially with Sillery's finding.

A search of the motel annex failed to turn up any weapons.

Almost the only thing that persons in the motel and law officers are agreed on is that the policemen burst into the motel about 2 a.m. The police said they were investigating sniper fire from the motel.

Paille, charged with slaying Temple, was released because of insufficient evidence. His defense attorney, Norman Lippitt, argued at the examination that all that had been proved was that Paille was in the motel that night.

No charges were filed in the death of Cooper. The evidence indicated that Cooper was the first to die in Room A-2. The other two were shot later in A-3.

On August 24 the county prosecutor brought conspiracy charges against Paille, a private guard named Melvin Dismukes, and Patrolman David Senak. August was named as a co-conspirator but not a defendant.

Cahalan charged that some of the lawmen in the annex had beaten, intimidated and abused the witnesses. He said they had engaged in excesses in obvious violation of the criminal statutes.

No trial date has been set on the conspiracy charges.

Senak was under investigation by Cahalan's office in two other riot deaths but was cleared of wrongdoing last week in the death of Joseph Chandler. Cahalan is still investigating Senak's part in the death of Palmer Gray.

Dismukes is also awaiting trial on a felonious assault charge involving the Algiers Motel.

4.　The Death Games at the Algiers Motel

John Hersey

During the revelations about the events at the Algiers Motel, John Hersey, the eminent author of Hiroshima, *became interested in the reports. Hersey spent many weeks in Detroit interviewing those involved: police and National Guard officers, the victims' families and their friends. His lengthy journal became* The Algiers Motel Incident, *a book that should be read and reread by all citizens of metropolitan Detroit. In two chapters, titled "The Death Game" and "The Death Game Played Out," Hersey deals with the core of the evening's events as they were relayed to him later by witnesses and from official records.*

Those who were present at the time Carl Cooper, Fred Temple, and Auburey Pollard died included Michael Clark, Lee Forsythe, James Sortor, Roderick Davis, Larry Reed, Juli Hysell, Karen Malloy, Robert Greene, an army veteran, private guard Melvin Dismukes, Warrant Officer Theodore Thomas of the National Guard, and Detroit police officers Ronald August, Robert Paille, and David Senak, plus, as Hersey had indicated, a large cast of others.

This material is present in Hersey's brief, rather staccato format, which lends itself to the illusion of a theater script.

John Hersey, "The Death Game" and "The Death Game Played Out," in *The Algiers Motel Incident* (New York: Knopf, 1968), 273–76, 277–80.

The Death Game

1 One at a Time

"Then," Lee [Forsythe] said to me, "they started killing us one by one."

"They were going to shoot us," Michael testified, "one at a time."

2 It Was All Right

"One of the Detroit officers," Thomas told the police, "pulled the 'big man'—Roderick Davis—out of the line and took him in A-4." In court Thomas was more explicit. "Officer Senak," he testified, "took the first man out of the line . . . into the front room, one to the left in front." "When they went in," Greene told Eggleton, [a member of the county prosecutor's staff] "he closed the door." Roderick Davis said to me, "They told me, 'Lie on the floor face down and if you make a move or say a word, we'll kill you.'" "I followed them to the doorway," Warrant Officer Thomas testified, "and Officer Senak told the man to lay on the floor and he fired a round through the wall. I seen him point the gun to the other direction. He didn't shoot him. He scared him. . . . He winked at me. He didn't say nothing." "I thought," Roderick testified, "he shot in the floor because I felt like vibration reaction by my feet." . . . "In the floor or through a chair or something," Roderick said to me:

Attorney Kohl; "Now, you were in a room with David Senak when he took a prisoner in there?"

Warrant Officer Thomas: "Yes, sir."

Kohl: "And is it not true that the told the man to lie down on the floor? He fired a shot but he didn't shoot at the man, did he?"

Thomas: "Definitely not."

Senak fired, Thomas testified, "right in the corner."

"He looked at me," Thomas testified, "and winked, indicating it was all right. . . . When we took the first man in I realized what he was doing. And it was better than letting these people be beaten; seriously. I felt somebody was going to really get hurt seriously, and I felt this was the best thing at the time."

"Then," Roderick told me, "they said, 'Don't budge an inch or you'll be dead.'" And the men left him alone in the room.

3 Want to Kill One?

"The warrant officer," Greene told Eggleton, "came out, and the policemen asked the other officer, 'Did he kill him?' And the officer said 'Yes.' " This was for the ears of the people in the line.

"This officer . . . " the Thomas synopsis said, "asked Thomas if he wanted to kill one. Thomas said 'Yes,' and took one of the men"—Michael Clark— "into A-4 and fired a rifle shot into the ceiling, forcing the man to remain in the room."

"I also took one person into that front room," Thomas testified. " . . . I used my M-1 rifle . . . I also told the man to lay on the floor, and fired a round through the ceiling . . . toward the corner so that anybody upstairs wouldn't get hit. I didn't think there was anybody upstairs around at the corner of the house.

"Let's see," Michael testified—once again he seems to err; even Senak's lawyer placed Senak in this role—"told the soldier to shoot me or something. Anyway, the soldier told me to lay down. Then he shot. I think he shot out the window or in the hall somewhere. Then he told me just to lay there and be quiet. And he said if I make any noise, he going to come back and shoot me for real."

4 Announcement

"Clark and an unknown man were taken into room A-4," the Sortor synopsis says of this first phase of the death game, "shots were heard, and the officers returned, saying, 'We killed those two.' " Telling me the story, Sortor said, "And so they said they were going to kill us, you know. They said they were going to kill us niggers, you know, so they picked Michael and this other guy out, so they said they were going to kill these two niggers, so they took them in this room in there, we heard two shots, so the police come out, so he said, 'I killed them two motherfuckers.' "

Karen told the detectives, "she believed the police killed Michael Clark." From the synopsis of Juli Hysell's statement: "They . . . made Hysell believe Clark was dead."

5 Rational, Reasonable Explanation

Thomas testified,"Immediately after the officer shot into the wall, into the floor, or corner, or wherever you want to call it, and laid the man down, they"—the people against the wall—"thought this man had been shot and they were willing to talk . . . I believe it was one of the girls—I wouldn't swear to it—said, 'Why don't you tell him about the gun? Carl is dead anyway.' And this is one of the statements I specifically heard to this effect."

"One boy spoke up," Juli testified, "and said that the boy that was dead was the one that had the pistol, and that's the only thing to my knowledge that was said about the pistol."

"One of the persons" Karen told Allen Early [an attorney who acted on behalf of Juli and Karen], "who had been in A-2 & come up to A-4 said, 'Go on and tell them anything you want because they've already killed him.' This was with reference to the blank pistol. This other person then said, 'The guy in there on the floor' (referring to Carl in A-2) 'had a blank pistol.' Policeman said, 'Why didn't you tell us that before we killed the other guy?' "

Having elicited from Juli, in the conspiracy hearing, an estimate that the ordeal in the hallway had been going of for about twenty minutes before this first mention of the starter pistol, Attorney Kohl asked, "Now, if in fact there was simply a blank pistol that had been fired, will you advise this Court, please, what rational, reasonable explanation there could be for not telling the police who would have the gun and who had done what for a period of twenty minutes?"

Juli answered: "Because everybody was scared."

6 Next?

Karen told Early, "The talking policeman then said, 'Who shall we get next?' "

The Death Game Played Out

1 I Want One?

"Then the first officer," the Thomas synopsis said, "asked the officer with the OCD type helmet (who was dark complx w/m),

'Do you want to kill one now?' He said, 'Yes,' and the first officer gave the gun to the second officer, who took a Negro youth from the line. . . . "

"He said it," Thomas testified, "loud enough for everybody to hear in the room, 'Do you want to shoot one?'—or to this effect."

Thomas testified that August had not been particularly active along the line-up. "Patrolman August," he said, "was very refined. He didn't say anything that I can recall." But it was August to whom Senak now turned; Thomas testified that Senak handed his shotgun to August and told him "to take a man into the back room or into a room."

"Then the guy next to me," Greene told Eggleton, "they took him to A-4. The officer told him not to take him to A-4. He said 'Take him to another room.' And he took him to A-5, I think it was A-5, that's the back room there." (It was A-3.)

"The game was going on," Thomas testified, "and I said, 'You can't kill any more in here. There are too many now.' And that is when I believe the other policemen handed Patrolman August the gun."

2 A Thing to Scare People With

Assistant Prosecutor Avery Weiswasser asked Thomas: "Did Senak hand a gun to August?"

"Yes, sir."

"What did he say when he handed him the gun?"

"To the effect this was a game. I mean, this is a thing to scare people with."

But in other testimony Thomas said, "I can't recall what was said. I know there was a conversation. I won't deny this. The idea was to give the impression that these people were being shot."

Yet again Weiswasser asked, "Did you know if anybody bothered to tell August it was only a game?"

"No, sir," Thomas replied.

3 Don't Shoot

From the Michael Clark synopsis: "Clark then heard someone take Pollard into Apt. A-2 and heard Pollard yell, 'Don't shoot. Don't shoot.' He then heard a gunshot."

From the Lee Forsythe synopsis: "Forsythe stated he heard Pollard yell, 'Don't shoot,' and a door slam, Forsythe believed in room A-3. A few seconds later, Forsythe heard a shot fired."

4   A Brush of Clothing

"Then I believe Officer August took this man to the rear of the room," Thomas, who followed August into the room, testified, "and I heard a shot. And Officer August had his back to me. I seen a brush of clothing, and I heard something fall. At this time I got scared."

"Did I see him fall? . . . " Thomas asked himself in testimony. "I won't say that. I seen movement. Officer August was standing between myself and him, and I seen a flash of clothing, what I thought was a flash."

Prosecutor Weiswasser asked at one point: "Did you hear any struggle going on prior to that time?" "No," Thomas answered, "I can't say I did."

"I want to be honest with you," Thomas testified later on. I have seen the pictures of the room after the two bodies were discovered in there. And I believe the man that Officer August took back there had a shirt on, dark gray shirt. And the pictures don't show this. And that is why I was confused on this point. You can see something or think you've seen something and think about it, and you don't know if you've seen it or not. And I thought I seen that flash of clothing. And it looked like a gray shirt."

5   Announcement

From the James Sortor synopsis: "A shot was heard and an officer returned, saying, 'That one didn't kick.' "

From the Robert Greene Synopsis: "Then a shot was heard and the Warrant Officer returned, saying, 'That nigger didn't even kick.' "

Sorter said to me, "Aubrey didn't lose his temper in that room; he was too scared. I figure if he would have lost his temper, he would have lost it when they was hitting him with the rifle. It was too quick for him to be in there tussling with the guy. It was too quick. He went in there, I heard the shot, and the guy came out, and he said, 'That one didn't even kick.' "

510

6 Strictly Their Business

"At this time," Thomas had said, "I got scared. . . . It scared me. I was scared. I will be honest with you. . . . As far as the conversation goes, I believe I told the policeman that this was strictly their business, and I called Henson [PFC Wayne Henson, a National Guardsman], who was outside at this time. And there was more shooting in the street. In fact, more shooting, and I told him we were going to leave. . . . "

5.　Integration's Last Hurrah: "Where Did Everyone Go To?"

William Grant

The coalition of labor/liberal political power effectively ended in April, 1970, when the adoption by the board of education of an integration plan for high schools provoked a recall of the liberal majority the coalition had achieved. This end of an era in Detroit political life was analyzed by William Grant, at that time education writer for the Detroit Free Press.

The stage here is set for what could become integration's last hurrah. Perhaps the final blow was struck in August when the liberal bloc that has controlled the city's board of education since 1964 was voted out of office in an unusual recall election.

The board had hired an egalitarian superintendent, aggressively recruited black teachers, promoted black administrators, and purged the schools of books that did not reflect a multi-racial society and did not adequately portray black contributions to history.

School boundaries were adjusted and student transfers were approved only if they improved integration. But the board was

William Grant, "Integration's Last Hurrah: 'Where Did Everyone Go To?' " *The New Republic* (12 September 1970): 20. Reprinted by permission of *The New Republic*, © 1970, The New Republic, Inc.

unable to integrate classrooms in a system that this year is 62 per cent black. A few high schools in the corners of the city were white enclaves. Last April 7 the board moved against them. Its plan involved redrawing attendance boundaries for half of the city's high schools. Protests, student boycotts and hurriedly called neighborhood meetings followed. When the board met, angry white parents chanted "Hell no, we won't go." Speakers denounced the plan for five hours, before the board voted 4–2 to adopt it.

"All the trouble was because for the first time we devised a plan that not only moved black students into white schools, but also required white students to go to black schools," said the board president, A. L. Zwerdling, a labor lawyer and former administrative assistant to the late Walter Reuther. Zwerdling was elected to the board in 1964, with liberals Peter F. Grylls, a Michigan Bell Telephone executive, and the Rev. Darneau Stewart, a black minister. The three joined Dr. Remus Robinson, a physician, who in 1955 was the first black elected to the Detroit board and who for a decade fought almost alone for integration.[1] Dr. Robinson was hospitalized when the April 7 meeting was held and died two months later; the critical fourth vote for integration came from Andrew Perdue, a black attorney elected to the board in 1968.

The plan involved boundary changes, not busing. But the board was accused of busing and of "forcing integration to drive the white people out of town." A Citizens Committee for Better Education was formed to organize a recall of Zwerdling, Grylls, Stewart and Perdue and to press the state legislature to overturn the integration plan. The committee produced 114,000 signatures on each of four separate petitions to get the issue on the ballot.

The recall survived three law suits in federal and state courts and was ordered on the ballot by the State Court of Appeals three days before the election. The legislature voted the citizen's group virtually everything it asked. The debate in the legislature was more emotional than in Detroit. The high school integration plan was companion to board action dividing the school system into seven regions for decentralization. Conservatives in the legislature attacked both decentralization and integration. The legislature stopped the integration plan, and significantly changed the decentralization plans.

If the board was startled by the action in the legislature, it was dumbfounded by the response of its usual supporters. Republican Governor William Milliken had a few ambivalent comments about the integration plan, and said nothing at about the recall. The mayor stayed on the fence. The United Auto Workers, long the cement in Michigan's liberal politics, managed to put up the money for the single newspaper ad opposing the recall when, as one union official put it, "we couldn't raise a dime anywhere else."

"Where is everybody?" Mr. Perdue agonized a few days before the election. "Where are the people who helped us get elected— the UAW, the NAACP and the others? Don't they care anymore?"

The four did managed to attract support from black voters on election day, but the recall carried by 59 percent in a city where white voters still hold a 58–42 edge in voter registration. Only 180,000 voters managed to make their way to the end of a long primary ballot and vote on the recall, and the percentage of whites voting on the issue was much higher than the black percentage.

The four will be replaced by interim board members appointed by the governor, and permanent replacements will be elected in November, as will members of regional school boards who will take office when decentralization begins next January.[2] The Citizens Committee for Better Education intends to stay around long enough to see that as many as possible of those new board members share its views. "We have a two-year battle ahead of us to take over this school system and turn it around," said Aubrey Short, a General Motors metallurgist who is the group's chairman.

"I had a right to fight," said a somewhat defensive Edward Zaleski, a policeman who was one of the early organizers of the recall drive. "My daughter was being sent to a black school. We knew we were going to win, because we were fighting for our children. They were only fighting for an idea."

Editor's Notes

1. The meeting of April 7, 1970, was stormy indeed, with several hundred people, unable to get into the room, packing the hallways and

crowding Woodward Avenue in front of the building. One moment of quiet came when the board secretary read Robinson's letter:

> To my fellow Board members—
> I am sorry that I cannot be with you as you make an important decision that will affect the educational opportunity of thousands of Detroit youngsters. I recognize that my unavoidable absence makes it impossible for me to cast an official vote, but I hope that my thoughts—arrived at after much searching of my conscience and my commitment—will be given serious consideration during your deliberations regarding the regional boundaries to be drawn in compliance with act 244.
> I have been a member of the Detroit Board of Education since April, 1955. During these past fifteen years I have tried—to the best of my ability—to serve fairly the needs of all children from all segments of Detroit's population. I have believed—and have tried to act always from that belief—that every youngster in the city of Detroit deserves to find in our schools the unprejudiced opportunity to develop his talents in such a way as to become a self-motivated, productive citizen in a democratic, pluralistic society. . . .
> I am deeply troubled by the forces within society—both black and white—which would continue to foist segregated regional patterns upon future generations of Americans. I cannot, with a clear conscience, submit to these doctrines.
> Therefore, I support the proposed plan as providing the best opportunity for quality, integrated education for our students and for effecting the most cooperation among the various racial, religious, and ethnic populations of our city. I believe this plan can work; I believe it is fair; I believe it is in the best interests of the total community. . . .
> This plan will enable more black and white students to attend senior high school together; it will also enable more citizens of the future to recognize—from firsthand experience—that in plura, and that in equal opportunity there is the possibility for all men to rise to the level of their best talents.
> My thoughts are with you.
>
> Sincerely,
R. G. Robinson

2. The change from citywide to local school districts was the first real use of that system since 1916, when the reformers of those days eliminated neighborhood "school inspectors."

Among the recalled board members, The Reverend Darneau Stewart channeled his anger into running for reelection, this time in his new local district, and won handily. Stewart served with distinction for several years until his death.

6.   The *Milliken v. Bradley* Dissent

Thurgood Marshall

       Known by many as "the school busing case," by others as "Bradley-Milliken," the suit begun by the NAACP in 1970 to desegregate the Detroit Public Schools was won by the NAACP and those who joined its efforts in two lower courts before reaching the U.S. Supreme Court on appeal as the "Milliken-Bradley" case. The court rejected by a 5–4 vote in August, 1974, that section of the lower courts' opinion that had called for a metropolitan remedy involving integration plans for both city and suburban school districts.

       Mr. Justice Marshall, with whom Mr. Justice Douglas, Mr. Justice Brennan, and Mr. Justice White join, dissenting:

       In *Brown v. Board of Education,*. . . (1954), this court held that segregation of children in public schools on the basis of race deprives minority group children of equal educational opportunities and therefore denies them the equal protection of the laws under the Fourteenth Amendment. This court recognized then that remedying decades of segregation in public education would not be an easy task. Subsequent events, unfortunately, have seen that prediction bear bitter fruit. . . .

       After 20 years of small, often difficult steps toward that great end, the court today takes a giant step backwards. Notwithstand-

Thurgood Marshall, Milliken v. Bradley, *418 U.S. Reports* (October Term 1973): 781–815.

ing a record showing widespread and pervasive racial segregation in the educational system provided by the state of Michigan
for children in Detroit, this Court holds that the District Court
was powerless to require the State to remedy its constitutional
violation in any meaningful fashion. . . thereby guaranteeing that
Negro children in Detroit will receive the same separate and inherently unequal education in the future as they have been un-
constitutionally afforded in the past.

I cannot subscribe to this emasculation of our constitutional
guarantee of equal protection of the laws and must respectfully
dissent. Our precedents, in my view, firmly establish that where,
as here, state-imposed segregation has been demonstrated, it becomes the duty of the State to eliminate root and branch all ves-
tiges of racial discrimination and to achieve the greatest possible
degree of actual desegregation. I agree with both the District
Court and the Court of Appeals that, under the facts of this case,
this duty cannot be fulfilled unless the State of Michigan involves
outlying metropolitan area school districts in its desegregation
remedy. . . .

We deal here with the right of all of our children, whatever
their race, to an equal start in life and to an equal opportunity to
reach their full potential as citizens. Those children who have
been denied that right in the past deserve better than to see
fences thrown up to deny them that right in the future. Our Nation, I fear, will be ill served by the Court's refusal to remedy
separate and unequal education, for unless our children begin to
learn together, there is little hope that our people will ever learn
to live together. . . .

Nowhere in the Court's opinion does the majority confront, let
alone respond to, the District Court's conclusion that a remedy
limited to the city of Detroit would not effectively desegregate the
Detroit city schools. I, for one, find the District Court's conclusion well supported by the record and its analysis compelled by
our prior cases. . . . The focus of this case was from the beginning, and has remained, the segregated system of education in
the Detroit city schools and the steps necessary to cure that condition which offends the Fourteenth Amendment. . . .

The State of Michigan, through its instrumentality, the Detroit
Board of Education, engaged in widespread purposeful acts of
racial segregation in the Detroit School District. Without belabor-

ing the details, it is sufficient to note that the various techniques used in Detroit were typical of methods employed to segregate students by race. . . . Exacerbating the effects of extensive residential segregation between Negroes and whites, the school Board consciously drew attendance zones along lines which maximized the segregation of the races in schools as well. Optional attendance zones were created for neighborhoods undergoing a racial transition so as to allow whites in these areas to escape integration. Negro students in areas with overcrowded schools were transported past or away from closer white schools with available space to more distant Negro schools. Grade-structure and feeder-school patterns were created and maintained in a manner which had the forseeable and actual effect of keeping Negro and white pupils in separate schools. Schools were also constructed in locations and in sizes which ensured that they would open with predominantly one-race student bodies. . . . [The evidence] showed that Negro children had been intentionally confined to an expanding core of virtually all-Negro schools immediately surrounded by a receding band of all-white schools. . . . [1]

The [district] court concluded that responsibility for segregation in Detroit city schools rested not only with the Detroit Board of Education, but belonged to the State of Michigan itself and the state defendants in this case—that is, the Governor of Michigan, the Attorney-General, the State Board of Education and the State Superintendent of Public Instruction. . . . Under Michigan law and practice, the system of education was in fact a *state* school system, characterized by relatively little local control and a large degree of centralized state regulation, with respect to both educational policy and the structure and operation of school districts. . . .

The District Court then turned to the difficult task of devising an effective remedy. . . . The District Court first considered three desegregation plans limited to the geographical boundaries of the city of Detroit. All were rejected as ineffective to desegregate the Detroit city schools. Specifically, the District Court determined that the racial composition of the Detroit student body is such that the implementation of any Detroit-only plan "would clearly make the entire Detroit public school system racially identifiable as Black" and would "leave many of its schools 75 to 90 per cent Black." The District Court also found that a Detroit-only plan "would change a school system which is now Black and White to one that would be perceived as Black, thereby increasing the flight of Whites from the city and the system, thereby increasing the Black student population." Based on these findings, the District Court reasoned that "relief of segregation in the public schools of the City of Detroit cannot be accomplished within the corporate geographical limits of the city, . . . [but that the court] must look beyond the limits of the Detroit public schools. . . ."

. . . The District Court's decision to expand its desegregation decree beyond the geographical limits of the city of Detroit rested in large part on its conclusions A) the State of Michigan was ultimately responsible for curing the condition of segregation within the Detroit city schools, and B) that a Detroit-only remedy would not accomplish this task. In my view, both of these conclusions are well supported by the facts of this case and by this Court's precedents. . . .

The State had also stood in the way of past efforts to desegregate the Detroit city schools. In 1970, for example, the Detroit School Board had begun implementation of its own desegregation plan for its high schools, despite considerable public and official resistance. The State Legislature intervened by enacting Act 48 of the Public Acts of 1970,[2] specifically prohibiting implementation of the desegregation plan and thereby continuing the growing segregation of the Detroit school system. Adequate desegregation of the Detroit system was also hampered by discriminatory restrictions placed by the State on the use of transportation within Detroit. While state aid for transportation was provided by statute for suburban school districts, many of which were highly urbanized, aid for intracity transportation was excepted. One of the effects of this restriction was to encourage the construction of small walk-in neighborhood schools in Detroit, thereby lending aid to the intentional policy of creating a school system which reflected, to the greatest extent feasible, extensive residential segregation. . . . When the Michigan Legislature amended the State Transportation Aid Act to cover intracity transportation [it] expressly prohibited the allocation of funds for cross-busing of students within a school district to achieve a racial balance. . . .

Michigan, unlike some other States, operates a single statewide system of education rather than several separate and independent local school systems. . . .

The state's control over education is reflected in the fact that . . . there is little or no relationship between school districts and local political units. To take the 85 outlying school districts in the Detroit metropolitan area as examples, 17 districts lie in two counties, two in three counties. One district serves five municipalities; other suburban school districts are fragmented into as many as six school districts. Nor is there any apparent state policy with regard to the size of school districts, as they now range from 2,000 to 285,000 students.[3]

Centralized state control manifests itself in practice as well as in theory. The State controls the financing of education in several ways. The legislature contributes a substantial portion of most school districts' operating budgets with funds appropriated from the State's General Fund revenues raised through statewide taxation. The State's power over the purse can be and is in fact used to enforce the State's powers over local districts. . . . The State also establishes standards for teacher certification and teacher tenure; determines part of the required curriculum; sets the minimum school term; approves bus routes, equipment, and drivers; approves textbooks; and establishes procedures for student discipline. . . .

Most significantly for present purposes, the State has wide-ranging powers to consolidate and merge school districts, even without the consent of the districts themselves or the local citizenry . . . Indeed, recent years have witnessed an accelerated program of school district consolidations, mergers, and annexations, many of which were state imposed. . . .

In sum, several factors in this case coalesce to support the District Court's ruling that it was the State of Michigan itself, not simply the Detroit Board of Education, which bore the obligation of curing the condition of segregation within the Detroit city schools. The actions of the State itself directly contributed to Detroit's segregation. Under the Fourteenth Amendment, the State is ultimately responsible for the actions of its local agencies. . . .

Under a Detroit-only decree, Detroit's schools will clearly remain racially identifiable in comparison with neighboring schools in the metropolitan community. Schools with 65% and more Negro students will stand in sharp and obvious contrast to schools in neighboring districts with less than 2% Negro enrollment. Negro students will continue to perceive their schools as segregated. . . . School district lines, however innocently drawn, will surely be perceived as fences to separate the races when, under a Detroit-only decree, parents withdraw their children from the Detroit city schools and move to the suburbs in order to continue them in all-white schools. The message of this action will not escape the Negro children in the city of Detroit. . . .

Desegregation is not and never was expected to be an easy task. Racial attitudes ingrained in our Nation's childhood and adolescence are not quickly thrown aside in its middle years. But just as the inconvenience of some cannot be allowed to stand in the way of the rights of others, so public opposition, no matter how strident, cannot be permitted to divert this Court from the enforcement of the constitutional principles at issue in this case. Today's holding, I fear, is more a reflection of a perceived public mood that we have gone far enough in enforcing the Constitution's guarantee of equal justice than it is the product of neutral principles of law. In the short run, it may seem the easier course to allow our great metropolitan areas to be divided up each into two cities—one white, the other black—but it is a course, I predict, our people will ultimately regret. I dissent.

Editor's Notes

1. Justice Marshall, as had Judge Roth before him, lacked a careful chronology of precisely when these acts of segregation occurred. For over fifteen years, progressive board members had fought for equality. *De jure* segregation was never the policy of the boards elected by the Serve Our Schools Committee. A thorough analysis of the time factors involved in Detroit discriminatory practices is available in Eleanor P. Wolf, *Trial and Error: The Detroit School Segregation Case* (Detroit: Wayne State University Press, 1981) Wolf also notes with cool accuracy the frustrations imposed on liberal efforts at integration both by bureaucracy and by the loss of integration as a goal by an important segment of black leadership. With careful detail, she notes areas in which the court records show that the truth remained elusive.

   Wrongs had been committed, however, in whatever year, and Justice Marshall's basic arguments stand on their merits.

2. *Public Act 48*, cited here, had begun as one of several bills that were introduced in the legislature by State Senator (later Mayor) Coleman Young, who had long pursued the idea of "community control" of

521

the schools. In the fall of 1970 the interests of community-control advocates coincided with those of white parents in outlying Detroit areas who wished to avoid any change within their all-white neighborhood schools. The bill abruptly became law. The part of it barring the use of the Detroit Board's desegregation plan was declared unconstitutional, but by that time the question was moot.

3. The number of 285,000 represents the enrollment in the Detroit public schools just before 1970. At this writing, it is about 110,000 less.

Part XV

Playing by New Rules: Grand Plans for Downtown

Playing by New Rules:
Grand Plans for Downtown

After the advent of the New Detroit Committee in the fall of 1967, most Detroiters became more conscious of the role of business and industry in shaping directions for the city and in choosing the players in the game. It was a role that they had always filled—it was clearly perceived by the French farmers of the 1830s when their lands were crossed by new roads—but it was a role ignored by many. Detroit's movers and shakers have in recent years been examined.

One critic is the young black artist and poet Leisia Duskin, who portrays in "Business" how some leaders, hopefully lesser ones, spend their days.

The political definition of the changes from the "city of homes" that Myron Adams saw in 1911 to the developers' game plan of the late seventies is set out for us by attorney Kenneth Cockrel in "Downtown Detroit," a section of a tour guide written for a field trip sponsored by DARE (the Detroit Alliance for a Radical Economy) in September, 1979. I note that former Councilman Cockrel's remarks on the lack of democracy in decision-making seem particularly valid, and are of the sort rarely heard in civics classes. (I *do* give government teachers full marks for effort, but this is not information easily obtained by anyone.)

The last of the "downtown" items is chosen from Wolf Von Eckardt's *Back to the Drawing Board: Planning Livable Cities*, in which he gives us an out-of-town architect's view of the Renaissance Center and bolsters the opinion of many Detroiters that the Emperor-Architect of the RenCen lacked a few stitches of clothing.

1.   Business

Leisia Duskin

the big shit office
workers and execs
get up early,
shower,
put on their corporate
dress.

They sign in early
in order to see
who will sign in late.
They read journals
for lunch and
listen to
MUZAK.

The rest of the
day spent staring out
windows perfecting
coffee and
cigarette butt dreams.

Leisia Duskin, *Lights Out in 10* (Detroit, 1986), 29.

2.   Downtown Detroit

Detroit Alliance for a Rational Economy

At the time Kenneth V. Cockrel prepared this material, he was serving on the Detroit City Council and frequently questioned tax abatements given to industry and to downtown developers, such as the backers of the proposed Millender Center and of the expansion of the Renaissance Center. The essay was written for the use of DARE (the Detroit Alliance for a Rational Economy). Attorney Cockrel gave his permission to reprint it here shortly before his death in 1989.

Introduction

People who don't come downtown much often are impressed with all of the new "developments." Something is always happening—new buildings are going up, and old ones are coming down. There are new public facilities, such as the Hart Plaza and the Joe Louis Arena. The amount of money being invested is considerable.

Since 1973, over $543 million was spent on downtown construction, with another $630 million earmarked for the next decade. There was never any question that there would be a Detroit "renaissance." The questions that faced the economic elite of De-

Detroit Alliance for a Rational Economy, Georgakas Collection, Box 2, file 21, Reuther Library, Wayne State University. Reprinted by permission of Kenneth Cockrel.

troit were when, how, and consistent with what priorities. But we must look beyond the glass, concrete, and glitter for the essence of the reshaping process.

The Major Goal

The present development of the downtown area pursues many of the same goals as were advanced by Mayor Cobo. The major objective is for Detroit to serve as the major administrative center for the region.

Downtown Detroit is still the most appropriate location for this center. All major roads and freeways originate downtown. . . . In addition, downtown is sufficiently compact to serve the particular needs of administrative and financial businesses. . . . These arrangements cannot be reproduced in the sprawling suburbs. . . .

How It's Done

The means for downtown Detroit's development is the much heralded private-public coalition. This unequal relationship combines the profit agenda of major investors with the political needs of the local leadership. . . .

To implement this new mechanism, a variety of hybrid organizations of business people and local political leaders has been formed. They have impressive titles: Detroit Development Authority (DDA), Economic Development Corporation (EDC), Detroit Renaissance, Inc., and Central Business District (CBD), to name a few of the most significant.

The single most important organization to downtown development is the Detroit Economic Growth Corporation (EGC). Its Board of Directors is appointed by the Mayor, and seats the chief executive officers of virtually every major area corporation. There is token representation from trade unions and the community, but the EGC is primarily directed by Detroit's corporate elite. The EGC was initially chaired by James Roche, of General Motors, and Lynn Townsend, of Chrysler Corporation. That power is now

[1979] in the hands of Arthur Seder, Jr., of American Natural Resources and Michigan Consolidated Gas.

The Economic Growth Corporation is a private corporation; its meetings are not open to the public. Nevertheless, its annual budget comes primarily from public sources: $375,000 from the State of Michigan, and $375,000 from the City of Detroit, but which is extracted from the Community Development Block Grant Funds!

This primarily publicly funded but privately controlled corporation also directs the work of two of the development agencies in Detroit: the Economic Development Corporation (EDC) and the Downtown Development Authority (DDA). To be sure, both are public entities. But the Executive Vice-President of the DDA and the EDC and all of their staffs are, in fact, employees of the EGC! They work under the direction of the EGC President; they are the people directly involved in downtown projects. . . .

These boards are justified as places where "coalitions" of powerful interests can be built, enabling them to work on projects in a coordinated fashion. Critical decisions are made by a few people who are insulated from public control. There are public officials and labor union leaders on many of these boards, but their priorities are clearly established by the business representatives. These organizations are not places where community input can be made, but are organizations whose primary function is to "facilitate" the investment of private capital in downtown Detroit.

The world of federal grants and special state legislation to aid investors is a complex one that has a language of its own. Words and phrases such as UDAG, P.A. 198, Urban Systems Grant, Community Development Block Grant, 22d Mortgage Loan, P.A. 255, P.A. 438, are casually used at these meetings, and the uninitiated will wonder what is being discussed. All of these deal with federal and state taxpayers' money. In the case of tax abatement plans . . . corporation developers are allowed to escape paying taxes, which means someone else must pick up the tab. While the language and details are often complex, the basic concept behind these grants and tax exemptions is simple: *to give public money* to private investors as inducements, thus foreclosing the use of these funds for services for the rest of us. . . .

What Is Downtown Detroit?

There are no signs or borders to mark the passage, but as we cross the Fisher Freeway, we enter a separate city. The Downtown Development Authority is a tax district separate from the rest of Detroit. Under a recently passed state law (Public Act 197 of 1975), all new revenues generated in the downtown development area after 1978 are given to the Downtown Development Authority to reinvest in that development area *only*! The result is that the increasing property tax revenues of the new private buildings are spent only within the borders of this separate city. . . .

3. Renaissance and *Risorgimento*

Wolf Von Eckardt

Perhaps it began in the New Detroit Committee. Suddenly there was a sense of power felt by community leaders, telling each other they could begin a new city in a world of change. Perhaps, as some said, the whole thing began with the restlessness of Henry Ford II, irreverently nicknamed by Detroiters "Hank the deuce." At any rate, in the mid-seventies a decision was made to tamper with the old city and its river on a grand scale. Suddenly great round towers were climbing skyward. As the work neared completion, average citizens, whose opinion no one had asked, began to wonder. What was it all for? Why the gray bunkers in front? Why was it so hard to walk around it?

It remained for architect and critic Wolf Von Eckardt to visit the scene and put together the thoughts of many.

If Detroit ever has a renaissance—and God knows it needs one—it will happen despite its flashy, new Renaissance Center. Completed in 1977, the skyscraping bundle of glass tubes on the Detroit River is really a counter-Renaissance Center. It is at best an example of modern city planning's exclusive reliance on the "perfection of physical equipment," as Mumford called it, without regard for the intricacy of the urban fabric. It cuts the city off from its river as effectively as the nineteenth-century industrial plants and warehouses. And, in keeping with LeCorbusier's and CIAM's misguided notions it concentrates and segregates one vital urban function—high-style commerce and tourism—from the rest of the city's life to the detriment of both.

Excerpt from *Back to the Drawing Board: Planning Livable Cities* by Wolf Von Eckardt (1978) reprinted by permission of New Republic Books.

At the time the Detroit Renaissance Center was built, New York city planners began the revitalization of a frisky, but declining (mostly lower middle-class) neighborhood in an altogether different spirit with altogether different methods. The *risorgimento* of Little Italy which is roughly between Greenwich Village and Chinatown in Lower Manhattan, is hardly comparable in terms of expenditure and scale with what was done in Detroit. But it illustrates a new approach to the rejuvenation of declining cities, an approach that preserves and strengthens the integration of a variety of people and activities that make neighborhoods and cities lively.

RenCen, as Detroiters call it, consists of a 73-story, 1400-room hotel; meeting rooms and halls for large conventions; four office towers with 2.2 million square feet of rentable space; parking for 6,000 cars; and a carnival of four movie theaters, 13 restaurants, a suburban shopping-center worth of shops, cocktail lounges, splashing water, greenery, glitter, and Muzak-drenched confusion.

All this obviously draws business, people, and vitality from Detroit's already decaying downtown, six or seven blocks away. Once you have entered RenCen, there is no reason to leave it again until it is time to go home, or your money runs out. But entering the glass doors is extremely difficult if you attempt it on foot. My excuse for being so maladroit in Detroit is that before my visit I had dinner with a friend nearby and there weren't any taxis. So, with much apprehension (Detroit has one of the highest crime rates), I negotiated several deserted and partly abandoned blocks of urban no-man's land until I came to a formidable barrier—ten-lane Jefferson Avenue, a nasty highway that clearly was not designed to be crossed by anything.

A pedestrian must pass two more tests before he may be admitted to architect John Portman's never-never megastructure. First, he must prove his courage by walking the driveway through a forbidding "berm," a concrete rampart that looks suspiciously like a Berlin Wall erected to keep the natives out, but built, I am told, to house heating and air-conditioning machinery. Next, he must prove his ingenuity by finding his way through a labyrinth of driveways, without signs or sidewalks, until he finds the all but hidden entrance into drive-in Portman-land.

The reward is that, once inside, you may plunk into any one of a myriad of cushiony seats on any of six levels—by the pond, under a waterfall, perching on a daringly cantilevered "cocktail pod"—looking up into dangling greenery or down into teeming humanity—and that at the flash of your credit card, an apparition will appear on a motorized refreshment wagon and sell you a drink.

The scene is at once lively and monotonous. You are inside the huge platform from which all the glass tubes sprout. It is an enormous, exciting space, filled with giant concrete columns that support the skyscrapers above, as well as elevator shafts, a multitude of escalators, spiral staircases that mesh the various levels and galleries and pods and ends. Portman is famous for these grand, somewhat adrenalized courts. He used them at the Peachtree Center in Atlanta, and the Embarcadero Center in San Francisco.

The space is monotonous once you walk around. In Detroit, the combined hotel lobby and shopping mall form a circle. You walk around and around expecting some surprise, but it is always the same. You get dizzy and confused. I never quite knew where I was. The poor graphics did not help.[1] Different shops and window displays might have helped. But at the time of my visit in the spring of 1978, few shops had opened, although the offices were renting well and conventions were booked for years.

RenCen is touted as one of the largest privately financed urban developments in the nation's history. It was launched on the initiative of Henry Ford II for the often expressed purpose of helping Detroit out of its despair, of showing confidence in the city. By the time it was finished, it showed over half a billion dollars worth of confidence. Ford was joined by fifty other corporations.

Wayne Doran, the amiable and frank spokesman for these investors, says the demonstration of confidence is as much psychological as physical. Psychologically, it may indeed have accelerated plans for other skyscrapers and shopping centers in downtown Detroit, and a federally assisted "people mover" system, linking the central business district with the cultural center—the Art Institute, the library, and Wayne State University with its various institutions—further up Woodward Avenue.[2] Psychologically, it is also true, no doubt, that the sight of the gleaming glass tubes makes many a Detroit heart beat faster, although the more impressive view of this fortress is from the Canadian side of the river.

But while Mayor Coleman Young is loudly and frequently praising RenCen, I heard much bitter talk about it on the part of Detroit housing and planning officials. Some see it as a capitalist plot against the city. The bitterness is understandable if you travel about in what one writer has called "the city of urban despair." Block after block of abandoned, looted, and burned cottages on weedy, littered plots look even more depressing than abandoned, looted, and burned-out tenements in Brooklyn. The shocking sight is one occupied house, in a sea of dead ones, with a horde of children playing in the debris of a broken-down porch.

RenCen does nothing for these children and Doran says irrefutably that it never promised to solve the city's social problems. It provides 3,000 jobs, he says, and is bringing thousands of conventioneers into the city. The trouble is, few of them venture across Jefferson Avenue.

The city, together with RenCen, will have to spend thought and money on building links to downtown, if the half billion dollar investment is to stop hurting Detroit and start helping. Well-lit greenways and walkways and minibus service to the restaurants and boutiques of Greektown and other attractions are imperative.[3] The sooner that silly "berm" is buried, the better.

I am sure the deplorable insularity of RenCen is not due to ill will, as some people charge, but to the naivete of American business in city planning and architecture. The riverfront site was easily available (although the city planners wanted it turned into a park). There was no need, as Doran pointed out, to displace anyone. It had a good view. Nor could Ford and his partners conceive of a manifestation of power and confidence that did not scrape the sky. Even Paris and London have succumbed to the Promethean temptation.

But just think what Henry Ford II and his 50 partners might have accomplished for Detroit if they had laid their half-billion dollar towers on end. It would have yielded at least 12-square blocks of new buildings—plazas, covered malls, greenery, splashing water, glitter, Muzak-drenched confusion, motorized barmaids, and all.

Editor's Notes

1. At the urging of merchants, those graphics were reassessed, and there have been some improvements. It is still possible, however, to get lost in the RenCen.

2. A beautiful, though smaller, People Mover opened in the summer of 1987. It has delightful art work by Detroit artists, but goes only on a downtown circuit—no runs to the Cultural Center.
3. Greektown is an enormous success, and everyone is happy to walk or ride the People Mover to it from the RenCen. Greektown pleases everyone, that is, except for a few old-time Greeks who remember the coffeehouses and grocery stores now displaced by rows of restaurants and the huge tourist center created in Trapper's Alley, the old Traugott Schmidt furrier's warehouse.

Part XVI

A Shrinking City

A Shrinking City

Detroit, within its city limits, is today unquestionably a shrinking city. Arguments about the accuracy of U.S. Census employees do not change the fact that there will be even fewer people in 1990. In 1950 there were 1,800,000; in 1980, 1,300,000. It is reasonable to project that Detroit may have less than one million in 1990. The loss of a half million people in thirty years was primarily due to the emptying of the central city, a six-mile square bounded by Livernois, McNichols, Conner, and the river.

It is useful to discard the widely quoted tales of suburbanites returning in great numbers to riverfront apartments. Some do return but never enough to cancel out earlier losses.

The six counties that roughly comprise the Detroit metropolitan area are something else again. Surprisingly, this area still maintains about the same level of industrial employment as it had during World War II. This is definitely not a "rust belt."[1]

Industrial employment has been relocated into many small plants with about five thousand to ten thousand workers. The new workplaces have spread out over a fifty-mile radius from the old city center. Detroit auto production has spread out into such places as Ypsilanti, Wixom, Flat Rock, and new sites north of Pontiac.

Along with scaled-down heavy industry, there are to be found in the outlying areas many corporate headquarters, principal retail activities, and newer growth industries. It is these service sector growth industries that are drawing newcomers to all southeastern Michigan. They include government administration, financial services, higher education, and the arts.

In contrast with the old smokestack industries of the city, which around 1900 became chiefly automotive, the new suburban workplaces do not need to look as ugly as the old, though they sometimes manage to. Most of the work is done behind glass and cement walls lining the major highways.

For a view of the movements of people and their work throughout southeastern Michigan, we turn to a research document produced by the Long Range Planning Committee of the Episcopal Diocese of Michigan, titled "The Emerging Pattern: A Regional Perspective."

As we have seen a number of jobs move to the suburbs and a number of Detroit factories close or leave town, there have been efforts to keep big industry here, or to entice it with tax abatements. The Cadillac plants in southeast Detroit are gone, the Burroughs Company is now Unisys and lives in Pennsylvania. Opinion is still divided about General Motor's effort to create a new factory in Poletown, but it is clear that employment goals there have been far from realized, though old neighborhoods, churches, and shopping areas were destroyed in Detroit and Hamtramck.

One of the most imaginative efforts to meet the challenge of the jobs and factories that have gone was a series of proposals by Dan Luria and Jack Russell in *Rational Reindustrialization*. Their sensible creativity has been largely ignored by the area's power structure in the several years since their study was written.

A city is, or should be, made up of homes. Detroit has come a long way since Myron Adam's 1911 exuberance over the city of homes and trees. For a current countdown of homes and statistics of our housing supply, we turn to the Catholic Interracial Council, which in a May, 1988, newsletter brought together statistics from several sources and tied them in with the current plight of the homeless.

Another view of the results of arson, vandalism, and official neglect is that of Ron Williams, editor of *Metro Times*, in "Detroit Loves a Good Demolition." Between them, Williams and the Catholic Interracial Council make clear that "gentrification" by young preservationists is not one of Detroit's problems; arson is. The largest item in the mayor's proposed "action grant" budget for 1988–89 was ten million dollars for the demolition of already half-destroyed and unsafe buildings.

Turning from shelter to another of the basic problems of people—hunger—we introduce the 1982 report of the Michigan Task Force on Hunger, written by Councilwoman Maryann Mahaffey, chairperson of the Michigan Statewide Nutrition Commission, for Congressional hearings.[2]

As Ken Cockrel strongly suggested in a previous chapter, the city's movers and shakers, its large committees, are reluctant to share power. Over the last year or two there has developed a short list of problems that the present mayor seems unwilling to address. When the responses of the city administration began to turn to charges of "white racism" on the part of its critics, a retired UAW staffer, himself black and experienced in political action, entered the arena. "Ernie" Dillard's call for accountability on the part of blacks in government and shrewdness on the part of black voters is here excerpted under the title "The Cry of White Racism."[3]

Editor's Notes

1. See reports of the Michigan Employment Security Commission, published under the titles *Detroit Manpower Review* and *Detroit Labor Market Review* (March 1974–March 1988). The 1974–80 reports had as their executive editor S. Martin Taylor, later head of the New Detroit Committee. There were certainly variations in manufacturing employment over the years, but overall the counties neighboring Detroit have maintained their manufacturing employment totals to an amazing degree.

2. A word about Councilwoman Mahaffey: Mahaffey has spent some years on the council, serving also as a professor of social work at Wayne State University. She has been active in the national and local Welfare Rights Organization and has served as president of the National Association of Social Workers. She is a persistent advocate of those who have no other place to go for help. In the last few years, she has been actively engaged in preparing handgun control, or "gun freeze," ordinances for the city, each of which, until a minor compromise resolution in July, 1989, was shelved by her colleagues

when it became clear that there was not enough strength to override the usual vetoes of Mayor Young. Mahaffey is liberal, but also practical; her understanding of the budget process goes well beyond several of her colleagues, and those who try to dismiss her as a "little lady" usually learn better, to their sorrow. Her quality shows in this hunger report.

3. Dillard and his wife, Jessie, who served for several years on the State Board of Canvassers, the agency dedicated to keeping Michigan elections honest, are shrewd and perceptive observers of the political scene and determined Democrats. Ernest Dillard, with years of political experience behind him in his work with the UAW, had clearly reached his boiling point when he wrote "The Cry of White Racism."

1. The Emerging Pattern: A Regional Perspective

Episcopal Diocese of Michigan

In 1987, the Episcopal Diocese of Michigan (then mainly composed of the eastern half of the Lower Peninsula) undertook a study of its people and their movements. The report, written by Merle E. Henrickson, is both history and projection.

There will continue to be urbanizing development in broad bands along the principal freeways, especially along I-94, I-96 and 696, I-75 and I-275. This urbanizing development will not necessarily result in net growth, but the greatest numerical growth in the state will occur in Livingston, Oakland, Washtenaw [Ann Arbor area] and *western* Wayne Counties.

The northern part of the lower peninsula may have the greatest percentage increase, but this will be in the range of 10,000 to 20,000 per county north of the Muskegon-Bay City line. It will consist of a combination of retirees and persons supported by the recreational use of the area.

Episcopal Diocese of Michigan, "The Emerging Pattern: A Regional Perspective," Report of the Demographics Task Force, Long Range Planning Committee (Unpublished MS, 1987), Episcopal Diocese of Michigan Archives, Detroit.

The inner core of both Detroit and other pre-World War II industrial cities will continue to decline.

The church will face a major separation and social stratification of people, with particular implications for the main line denominations.

The acquaintance with the world for young newly formed families living along the individual corridors will have been formed from television and shopping malls. They will be without memory of depression, sit-down strikes, war and the social unrest of the sixties. Their computers will flash, "Document not found."

Many older retired people and much rural poverty will be located in the area north of the Muskegon-Bay City line. A residue will remain in the old inner city areas of people who can not make their way in the society in which they are living. The highest incidence of unemployment, under-employment and dependence on various welfare programs will be in these areas.

Changes since World War II in the organization of the industrial work place, as well as changes in the transportation of materials and workers to that place, have profoundly affected the patterns of industrial and residential location in the Detroit Metropolitan area.

Industrial plants built in Detroit prior to World War II were dependent on water and rail transportation to receive their essential raw materials and to ship their manufactured products. Industries in Detroit were located along the Detroit or Rouge Rivers, or along the railroad belt lines which were roughly parallel to Grand Boulevard and the circle with a six mile radius formed by Livernois, McNichols [old Six Mile Road] and Conner Avenues.

Prior to World War II there were 400,000 to 500,000 industrial work places in the Detroit area, and 85% of them were located along these railroad lines. Industrial plants were sometimes enormous concentrations of work stations, with 75,000 employed at the Ford Rouge Plant and 40,000 at the Dodge Main Plant.

The people who worked in these plants depended principally on public transportation for the trip to work, and lived as close as possible to street car or bus lines. During World War II and until 1950, there were over 1,300,000 people who lived inside the Livernois, McNichols, Conner belt in Detroit, Highland Park, and Hamtramck. Another 600,000 lived within the city of Detroit outside this belt, and the balance of the metropolitan area population consisted of 1,000,000, mostly living beyond the Detroit city limits.

Beginning with World War II, new industries broke from their reliance on railroad transportation, and came to use trucks to move materials to and between plants. Construction of freeways extended to fifty or seventy-five miles the distances which plants might be separated from their related and supplier plants. At the same time the functioning size of major industrial plants was generally reduced to a range of 3,000 to 10,000 workers.

The number of industrial jobs in the metropolitan area has remained substantially the same—in the 400,000 to 450,000 range. However, the location pattern is now reversed. At least 80% of the work places have moved outside the city and less than 100,000 remain along the old industrial corridors.

With work places moved twenty-five to fifty miles out of the city, and little public transportation, workers traveled to work in their own cars, and parked in lots provided by their employers. As new families formed, they sought homes near their work places, and gradually emptied out the old city with its housing crowded into two and four flat units. Between 1950 and 1980, the area between the Livernois, McNichols, Conner belt lost half its people—about 650,000. Over that same period, Oakland County added 600,000, *western* Wayne County added 550,000 and Macomb County added 500,000.

The outward movement was selective. People who bought new houses had regular income, either as industrial or white collar workers, frequently with two incomes in the family.

Four groups of people remained in the inner city, which experienced the greatest population loss:

Those persons who could not afford to buy a house, who had to remain where rental housing of some sort was available. Since the principal supply of rental housing in Detroit has been the two and four family flats built in the 1920's, these were the places that were available. However, the oversupply resulting from a 50% population loss meant that many were vacant, became vandalized, and have been demolished.

The elderly who chose to remain in their old homes, but also the elderly for whom new senior citizen housing was scattered around in the older part of the city.

People released from institutions for whom many of the large older houses were taken over to become adult foster care homes, or unregulated rooming houses.

A few middle class families who lived in new housing on urban renewal lands near downtown or along the Detroit River.

2.   Rational Reindustrialization

Dan Luria and Jack Russell

In 1981 Luria and Russell outlined a plan for redeveloping Detroit industry through new products, mainly "energy hardware" such as natural gas drilling and coal gasification equipment. They urged an immediate inventory of Detroit's capital goods, believing that it would show both tools and industrial capacity adaptable to these uses. They suggested that new industries might well exist in old buildings threatened by the wrecking ball, and that these industries could provide jobs for the still-available pool of highly skilled workers.

Detroit is wounded. For thirty years we have bled jobs and capital to the suburbs, to the South, and overseas. During the past five years, Detroit's condition has become critical. New wounds have been opened. We have hemorrhaged economic life as never before. In the 1980's, a city once the vital hub of America's Great Lakes industrial heartland is becoming a grim monument to the waste of an unplanned economy. While the mayor exhorts the taxpayers to save our City, a Presidential Commission has concluded that America's Detroits are disposable containers of economic activity which, now nearly empty, may be cast aside.

Detroit's economy is being killed by industrial disinvestment. Detroit's major manufacturers have not returned to the city the

Dan Luria and Jack Russell, *Rational Reindustrialization: An Economic Development Agenda for Detroit* (Detroit: Widgetripper Press, 1981), 5–12.

547

wealth we have created. On the contrary, the profits produced by Detroit labor have built new factories elsewhere, or been distributed to stockholders, or funded often ill-advised corporate adventures. In 1947, the city held over 280,000 manufacturing jobs in some 3,300 firms. Today, Detroit hosts less than 100,000 such jobs in fewer than 1,700 firms.

This industrial disinvestment has eroded our tax base and distorted our expenditure priorities. It is *the* fundamental cause of the municipal fiscal crisis we now confront and with which we will continue to struggle for years.

Proclamation of Detroit's Renaissance will not end the trauma of industrial disinvestment. Downtown recommercialization can replace neither the number nor the quality of the jobs lost as our industry dies. The family of the unemployed auto worker is not saved by employing one daughter as a file clerk at Renaissance Center or one son as a security guard at Riverfront West. . . .

We believe that the 1980's will determine Detroit's fate: either industrial Detroit will be rebuilt and recover an important position in the national economy, or disinvestment will destroy the life chances of our youth, our capacity for local self-government, and much of the useful wealth created by three generations of Detroiters. By the 1990's, Detroit will either be a diversified manufacturing center of a new kind, or it will be a discarded city of vacant factories and abandoned homes from which the remaining affluent shield themselves in residential enclaves and a well-fortified downtown.

If Detroit is to survive as a city in which working people can prosper, we must redefine and reorder our development priorities. We believe that a rational economic development program for Detroit must be a least-cost program to retain and create tens of thousands of high-wage, cyclically insensitive industrial jobs. This essay is a first sketch of such a program. . . .

First, we are not opposed to the relocation of investment capital within cities of a metropolis, regions of a nation, or even the nations of a world. We oppose only its unplanned, socially wasteful, and privately controlled movement. Once the relatively high wages enjoyed by Detroit auto workers had filled up the city's available space with single family homes, it was inevitable and desirable that those forms of auto production requiring extensive space would subse-

The flag left behind: scene in an abandoned factory. (Courtesy of Bob McKeown, 1988.)

quently be built in suburban and rural greenfields. But it was neither inevitable nor desirable that metropolitan Detroit be politically balkanized into hostile municipalities differentiated by class and race; that metropolitan tax base sharing would thus become impossible; that a powerful auto/oil/construction/consumer durables lobby would decree the federal highway and mortgage policies that replicated the suburban phenomenon section by section to 26 Mile Road and beyond; that Detroit would be gutted by freeway trenches rather than served by mass transit; nor that the city's commerce would be mauled by the placement of major shopping centers just beyond its borders. The spatial catastrophe of metropolitan Detroit is a sufficient argument for greater social control of investment.

Similarly, the siting of some new auto plants in the West and the South has been a logical and desirable response to regional growth and the development of new markets. But it is hardly in the interests of society as a whole that some firms leave Michigan because unionized workers can claim a greater share of the wealth they produce and because our citizens have organized politically for better protection from unsafe work and the vagaries of the capitalist business cycle.

We will not advocate the socially irrational imprisonment of private capital within Detroit or southeastern Michigan. We *will* argue for radically increased government authority in the economy. . . .

Second, we are not opposed to Detroit's Renaissance. We *do* believe it should be demystified. The much-celebrated re-birth is in essence an attempt to protect the value of existing investments and future profit opportunities in the downtown hub. The banks, retailers, utilities and other businesses downtown have been threatened by the disinvestment of Detroit, especially since 1967. The Renaissance was their self-interested redevelopment strategy, long before it became the keystone policy of the administration of Mayor Coleman Young. By logic and law, many of the downtown businesses are less mobile than industry. They must stay and protect their futures. We hope they build and succeed.

We do challenge, however, the terms they offer for development, the logic of their strategy, and the absurd conceit that somehow their success will be the salvation of a city ravished by industrial disinvestment. . . . When and if just the beachhead projects (Trolley Plaza, Riverfront West, the Millender Center, and the Cadillac Mall) are completed, hundreds of millions of federal and local public revenues will have facilitated these private developments.

Even with this huge taxpayers' subsidy, the downtown commercial renaissance is a risky business. . . .

The grand designs for the future development of downtown Detroit are based upon the questionable belief that many thousands of salaried professionals and managers can be induced to settle there with their families. Some will surely be attracted to the amenities of the river and the hub, but with Detroit's extraordinary upper-middle-class home bargains and the comfortable, secure suburbs just minutes away by freeway, we believe the downtown Renaissance may well abort. Given the high risk, the developers' current terms, the narrow strata of the population served, and the limited impact on the local economy, we do not believe that the downtown strategy should have priority claims on the City's precious economic development resources. . . .

Unfortunately, even a booming commercial Renaissance on the riverfront and downtown would not meet the needs of working class Detroit. It would not deliver the jobs. . . . It is fantasy to hope that hotels, a shopping center, some office buildings, and the service needs of wealthy condominium owners will be able to employ the workers, the children of workers, who have been discharged from our closed factories. Moreover, the jobs that the commercial Renaissance may provide will contribute far less to the families of the employed and to the economy of the city than have the high-wage, national market, industrial jobs they "replace."

During the past 30 years, Detroit has lost 27% of its population but nearly 70% of its jobs in manufacturing. In 1981, over 400,000 Detroiters—one in every three—receives some form of public assistance. . . .

Third, we acknowledge the important efforts at community development in Detroit, but argue that these efforts at best only partially balm the wounds of disinvestment; they do not constitute a cure for the disease. Detroit needs all the housing dollars and programs we can get, but we should understand that the neighborhoods created by a high-wage, high-employment industrial economy between 1910 and the 1950's will not be renewed, especially at today's costs, in an economy based on transfer payments from the federal government and on low-wage service employment. The best housing program for Detroit would be one that reopens our plants and employs our homeowners.

Similarly, most neighborhood commerce cannot survive drained by the suburban malls and dependent on the Detroit poor. If Detroit can reindustrialize and employ our people, then neighborhood merchants will have a chance. If industrial disinvestment continues unchecked, we will have boutiques for the downtowners and party stores for the people.

What *will* rebuild [Detroit's economy]? . . . Let us begin with a paradox: the very severity of Detroit's industrial disinvestment may create an opportunity. . . . Tens of thousands of workers have been permanently dismissed. Several major plants have closed; more will follow. Smaller plants that built components for obsolete technologies or products have been abandoned. Orders from smaller parts suppliers have ceased. Tool and die shops are without work. In less than 30 months, multiple shocks have broken many of the crucial links that held together Detroit's ailing but still viable automobile industry.

Are these links permanently broken or can they be reforged? In some quarters, optimism about *Michigan's* future in the automotive economy runs high. Transport economies and attempts to emulate Japanese-style inventory management may recentralize in our State some of the previously lost major elements of the industry. Southeastern Michigan still has important comparative advantages in labor skills, transport infrastructure, abundant water, and the substantial remaining share of auto production. But *Detroit* cannot hope to win back what *we* have lost; our built environment is a huge barrier to major new industrial construction. The staggering public costs borne to prepare the new Cadillac Plant site indicate the price extracted for merely retaining 6,000 of the 14,000 Cadillac jobs we had less than a decade ago. . . .

Much of our auto industry, then, is gone or going. . . . Capital leaves, but labor skills remain. Plants are closed, but not razed. Railways and freeways still tie the factories together and connect them to the nation. The links between the hundreds of small- and medium-sized vendors and the major facilities are damaged, but not broken beyond repair. The engine of production that was built over the span of half a century has not yet been scrapped, nor should it be. Detroit can still bend metal. . . .

We believe that currently there exists *no* workable program for inducing privately financed economic development. There is, moreover, no self-correcting process by which urban disinvestment creates the conditions necessary for expanded reinvestment of the kind and on the scale required. From this outlook flows the need to project our own concept of "rational economic development," one which transcends wishful thinking about an orderly transition from an industrial economy to a service economy and seeks to build upon the actual history of Detroit as a producer of durable goods for the national and international economies.

Others before us have, to be sure, seen the need to preserve and revitalize Detroit's aging industrial base through planned conversion to the production of socially useful goods needed by America and the world. Walter Reuther, for example, popularized demands for reorienting facilities supplying the 1941–1945 war effort to making building supplies for low-cost housing. Our effort seeks to supply this legacy of intent to the now very much more difficult circumstances of Detroit in the 1980's. . . .

3.   Conscience and Housing

Catholic Interracial Council

In May, 1988, the Catholic Interracial Council of Detroit, a small but highly respected group, issued a newsletter containing the results of a study of housing and the homeless. Mainly the work of Robert Selwa and Marie Oresti, it is reprinted here.

Will Housing Opportunity Grow or Diminish for Detroit?

The 1980 census showed that Detroit had a net loss of 58,696 homes! This was the largest loss of housing for any city in the United States. Detroit has had this enormous loss while other older northern and eastern cities were expanding their housing opportunity.

Detroit: net loss of 58,696 homes. *New York:* net gain of 21,000 homes.

Toledo: net gain of 13,000 homes.

Philadelphia: net gain of 11,000 homes.

Catholic Interracial Council of Detroit (May, 1988). Reprinted by permission of Robert Selwa and Marie Oresti, editors.

Boston: net gain of 8,000 homes.

Milwaukee: net gain of 7,000 homes.

Detroit's staggering rate of destruction of its homes is continuing throughout the 1980's. Here are the annual housing reports on Detroit by the Southeast Michigan Council of Governments:

Year	New Homes Built In Detroit	Homes Demolished In Detroit	Net Loss In Homes In Detroit
1980	928	4,387	-3,459
1981	1,372	6,002	-4,630
1982	1,263	3,814	-2,551
1983	165	4,037	-3,872
1984	69	3,656	-3,587
1985	217	4,301	-4,084
1986	223	5,016	-4,793
1987	262	4,796	-4,534

In the entire city of Detroit, a city of 140 square miles, during 1987 only two single family homes were built! There were 260 multiple housing units built. And there were 4,796 dwellings destroyed, for another enormous loss in housing of 4,534 homes.

This is while thousands of homeless people wander the streets of Detroit. This is while housing destruction is practiced in Detroit instead of housing rehabilitation. The net loss in housing translates into this fact: on the average, another 12 homes are destroyed every day in Detroit!

To shelter the homeless is one of the Corporal Works of Mercy. To expand housing opportunities is one of the goals of this country. What are we going to do about reaching this goal in this city? How are city, state and federal governments going to address this problem? How are business, civic groups and individuals going to address it? Are we going to let the dream of Dr. Martin Luther King die in the rubble of a bulldozer?

4. Detroit Loves a Good Demolition

Ron Williams

Detroit maintained until recently a unique disregard for the elegant but rotting Gilded Age mansions remaining near downtown and the great architectural triumphs of the twenties. Commenting on the recent successful effort of Detroiters to save Orchestra Hall, Ron Williams, editor and publisher of Metro Times, Detroit's strong alternative weekly, wrote the following.

       In 1970, when Detroit Symphony bassoonist Paul Ganson learned that Orchestra Hall was targeted to make way for a pizza parlor, he became very angry. And determined.

Mustering a group of equally angry and determined musicians and preservationists, Ganson succeeded in having the venerable hall—which just happens to be a shade this side of acoustically perfect—placed on the National Historic Register in 1971. Then the chamber concerts began, the preservation jazz series and much later the guest concerts by the DSO itself. In that sorry excuse for a decade, with the city crumbling down around them, a small group of Detroiters dug in their heels and simply said no. They said, "Save Orchestra Hall."

Ron Williams, "Detroit Loves a Good Demolition," *Metro Times* (25 February–3 March 1987): 18–20.

The Feb. 20 [1971] press conference was very crowded. . . . Some of Detroit's most powerful movers and shakers, all smiles and with good reason: they were there to announce something very right. The DSO was coming home to Orchestra Hall. Sure there had been talk of a state-of-the-art performing arts center on the riverfront with a revolving something or other. But the symphony board—which means a cross section of the most influential citizens in our community—chose to dig their own well-heeled shoes into one of the most ravaged and desolate stretches of urban landscape in a city which has virtually redefined the meaning of the words urban renewal. I hope Paul Ganson was there. He should have had the biggest smile of all. . . .

The city of Detroit is rotting. Its roof is caving in—plaster, dust and debris occasionally shower down through the sunlight and pigeon feathers admitted by the hole in the roof. Mildew and dry rot are in control now. Much of the time plywood is a formality easily dispensed with. "Detroit's buildings are getting debricked to provide patios in Dallas," says Preservation Detroit President William Colburn.

Detroiters stopped caring about their city a long time ago. When the Republicans came to town in 1980 to nominate Ronald Reagan, we boasted through bloodshot eyes and stupid grins that Detroit loves a good party. Well, the sad fact of the matter is that what Detroit really loves is a good demolition.

There is probably not another city in this country with a more shameful track record in preserving its past. Go ahead. Wander into the Burton Historical Archives of the Detroit Public Library in the cultural center and discover the truth for yourself. Or if the library isn't your style, head down to one of my favorite watering holes, Old Detroit on Beaubien in Bricktown. Order a Signature and take a hard look at the photos on the wall. It should come as no surprise that half the magnificent buildings pictured were razed long ago to make way for yet another parking lot.

History, you say? Wrong. For every Orchestra Hall, there are 20 other historically significant structures steadily degenerating, moving precariously closer to the point of no return.

> The white financial structure isn't giving mortgages to restoration efforts. They are liars if they say they aren't redlining.

(Michael Farrell, University of Windsor; art history professor and urban pioneer)

There is no other conclusion to be drawn: Detroiters, urban and suburban alike, have permitted the physical soul of this community to be decimated. Now, as a small vanguard of preservationists and developers have begun to take stands across the city to save what is still left, the weight of decades of indifference is being felt. Detroit's financial community reflects the attitude of the people of this city and, down to almost the very last institution, turns away those proposals.

I accuse the Detroit financial community—and specifically the banks of this city—of willfully redlining preservation and restoration projects. As developers and financial analysts trip over each other to assemble projects in Oakland County, world-class theatres and historically important structures of all kinds are literally rotting in this city. What has changed in the last decade? The presence of urban pioneers, preservationists and developers of every stripe with sophisticated and viable packages who simply cannot get a penny from Detroit banks. We are allowing our own institutions, holding our money, to pursue lending policies that continue to weaken this community. Detroit banks will not lend money to Detroit.

> The Monroe block has been a long learning process. We'll preserve the facades. . . . 10 years ago, we could have preserved the whole buildings. (Dorothy Wrigley, Co-developer of the Monroe Block project)

The buildings in question are some of the oldest left standing in Detroit: Civil War-era structures adjacent to the Kern block. It took a progressive Cleveland-based developer (Forest City Dillon) joining the project to finally give it the right chemistry of public and private funding to move ahead. Also included in that historic block and incorporated into the Monroe redevelopment is the National Theatre. Built in 1911, it is the only theatre designed by internationally renowned architect Albert Kahn and is on the National Register of Historic Places.

Indifference and redlining are just terms. What they have done to this city can be viewed in stark relief . . . [at the National Theatre today]. That is what Detroit has done to its heritage.

An exception, you say? A few blocks away from the National on Bagley sits the empty United Artists Theatre. Some say water damage has made demolition inevitable; others hold out hope. Built in 1928 and designed by architect C. Howard Crane (who also designed Orchestra Hall), the United Artists could face, if not outright destruction, a far worse fate. For only a block south of the United Artists is what is perhaps the perfect metaphor for Detroit's dark struggle with its past—the remains of the Michigan Theatre, now a parking structure. Words cannot describe the feeling one gets to see the spectacular art deco ceiling and then the rows and rows of cars parked beneath. The Grand Circus Theatre . . . ? Shuttered. The Madison Theatre? Dark. All threatened.

What happens when someone comes forward, puts their own money where their mouth is and looks to Detroit's financial community for support? Chuck Forbes and his son Jim purchased the Fox, State (formerly the Palms) and Gem (formerly the Vanguard) theatres in the historic theatre district north of Grand Circus Park. After stabilizing the structures with new roofs, adequate winter heating, etc., they have searched locally and nationally in vain to secure financing to move ahead with their dream of a revitalized entertainment district. Their plan is viable. The Fox alone is inarguably one of the top two or three historic theatres in this country. But no Detroit financial institution will touch them.[1]

Debbie and Joe Grella bought the historic David Whitney Building several years ago with earnings from New York real estate transactions. With a stunning four-story marble atrium, a solid tenant base and an interior People Mover stop, the Grellas set out to refinance the building. Although, according to Debbie Grella, they had financed $300 million worth of projects in New York city, she and her husband were turned down by over 70 lending institutions when it came to this project in this city. Financing was recently acquired through an innovative Build America Bond, the first such bond sale of its kind in Detroit.

Even the prominent and powerful Southfield-based Shostak Brothers real estate firm may have met its match in the city. Despite commitments from Michigan Bell and Blue Cross / Blue Shield to lease office space, the Shostak plan to convert the old flagship Hudson's store (itself saved by preservationists in the late 70's) into luxury atrium office and retail space, perhaps downtown's single most pivotal redevelopment project, appears stalled. The reason? Lack of adequate financing. . . .

In 1981, Mike Farrell purchased a threatened Gothic home just three blocks south of Orchestra Hall. Built in 1868, the house is listed on the National Register of Historic Places.

The mansion on Alfred Street is resplendent in leather wallpaper, marble counters, hand-carved ebony bookcases and 25-foot ceilings. It is a veritable castle surrounded by a moat of modern antagonists—crack houses, prostitution dens, plasma donor centers, boarded-up buildings, rusting auto carcasses, dead hotels and weed-choked fields. "When our house was broken into, the cops said 'tough luck,' we were nuts to live here anyway," Farrell said. "Some sympathy for all the money we've spent on restoration."

Farrell needs to lower the monthly payments on the mortgage so he can replace the roof and stabilize the house. He has been to one bank three times, a second twice and tried a third bank once. He talked to officers at other banks and savings and loans. While he says the inspectors the banks send invariably fall in love with the house, when the formula for financing is run through the computers back at the office, the answer is always the same.

To most of us, that home may be viewed as an important link with the past, part of this city's heritage that should be respected and restored. . . . [Farrell sees] it as something more. "That building is the future of Detroit. And the banks don't have faith in the future of Detroit."

Editor's Note

1. Since then Michael Ilitch, owner of Little Caesar's pizza chain, has purchased the Fox from Forbes, and completed its restoration in the grand style Detroiters remember. Mr. Forbes remains an interested owner of other properties in the old theater district.

5.   Hunger in Michigan

Maryann Mahaffey

I am a member of the State health coordinating council, tenured professor of the School of Social Work at Wayne State University. I did research into hunger in Detroit in 1969, and as a result, became the founder of both the Detroit and the State nutrition commissions.

Today the unemployment rate in Detroit, Mich., actually in January 1982, was 20 per cent. It is estimated that two-thirds of our black youth in Detroit are unemployed. On February 25, 1982, we were informed that two General Motors plants in Detroit will close before the end of the year, laying off 2,100 work-

Maryann Mahaffey, *Oversight Hearings on the President's 1983 Budget Recommendations for Child Nutrition: Hearings before the Subcommittee on Elementary, Secondary, and Vocational Education of the Committee on Education and Labor, House of Representatives*, 97th Cong., 2d sess., 16–18 March 1982, 111–15.

ers. McLouth Steel Co. in southeast Michigan may be saved if the creditors agree not to foreclose.

In December, 1981, we estimated—based on our 1980 population—28 per cent of Detroiters were receiving either AFDC, general assistance, or supplemental security income. These figures do not include those working at the minimum wage who are eligible for food stamps or other benefits.

Of the 9.3 million people in Michigan, currently 34.7 percent can be presumed to be economically vulnerable and barely capable of providing for their own maintenance.

. . . The most recent report documents that the highest unemployment in Michigan is not in Detroit. It is in Flint, followed by Muskegon, Saginaw, and Pontiac, with Detroit as No. 5. The Michigan Department of Commerce's slightly different approach to measuring the statewide economic distress released in November 1981, showed 15 cities in Michigan with a per capita income of less than $4,087 in 1980, and 15 with an unemployment rate above 19 per cent in 1980, including the cities of Pontiac and Flint. Using the department of commerce 1980 data, more than 15.4 percent of the population of 15 cities lived below the official poverty level. Of the estimated 18,000 terminated [from Michigan social service benefits] in Michigan last fall, 77 percent live outside Detroit.

. . . A study by the Michigan Statewide Nutrition Commission of emergency food depots and kitchens in June 1981 documented that all of them across the State of Michigan were out of food by the end of the month, most of them by the middle of the month. . . .

The end result is that some of the emergency food depots get much more restrictive as to who is admitted, and they draw their boundaries across smaller and smaller territories.

The Detroit School Board fed almost 20,000 children in the summer school lunch program. . . . We face a number of problems for the summer of 1982. The program's financing has been cut, we understand, from $122 million to $61 million. Last Year Detroit had $1.5 million to operate the program. USDA representatives told our Detroit Health Department the other day that we will receive one-half of our 1981 allotment for 1982, and yet the problem is increasing. More layoffs are occurring, and more people are running out of their unemployment benefits. . . .

In Detroit, the board of education has told us that 80 to 85 percent of our school-age children in Detroit qualify for free meals. The new regulation that, in effect, eliminates private, non-profit organizations as sponsors will wreak havoc in Michigan. In the summer of 1980 in Michigan, 23 churches served an average of 4,274 children per day. Eight community action agencies served 10,142 children per day, and 53 other private, nonprofit organizations such as Boys' Clubs served 23,499 meals per day. That's 84 private nonprofit sponsors serving 38,000 children every day across the State of Michigan, and they cannot be sponsors and serve the children meals in the summer lunch program in 1982 in Michigan or anywhere else in the country. . . .

The administrative costs [under new regulations] will go up, and if we don't come up with the extra money for monitoring, we could be accused of not following the regulations and face further cuts. Detroit passed an increase in its income tax last June to show that we are willing to sacrifice to save our beloved city. We have continued to lay off city workers. We had about 33,000 workers on the city payroll in the 1950's and now have 18,000.

The drop in our population is not enough to account for that much loss in workers other than representing the cutbacks in services to our citizens.

Thus, the new regulations and assignments lead us to believe that there are those who would like to find reasons to justify more cuts at the same time that we face more unemployment and more need. . . .

The program has benefits beyond the serving of meals to children. In Detroit and Michigan we have relied on volunteers as well as hiring people to work in the program. In Detroit, we have employed 40 to 50 people with 20 to 25 of those in college and high school. For many, it's their first job; it also makes it possible for them to continue in school. This is crucial for many, given the severe cutbacks in loans and grants. . . .

Why is the summer lunch program so important in meeting a child's health and nutrition needs? A nutritionist who operates the WIC program in a health center in a community southwest of Detroit has reported that the children she sees suffer primarily from anemia. A vitamin supplement is not only expensive, it is not a substitute for an adequate nutritious diet. If the children the nutritionist sees were not getting the summer lunch program, in addition to the school lunch program, they would be eating only one meal a day, and inevitably, their anemia will worsen.

A mother in another southern Michigan city reported that she sends her children to her sister's house during the summer to get the summer lunch. She does not have one in her area, for less than 50 percent of the children in her community are classified as "needy."

I worry about the children who do not have aunts or contacts in an area with 50 percent of the children classified as "needy."

When asked what she would do if the children could not get the summer lunch, the mother said they would be reduced to one meal per day. The nutritionist pointed out that summer is the time when children burn up energy and need this program. Obviously, we are also dealing with the interrelationship between programs. The food stamp allotment is inadequate. Commodities are not the answer, either, whether cheese, peanuts, or peanut butter, whatever it might be.

A study, conducted since 1978, by Shirley Nuss, Ph.D., Detroit, documents that when people face reduced incomes they first pay the rent and utilities and cut back on food. Parents generally cut back on their own food intake in order to feed their children. One father reported in the food survey this year that he takes Tylenol to cut his hunger pangs so he will eat less in order to more properly feed his children.

The need to insure a roof over one's head is exemplified in another case that we were presented with this fall, where the mother spent the rent money on food for a sick baby. Her husband, who had carefully gathered the money together to pay the rent, when he found out she had used it for food for the baby and not to pay the rent, blew up and walked out: family breakup.

When people do shift from meat to such items as noodles and rice, or using them as fillers, they often do not have access to enriched noodles and rice in their local groceries. The Michigan Statewide Nutrition Commission has advocated legislation to restore nutrients [to] processed food through the enrichment processes. But Michigan, along with a number of other States, has still not acted. It would be lovely if Congress would do so.

The lines of people selling their blood are getting longer. Grocery store personnel across the State report layoffs as food sales are down.

In the meantime, more people in Michigan are going through the McDonald's "Golden Arches" garbage for food, and the managers are complaining about people coming into their restaurants and begging for money to buy food, people who come in and eat what is left over on somebody's plate. . . .

How on Earth can anyone contemplate reducing the summer lunch program or eliminating it? Or any other nutrition program?[1]

Editor's Note

1. On December 9, 1983, Mahaffey attacked old myths that sought to place the blame on the victims of hunger. "Yesterday, Edwin Meese, White House Counselor [later attorney-general], stated that there are lines in soup kitchens simply because the 'food is free.' Mr. Meese went on to say that many of the recipients are working, and that it's easier to go to a soup kitchen than it is to shop for food. We are outraged by this cavalier approach to the problems of the unemployed and poor families. . . . I propose that a moral society will not reduce its population through starving people."

6.   The Cry of White Racism

Ernest Dillard

Since blacks have held the highest political offices in this city for 15 years, the questions voters should ask about political power in Detroit are:

Has it provided Detroit citizens (70-percent black) safety and security for their persons and property?

Has it provided clean, safe, decent and reliable public transportation?

Has it provided well-kept litter-free public parks and safe, sanitary and open rest rooms?

Has it provided safe, dope-free and properly maintained public housing for the homeless and poor as well as management that administers these complexes in compassionate but firm, business-like fashion?

Ernest Dillard, "The Cry of White Racism" (unpublished MS, 1988), 1–3.

Has it cut down the increasing rate of black infant mortality?

The answers to these questions are no. What reason tends to be given? "White racism." (Yet) the constituency is predominately black. Mayor Coleman Young has often blamed "media hype" or "white racism" when troubling issues such as crime, housing and black unemployment are raised.

But are these problems caused by "white racism" or is this cry a vote-getting, political ploy? The latter seems more plausible. Because of the long history of real racism in this country even in the best of circumstances blacks are likely to charge "white racism" before distinguishing fact from fiction.

Consider, for example, that there is a hemorrhaging exodus of the black middle class from Detroit to the suburbs. Is this caused by "white racism"? The participants in the "black flight" will not hesitate to tell you that they are leaving because the elected black political leadership has failed to provide protection for them and their families.

It is common knowledge that a significant percentage of black teachers in Detroit public schools send their own children to schools in the suburbs. . . . The parents say they fear the violence in Detroit schools.

At some point, black politicians must be held accountable. In the case of Detroit, the city charter centralizes much of the power in city governance in the office of the mayor. He appoints department directors, including the chief of police, who is black.

If this is not enough, there are more than 30 black judges in Detroit's criminal justice system. There are also 14 black state representatives, three black state senators and two black U.S. representatives. This Detroit juggernaut of black political, police, judicial, and legislative power is unmatched in the nation. Nevertheless, the hoodlum element in Detroit has been allowed to impose upon its citizens a citywide curfew that kicks in at sundown.

The problem is that the black community views the election of black public officials as tantamount to solving problems that plague the black community. Being black, candidates will be more sensitive and dedicated to the "struggle" because they "have been there." Yet, upon the slightest criticism, black elected officials tend instinctively to respond "the white folks did it," and black voters fall into this "white" trap.

What black voters are forgetting is that the reason they voted for blacks in the first place was that they didn't like what the "white folks" were doing. Yet Detroit black voters have not held black elected officials accountable for their actions. If the office of the mayor of Detroit were held by a white mayor under the circumstance of today, there would be wall-to-wall blacks marching around the City-County Building with clenched and upraised fists demanding the mayor's head.

Besides holding black politicians accountable, there must be an honest effort by black politicians to work with white mainstream groups to help improve the condition of the white and black underclass. After all, poverty and welfare are not a "black problem." True, the percentage of blacks in poverty is higher than that for whites in Michigan. But the number of whites in poverty is much greater than that for blacks.

Unfortunately, the misperception of poverty being "a black problem" allows white politicians—under the guise of fighting "big government" and "runaway welfare costs"—to vote against effective social legislation, which their white constituents sorely need. Through widespread educational programs in the white community, whites and blacks would recognize the common denominator of their need—jobs for those willing and able to work.

This would enable well-intentioned but politically sensitive white candidates or public officials to work with blacks on finding solutions to today's problems. It could significantly mute, if not silence, the cry of "white racism." And it would refocus attention on a principle that Martin Luther King introduced long ago: "Color has nothing to do with the contents of a man's character."

Epilogue: Trade-Offs and Hopes

All of us tend to ignore the lessons of history. Among the folktales related by Marie Hamlin in *Legends of le Detroit* is that of a little red creature, *le rouge nain*. Call him trickster, imp, or devil, what you will. All the peoples of the earth have one in their folktales. Cadillac was warned by the voyageurs on his arrival at Detroit to beware of offending the red devil. In spite of this, when he saw a small ugly dwarf in his path as he was leaving a large banquet in his honor, he kicked the creature out of his way, to the horror of Madame Cadillac. She reminded him that the imp had the power to put a curse both on him and the entire settlement. Cadillac refused to listen. Soon his fortunes took a sharp turn for the worse. He lost money, position, and reputation. The French blamed it on the red devil.

How effective or long-lasting the curse of *le rouge nain* on Detroit was is still uncertain. An intermittent curse at most, I think, for the city has had its share of good fortune. The legacy of unthinking arrogance epitomized by Cadillac has, however, remained over many periods of Detroit's history.

All in all, the condition of Detroit is not good as it enters the 1990s. Its major perceived troubles are crime and drugs, especially crack cocaine; poor health conditions; its schools, seen to be ineffective and prone to violence; its burned out and vandalized homes; the despair of joblessness; and a widening gulf of black-white antagonism, augmented by talk of racism.

These are the most widely perceived problems. No one can deny their existence, but there may be different shadings of reality.

My own list to examine begins with the nature of unemployment, moves to crime, including arson and "drug-related" crimes, then physical health, especially that of children. Only then do I look at the schools, which exist to serve those lucky enough to survive to age five. I propose to return last to the damage to the beautiful natural world Cadillac described, and to the river where it all began.

Each of these troubles must be considered within the context of where it occurs, the pattern of decision-making that led to it, and whether there are, even now, some ways to alleviate it. The question of where becomes all-important when we recall the tremendous growth of suburbs in the six counties surrounding Detroit proper. Executive recruiters admit to working skillfully to conceal Detroit city destinations from the outside talent they are hiring.

As indicated in "A Shrinking City," heavy automotive industry has all but vanished within the city proper, and has largely been replaced by service and high-tech industries throughout the metropolitan area. Unemployment, however, is not a significant problem in the suburbs. The shift to service industries has lined the highways with new office buildings: corporate head offices, insurance and banking firms that have migrated from Detroit's financial district, and many new hotels specializing in serving the executive traveler. For Detroiters, the problem of access to suburban jobs, especially at entry level, is acute. In August, 1989, an official in southeastern Michigan's transportation authority had an innovative idea—that buses should be rescheduled to provide more opportunities for Detroiters to reach suburban workplaces! Although determined corporations, such as K-Mart, which has its world headquarters in Troy, Michigan, have been able to negotiate outward transportation for their workers, the general pattern has been to take suburban clerical workers into Detroit workplaces, and take a few household helpers to wealthy suburbs. The late Senator Philip Hart's mass transit hearings in 1974 should have been required reading for all transportation planners since then. Senator Hart's committee saw the dangers of an isolated work force dependent on the automobile.[1]

The city government of Detroit has paid its full share, and more, in job creation by tax benefits to employers. Among significant lapses has been the city's failure to take seriously the notion of readapting its sleeping industrial capital, as described by Luria and Russell in the section from *Rational Reindustrialization*.

There are jobs in the suburbs, good jobs, but lack of access defeats many. It is the problem of which Zachariah Chandler despaired in his struggles with Congress for access to livelihood. Chandler would not hesitate to call today's situation racism.

Drugs are involved in the city's high crime rate. Yet even the city's epidemic of crack cocaine, a cheap profit maker that builds violence into its users, is not the whole story of crime. Crack has created new developments, however. Among them are more teen-age killings; children are not only victims but often killers. An element of shock and horror seems to add a depth of mystery to the new local crimes. A decade ago, citizens were aware of an increasing crime rate, yet the sad happenings were almost predictable. There were purse-snatchings, muggings, car theft, and a murder rate that drew national attention, yet was described by local police as mainly involving acquaintances. Detroiters, women in particular, gave up the evening, gave up downtown, gave up the choice of solitude away from home. Today, by contrast, crime has entered a far less predictable phase. Crime has intruded into homes, particularly those of the elderly. Child abuse, or public awareness of it, has been growing. So has the number of abandoned babies. Teen-age drug dealers are said to be commonplace; a ten-year-old dealer is found sitting on a pile of heroin in a closet. Everyone talks of his age as if it were a first-ever item. Yet there were eight- and ten-year-olds determined to murder during the Faulkner riots of 1863.

The new, improved modern crime leaves no margin for error or lack of judgment by law officers. The revitalization of the police department by Mayor Coleman Young appeared to be one of the greatest accomplishments of the 1970s. Integrated and efficient, the department went far toward wiping out memories of brutality and racism. It is only recently that there are questions. There are rumors that some officers have been involved in the drug trade. There are absolute certainties that young off-duty officers with guns can play the part of fools.

Possibly the police cannot win against the current random crime. Expressway bridge shootings, street corner shootings, gun shots from a passing car, the bullets sweeping across children on a front porch—many of these will probably remain insoluble. A partial solution would be the control of handguns. Ordinances have been proposed several times in the council (usually by Maryann Mahaffey), but until the summer of 1989 even the weakest of them, asking simply for gun registration and training for

571

owners, failed to receive a majority or has lost by a veto or threat of veto from the mayor.

As with many other city functions, the difficulty in getting crime information seems worst of all. Ordinary citizens and the council alike feel powerless.

A crime not ignored by the police and fire departments, but quickly forgotten by the public, is arson. Arson is responsible for the destruction of an unknown number of vacant homes and the loss of potential housing stock throughout the city. A decade ago, much of it was blamed on insurance fraud, as apartment after apartment disappeared along the inner city's Cass Corridor. Now it is simply the fire in the night, the end result of drugs, vandalism, or, latest of all, neighborhood anger that an empty house, open and dangerous, has stood too long.

Health can be defined by the infant mortality rate, which is one of the worst in the western world; in 1983, thirty-four per thousand. In one inner-city area, infant and neonatal deaths reached sixty-three per thousand. Death comes more certainly to babies who are black, who are poor, or whose mothers are under twenty and failed to finish high school. Many are also listed under the Health Department euphemism I.F.U. (Information on Father Unknown). This means only that the couple had not married at the time of birth, usually because they didn't believe they could afford to. All too often, the insecurity is prolonged and results in another single-parent family.

> Another summer
> Browns to fall, children grow up
> calling grandma
> "mama" and
> themselves grown.

> —Leisia Duskin

A spokesperson for Hutzel Hospital's neonatal clinic reported in September, 1989, that they were seeing a record percentage of mothers who had no prenatal care before coming for delivery.

As with other Detroit trouble spots, the difficulty of getting information makes reform more difficult. In a 1988 request for information, the council learned that for the second successive year, money they had appropriated for maternal and child health care had not been spent by the Department of Health.

Those 1983 statistics for infant mortality were used here because in 1988 they were the latest available. Credit should go, however, to a team on the Department of Health's Substance Abuse Division for its effort to bring together data from its own department and other public agencies.[2]

As for the schools: at best, the city has lost belief in them. The media clearly see the schools as a shambles and a drawback on the city's image. It was the fiscal irresponsibility and arrogance of board members that brought the general public to the breaking point.

In the fall of 1988, four board members were replaced by a slate committed to reform. The exact nature of the change remains cloudy. There has been almost total acceptance by the media and the public of the notion that principals should have more power. Most citizens seem to favor simplistic reforms, such as more stress on basic skills. As in Mathilde Coffin's day, there is a large coterie who wants the minimum for entry-level jobs. Low test scores draw attention, but methods of testing or the self-defeating emphasis put upon tests are rarely questioned. The high school dropout rate is deplored by all, but in-house research and some workable staff proposals to cut it have been ignored by the bureaucracy and are unknown to the citizenry.[3]

The newly elected board soon replaced the superintendent and initiated sweeping changes. Sadly, many excellent programs of the former superintendent, Arthur Jefferson, had lost by one vote. After first insisting that he would not accept the position without total board approval, John Porter, former state Superintendent of Instruction, became superintendent by a narrow margin and has since also won or lost a few key issues by a margin of one vote.

We do not see among the proposed reforms any true awareness of the despair of teachers in the face of the continued nepotism and cronyism that controls their careers. There has been an adversarial relationship between labor and management in the schools for about fifteen years.[4] (The plan to "empower principals" is seen by many teachers as opening the gate of the chickenyard to the wolf.) There is also confusion. Principals are urged to apply uniformly the rules contained in the vague and unrealistic "Student Conduct Code." It seems not to have occurred to anyone that a valued power of any principal should be the right to form judgments on students, and even sometimes to use the quality of mercy.

There are strains in the parent-teacher relationship. Detroit has never been a take-a-teacher-to-lunch town. On the other hand, most major school ills go with society's failure to give meaningful support to the single-parent family.

Recent added stress comes from the political strength of some parents in some districts. Regionalization created power that was quickly seized upon by parents in disadvantaged districts. This was to be expected and appropriate. Less expected was the continuance of many of the same parents of self-perpetuating school committees for almost two decades. Many have long since ceased to be volunteers and are entrenched in lower-level staff positions. These parent groups have successfully upset recommendations of the superintendent, board, and staff at angry board meetings. School closings are tense; so is the placement of a program for unmarried mothers.

As to the "excellent suburban schools," as the executive recruiters term them, some are wonderful, but they vary as much as schools anywhere and suffer mainly from the racial isolation predicted by Thurgood Marshall. So, of course, do Detroit children. At this writing, the chance of Detroit schools becoming once again places of "good learning" is uncertain.

The natural environment of metropolitan Detroit has of course changed, but there has been more effort spent to maintain it than in many other parts of the country, beginning with the brave purchase of Belle Isle. Anger still flares quickly at the suggestion of any change there. An ill-advised comment by Mayor Young early in his first term that it could be a wonderful site for apartments led to the formation of the Friends of Belle Isle, fighters every one.

In the suburbs there are well-organized efforts to retain the natural heritage. Here there are the Sierra Club, SEMEAC (the Southeast Michigan Environmental Action Council), Michigan Audubon, the Nature Conservancy, and others, all struggling to preserve green space against the encroaching ugliness of glass-walled office buildings. The struggle here is to enforce state laws protecting the wetlands. The enemy is the developer.

Within Detroit, there are many enemies. It is easy to blame those who don't pick up litter. That absolves everyone else. But

Fisherman, west side Detroit. (Courtesy of Bob McKeown, 1988.)

how much blame need Detroiters accept for the frequent lack of trash bins? The most common complaints of Detroit's neighborhoods concern the irregularity of trash pickup and accusations that ordinary neighborhoods are passed over for wealthy ones.

Still more basic to the environment is land use and the river. The trend noted by Kenneth Cockrel has continued unabated. The profits of developers have fueled the growth of downtown at neighborhood expense and have determined many of the decisions made about the shoreline of the Detroit River. However, with the help of a determined Canadian government, the expansion of Cobo Hall into the Detroit River was partly cut back from its original encroachment.

In spite of the growth of Detroit shoreline parks, ordinary pedestrian access is increasingly barred in other places. The explanation given is always "security." Only the personal intervention of owner/developer Peter Stroh made possible a public walkway connecting city-owned parklands on either side of his riverfront development. Riverfront West, in contrast, permits no pedestrian access whatever to any part of its lavish apartment complex. In

575

general, along the river both public access and public decision-making have been minimal.

The river is a showcase for the general sense of powerlessness felt by Detroiters. In the areas we have discussed, there is little access to power and barely access to timely information that might strengthen the citizenry. Yet there is a sense of awakening. We note that the arts have benefited from controversy and excitement for several years. There may be a stirring in the body politic as well. The board of education was one symptom. A lively mayoralty campaign is another. Who knows what the city might become if one-twentieth of the media attention given to professional sports were diverted to government? Perhaps the catalyst will be the emerging struggle over whether the people of Detroit will be allowed to keep their beloved ballpark, Tiger Stadium, or be faced with yet another developer's bill.

Still, Mayor Young, at the urging of the Central Business District Association, arranged for festoons of light across the Ambassador Bridge to Canada. For that good deed we thank him, remembering Clara Ward's saying: "La belle Paris is not more beautiful than Detroit when the lights are shining on the river."

Editor's Notes

1. U.S. Congress, Senate Judiciary Committee, Antitrust Sub-Committee, *Hearings on S. 7767*, 93d Cong., 2d sess., 1839–51.
2. *Detroit Youth: "Harmonies of Liberty" or "Drunk with the Wine of the World?": A Summary and Interpretation of the Data Recorded by Public Institutions* (Detroit: Department of Health, Bureau of Substance Abuse, 1987).
3. Most school leavings occur at the ninth-grade level, and for that reason the catchall phrase "high school dropout rate" is often heard. It is, however, misleading, as it is subject to many statistical variations in computing it. More useful and no less grim is the fact that among students who enter the Detroit Public Schools approximately 40 percent graduate. Some of the others, of course, have successfully completed the twelfth grade in private schools, or have received an alternate diploma under the schools' GED program. Still, it is estimated that both of these groups together do not exceed 10 percent of the whole.

4. This period does not coincide at all with the earlier arrival of the Detroit Federation of Teachers, but rather with the appointment of a strongly antiunion deputy superintendent, who during his term in office managed to make a number of executive appointments and set a certain tone of contentious hostility to labor. That union negotiations have been unnecessarily difficult is only one result. The schools were probably more deeply affected by a growing reluctance to listen to suggestions from the lower ranks of staff.

Bibliography

Abrams, Charles. *The City Is the Frontier*. New York: Harper, 1965.

Anderson, Carlotta. "Jo Labadie, Detroit's Gentle Anarchist." *Michigan History* (June-July 1986): 32–39.

Angelo, Frank. *Yesterday's Detroit*. Miami: E. A. Seamann, 1974.

Ashworth, William. *The Late Great Lakes*. Detroit: Wayne State University Press, 1988.

Babson, Steve, with Ron Alpern, Dave Elsila, and John Revitte. *Working Detroit: The Making of a Union Town*. Detroit: Wayne State University Press, 1986.

Bald, F. Clever. *Michigan in Four Centuries*. New York: Harper & Row, 1954.

Barnard, Harry. *Independent Man: The Life of Senator James Couzens*. New York: Charles Scribner's Sons, 1958.

Barone, Michael, and Grant Ujifusa. *Almanac of American Politics*. Washington, D.C.: National Journal. [Issues of 1974–1990]

Bingay, Malcolm W. *Detroit Is My Own Home Town*. Indianapolis: Bobbs-Merrill, 1946.

Bluestone, Barry, and Bennett Harrison. *The Deindustrialization of America*. New York: Basic Books, 1982.

Boggs, James. *The American Revolution: Pages from a Negro Worker's Notebook*. New York: Monthly Review Press, 1963.

Bontemps, Arna, and Jack Conroy. *Anyplace but Here*. New York: Hill and Wang, 1966.

Boykin, Ulysses. *A Handbook on the Detroit Negro*. Detroit: Minority Study Associates, 1943. [Available at BHC]

Burton, Clarence M., William Stocking, and Gordon K. Miller, eds. *City of Detroit, Michigan, 1701–1922*. 4 vols. Chicago: S. J. Clarke, 1922.

Capeci, Dominic. *Race Relations in Wartime Detroit: The Sojourner Truth Housing Controversy of 1942*. Philadelphia: Temple University Press, 1984.

Casey, Geneviere. *Father Clem Kern, Conscience of Detroit*. Detroit: Marygrove College Press, 1989.

Conot, Robert. *American Odyssey*. New York: Morrow, 1974. Reprint. Detroit: Wayne State University Press, 1986.

Cornell, George, James M. McGlurken, and James A. Clifton. *People of the Three Fires: The Ottawa, Pottawatomi and Ojibway of Michigan.* Grand Rapids, Mich.: Grand Rapids Inter-Tribal Council, 1986.

Crathern, Alice Tarbell, ed. *In Detroit Courage Was the Fashion: Women in the Development of Detroit from 1701 to 1951.* Detroit: Wayne University Press, 1953.

Dain, Floyd Russell. *Every House a Frontier: Detroit's Economic Progress, 1815–1825.* Detroit: Wayne University Press, 1956.

Dancy, John. *Sand against the Wind.* Detroit: Wayne State University Press, 1966.

Detroit Department of Health, Bureau of Substance Abuse. *Detroit Youth: "Harmonies of Liberty" or "Drunk with the Wine of the World?": A Summary and Interpretation of the Data Recorded by Public Institutions.* Detroit: Department of Health, Bureau of Substance Abuse, 1987.

Detroit Free Press. *Great Pages of Michigan History from the Detroit Free Press.* Detroit: Wayne State University Press, 1987.

Edwards, George. *The Police on the Urban Frontier.* New York: American Jewish Committee, 1971.

Ewen, Lynda. *Corporate Power and Urban Crisis in Detroit.* Princeton, N.J.: Princeton University Press, 1978.

Farmer, Silas. *History of Detroit and Wayne County and Early Michigan.* Detroit: Farmer & Co., 1890. Reprint. Detroit: Gale Research Co., 1969.

Fine, Sidney. *Frank Murphy: The Detroit Years.* Ann Arbor: University of Michigan Press, 1975.

Fountain, Clayton. *Union Guy.* New York: Viking, 1949.

Gabin, Nancy. "Women Workers and the UAW in the Post-World War II Period, 1945–1954." In *The Labor History Reader,* edited by Daniel J. Leab, 407–32. Urbana: University of Illinois Press, 1985.

Georgakas, Dan. *Detroit, I Do Mind Dying.* New York: St. Martin's Press, 1974.

Georgakas, Dan, and Albert Blum. *Michigan Labor and the Civil War.* Edited by Sidney Glazer. Lansing: Michigan Civil War Centennial Observance Commission, 1964.

George, Emily. *William Woodbridge, Michigan's Connecticut Yankee.* Lansing: Michigan Department of State, Michigan Historical Division, 1979.

Grant, William. "The Detroit School Case: An Historical Overview." *Wayne Law Review* (March 1975): 851–66.

Grier, Eunice, and George Grier. *Privately Developed Interracial Housing,* 133–43. Berkeley: University of California Press, 1956.

Hamlin, Marie C. Watson. *Legends of le Detroit.* 2d ed. Detroit: Thorndike Nourse, 1884.

Hanawalt, Leslie L. *A Place of Light: The History of Wayne State University.* Detroit: Wayne State University Press, 1968.

Hill, Daniel G. *The Freedom-Seekers: Blacks in Early Canada*. Agincourt, Canada: The Book Society, 1981).

Holli, Melvin G. *Reform in Detroit: Hazen S. Pingree and Urban Politics*. New York: Oxford University Press, 1969.

Howe, Irving, and B. J. Widick. *The UAW and Walter Reuther*. New York: Random House, 1949.

Jackson, Kenneth T. *The Ku Klux Klan in the City, 1915–1930*. New York: Oxford University Press, 1967.

Jacobs, Jane. *The Economy of Great American Cities*. New York: Vintage, 1961.

Jameson, Anna Brownell. *Winter Studies and Summer Rambles in Upper Canada*. Toronto: Thos. Nelson and Sons, 1837.

Katzman, David. *Before the Ghetto: Black Detroit in the Nineteenth Century*. Urbana: University of Illinois Press, 1973.

Kraus, Henry. *The Many and the Few*. Los Angeles: Planta Press, 1947.

Larrie, Reginald R. *Makin' Free: African-Americans in the Northwest Territory*. Detroit: Blaine-Ethridge Books, 1981.

Lee, Alfred McClung, and Norman D. Humphrey. *Race Riot*. New York: Dryden Press, 1943.

Levine, David Allan. *Internal Combustion: The Races in Detroit, 1915–1926*. Westport Conn.: Greenwood Press, 1976.

Linck, Orville E., ed. *Kelsey the Commentator: The Affirmations and Dissents of a Distinguished Columnist*. Detroit: Wayne State University Press, 1963.

Locke, Hubert. *The Detroit Riot of 1967*. Detroit: Wayne State University Press, 1969.

Lodge, John C., with Milo M. Quaife. *I Remember Detroit*. Detroit: Wayne University Press, 1949.

Lovett, William P. *Detroit Rules Itself*. Boston: R. G. Badger, 1930.

Luria, Dan, and Jack Russell. *Rational Reindustrialization: An Economic Development Agenda for Detroit*. Detroit: Widgetripper Press, 1981.

McLauchlin, Russell. *Alfred Street*. Detroit: Conjure House, 1946.

McRae, Norman. *Negroes in Michigan during the Civil War*. Edited by Sidney Glazer. Lansing: Michigan Civil War Centennial Observance Commission, 1966.

Mary Rosalita, Sister. *Education in Detroit Prior to 1850*. Lansing: Michigan Historical Commission, 1928.

May, George S. *Michigan: An Illustrated History of the Great Lake State*. Northridge, Calif.: Windsor Publications in cooperation with the Historical Society of Michigan, 1987.

Meyer, Katherine Mattingly, ed. *Detroit Architecture: AIA Guide*. Rev. ed. Detroit: Wayne State University, 1980.

Michigan Department of Labor. *Annual Reports*. 1891–1906 and 1912–17. Lansing: Michigan Department of Labor.

Moehlman, Arthur. *Public Education in Detroit*. Bloomington, Ill: Public School Publishing Co., 1925.

Moran, J. Bell. *The Moran Family: 200 Years in Detroit*. Detroit: Alved of Detroit, 1949.

Motley, Mary Penick, ed. *Invisible Soldier: The Experience of the Black Soldier, World War II*. Detroit: Wayne State University Press, 1975.

Mowitz, Robert J., and Deil S. Wright. *Profile of a Metropolis: A Case Book*. Detroit: Wayne State University Press, 1962.

Myers, Gustavus. *History of the Great American Fortunes*, 93–121. New York: Modern Library, 1937.

National Advisory Commission on Civil Disorders, Chairman Otto Kerner. *Report*. New York: E. P. Dutton & Co., 1968.

New Detroit Committee. *Progress Report of the New Detroit Committee*. Detroit: New Detroit Committee, 1968.

Palmer, Friend. *Early Days in Detroit*. Detroit: Hunt & June, 1906.

Parkinson, Almon Ernest. *Historical Geography of Detroit*. Lansing: Michigan Historical Commission, 1918.

Player, Cyril Arthur. "Pingree." BHC, Detroit Public Library. Typescript.

Rich, Wilbur. *Coleman Young and Detroit Politics: From Social Activist to Power Broker*. Detroit: Wayne State University Press, 1989.

Rogin, Michael Paul. *Fathers and Children: Andrew Jackson and the Subjugation of the American Indian*. New York: Random House, 1976.

Ross, Robert Budd. *The Patriot War*. Detroit: Detroit Evening News, 1898.

Ross, Robert Budd, and George B. Catlin. *Landmarks of Detroit*. Detroit: Detroit Evening News Association, 1898.

Satz, Ronald N. *American Indian Policy and the Jacksonian Era*. Lincoln: University of Nebraska Press, 1975.

Schoolcraft, Henry. *The Literary Voyager, or Muzzeniegun*. Edited by Philip Parker Mason. East Lansing: Michigan State University Press, 1962.

Schucter, Arnold. *Reparations: The Black Manifesto and Its Challenge to White America*. Philadelphia: Lippincott, 1970.

Serrin, William. "God Help Our City." *Atlantic Monthly* (March 1969): 115–21.

——— . *The Company and the Union: The "Civilized Relationship" of the General Motors Corporation and the United Auto Workers*. New York: Knopf, 1973.

Sexton, Patricia, and Brendan Sexton. *Bluecollars and Hard Hats: The Working Class and the Future of American Politics*. New York: Random House, 1971.

Shaw, Virginia W. V. *O, Call Back Yesterday*. Detroit: Privately printed, 1936. [Available BHC]

Sinclair, Upton. *The Flivver King: A Story of Ford-America*. Emaus, Penn.: Rodale Press, 1927.

———— . *The Goslings: A Study of the American Schools*. Pasadena: Privately printed, 1924.

Streeter, Floyd B. *Political Parties in Michigan, 1837–1860*. Lansing: Michigan Historical Commission, 1918.

Sward, Keith. *The Legend of Henry Ford*. New York: Rinehart, 1948.

Sword, Wiley. *President Washington's Indian War: The Struggle for the Old Northwest, 1790–1795*. Norman: University of Oklahoma Press, 1985.

U.S. Congress. Senate Judiciary Committee, Antitrust Subcommittee. *Hearings on S. 1167*. 93d Cong., 2d sess., 1839–51. [Hearing on mass transit]

Warren, Francis H. *Michigan Manual of Freedmen's Progress*. Lansing: State of Michigan, 1915.

Washington, Forrester. *The Negro in Detroit: A Survey of the Conditions of a Negro Group in a Northern Industrial Center during the War Prosperity Period*. Detroit: Associated Charities, 1920. Detroit Public Library. Typescript.

———— . *The Negro in Detroit, 1926*. Report of the Mayor's Interracial Commission. Detroit: Bureau of Governmental Research, 1926. Detroit Public Library. Typescript.

White, Walter. *How Far the Promised Land?* New York: Viking, 1955.

Widick, B. J. *Auto Work and Its Discontents*. Baltimore: Johns Hopkins University Press, 1976.

———— . *Detroit: City of Race and Class Violence*. Rev. ed. Detroit: Wayne State University Press, 1989.

Wolf, Eleanor P. *Trial and Error: The Detroit School Segregation Case*. Detroit: Wayne State University Press, 1981.

Wolf, Eleanor P., and Mel Ravitz. "Lafayette Park: New Residents in the Core City." *Journal of the American Institute of Planners* (August 1964).

Wolf, Eleanor P., and Charles LeBeaux, with Shirley Terreberry and Harriet Sapirstein. *Change and Renewal in an Urban Community: Five Case Studies of Detroit*. New York: Praeger, 1969.

Woodford, Arthur M. *Detroit and Its Banks: The Story of Detroit Bank and Trust*. Detroit: Wayne State University Press, 1974.

Woodford, Frank B. *Lewis Cass: The Last Jeffersonian*. New Brunswick, N.J.: Rutgers University Press, 1950.

Woodford, Frank B., and Arthur M. Woodford. *All Our Yesterdays: A Brief History of Detroit*. Detroit: Wayne State University Press, 1969.

Woodson, June Baber. "A Century with the Negroes of Detroit: 1830–1930." Master's thesis, Wayne State University, 1949.

Wylie, Jeanie. *Poletown: Community Betrayed*. Urbana: University of Illinois Press, 1989.

Zunz, Olivier. *Beyond Inequality*. Chicago: University of Illinois Press, 1986.

Index

Wilma Wood Henrickson is a historian and free-lance writer. She holds the B.A. and M.A. degrees from Wayne State University. For fifteen years she was chairman of the social studies department at Murray-Wright High School, Detroit, and is currently active in a number of historical, cultural, civic, and political organizations.

The manuscript was edited by Robin DuBlanc. The book was designed by Mary Primeau.

Manufactured in the United States of America.